TRIPPIN' WITH KIDS

PETER + BRIDGET HELLIAR

Hardie Grant

TRAVEL

INTRODUCTION
vi

ALL YOU NEED TO KNOW
xii

Travel tips for different ages 2
Before you go 5
Packing 11
Planes, trains and automobiles 17
Your holiday is go! 22
Heading home 29
Types of holidays 30

AUSTRALIA
34

Victoria 39
Christmas, Camping and Cricket 42
Melbourne 43
Mornington Peninsula 47

New South Wales 49
Sydney 52
Blue Mountains 56
Byron Bay 57

Australian Capital Territory 59
Canberra 60

Queensland 65
Brisbane 68
Gold Coast 73
Sunshine Coast 76
Fraser Island 78
The Tropical North 79

Western Australia 82
Perth 85
Margaret River 89
The Kimberley 90

Northern Territory 93
Darwin 94
Kakadu 97
Katherine 98
Alice Springs 99
Uluru 100

South Australia 102
Adelaide 104
Kangaroo Island 108
Mount Gambier 109

Tasmania 110
Hobart 113
Freycinet Peninsula 117

NEW ZEALAND
118

Wellington 121
Auckland 123
Elsewhere on the North Island 126
Christchurch 127
Queenstown 128
Wanaka 129
Elsewhere on the South Island 130

BALI
132

FIJI
138

Oscar's day not to be remembered 142

SINGAPORE
144

THAILAND
150

Bangkok 153

VIETNAM
156

Hanoi 159
Da Nang 160
Hoi An 160
Nha Trang 161
Hue 161
Ho Chi Minh City 162

JAPAN
164

Tokyo 170
Kyoto 174
Osaka 178
Hiroshima 180

UNITED KINGDOM
182

England 184
London 187

Scotland 192
Edinburgh 194

Northern Ireland 196
Belfast 196

IRELAND
198

Dublin 203

FRANCE
206

Paris 209
Paris degustation 214
Normandy 216
Toulouse 216
Côte d'Azur 217
Burgundy 218
French Alps 219
Collingwood versus France 221

ITALY 222

Rome 225

EASTERN EUROPE 250

Prague, Czech Republic 252
A night at the theatre 254
Krakow, Poland 255
Budapest, Hungary 259

GERMANY 230

Berlin 235
Hugo's has a dress code 238
Munich 239

USA 262

Los Angeles 270
San Francisco 274
Las Vegas 278
New York City 282
Boston 285
Chicago 288
New Orleans 290
Hawaii 292
Hawaiian missile crisis 295

DENMARK 240

Copenhagen 244
LEGOLAND 248

About the authors 297

Index 298

INTRODUCTION

YOU CAN DO IT

This book is not your regular travel guide book. We wrote *Trippin' with Kids* to encourage you, parents with children (of any age), *not* to put off travelling until the kids have flown the coop. Our boys, Liam, Aidan and Oscar, are getting older by the day (which is totally normal we are told) and we treasure the times we had travelling with them when they were younger – and hope those days aren't over quite yet.

The thing is, if you put travel off, there's a good chance you'll just keep putting it off. We all know that life gets busy, excuses can disguise themselves as reasons and before you know it your oldest is in Year 11 and you can't easily take them out of school. Or, worse, they don't want to travel with you because their best friend Scabby's parents own a holiday house down the coast and that's much more appealing.

We want to help you see that you *can* do it now. Even with little ones! You don't have to start with month-long trips overseas – weekends away are a great way to get the kids used to travelling and are also much easier on schedules and budgets (and sleep-deprived parents!). So we begin the book with our wonderful country and our pick of what you can see and do without leaving Australian shores, before talking about some of our favourite kid-friendly overseas destinations.

Our hope is that, among the practical advice, helpful tips and personal anecdotes in this book, you will find inspiration – inspiration to call a travel agent, to get on the road, to start planning a wonderful memorable family adventure.

Lastly, when reading this book, just keep thinking: *there is no reason why we can't do this*. Go for it. It's worth it. The world is waiting for you … and your rugrats!

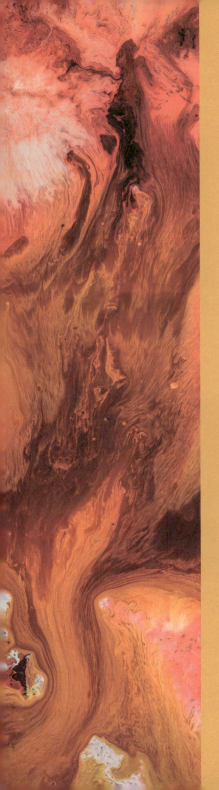

A CHOICE WE MADE

For us, it was definitely worth it – we'll explain why. Six years into our marriage we decided we needed to hit refresh. We wouldn't call it a rut as such, but perhaps it was knowing that the infamous seven-year itch may or may not have been just ahead of us – we decided to take pre-emptive action. A friend of ours suggested a marriage counsellor, which sounded *way* over the top to us; we thought that counselling was for couples trying to desperately cling to the final threads of their relationship. That was not us. We were good. We just wanted to be *better*. Turns out that's actually the perfect situation for relationship counselling – you don't wait for the bitter end to save something you love. So we had a few sessions and found we enjoyed investing the time to talk honestly about our marriage, our relationship, how we got here and, most importantly, where we wanted to go.

What we quickly realised was that we wanted to bring travel into our marriage. We had always thought that we would wait for our three boys to get older before we all travelled overseas, but after talking about it we decided not to wait any more – if we waited for the kids to get older then we would be older too. We didn't want to explore the Pyramids on walking frames, so we got cracking, opened a bottle of bubbles and started pitching destinations, dates and a budget.

It was instantly thrilling. Suddenly our marriage wasn't just about these four walls, endless laundry, Saturday sport and school lunches. It could be vineyards in France, pizza in Rome or Central Park in New York. We could chase summers, hike Tibet or run with the bulls in Pamplona (although running with the bulls with a BabyBjörn is highly discouraged – or just running with the bulls at all to be honest!).

After spinning globes, eyeing maps and consulting with the kids, it was decided the Helliars would travel to France in October 2010 (a week after the AFL Grand Final) with our three boys: Liam, who was eight, Aidan, five, and Oscar, two. We had taken two of the boys to Fiji when they were young but six weeks in France with three kids was an all-together different ballpark.

It was actually no surprise that travel provided a tonic for us: we have always loved travel and, even before we met, it had been a big part of our lives. Pete had travelled to Europe straight out of school after making some fast cash working down at the Melbourne docks (he calls these his Bon Jovi years even though he packed 25kg bags of sugar into shipping containers for no more than three months). Brij had backpacked through Europe several times and travelled to the United States and Asia too.

Ironically, we actually met, if you can call it that, at an airport. Gate Lounge Two at Sydney in fact. Waiting for his plane to Melbourne, Pete saw an attractive woman reading a book across from him. Pete didn't speak to her, instead hoping that luck may play its part and miraculously seat him next to her on the plane. Luck said, 'You're dreaming, Helliar!' and seated the woman a safe distance from the up-and-coming comedian. When they landed in Melbourne, Brij was met by her family and Pete took the shuttle bus to his car.

And that was that.

But it wasn't, was it? Of course it wasn't. This book wouldn't exist if that was that.

So, this is that ... A few nights later Pete was booked to perform a stand-up comedy set. Before his set, he spotted a friend of his, Anna, at the bar, and worked his way through the crowd to say hi. Then he saw that Anna had a friend with her – that friend, believe it or not, was the girl from Sydney Gate Lounge Two.

And we've pretty much been together ever since.

The boys eventually took their surfboards to the waters of Waikiki, Hawaii

LIAM'S OSKAR SCHINDLER STORY (OR, WHY WE TRAVEL)

Our trip with the kids to France was such a success that we started planning and saving for a new overseas adventure, even though it meant taking the boys out of school again.

Of course, it's up to every parent to consider the benefits of travel against the time a child will miss in the classroom. For us, though, it was this next trip that confirmed we'd made the right decision and it has shaped the way we look at taking the kids out of school for travel.

During our trip to Poland in 2012 we had decided to spare our kids the heaviness of a trip to Auschwitz but, after doing some research, we discovered that the Oskar Schindler Factory in Krakow was a great middle-ground.

Sure, there were still some facts to discover that ranged from unpleasant to horrifying but this museum, set in the old factory where Schindler worked to save 1200 Jewish men and women from the camps, is more than anything a place of hope.

Liam, our eldest, had just turned ten, Aidan was seven and Oscar, four. They all approached the museum differently. Oscar zipped through it like he was trying to win a race. Aidan checked out artefacts and looked at photos of Krakow during the time of Nazi Occupation. But Liam – well, he took longer. He spent time reading the stories behind the photos and the artefacts. He read letters from children living in the ghettos. He learnt about Oskar Schindler's mission. He took it *all* in. Pete, standing outside the museum after chasing Oscar to deliver the news that this wasn't in fact a race and that there would be no award ceremony, had to wait and wait for Liam and Brij before they finally emerged.

After our visit, we debriefed over some delicious golonka (stewed pork knuckle). We wanted to make sure the kids were taking the right messages from the experience, that rather than focusing on the ghastly images of concentration camps they could see that even in our darkest hours there is light. It was a good chat and we patted ourselves on the back for providing them with such a valuable experience. But it wasn't until we got back to Australia that the full value of those two hours was revealed.

Liam had been back at school for less than a week when his class was asked to write a short essay on somebody they considered a hero (we can only assume parents were off limits as Liam didn't seem to consider us an option). Many of his classmates had decided to go for their sporting heroes: Aussie cricket captain Ricky Ponting, then Collingwood footballer Dale 'Daisy' Thomas and athlete Cathy Freeman were popular picks. Liam, his travels still fresh in his mind, chose Oskar Schindler. Many in his class understandably didn't know who Oskar Schindler was so Liam stood in front of his peers and told them as much as he could remember about Oskar Schindler.

It obviously made an impression because the next day more than half the kids came to school with new heroes in mind for their essays. It seems that the kids went home, talked about Schindler and what makes a hero with their parents, and came back to school with new non-sporting heroes. War surgeon and prisoner of war Sir Edward 'Weary' Dunlop, aviation pioneer Amelia Earhart, Paralympian and Kokoda Track 'crawler' Kurt Fearnley and esteemed eye surgeon Fred Hollows were some of the kids' new heroes.

Liam's project was pinned up proudly in the school library and has also gone down in our family legend as one of the reasons we travel. This is just one example of the wonderful experiences that can come from travelling with kids and it's why we want to encourage you to get on out there. So go for it!

(By the way, Pete is *still* waiting for Liam to do a project on him.)

FIND YOUR LUKE AND LIZ

'Who are Luke and Liz?' we hear you ask. It's a perfectly reasonable question, but the thing you have to know first is that everyone needs a Luke and Liz.

Maybe you are the Luke and Liz for your friends or maybe your Luke and Liz go under different names, such as Steve and Jazz or Shaun and Sam or Kylie and Dan. Whatever their names, they can be vital to you getting off the couch and out of your comfort zone.

We know. We, annoyingly, still haven't answered the question: who the bloody hell are Luke and Liz?

Well, our Luke and Liz are actually called Luke and Liz. Luke is Brij's brother and Liz is Brij's sister-in-law. Luke works in the family business, Liz works in psychiatric care; they are salt-of-the-earth kind of people. But being earth-salt people isn't enough to get you mentioned in this book. No way. Perhaps the next book, when we're struggling to make the word count, but until then you need to be totally book-worthy to make these pages and Luke and Liz definitely are. Now we will, finally, tell you why.

We were both busy with work and seemed to have no interests or hobbies outside of our jobs and the kids (well, Pete did play a bit of golf but realistically his 18 holes resembled a nice stroll that had gone terribly wrong). We mentioned this to Luke and he said, 'You guys should come skiing with us this winter.'

'What about the kids?' we asked Luke. 'Won't it be a nightmare with the kids?'

'It's perfect for the kids. They learn to ski and there's even a ski school and ski creche. Don't worry about a thing,' he said. 'Liz and I will help you out.'

And that's why it's handy to have a Luke and Liz. Ski culture and planning a skiing holiday can be intimidating so to have friends who had our backs, who provided a safety net and who filled in the gaps in our knowledge was a huge help.

That was 2010 and we haven't missed a ski season since. We now get to the mountains as much as we can during the Aussie winter. Our boys ski and snowboard like demons and we go at our pace and enjoy well-earned beer and wine at the end of each day.

Try to find your own Luke and Liz – people who will help you get to the places you may have dismissed as being too hard, people who will encourage you to say 'yes' to that trip outside your comfort zone, people who will say, 'It's okay, we'll help you out.'

And after enough trips, who knows, you may become someone else's Luke and Liz.

ALL YOU NEED TO KNOW

TRAVELLING WITH KIDS CAN REQUIRE A LITTLE MORE ORGANISATION AND PLANNING THAN TRAVELLING KID-FREE, SO IN THIS CHAPTER WE GIVE YOU ALL THE INFORMATION YOU NEED TO KNOW TO PLAN FOR AND ENJOY YOUR HOLIDAY FROM BEGINNING TO END.

TRAVEL TIPS FOR DIFFERENT AGES

Before you start booking your holiday, consider what will be best given the ages of your kids.

BABIES

Like changing the batteries in the smoke alarm or performing a single one-handed push-up, travelling with babies is easier than you think. They do, however, require a lot more stuff, so lugging the extra around can be tiresome. Your main priorities will be security, sleep, nappy changes and food. We found the easiest thing was to use a baby carrier: you can see the sights you want to see and your bub has what it needs – you (and the food and nappies). Also ensure you never go for full-on days when travelling with babies; always have breaks and allow quiet times for the baby to sleep.

Planes are a good option when travelling with babies, especially with the bassinet option (but book the bassinet as soon as you can because they go very quickly). Take-offs and landings are tough enough on big ears so they will be tough on little ones too. Brij would breastfeed our babies on take-off and landing and that helped. Get them sucking one way or another; if they're not breastfeeding and don't need a bottle, try getting them to suck your clean hand or if they have a dummy try that. Don't worry about a crying baby – most people just ignore it or will politely help if they think they can offer something. The crying doesn't last forever and it won't ruin anyone's trip.

Baby naps will be the hardest thing to keep to schedule if you or your bub need a strict routine. You can, if you think it will help, start changing their nap times a week before you leave to fit in with your destination. We found that a bit difficult so our little ones simply slept when they could or wanted to – we just watched for tired signs.

TODDLERS

For us, travelling with a crawling toddler was the hardest – as you probably know, they want to be everywhere and investigate absolutely everything. It's just so demanding, and once they know how to crawl they can be so fast! Toddlers are entertained by whatever they don't have, so you have to be switched on when you are out. The type of trip doesn't matter: as long as you can keep them safe and healthy, they will have lots of fun. We preferred to stay in apartments when travelling with a toddler; they can have a safe crawling area and a day nap (and parents can too). But do check the accommodation is safe: cover low power points and lock balcony doors.

Toddlers on planes are a bit more work, but it is possible. Allow some settling in time and walk around the cabin with them. You can also play games. Just try to get them not to kick and pull on the seat in front of them.

Toddlers will get more out of a visit to Disneyland than the Louvre Museum, but that doesn't mean you can't visit some incredible museums – just don't take as long as you would travelling without kids. A lot of museums and galleries are free or much cheaper for children, so they are still worth visiting even for a short amount of time.

Our other tips for toddlers include:

- Have at least one extra outfit on your travel day and pack lots of wipes and tissues.
- Go to the doctor before leaving. If vaccinating make sure you are up to date and have any remaining vaccinations at least a week before you leave.

- Have plenty of snacks on travel day (limit the amount of sugary snacks).
- Request a kid's meal for the plane.
- Find accommodation that is easy to get to and close to a supermarket and a park if possible. If staying on a high floor, check there is a lift (and ideally avoid accommodation at the top of a huge hill).
- Kid-sized headphones are helpful for long journeys. Plan ahead by downloading kids' movies, audio books and so on.
- Get the kids excited with maps and books about your destination.

PRIMARY SCHOOL

This is the best age to travel with kids. It's easy to take some time away from school and there are plenty of ways to keep them on top of schoolwork while away. They are eager to learn and see new things around this age. The world is still so big and exciting that everything will be entertainment for them. They don't need a whole suitcase of extra items and they can carry or pull their own luggage. When we took our three kids backpacking in eastern Europe and the two older boys had their own backpacks to look after and managed the task well.

Long distances are easier with kids at primary school: they all fit in the back seat of the car, they can handle long plane journeys and they don't care about missing things back home.

Our other suggestions for travelling with kids this age are:

- Consider taking them out of school to avoid busy school holiday travel periods.
- Research the kids' clubs if available.
- Download some age-appropriate learning apps for maths, spelling and English.
- Get them to write a diary or blog.
- Get them to act out something they found fun on a trip with finger puppets.

Prams can't go everywhere

HIGH SCHOOL

We love travelling with teenagers because they are helpful and you can have some pretty awesome conversations with them. However, travelling with teenagers can be more difficult: school is more important, as are friendships, social life and time to themselves. It's harder to drive long distances with three growing (and taller than you) teenagers in the back seat.

Involving your teenagers in planning the trip will be an important part of its success. By the time kids are teenagers, they usually have a say in many things the family does, so why wouldn't they have a say in your holiday destination? Are they adventure-seeking teenagers with abseiling and whitewater rafting in mind? Or are they theme park diehards with thrill rides on their must-do list? Planning and talking together means you're more likely to include everyone's ideas on your trip. For things you want to do that your teenagers are not keen on, keep it short: if you're going to a gallery or museum, go to the parts you're most interested in and if the kids want to sit on the steps out the front halfway through, let them. Also, have a teenage-friendly activity planned afterwards. Mix and match your activities so it's one for you, one for them. And then one for all of you!

The older your teenagers are, the more challenging it will be taking them out of school. Will they be doing homework? Make sure you have wifi or data for this to happen and all the right books. Don't take Year 11 and 12 students away from school days if possible. Even some school holidays can be hard for this age group with study expectations; you know your child so if you think they are going to be anxious about not doing homework for two weeks in January and there is no wifi, maybe put camping off-grid on hold for a year or two.

It's also the time for serious discussions. Are you ready to let your teenager do some things without you? Talk about boundaries before you book the trip. You also need to make sure your older teenagers know how to be safe when on holiday, so talking about sex, drugs and new friends is important.

Our other tips for travelling with teens are:

- Have a pack of cards in your bag at all times and teach them some new games (long journeys will be more fun playing cards together than having your kid spend the whole time looking at their phone).
- Get them to buy the train tickets and validate passes for the family (with you watching).
- Go to different theatre productions.
- Encourage them to look up the place you're visiting and find something they want to do.
- Get them to work out the currency exchange if overseas.

BEFORE YOU GO

When you're sitting down to discuss destinations, talk about what you and your family want to get out of the trip. Are you after adventure, relaxation or cultural immersion, or all of the above? Write a list of all the things you want to see and do, but don't be disappointed if you don't get to every single one. If there's one thing that travelling with kids teaches you, it's to be flexible and go with the flow when necessary. Making sure the trip is fun and relaxing is better than getting through to the end of a must-do list. Kids will need naps and quiet time, and you will probably need some downtime too. Once you've worked out where you want to go, here are certain things to consider.

TRAVEL AGENTS

What do fax machines, car stereos and landline telephones have in common? They are largely unnecessary in the modern world. The same cannot be said of travel agents despite the apparent ease of hopping online and booking your own holiday. Travel agents are still a thing and we use them every time we travel overseas.

Of course, when travelling in Australia for an extended weekend, it's not a big deal. We like to book our own travel and accommodation direct rather than use an online booking agent – usually the prices are similar and if you book direct you are more likely to get a free add-on or an upgrade if available.

Travelling overseas, however, is a whole different ball game. We book through a travel agent for the simple fact that, if something goes wrong, they have your back. And if you have chosen a good travel agent, they won't let you down. So many unexpected things can happen, from volcanic ash clouds or gas leaks in the apartment you booked to a stuff-up with dates meaning your hotel isn't expecting you until next year! When travelling abroad it's best to hope for the best but prepare for the worst – a good travel agent is a significant part of this plan. Your agent will do everything (other than remove volcanic ash from the sky) to ensure you all have the trip of a lifetime.

While booking your trip may be cheaper without an agent, booking through a travel agent provides a safety net. Many will also look for cheaper deals and most will match online accommodation prices if you show them the deals. They will help you choose the holiday, tour or cruise that is just right for your family.

Travel can involve lots of forms, and your travel agent can help you with this. Do you remember those pre-internet days when you would have to drive across town to physically pick up your travel visas from international embassies? At least nowadays, many of these can be organised online, but your agent will also help organise your visa requirements for your destinations.

Some agents try too hard to find the cheapest deal they can. While this is admirable there are some things we tell our agent not to skimp on. Take the time to work out what you're willing to pay for and what's less important to you. Here are our priorities:

 Transit time. We don't want to save $100 on a flight if it means our transit time is longer. Twelve hours at Dubai airport isn't worth $100, especially with kids. Get to your final destination as quickly as possible.

- Travel insurance. When it comes to travel insurance, we check boxes like we are drunkenly ordering from the hotel breakfast menu. (See the next section for more on what to look for with your travel insurance.)
- Airline choice. We refuse to travel on certain airlines regardless of their amazing deals. Some airlines are happy to seat children away from their parents, and it may not just be the seat behind. On one trip, all five of us were separated and the boys (including Liam, who suffers with anaphylaxis) were each at least six rows away from us. Before you book, check with the airline on their seating protocols. Log in to their website and try to choose your seats as early as possible.
- Day one. Add extra funds to day one to ensure everything goes smoothly. Having to transit in a snowstorm at minus 22 degrees Celsius sounds like the beginning of a Liam Neeson film rather than the start of a family holiday. Ensure you know where you are going and, if you can afford it, have your agent arrange transfers. Some hotels will offer these free.
- Location. Let's face it: whoever coined the phrase 'location, location, location' was right, especially when travelling with kids. If possible, stay somewhere close to transport, shops and places to walk or play. Easy access to a supermarket is very helpful, especially if you are running very low on nappies.

INSURANCE

Yes. We know. We hear you. Insurance is boring. Okay. Calm down. Yes, we know you could spend that money on pizza in Rome. But, seriously, don't even think of travelling overseas without insurance. It's worth paying attention to what you are being offered and what you are entitled to.

First up, you have to mention everything when organising insurance. Remember to tell the insurance company all the places you will be visiting as this could change your policy. If your plans change as you travel because you are just 'so in the moment', it's important to adjust your insurance accordingly (perhaps not such a fun thing to do when you are 'so in the moment' but it could save you in the long run).

Consider pre-existing conditions. Just check with the provider if a pre-existing condition isn't covered and pay a little extra to cover it if you can. Insurance for travelling to places like the United States will cost more but it will be nothing compared with the cost of an overnight stay in a hospital after anaphylaxis that you didn't mention to your insurance company.

If your holiday includes some thrill-seeking adventures, then ensure you are covered for adventure sports (even things like snow skiing, motorbike riding and hot-air ballooning). You can shop around for a better price, but just make sure you are covered for the holiday you are actually planning.

Are you hiring a car? Will your insurance cover you in an accident or cover your excess? (Remember you might be driving on the opposite side of the road.) Are you covered for lost luggage? As much as it still amazes us that suitcases make it from the check-in desk to a conveyer belt on the other side of the world, airlines will occasionally lose your luggage. It's worth covering yourself so you're not hiking Everest in the pyjamas you decided to wear on the plane. Also consider cover for emergency evacuations. Many Aussies have been caught out by volcanic ash in recent years and even though an unexpected extra stay in Bali sounds delightful it can be bloody expensive. Cancellations may not be covered, so make sure you are aware of the terms for all of your accommodation, flights and hiring.

Even with top-level insurance, you will not be covered for certain things so check your insurance before you leave. Things not covered can include damage to skis while in use, general wear and tear to suitcases, and stolen property if it was left unattended. Natural disasters are not covered if it is a known or forecast event. Or if you have an allergy to tomatoes and are in La Tomatina in Spain for the traditional Tomato Fight, it's unlikely you'll be covered if you have an allergic reaction (you really should have seen that reaction coming!). In the event of a terrorist attack, some medical costs are covered but not financial losses.

Yep, we hear you – travel insurance can be expensive. Shop around for the best travel insurance at the right price. Visit the Australian government website smarttraveller.gov.au for information on how to get the right travel insurance for your family. If you travel more than once a year it may be worth buying annual travel insurance; look into some of the yearly options on offer. With this kind of yearly insurance, you don't need to let the company know when and where you are going – you just go (which makes it easier to be 'so in the moment'!).

ELECTRONICS

Even if you are planning a largely tech-free holiday and hope to sample the Amish way of life, there may still be some tech and devices that you may want to consider (just in case you change your mind).

Power adapter: Use a multi-USB charger, find the fastest output available for multiple devices and get those phones charged quickly. When travelling with kids you are more than likely going to have several devices; while it frustrates us how much our kids want to be on them, devices are a helping hand when there are delays and downtime days. Get adapters for the countries you are going to. We have travelled with a power board plugged into the adapter (it looks like an electrical hazard but can be helpful in public areas where people have already nabbed nearly all the electrical points).

Portable phone charger: These are super helpful for those long days of adventuring. Choose one that's highly compact and high capacity, and check that it's laptop compatible if you need it. Keep your phone charged for maps and checking out local places to eat, and keep an eye on the battery level as taking holiday photos and videos will run the battery down. When we head out for the day, we flick the battery-saving mode on even when the battery is at 100 per cent to help us get through the day.

Personal or portable wifi: Only buy these from a reputable company, with a high-speed connection, multiple device connection and easy pick-up/drop-off service. We used one in Tokyo recently and it was awesome. In Italy you can pick them up at the airport, in Japan and Singapore they can be sent to your hotel and in France there are post-office pick-ups. Some companies will even deliver to Australia. We love personal wifi because it's great for looking at maps and train schedules when we are out and about, searching for things to do on the go and finding out about a random place we may have stumbled on. We get unlimited data, which means everyone can log on when needed. When travelling in Australia consider increasing data for the time you are away if you need it. If you don't have personal wifi, you can download a Google map when you have internet access and then refer to it later

Phone data: Get an international pass to save on money (and stress). For example, Telstra offers 200GB per day and unlimited calls, so ringing home and receiving calls won't cost a fortune.

Apps: Download various city apps and metro maps for the places you're going. Most cities have great free apps to get around, with many able to be used offline as well.

ENTERTAINMENT

Yes, we know travel isn't about being glued to your screens and tablets but, as we noted above, electronic entertainment can come in handy and may provide some much needed respite for everybody. Whether it's for winding down after the kids are in bed or to keep the children content as you wait for your connecting flight, it doesn't hurt to have some options. Audio books are a great thing to download before you leave. You can also use them at night to send the kids to sleep if you are too tired to read a book. Most streaming apps allow you to download movies to your tablet or phone, which can be great for transit delays and long journeys. It's still a good idea, though, to watch how much time the kids are on devices, just as you would at home. When in transit, there is still value in allowing for some 'looking out the window' and 'getting bored' time.

Old-school games and activities are also good – think card games, painting with water, gel stickers and roll-up crayons (avoid lids). Of course, the classic I-spy never gets old – until it does after you spend 15 minutes looking for something beginning with L only for it to be 'aeroplane' (remember, two-year-olds cannot be relied on for accurate hints).

We have a few favourite word games, such as having to find ten things starting with W (or any letter) in 30 seconds, or a 'find the alphabet' game starting at A – for example, A, I see apple; B, I see a bee ... and so on (please note, if you do see a bee while on a plane perhaps let the flight attendant know). For a great picture game, draw half a picture on a page. Fold it over with just a few markings on the other side. The other person finishes off the picture without seeing the whole thing. We've played this for years and it still gets a go.

We had finger puppets on the trains around Europe that we used to re-enact experiences from our trips. One lovely Italian woman thought our puppet plays were great – we think she was hoping for a matinee.

VISAS

There are many countries that will allow a 90-day visit without a visa but don't get stuck at the last minute with the ones that don't. Check with your travel agent or smarttraveller.gov.au when booking. For entry into the United States, ESTAs (Electronic System for Travel Authorizations) have been required since 2010, yet we still hear of people getting to the counter in Australia without their completed ESTA for entry into the States. Be prepared for the countries you visit.

PASSPORTS

A wise man who wishes to remain anonymous once said, 'A passport is like a passport to travel.' (Brij suspects Pete is the anonymous wise man.) Now, as much as most of us hate getting a new passport – one, because the old passport can represent so many memories and, two, because it requires a photo that is exactly ten years older than the last one – you must be careful not to get caught out. Passports need at least six months validity or you can't leave the country. Yes, we can argue we pay for a ten-year passport and get only nine years and six months – maybe we can all organise a protest march about that one day – but in the end, your travel plans will be stuffed. So check the expiry dates of all your family's passports (as they may expire on different dates) and renew well ahead of your departure.

Kids' passports are so damn cute you can forget they are serious, proper documents that need to be in order. Children need to be fully renewed every five years up to the age of 16. From 16 they can get a ten-year passport too.

Keep a copy of your passport somewhere when travelling; if you lose it, it will help when trying to apply for a new one. Apps like Turbo Scan are good for quality photographs of documents, also allowing you to send PDFs to your travel agent and to anyone else you think needs it.

HEALTH

Vaccinations are recommended for some countries and you may be required to provide proof of the vaccination. Check smarttravelller.gov.au for advice on your destination. Your doctor can also guide you on the appropriate vaccinations (some may involve a few doses, so plan ahead).

If you take regular medications, make sure you have extra scripts and, ideally, a letter from your doctor. Always carry your medications with you on the plane.

If your kids have allergies, it's really useful to get allergy cards in the local language for non-English-speaking countries. Another option for allergies or medical requirements is, if you are staying in a hotel, to ask the concierge or receptionist to write down in the local language what your requirements are. We have found everyone was helpful when dealing with allergies (we even took a chocolate bar to reception to ask if they could read the ingredients for us). To manage Liam's allergies, we also always get his extra EpiPen from school so we have both EpiPens with us on the trip. Always carry all your EpiPens and antihistamines on you, especially on planes.

We always go to the doctor before we leave, just to make sure we have a script for any asthma and allergy medications. Before our trip to Denmark, we went to the doctor for a check-up for Liam. While we were there the doctor noticed that Aidan had a cough. We said we thought it was just a cold and he'd be fine (based on exactly zero years of medical training!). Thankfully, the doctor looked at Aidan anyway and it turned out he had a bad chest infection requiring antibiotics and Ventolin. This was the day before we had to get on the plane. By the next morning the antibiotics were starting to work and we got the okay to fly from the doctor much to Aidan's relief. We were just so glad we had gone to the doctor and now have check-ups before every trip.

ETIQUETTE

Check the customs or traditions of the places you are visiting before you leave home. This way, from the moment you arrive, you'll be prepared and have an understanding of local customs, which can relate to anything from clothing to disciplining children in public and breastfeeding. Remember to respect the local ways and explain them to your kids – you'll all gain a better understanding of the local culture and have a much more relaxing time.

LEAVING HOME

Leaving home for a holiday is exciting but so is coming home to a house that's exactly as you left it. If you have great neighbours, let them know your travel plans as well as if anyone will be visiting the house while you're away and any plans you have for security. Here are a few more things to check before you go:

- Find someone to pick up your mail, take out the bins and bring them back in.
- Make sure you have someone organised to look after your animals.
- Consider turning off the water if you're away for a long time. Brij's parents turn off the water if they are going away for a while (returning to a flooded laundry after one trip was a valuable lesson).

- Check you have turned off the heater, iron and other appliances, and switch off computers and remove the plug from the socket. It's always good to unplug any electronics that won't be needing power.
- Seal all open boxes in the pantry.
- Put a good healthy meal in the freezer for the night of your return.
- Clean the house, clean out the fridge and pantry and empty all the rubbish bins.
- Do you have timers? Automatic lights can ward off unwanted attention. Get a watering timer for your garden so you don't come home to a sad garden.
- Double-check you have locked all windows and doors.

HELPFUL WEBSITES

You'll find you can do a lot of planning online before your trip. Here are some great websites to use.

- **smarttraveller.gov.au:** a great Australian government travel advice website (you can register your travel plans online to receive safety alerts)
- **health.gov.au:** for advice on vaccinations required when travelling
- **passports.gov.au:** apply or renew online, plus find other passport information
- **seatguru.com:** a good way of sussing out the best seats on most plane models
- **rome2rio.com:** one of the best ways to get information on all forms of transport from A to B worldwide
- **roadtrippers.com:** for help with planning, booking and navigating your trip
- **hopper.com:** for cost-saving ways to book flights and hotels
- **translate.com:** a must-have when travelling in non-English-speaking countries
- **tripexpert.com:** the place for honest reviews of hotels, restaurants and attractions
- **wires.org.au:** for rescue of injured wildlife in New South Wales (the website lists contact details for rescue organisations in other states)
- **bom.gov.au:** check the weather of your Australian destinations.

PACKING

We have to ask a question first: why do 90 per cent of us buy black or navy blue suitcases? At least that's what it feels like when you are trying to spot your needle in a stack of needles. If you need to buy a new case for your trip, consider being bold with your colour choices. Or you can use ribbons to make your bag stand out. We are a proud ribbon family – not only does it make it super easy to find your luggage, it also makes it less likely someone will accidentally take your black bag. And don't forget to attach a luggage tag with your contact details in case the luggage gets lost.

Brij read an article on how to pack the lightest suitcase. She thought it was fantastic until two paragraphs in the author mentioned zip-off pants. Zip-off pants might be great for a hiking trip, but they don't really suit the streets of Paris or New York. Regardless, packing light will nearly always make your trip easier. If you are backpacking, packing light becomes an art form. Even with a suitcase, keep it light: while dragging your family's five heavy suitcases up three flights of very narrow stairs is an excellent work-out, it's not actually much fun.

When you're travelling with kids, it's worth being super organised with your packing. (Once we forgot to pack undies for Oscar when he was three. Luckily we were heading to Paris, so we could grab some emergency ones and Oscar didn't have to free-ball in the City of Light.) One thing we also do is pack brightly coloured clothing for the kids – this way you can find them easily.

It sounds a little crazy, but packing twice can be really helpful, especially with kids. We put everything out, make sure everything's there, check the shoes and then pack. Then Brij will take it all out again, count how many days we're away for and figure out if she can lighten the load. Then repack! This also helps you make sure you haven't forgotten an essential like undies (sorry Oscar!) – you'll usually notice anything missing second time around.

Check the temperatures of your destinations before you leave. Are you travelling cold to hot? Our trip to the United States involved temperatures ranging from minus 15 degrees to 30 degrees Celsius and we had to make sure we had sufficient gear to cover both of these extremes.

When you're on the road with kids it's good to pack some fun and games. We will always spend time in various parks so pack small items such as a frisbee, tennis ball, blow-up ball and a small bat. Balloons are great for inside play – we've even taken fly swatters so the kids can play balloon-tennis.

Brij has kept packing lists on her phone from over the years of travelling with the kids, from skiing to weekenders. We have included two examples on the next page and adjusted them to work for boys and girls. She prints them off for the kids and they pack themselves now – this is a great way to get older kids involved in the holiday planning. Brij packs general toiletries like toothbrushes and toothpaste, but the kids look after anything else they need. If it's a big trip or something like skiing we always double-check that they have packed everything, because sometimes kids just want to get back to playing Fortnite with their mates, which can mean they end up not having ski pants at the snow. Weird that.

PACKING LIST – WARM LONG WEEKEND WITH FLIGHT

- Raincoat 1
- Pants 1
- Shirt/dress to wear out (short sleeve is best) 1
- T-shirts 5
- Shorts 4/Skirts 2
- Undies 6–7
- Socks 6
- Jumper 1
- Track pants 1 (for plane) plus T-shirt
- Swimmers
- PJs 2
- Thongs
- Runners
- Backpack for plane
- Book
- iPad or other
- Charger
- Notebook and pen
- Hat
- Deodorant
- Hair product
- A smile and your excitement

PACKING LIST - USA WARM AND COLD

Gather items and put aside – do not pack into bag.

- All thermals – check they still fit
- Undies 10–12
- Socks 6 or so (warmest)
- Jumpers 3 (warmest)
- Long top for under jacket 1
- Beanies 2
- Track pants 1
- Winter PJs 2
- Ski jacket
- T-shirts 7
- Shirt/dress to wear out 1
- Jeans/pants 2
- Swimmers
- Shorts 2/Skirt 1
- Boots 1
- Thongs 1
- Runners 1
- Deodorant
- Sunglasses
- Chargers
- Book
- iPad or other
- Games

BRIJ'S GENERAL PACKING ESSENTIALS

Here are a few of my essentials when packing for your trip.

Dryer sheets: I don't use the term *must-have* very often but dryer sheets are simply a must-have when travelling. I know many people who didn't know they existed until I started raving about them. Simply throw some in your suitcase to keep everything smelling nice rather than stale and dirty. Plus, they are phenomenal multi-taskers! They remove stains, clean your glasses, remove deodorant stains, freshen shoes, remove sand stuck to your feet, repel insects (I'm yet to try this), clean electronic screens and freshen a musty room.

Zip-lock bags: Take a selection of sizes. Put your bottles in one to avoid leaks. I always pop our toothbrushes in one. I carry extras as you will always find uses for them, from storing LEGO to saving food. Zip-lock bags are also great for the beach: pop your phone in one and it's safe from a water-bottle leak or a sunscreen spill.

Teabags: If you are a tea lover and don't drink coffee you'll appreciate this little reminder. Coffee can be found everywhere, but good tea often can't. I have even been known to travel with a little kettle, as many coffee-loving countries think a coffee machine will suffice as a kettle (it doesn't, because who wants coffee-flavoured, lukewarm tea?).

Luggage scale: It's not much fun having to unpack and repack your suitcases at the check-in desk in front of everyone (trust me, I've had to do it), so it pays to keep an eye on the weight of your luggage. Travelling with a luggage scale will help you throughout your trip (it will also help you keep a check on any shopping).

Fold-up travel bag: Leave this at the bottom of your suitcase. That way, if you have a last-day shopping fix and can't fit it all in, an extra bag is waiting for you.

First-aid kit: It will always be needed when travelling with kids, even if just for a bandaid. In your kit include antiseptic, basic dressings, bandaids, hand sanitiser, insect repellent, sting treatment, water-purifying tablets, pain relief (both adult and child), allergy meds, multivitamins, lozenges, indigestion and motion sickness remedies, sunscreen and lip balm. Don't forget any prescription medications along with a letter from your doctor and extra prescriptions if needed. Depending on where you're going, it may also be worth including anti-diarrhoea medications, some probiotics and electrolyte replacements.

Smaller items: I find it helpful to include:

- masking tape (great to put over power points)
- scissors (not for hand luggage)
- a black marker-pen
- a plug-in night-light for younger kids
- binder clips (helpful for cords, headphones and shavers).

ESSENTIALS FOR THE LITTLE ONES

These are the key things we've found you need when travelling with kids.

Nappies: Pack plenty of nappies in both your hand luggage and suitcase – it's best to plan for not getting to a supermarket in the first two days. Remember to bring plastic bags to put the dirty nappies in (the bags are also handy for wet bathers or a thrown-up-on shirt). If you are heading to places with pools, beaches, rivers or lakes, remember to pack swimming nappies. If you prefer reusable nappies, make sure you have the ability to wash them.

Wipes: Pack wipes in both your hand luggage and suitcase. Wipes are handy for everything, not just baby bottoms. Not every plane you get on or place you eat will be spotless and, if you're a bit of a germaphobe like Brij, wipes can put your mind at ease.

Changing pads: Disposable ones are great for the plane and reusable changing pads are perfect for your destination.

Blanket: Pack a blanket if your baby or child gets cold or likes to snuggle up (especially for road trips where your luggage isn't as limited). The thickness will depend on the weather, and don't forget the security one if needed. Take ones that you don't mind getting lost, stolen or ruined.

Pusher or stroller: If you need a pusher or stroller, choose the cheapest, lightest and most compact stroller available (but make sure it is still comfortable). Keep in mind that places or paths with rough terrain won't suit a stroller. Slings and backpack carriers have their advantages but if you're heading to a hot and humid destination, baby-wearing can be uncomfortable for both you and your bub.

Bottles and food: Don't forget the sippy cups or water bottles for your little ones – it's so important to ensure they stay hydrated when you're travelling and out of your usual routines. If you are travelling with a bottle-fed baby, there are many options on the market to make this a bit easier. First ensure you have enough formula for the trip, and take a little extra just in case. For the plane you can get compartmentalised storage containers, so you don't need to take a whole tin. There are single-use bottles available; these are not environmentally great but if you don't have the ability to clean or your baby needs sterilised bottles and you don't have a steriliser then they're worth looking into. To keep the bottle warm, you can buy portable travel warmers. Remember to pack all the cleaning items required for bottles and a steriliser if you're able to use one. There are also water purification tablets available, where water is drinkable in 30 minutes. It's worth having a pack just in case.

Plastic cutlery: Sometimes little spoons aren't available and if you're travelling in countries where chopsticks are the local utensil of choice, it's a good idea to have spoons and forks on hand.

Travel booster seat: We had a fantastic travel booster seat that self-inflated and strapped onto any type of dining chair – we used this everywhere and anywhere. There was no highchair taking up room at the table and the kids felt like they were just like everyone else. These are not for use in a car.

Floaties and life vests: If you are travelling anywhere with water, have the right gear for those little ones to get into the water safely. Blow-up floats for pools, vests for the lakes, oceans and bays and a full life vest for rivers. A life vest is the best choice for any child who isn't a strong swimmer. When choosing a life vest for the little ones go with one that has head support, which keeps their head facing the sky (it will help kids to float face up). It's good to have one with a grab strap as well. For more swimming safety tips, *see* p. 37.

Kid's backpack: It's not a must-have really but, depending on the age of your kids, it's a great idea to give them their own little backpack. They can carry their cuddly toys (Oscar carried his teddy bear, Rosy, in his little daypack. Rosy was lost in Prague and then thankfully was sent back to Australia, only to get lost back home). They can also carry activities, books and snacks for travelling. It's better to pack healthy, filling snacks rather than lollies. In startlingly breaking news, sugar *isn't* the greatest thing to keep shoving into the gobs of kids. We don't go completely sugarless but do try to include healthier snacks that will also fill them up.

Other things to consider: There are so many amazing little gadgets to buy for little kids when travelling these days and we've had our fair share of 'Why didn't we think of inventing that?' moments. But with all those awesome travel gadgets comes the fact you have to carry them as well as your baby. Figure out what you can do without: for example, that colourful mat with a toy canopy will be a much hated item if you are on the move. Is that ride-on scooter suitcase going to be as fun on cobblestone streets as it is in the airport? Do your research and decide on what you really need. We took a great cot on one trip after much consideration – it had a self-inflating mattress, blow-up sides and a sleeping bag, weighed less than 2kg and folded up smaller than a backpack. It was fantastic for places that didn't offer cots or had rooms that were too small for a normal one. What about car seats? Well, we have never travelled overseas with our own car seats. If you are travelling in a hire car, you can book a car seat to be included (see if the company will fit it for you).

BRIJ AND THE TWO-DOZEN KOALAS
(BY PETE)

Among the tins of baby formula, bottles and nappies in our luggage before our French adventure I noticed an unanticipated addition. Shoved between the nappies and Oscar's jeans were two packets of koalas. Not real koalas and not the type full of delicious smooth caramel; instead they were novelty furry koalas with clip-on claws allowing them to attach to whatever you may want to attach a toy koala to.

I wasn't completely surprised that Brij had packed novelty koalas thinking that the kids might find some value in having one each, a fun reminder of home to provide entertainment on the long flights and car drives ahead. But there weren't three clip-on koalas, there were 24!

'Do we really need 24 clip-on koalas?' I asked Brij, who looked sheepish. See, Brij had an idea. An idea that came from the goodness of her heart. These koalas were not for our kids but to be gifted to kids we met on our travels. She envisaged our boys playing with French boys and girls under the Eiffel Tower, kicking soccer balls and swinging off monkey bars.

Turns out we didn't meet many kids who were koala-worthy. And we always seemed to meet the ones who *were* worthy of the honour of a clip-on marsupial when the koalas were left back in our apartment.

We returned to Australia after six weeks with exactly two-dozen clip-on koalas. But it's the thought that counts, right?

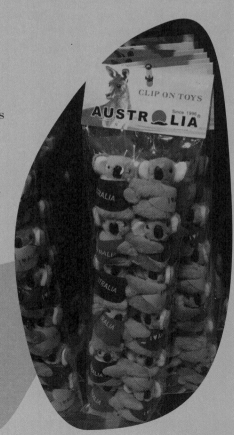

PLANES, TRAINS AND AUTOMOBILES

There are so many ways to get from A to B on your holiday and often it comes down to what's available, what works for your budget and what your personal preference is. Whatever transport we're taking, Brij loves to allow plenty of time for transit. Pete, for some reason, doesn't agree with this – his preferred method is to leave as little time as possible, sometimes even missing flights. Allowing more time means that if anything goes wrong, like you get to the wrong airport, or security is busy, or your train changes platform, you won't be worried and you'll have time to figure everything out. So aim to make transit as relaxing as possible – when you're relaxed, the kids are more likely to be too.

PLANES

Whenever the idea of travelling abroad with kids comes up, it is usually the thought of the plane trip with the kids that causes parents to curl up into the foetal position. Actually, the plane ride can often be the easy part. There is probably a tricky age where older bubs and younger toddlers are more challenging to manage but they will get tired soon enough. Older kids are just happy to have access to their own screen all the way to Europe! Aidan once famously did an all-nighter, watching *Diary of a Wimpy Kid* five times in a row, on the way to Denmark, which led him to be so sleep-deprived he walked straight into the glass foyer doors at our Copenhagen hotel. Oh, how we wish we had filmed that! So don't let a long flight put you off from seeing the world. Here are some tips that'll make the journey easier.

Being organised will help with plane journeys big and small. We pack our hand luggage a few days before we leave, so we can check off all necessary items:

- passports
- wallet, with unnecessary cards removed (you won't be using that Video Ezy VIP membership)
- house keys placed somewhere safe
- single-use eye drops
- lip balm
- moisturiser
- hand sanitiser
- hand wipes that are actually body wipes (so you can freshen up quickly)
- face wipes
- medications
- barley sugars to help with ear-popping
- tissues
- book
- tablet/device (if you want it)
- phone
- notebook
- pens
- headphones with appropriate adapters
- kid-size headphones
- phone charger/USB cable.

Choose your seats on the plane as soon as you can. Aisle seats are great for the parents because little ones can't easily escape. Use a seating site, such as seatguru.com, to help you choose ones away from the toilets or galley where they prepare meals. When flying with babies, book in a bassinet as soon as you book your flights. That bassinet is gold on long-haul flights; even if your bub doesn't actually go to sleep in it, you get space and maybe some rest to free up your hands.

Travelling with younger ones will always require more items in your carry-on. Don't forget to pack more than enough nappies and wipes. Carry a second set of clothes for the little ones. Brij also always packs an extra set of clothes for herself. She has been thrown up on, had juice and water spilled on her; melted chocolate on her seat and probably so much more she somehow manages to forget – yes, it's one of the joys of sitting next to Pete. And if it happens twice, hope the first set has dried.

Parents, please, please take notice of what your children are doing to the seat in front of them. Constantly kicking, grabbing onto the headrest and putting the seat tray up and down is very frustrating for the poor person in front. If it does happen, apologise to the person – it will go a long way to help. Of course, one of the things people most worry about when travelling with a baby or toddler is the possible crying and how it might affect other passengers. Most people will understand and most people have headphones (often noise-cancelling ones too).

Before hopping off the plane we all try to do a wake-up ritual. About 90 minutes before landing (before the toilets get crowded), we all brush our teeth (but don't drink or use the water from the bathroom; use bottled water instead), use wipes to freshen our faces and hands, and start packing up our carry-on bags. We have managed to encourage the kids to do the same thing – it's really important for them to pack everything and check their bag for their iPad, jumper, shoes and so on (we have had to run back to the aircraft and grab something before heading through Customs and it was a little bit stressful!).

Being organised certainly helps when disembarking with children. Remember, you don't have to be the first off the plane. Take time to gather all the little belongings if your kids are too young to pack up their own bag and double-check the overhead compartment and seat pockets. Take your time getting to the luggage carousel and let the kids burn off any stored energy.

There is so much waiting to be done in airports, and exiting can have just as many things to wait for as entering. Having those Customs entry forms filled out during the flight is a must. Five passport numbers and five forms for some countries is too many to try to fill in while in the Customs queue. We share the duties between the adults.

And a bit of fun – we play the luggage carousel game every time we fly (even if it's just the two of us). The rules are simple: first bag out wins. There are no rewards, it's just about taking the bragging rights.

TRAINS

Train travel is our favourite transport on holiday: it's relaxing, you see the countryside, you can walk around and trains are generally very comfortable. Not needing to be at the station three hours before departure or go through security is a bonus you don't get at airports. There are some small downsides, like having to lift a 33kg suitcase above your head to get to the luggage rack (though some trains have places at each end of the carriage for larger cases).

Travel agents can help you with all your train travel needs. There are so many options with trains around the world, so get some good advice from people who have probably done it themselves.

When booking, check out seat availability and make sure you can all sit together. For Japan get your JR Pass before you leave Australia. We find that Europe is very easy to get around but if you know the dates you'll be needing the trains it's best to get organised and book tickets before you leave. If we can manage it, we like to add first-class or a sleeper carriage to our budget when travelling longer distances – this way you have a seat assigned and it's a nice experience. The cost isn't overwhelming like it is for a first-class plane ticket so it can be affordable.

When travelling overnight, if you don't purchase a sleeping cabin with your own conductor, remember the carriage may not always be safe: there is a chance of theft occurring while you are asleep. Make sure your passports are locked away and remove anything lying on the ground. Get the kids to keep their

BEATING JET LAG

Setting your body clock to a new time zone isn't always easy, especially if you have crossed several time zones, but here are our tips to get you and the kids going.

No other way of putting it – this is Oscar absolutely cracking it in Dublin

Hydration is key. Drink plenty of water before, during and after your flight. Check the kids are hydrating regularly too. Limit alcohol or caffeinated drinks and sleep whenever you can. We wouldn't recommend taking sleeping tablets for adults or kids as medication does have side effects and does not help with jet lag.

As soon as we get on the plane and settle in, Brij sets her wristwatch to the local time of our destination. Tell the kids what time it is in the destination too so they get used to the idea.

You can read up on plane food – many of the experts say not to eat the food at all. There are no Michelin stars heading the way of any in-flight meal anytime soon but the meals are better than they use to be. Yes, the overload of carbs and processed food will not help with jet lag, but hungry is hungry, especially for kids. The answer is to opt for eating less. Perhaps don't touch the bread roll (they usually feel stale anyway) and decline the dessert, ice-creams, juice and chocolates on offer. On shorter flights, just don't bother – it's best to pack some snacks, drink water, have a mint and wait until you land for a proper meal.

Wear loose clothing and stretch, walk and move as much as you and the kids can. Put on extra socks when you take off your shoes as the cabin will get cold (but please put your shoes back on when going to the bathroom – just google 'dirty airline bathrooms' and you'll never go there in your socks again).

We always take eye masks, good headphones and earplugs. The earplugs may fall out once you're sleeping but they will help you actually *fall* asleep so they're worth it. Kids benefit from using eye masks too. For the younger ones, we put them into some PJs, brush their teeth and read them a book, because mimicking their bedtime routine does help.

Once you land, hit the ground running – well, not running but briskly walking. Daylight is helpful for jet lag and convincing the body clock that you're not ready to head to bed. We arrived in Tokyo at 6am and, of course, the hotel room wasn't ready. We had barely slept on the plane but we went to the bathroom in the hotel foyer, freshened up and changed clothes before we left our luggage – then we were ready to hit the streets. We had breakfast, checked out our neighbourhood, worked out the metro and got some much needed exercise. We came back that afternoon when our room was ready, had our showers and went out for dinner. It was the perfect way to ignore the sleepiness and plus exercise is a great way to rejuvenate.

belongings in their backpack locked above when asleep. It's better to be aware of these possibilities than to regret the outcome. Brij once had her sleeping bag cover stolen; it had fallen to the ground and the thieves crawled under the seats while she was asleep. Thankfully, they didn't care much for her sleeping bag cover and dropped it in the next carriage, but they got away with cameras, passports and wallets from her fellow passengers.

Talking security, be relaxed but aware, alert but not alarmed, at train stations. Keep all your belongings with you or in a locked locker. Watch the kids at all times and don't stand in large groups. Being distracted will make it easier for people to steal from you.

Don't be late for your train – it won't wait! Arriving about 30 minutes before departure will be enough time to find your platform and get organised. If the station is a big one or is confusing, get there a little earlier to find your way around. Also make sure you have enough time between connections (usually 30 minutes is enough) to change platforms and allow for a delayed initial train.

This may seem obvious but if possible avoid travelling at busy times; trains will be full and it might be harder to sit together. If you have to travel during a peak time, choosing first-class on most trains will reserve seats and guarantee the whole family is sitting together so you can happily annoy each other without having to reach or shout over fellow commuters.

Taking water and snacks is a good idea, though you can usually buy food on the train and some first-class tickets offer free snacks. Letting kids choose their own snacks – within reason – can be a good use of excess time.

Most importantly, put the iPad down and look out the window. We know it's a radical idea worthy of its very own TED Talk but it's truly worth the effort of looking up, we promise you. Experience the sight of snow in Massachusetts, smell the scent of the tea plantations in Sri Lanka or take in the beauty that is Mount Fuji in Japan. Train travel is beautiful if you look up.

AUTOMOBILES

You have a few options if you're wanting to get around by car. You can hire a car for a few days or longer, or for short trips use taxis or ride-share services.

HIRE CAR

We recommend hiring the smallest car you (and your luggage) can all fit in. The smaller the car, the more money you'll save on petrol and the easier you'll find it driving around in strange cities (for example, some European cities and towns are much harder to drive in with bigger cars). With that said, this is your holiday and if you've always dreamed of exploring the Amalfi Coast in a Porsche SUV rather than a Ford Festiva, then go for it ... but good luck with parking.

Book your hire car in advance. Also book any car seats or booster seats you will need for the kids. If you want to save money on the hire car, buy your own GPS; you can get one from the car-hire company but book it at the same time as you book the car because companies often have a limited number of GPSs available.

When you first pick up your car, check it thoroughly for damage; if there is damage, take photos of it while you're still in the company's carpark. Don't assume the car is covered through your travel insurance. Put all drivers on the hire agreement so the company can't argue with you about who was driving.

You need to return the car with a full tank. If you're in a rush or there isn't a convenient petrol station nearby, don't panic – it just means you'll pay an inflated price for the petrol through the car-hire company. Some policies will be different: some options may include a fuel service or a pre-paid fuel service.

Sometimes it's convenient to return a car to a different location (for example, once we hired a car in Denmark and dropped it off in Berlin). It can cost a little bit more but this will balance out if you would have had to get tickets for a flight or train anyway.

TAXIS

Taxis can be convenient (but expensive) when getting around cities. The key thing with kids in taxis is to work out whether you need a car seat or not. The regulations for taxis are different from private cars, so check the rules for the countries and cities you are visiting before you arrive.

In Australia, rules differ across states. In Victoria, taxis are not required to provide car seats but do need to provide an anchorage point in case you bring your own. Also in Victoria, children aged under one must travel in the back seat, but do not have to use a child restraint, whereas in New South Wales children under one are not permitted to travel in a taxi unless they are secured in an approved car seat. Children over one can sit in the back seat using a seatbelt (though if possible it would be better to bring your own car seat). In New South Wales, you can book taxis with car seats (and all wheelchair-accessible taxis carry an approved child car seat) or use your own car seat (all taxis should have anchorage points). Generally at airports most information desks can help you book a taxi with a fitted car seat.

RIDE SHARING

Australian law states that all children travelling in a motor vehicle who are under seven years of age must be restrained in a suitable and properly secured restraint. A ride-share vehicle is just like any other private car and requires child restraints to be installed to transport children under seven. Ride-sharing services can be useful, though, and some offer worldwide services so your Australian account can be used anywhere. Or sign up to the most appropriate service for that country.

'I know the camera is on me so I'm looking adorable!' Oscar, Paris

YOUR HOLIDAY IS GO!

You've done the planning, you've all survived the journey and now you've arrived – congratulations! First, understand the city you are arriving in: it's good to have a sense for what will happen once you've landed, where to go and how to get from the airport to your accommodation. We always try to have a quick look at the airport map before we've left home so that if we have to find a hire-car desk or something similar, we can find it easily (this is because on arrival we're usually exhausted and the thought of walking around airport terminals lost and looking for a hire-car counter is as appealing as listening to an audio book narrated by Elmer Fudd). We always have our exit organised (usually co-ordinated by Captain Brij). Questions to consider when planning include: Does the hotel have a shuttle? Can we get five plus luggage in a cab? Is the train an easier option? Why didn't we learn this language from birth?

Sometimes the cheapest transport option isn't the easiest or best idea. If you are heading into a big city in peak hour, the central city trains will be packed and you'll be loaded with suitcases. It's the least fun you can have on a train: three kids, five suitcases and 200 people all pressed up on you. Consider a shuttle, if available, where peak-hour traffic won't affect your fare like it will in a cab. Be careful of unauthorised taxi drivers as you pass through security; they can end up costing you a fortune.

One thing we always do when hiring a car from an airport is that one parent lines up for the car and the other goes to the carousel for luggage. Hire-car lines can be long and it can take ages to process each person. Aim to have a car booked before arrival and keep your booking information handy. Being organised will make it easier because, after long-haul flights, kids are tired and you may be carrying one or more of them.

Liam and Aidan overlooking the Danube River, Budapest

GETTING OUT AND ABOUT

Culture shock can happen in the most unexpected places and to anyone. Brij's one and only experience was landing in Hanoi, Vietnam. The constant honking of the cars, complete lack of recognisable road rules, sheer abundance of people, general chaos and stifling humidity made Brij suddenly highly anxious. Luckily, her hero (this has been fact-checked three times and Brij is in fact referring to Pete here!) got her to the hotel room and talked her through it. Pete offered Brij a few options on what to do next and gave her time to regroup. Within 30 minutes we were back walking down that same chaotic street on the way to lunch and we never looked back. Sometimes you just need to take a moment.

Our kids haven't experienced culture shock to this point. We prepare them by talking about what the trip will involve, the culture they'll experience, what they'll see and what will happen when we land. For us, it's important to share the organising of a trip with the kids – this helps them to feel safe in a new environment.

The fun of visiting new places is finding those little gems that are often accessed only via a local guided tour. Having a local who speaks the language, who can take you to the best and most authentic spots to eat and who knows the history and culture of the place can be extremely rewarding. Many cities have family- and kid-focused tours available too. But remember you can do cities and countries by yourself – it just takes a bit of extra planning with kids.

If you decide to travel around a country, schedule time for kids to rest and recover. We do our washing and other tasks when the kids need a day off. Try to spend three to four days in each city or town when you're on a long trip. Having said that, one-night stopovers can be fun: we drove three hours to get to Carcassonne in France just to stay in a walled castle that dates back roughly 2000 years (it was an amazing experience but getting back on the road the next day was tiring for the kids, so we had to look for a longer stay at the next destination).

Don't fear a language barrier. Learn some key phrases to get you going (and it's a good idea to learn the possible responses too). Be prepared to eat a meal that you thought was spaghetti Bolognese but was actually marinara. It's all part of the fun.

We have done so many different type of trips with the kids and they have all been adventurous, exciting and sometimes a little bit nerve-racking. If we are about to do something that we haven't done before or that seems like it might be a bit out of our comfort zone, we find friends or family who have done it. We ask questions and make sure we're extra prepared – that way we don't miss out on new adventures. Remember, find your Luke and Liz (*see* p. xi if you skipped the bit about Luke and Liz earlier!).

STAYING SANE

Ah yes, one of the great challenges of travelling with kids: maintaining your sanity. Travelling with your little ones can definitely take its toll on your patience and energy levels, and we have, more than once, found ourselves with a crying baby and fighting toddlers in a long queue or at a busy train station or cafe. Most people will sympathise with your plight and generally people will want to help you (even if it's partly self-serving so they don't have to listen to a child screaming!). Our approach is to always be polite and smile. As hard as it may be in the moment, try to smile through it. We find sometimes apologising for the craziness can inspire people to help you out. People tend to want help nice, friendly people; it's human nature to not want to go out of your way to help rude people. Try to stay calm, explain what is happening and ask for help.

You can be completely organised, bags packed perfectly and tickets in hand. Yet the stresses of holidays can creep in and make it about as much fun as a beach holiday for a polar bear. Sometimes just getting everyone to the airport has the potential to be the biggest 'fight day' of all; there will be so much nervous energy and excitement, so word-up the kids early on how important it is for everyone to pitch in. As the adults, remind yourselves to breathe and be prepared for not everything to go perfectly. This way it will be a lovely surprise when things do go smoothly (which we are sure they will!).

For some reason Pete becomes a game show model whenever he orders a whisky. Taken in Tokyo.

Here are some of our quick tips to keep your kids (or you!) from having a meltdown in the middle of Times Square:

- Little kids need rest. Don't push them beyond their limits. Be realistic about their coping abilities. Heading back to the hotel for breaks or finding a park to rest for a little while can be the best thing to do.
- When kids are getting a bit over their siblings, split up and go for a walk.
- On the road? Try to cook some home meals because often kids' menus can be as dull as a flat basketball.
- Make sure you're carrying plenty of water. Sometimes you might also need electrolytes, particularly if travelling in humid conditions (or particularly if you opened that second bottle of pinot after the kids went to sleep last night).
- Get some alone time and have an adult conversation. These holidays are not just about the kids. They are just as much about you as an individual and as a couple.
- Stay in decent accommodation. It doesn't have to be six-star but it will be your sanctuary at times. You don't want to exchange the hustle and bustle of Shanghai for the hustle and bustle of a cramped and dirty hotel room.
- Be open to diversions, mishaps and experiences. Embrace these where possible. Leave expensive things at home, then you don't have to worry about losing things.
- Let kids vent. As wonderful as the memories of your trip will be, it can be stressful or overwhelming at times.
- Don't stress about screen-time rules. Every family will have their own ideas of how much screen time they are prepared to tolerate but chances are if you are getting out and about and seeing the world, your kids will be on their screens *way* less than they would be at home.
- Be patient with tough times. Whatever the frustrating situation you are in, it won't last forever. So many things have gone 'wrong' for us when travelling but now we laugh at those memories the most. Remind yourselves in the moment – even say it out loud so you can all hear – 'We will all laugh about this one day.' You'd be surprised how much it can help defuse the tension in the moment. We sometimes go a step further and try to put a timeframe on *when* exactly we will begin laughing at this horrid moment.
- Rest when tired and consider omitting something from your list of places to visit. Part of travelling as a family is just being together, whether it be out and about or lounging around a hotel swimming pool or even the hotel room. These are good times to get the kids chatting about what they have seen and even what they are missing from back home.
- Let the kids sleep in sometimes … if they can. Feel free to do the same occasionally … if you can.

KEEPING COSTS DOWN

Whatever budget you are on, you want your dollars or yen or dong to go as far as they can. By saving here and there along the way you may be able to have that fancy dinner at that uber cool restaurant they once mentioned on *MasterChef*. Here are our budgeting tips:

- Make your own breakfast in the room and/or pack lunch. Pack your own snacks and water for the day out.
- Pre-purchase tickets where possible.
- Park passes for theme parks can save money.
- Look into multi-day tourist passes for public transport.
- Travelling outside school holidays is cheaper (though not recommended for students in Years 11 and 12).
- Some days of the week will be cheaper to fly on than others.
- Local deal websites often have good deals for travellers, but always check the fine print to make sure that the vouchers can be used in the time that you travel.
- Limit the number of times kids ask 'Can I have …?' by giving them a certain amount of money to spend. It's a great learning curve for the quick spenders to watch their saving sibling buy something better by waiting later.
- If driving, keep fuel costs lower by packing light.
- Do your own washing in a laundromat if you can.
- Look into memberships of caravan parks, airlines, hotel chains and so on.
- Consider the type of holiday that suits your budget. Camping is cheaper than a resort extravaganza. Theme parks are more expensive than city exploring. Beach holidays are dearer than inland getaways.
- There are many deal websites that offer cheap airfares or will watch the prices for you (iknowthepilot.com.au and secretflying.com are two examples).
- For ski trips book your accommodation well in advance.
- Look for ski-pass discounts for children and half-price days for everyone.
- Check to see if buying a ski pass in advance is worth the savings.
- Get a fuel map app for Australia.
- Eat away from tourist streets when dining out. You'll get some great local atmosphere as well.
- Book all-inclusive resorts but double-check (Brij says triple-check!) if it really is all-inclusive.
- Look for free or half-price museum days.

TRAVELLING WITH OTHER FAMILIES

This can be a fun holiday option but, no matter how well you know each other or how closely related you are, everyone travels differently. And everyone parents differently. Here are our tips to travel well with other families:

- Keep to your sleep-time routine and remind your kids of this at the beginning of the trip before you meet up with the other family.
- Organise a few separate family meals if needed. It's a good time for the kids to wind down. Just like adults, sometimes kids need a break from other kids.
- It's helpful to have similar interests. If a family hasn't done this particular kind of trip before, assist them without doing it all for them.
- Go for a walk if someone is irritating you. Decide whether your irritation can be put aside for the betterment of the holiday. Holidays and confrontations are not happy bedfellows.
- Before booking, consider whether all the kids actually get along. Be open and honest. Ask your kids if the idea of going to Fiji with the Burke clan excites them or would they rather eat a bowl of fire ants? And, of course, consider if both of you like the accompanying adults enough. Or has one of you simply been tolerating Trudy's hubby and his endless tirades about the fake moon landing?
- Keep costs separate and when dining out pay for your own family. Spilt the bill for shared groceries between families. Have an open discussion about this early on.
- Remember you don't need to spend every waking moment together; it's good to get out and about with just your family. This should be something that you are open about early in your planning – that you will have days or nights doing your own thing.

Fun along the Seine, Paris

ACCOMMODATION

We have stayed in almost every means of accommodation available. Hotels are good for housekeeping but bad for making your own breakfast. Apartments are brilliant for eating in and bad for housekeeping. Airbnb and other similar sites are fantastic for local living. No matter the type of accommodation we choose, we always want a place that's easily accessible to public transport. If you want accommodation with a kitchen, choose a place that is within walking distance of a supermarket.

Don't forget young kids need to rest, so plan your days to ensure you can get back to your accommodation for naps or downtime then, once rested, head back out. Your trip will be determined by how much your youngest can handle, so take time out for meals, naps, rest and more toilet stops than you are in the mood for.

If your toddlers usually sleep with a bed rail, a quick tip is to roll a towel and place it lengthways under the bed sheet (one on both sides if needed) to stop the little one from rolling out. Some people take a cut-down pool noodle, but we think that takes up way too much precious packing space.

BABYSITTERS

You're on holiday with your kids, but it's understandable that you might want a night out. Finding the right babysitter is important. We have used them cautiously – we always choose a reputable company or a service recommended by our travel agent or hotel and spend time with the babysitter before we head out. Cruises and resorts have kids' clubs and nanny services available. If you don't want a babysitter, get a room with a balcony so there's an adult space for you once the kids have gone to sleep. Adjoining rooms are also good to get some time without *Bluey* on the TV.

Oscar – drunk or tired?

LAUNDRY

Figure out how many times you can get laundry done and plan your packing around it. Places like Bali and Fiji have a daily laundry service (our favourite hotel in LA offers it too). Pack less and get your laundry done daily. Bear in mind, though, that most hotel laundry services in big cities are crazy expensive so find an alternative. Some countries, such as Japan, have fantastic fluff-and-fold businesses – you drop off your laundry and they return it to your hotel, all wrapped up in paper with a nice little bow. If all else fails, spend a few hours in a laundromat and fold it yourself (no paper or bows but clean clothes are oh so good).

On a practical level, a compact travel clothesline is very handy. Take a little bit of powdered washing detergent or laundry soap (if you plan on doing your washing in a laundromat, powder is best). Also pack a cloth bag for your dirty washing. Not only is it easier to organise when washing day comes around, but you can throw a dryer sheet in the bag and your dirty washing smells delightful.

HEADING HOME

At the end of your trip, consider donating items, such as clothing, that you won't have any further use for. If you can do this at the city you're departing from, you'll save on luggage too.

When leaving a country, we often have a pocket full of coins and usually donate any leftover currency to UNICEF or to the homeless (you'll find donation points at airports).

On arriving back in Australia, remember to declare for inspection all food, plant material and animal products to ensure they are free of pests and diseases. For more info visit australia.gov.au/information-and-services/passports-and-travel.

We know the idea of declaring something seems like it will take longer, but if you are honest and go through the right area it can take less time than the nothing to declare line, especially if there are a few big planes exiting at the same time. Do the right thing and make sure you are not bringing in anything you shouldn't.

And finally, celebrate that the fact that *you did it* – you just went trippin' with your kids and had a family holiday to remember!

TYPES OF HOLIDAYS

There are endless types of holidays, but here are three popular types you may want to consider.

CAMPING

Camping can be such a simple and enjoyable family holiday, especially for kids, and a great way to get 'back to nature'. Regardless of your camping experience, preparation is key. Here are our tips.

There are so many different ways to camp, but make sure you have comfortable accommodation. Check your tent for damage, including zips and floor. There are lots of bugs and slithery things in the bush and you don't want them in your tent. Our boys have their own off-ground swags, which they love (and it means they're away from creepy-crawlies on the ground). Make your sure bedding is enough to keep you warm and dry. It can get cold anywhere, so take extra blankets or sleeping bags and a good jumper. Beyond the tent, figure out what shade you'll need – for example, tarps or a super-easy gazebo (try to get instant-up, or at least easy-up, for any shelter you bring). As important as shelter is, ground cover is too. Keep the dust from coming into your home away from home. Good ground covers are reasonably priced; get ones that can be used on all terrain (just be aware that some caravan parks only allow certain types, such as breathable ground covers, to ensure the grass doesn't die off).

If you don't want to pitch a tent, you can hire caravans and camper trailers. Check with the company you hire from that you are allowed to travel to certain places (some won't allow you to travel on dirt roads, for example).

Have you ever tried glamping? Glamping options are popping up everywhere and many are starting to accommodate families. It's Brij's mission to have the best glamped-up campsite on the river by 2024.

In terms of what to pack, on top of our must-haves list are mozzie coils and a pack of cards. You'll also need lamps, torches and lanterns, and take extra batteries. Have extra tent pegs and rope too – you never know what you'll need to MacGyver. Apart from the obvious kitchen items, remember to take fuel, lighter, bottle opener and corkscrew. Other useful things to include are marshmallow sticks for the fire, a sharp knife and paper towel.

If you are planning on taking your dog, check your destination. National parks and some free campsites don't allow dogs.

If you're going hiking, remember to wear in your boots well in advance, take a raincoat and get a pack cover or line your pack with a good quality garbage bag (there's nothing worse than wet clothes or a soggy sleeping bag).

CRUISES

Cruises can make for great family holidays and usually provide a good mix of fun activities for kids and relaxation for adults. If you're keen on booking a cruise, here are some of our practical tips.

Getting on and off the cruise is fairly straightforward. Remember to check that you have your passports in your hand luggage before the port-person takes your luggage away. Brij had to desperately chase our portman down before he put our bags on the ship on a trip to Jamaica from Florida after we forgot to do this.

You will receive an allocated check-in time. There is no point going any earlier and trying to score an earlier boarding time – it's just not how it works. Arrive at the time they've allocated or perhaps ten minutes earlier, but not much more because you could be waiting for ages at a boring port that does not have the shops, cafes or lounges that airports do.

Arrive in the city or town of departure the day before your ship is due to leave. It is way more relaxing to know you are just up the road from your departure point and won't miss the ship. Like any other form of public transport, ships won't wait for you.

What type of cabin do you need? Do you want a balcony? These are great for people prone to motion sickness. Do you need connecting rooms? If you book in advance you can get pretty much everything you need. Remember, the cabins are pretty small and squishy so packing lighter will be helpful. It is good to pack a power board because there aren't many power outlets in the room.

Brij struggles with motion sickness badly. Getting on a cruise ship with severe motion sickness issues is terribly frightening. Your doctor or pharmacist will recommend motion sickness tablets but remember you do need to start taking them before you get on the ship. You can also get some herbal remedies that might be helpful and usually the purser's desk will have sea-sickness tablets too if you run out. There are other things you can do too. Our amazing travel agent booked us in the middle of the ship for sleeping so Brij had fewer issues. Going lower in the ship made her sea-sickness worse and seeing the water splashing in the pools wasn't helpful either. Things that did help Brij included looking at the horizon a lot and wearing a motion sickness bracelet. Brij also ate ginger anything (you can get ginger in cocktails, you know!) and tried not to think about feeling sick.

Many cruises have nurseries or babysitters for littlies and a kids' club for older kids that will usually have long opening hours. Oscar asked if he could go back to his at 3am as they were going to do something so fun. He was pretty upset when we told him we'd all be sleeping.

If you have teens on board, the older teens often have access to a teen lounge, but it's a 'come and go as you please' type scenario. Set responsible rules for older teenagers too; the ship is a fun place to explore and will have lots for teens to do, but the usual teenage dangers exist even when at sea, such as alcohol, drugs, indecency and bullying. Just to be clear and not besmirch our sons' good names (thus far), this was not an issue for any of our boys.

In terms of health, the golden rule is to always wash your hands. Keeping your hands clean stops you getting sick and stops anything spreading. You have probably seen it on the news occasionally: massive gastro outbreak on a cruise ship turns dream trip into the holiday from hell. Well, you can do your bit. Wash your hands *all the time*. At *every* opportunity. Cruise ships have hand sanitiser readily available at almost every doorway. Use it and stay well.

Do your sums on the packages offered – will the drinks package be worth it? A money-saving tip from cruise regulars is to take your own wine on board. Liquor and beer are not allowed but each person of legal drinking age is allowed one bottle of wine each. Bring that extra special bottle of champagne with you to celebrate rather than pay a ridiculous price on board.

Some cruises have free or minimal-cost room service, which can be a nice break from the crowds in the main dining room, especially for the kids.

Most of the time you won't need to add a tip to your bill as it is automatically added. Tipping every time you come in contact with staff could lead to a big bill upon disembarking.

Remember you don't need to get off the ship at every port. Stay on board instead and you'll find spas sometimes offer discounts, lunch is quieter and you'll get lounges at the pool without any hassle.

SKIING

As you'll discover further on in this book, we *love* skiing holidays! (*See* pp. 169 and 220 for some of our favourite skiing spots.) If you're planning a skiing trip, there are a few things to consider. Are you prepared to take all your own gear if you have it? Are you visiting other places beside ski resorts? Some places have daily pick-up ski hire so you don't have to trek the gear home or to other mountains (carrying the kids and their gear after a long day on the slopes is hard work).

If you don't have all the necessary items to keep you warm, you can easily hire them. Just don't forget goggles, neck warmers and quality gloves (we would recommend two pairs for the kids because they will be picking up snow all the time). Take some winter gloves for going into town too, as you'll need to keep those little hands warm all the time.

Bros before snows... Liam and Aidan taking on the mountain

CARING FOR OUR WORLD
(BY BRIJ)

When I started travelling it was all about the adventure and not so much about what I left behind. As I get older, I travel with more awareness and care, and I hope I'm teaching my kids to respect what we have in this world.

ANIMAL TOURISM

Something that we have become more and more aware of in our travels is the need for ethical animal tourism. Usually cruelty to animals is hidden from tourists, so simply remember this: if you can ride the animal, take a photo with it or touch it, it's most likely occurring under duress and causing harm and suffering to the animal. For example, a wild elephant would never normally let a human ride it. According to a study carried out by World Animal Protection (WAP), tourists visiting elephant attractions in Asia are fuelling a rise in the number of elephants captured from the wild and kept for tourism and entertainment. The number captured in Thailand has increased by almost a third over the last five years. The elephants are forced to live in terribly cruel conditions and perform unnatural behaviours for the sake of entertainment.

Instead of riding an elephant, visit an elephant sanctuary and teach your children the importance of looking after wildlife. Choose animal encounters that do not disrupt or disturb the animals. Visit national parks and take wildlife tours where the animals are kept at a safe distance. If you want to get up close and personal, buy a zoom lens.

There are so many exploited animals all over our globe – animals treated badly or captured horrifically just for the price of tourism. We visited an aquarium where two killer whales were swimming in what was an incredibly small pool for them. It broke my heart – I was so disappointed that I had taken my children there for them to see such a sad situation and paid money for it to continue. I have also seen the horrible sight of monkeys in Bali chained to trees purely for entertainment purposes.

After seeing *The Cove*, a documentary about Japan's horrific treatment of dolphins, killed for their meat or captured for international sale, we have never gone back to America's SeaWorld, which is one of the biggest companies that buys these dolphins. This is why we don't mention visiting SeaWorld. We also don't mention activities where we feel animals are exploited for the sake of tourism. There are so many available but we hope you will consider animal rights and try to be involved in animal-friendly tourism.

ETHICAL TOURISM

Buy souvenirs that are locally made and buy locally sourced products. Support family-owned shops and local tour companies. Avoid visiting slums or orphanages unless you have a reason to be there (other than to simply gawk). Instead, consider donating time, clothing or money to places that need it the most.

ECO-TOURS

If you're taking an eco-tour, check before you book that the tour meets any necessary requirements (most countries have some kind of eco certification). Make sure the tour company protects native wildlife, has leave-no-trace principles, supports local communities and runs smaller size groups.

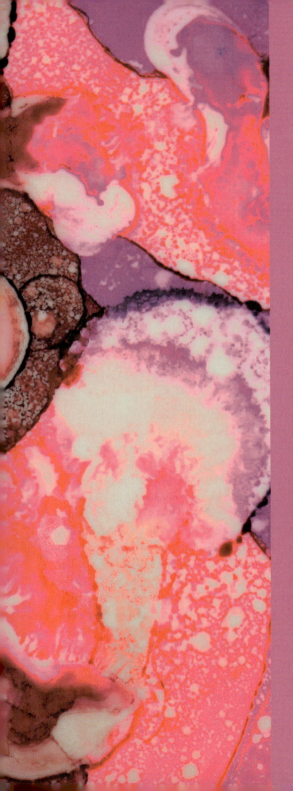

AUSTRALIANS OFTEN LAMENT THE FACT THAT WE USUALLY VENTURE OUT TO SEE THE WORLD BEFORE WE EXPLORE OUR OWN BACKYARD.

Well, we can see both sides of the coin. Born with wanderlust, Aussies are always going to want to travel overseas (after all, we're stuck on an island or, in the words of a former prime minister, 'at the arse end of the world'). Yet Australia has more to offer than an over-caffeinated game-show host – from surf to snow, waterways to desert, mountains to the lights of our beautiful cities.

We want to inspire you to go tripping around Australia with your kids. This incredible country has so much to offer families, whether it's for a weekend away or six months on the road. Every corner, every town, every city has an experience to offer. From Christmas at the beach to winter in the mountains, we find something new every time we travel and we want you to see it all too. For each state and territory, first we touch on its overall top attractions, then explore its capital city and finally mention a favourite region or two. Sadly, there is no way we can cover everything (sorry, Australia, but how heavy do you want this book to be?), so we focus on our favourite things to do and those that come highly recommended. But before we get stuck into some of the many reasons staying homebound is a cracking idea, here are some things you may not know about your own backyard.

Did You Know?

- The venom of the male platypus is strong enough to kill a small dog, so hold off buying a pet platypus until your dog is big enough to fend for itself.
- In Australia, horses are responsible for more deaths than venomous snakes and spiders.
- Australia has a killer plant called the Gympie-Gympie stinging tree. Get stung by this tree and it will feel like you have been burned by acid and electrocuted *at the same time* (or so says scientist Marina Hurley and she should know – she's been stung many times while researching the tree). So, you know, best avoid.
- Australia gets more snow than Switzerland. But they have more chocolate so we'll call it a tie.

Stating the obvious, Australia is a huge country. You can fly from Melbourne to Perth faster than you can fly from the top of Western Australia to the bottom, and the climate can change rapidly from place to place and season to season (or on any given day in Melbourne). So, be aware of the seasonal weather conditions and remember to stay updated with the local weather, especially in the outback. Preparation is key – while many Australians may not know the words to our national anthem, we're familiar with the words *Slip! Slop! Slap!* As residents of this sunburnt country, we know to slip on a T-shirt, slop on some sunscreen and slap on a hat pretty much at all times. This applies to travelling too – always wear appropriate clothing, carry hats and sunscreen, and take water and snacks for energy. In the northern parts of Australia, the climate can be extreme and you may need to drink more water than you are used to; always carry extra water when heading out and always tell someone where you're going and when you expect to return.

At the time of this book being published much of Australia was experiencing unprecedented bushfires, with many country towns and tourism destinations devastated. This saw a flood of support from Aussies in the way of vital fundraising and donations of food and supplies, as well as an outpouring of love and care. These towns and communities need our continued love and support as they rebuild their houses, restore their hotels, re-model their cafes and re-imagine their pubs. What they'll really need is people *visiting* these hotels, pubs and cafes. Pouring tourist dollars into their local economy will provide a much needed morale boost and show them that our solidarity was more than a Facebook post. When you're planning a trip – whether it's a two-week holiday or a weekend getaway – we encourage you to consider visiting the fire-affected communities.

FANCY A DIP?

Australia has more places to swim than a crocodile has bad intentions, from sparkling oceans and bays to beautiful rivers, lakes and waterholes, so knowing how to stay safe is vitally important. Obviously our beaches are a huge reason tourists flock to our shores each year, but it takes only a quick peek at *Bondi Rescue* to see how dangerous the ocean can be. Always swim at a patrolled beach – most popular beaches are patrolled in summer and some are patrolled year-round. If possible, swim with a group (but be aware of each member's ability), particularly because some beaches have no mobile phone service. If you are up for surfing, always check conditions with locals first. Sharks are common in our oceans so always heed any warnings. Learning how to spot a rip and how to get out of one are great skills to have. Be aware of the tides when swimming near rocks, and never swim at a closed beach – it's closed for a good reason. Lifeguards are there to help, but if you swim irresponsibly you will put other people's lives in danger, not just your own. See beachsafe.org.au/surf-safety for more information on identifying rips and surf safety.

When swimming in rivers and lakes, watch out for currents, submerged objects, slippery banks and any undertow. Be mindful that a calm surface may hide rocks and tree branches, and that the water might be very cold. A good rule for both kids and adults is to wear a life-vest when in a river (younger children should have an appropriate life-vest on at all times). See royallifesaving.com.au/programs/respect-the-river for more useful information.

In the northern parts of Australia check with the locals about good places to swim because you'll definitely want to avoid crocs and stingers – neither are much fun (particularly avoid swimming in northern waters between October and May). The town locals will be able to point you to family-friendly swimming spots.

A school of Helliars down at the Mornington Peninsula

THE FIRST PEOPLE

Australia's Indigenous people have the longest continuous history of any people in the world – thought to be around 65,000 years. Before white settlement there were many hundreds of different Aboriginal and Torres Strait Islander societies or clan groups around the continent, each with their own distinctive cultures, beliefs and languages. Today Indigenous people make up just over three per cent of the total Australian population and they hold specific rights as Australia's First peoples, set out in international law.

Across the country, many Indigenous people maintain strong connections to their culture, languages and traditional lands, while also contributing to the environmental management and cultural identity of our nation. Our understanding and appreciation of Indigenous culture is growing but there is more to be done. Learning about Indigenous history and tradition helps improve our understanding and there are many opportunities to explore Indigenous culture on holidays with the kids. On a recent getaway to Queensland's Port Douglas, we took the kids on the Ngadiku Dreamtime Walk in Mossman Gorge. A local guide, who was both knowledgeable and funny, took us for a walk through the rainforest, pointing out significant cultural landmarks, telling stories of Kuku-Yalanji culture and traditions, and including us in a smoking ceremony. We also learnt how to make soap and ochre paint, and enjoyed tea and damper at the end of the walk. It was an hour and a half and it really engaged the kids; the only downside is there's no wheelchair access and we would avoid having a pusher on this walk. (*See* p. 79 for more on our adventures in north Queensland.) Around the country there are many of these Indigenous cultural experiences on offer, and adding an experience like this to your trip will be special, a lot of fun and a great learning opportunity.

VICTORIA

Victoria is the smallest mainland state, but has the second largest population in Australia. We haven't explored everything this wonderful state has to offer, but love driving to its snow fields in winter, and a river, beach or lake in summer.

Not only famous for its sporting passion (go the Magpies!), Victoria is also considered the birthplace of the Australian culinary explosion, and the state's small country towns now offer restaurants of a quality you once only found in the big cities, but with the added bonus of quintessential country charm and plenty to entertain children of all ages.

ATTRACTIONS

- As far as natural beauty goes, nothing in Victoria surpasses the **Great Ocean Road**. A 243km stretch of road, it showcases the gorgeous coastline between the surf capital **Torquay** and **Allansford** (which houses a Cheese Museum). They're the official start and end towns, though most people begin the drive at Geelong and continue all the way to Port Fairy. The first ever ute was made in **Geelong** (presumably by a bloke with a stunning mullet). Don't just drive through Geelong – stop at the Geelong waterfront, go swimming in the ocean pool, visit **Poppy Kettle Playground** for little adventurers and walk the famous bollard walk. Torquay is home to **Surf World**, a surfing museum, and world-famous **Bells Beach** – catch a wave if you're game. The **Twelve Apostles** are the jewel in the Great Ocean Road's crown, a collection of eight limestone stacks off the coast of Port Campbell. (We suspect limestone Judas may have been responsible for the missing four.) It's truly a remarkable drive and offers plenty of opportunities to stop for ice-creams, fish and chips, or some of the best-ever vanilla slices. Keep in mind that some towns along the Great Ocean Road can get crowded during school holidays, especially in summer, so travel outside holidays or make sure you book your accommodation well in advance. The traffic entering towns and around beach carparks can also be crazy during the summer period, so getting accommodation within walking distance of the beach or town centre will be more relaxing for all of you.

- Rug up for the famous penguin parade at **Phillip Island**. Be warned: you'll need to get there in plenty of time for the best vantage point and those tuxedoed waddlers can take their sweet time strutting their stuff across that windswept beach. Bring a blanket, a cushion to sit on and a thermos of something hot – it's worth it, though, as the kids will get a serious kick out of it.

- Only about two hours from Phillip Island is the wild **Wilsons Promontory National Park**. This is a great place to take the kids for a bushwalk, a play on the beach or some wildlife watching. The Big Drift is a good walk for smaller kids and doesn't require too much effort (it's around 2km). Mount Oberon Summit is a good walk (3.4km), a steady climb and beautiful scenery, but it requires a little more effort (you're climbing to a summit after all!). It's best on a clear day so you can enjoy the views, and is not ideal for toddlers as there are some cliff edges.

- The legend of Ned Kelly looms largely and perhaps controversially over Victoria's bushranger past. Get your Kelly fix at **Glenrowan**, just near Wangaratta, home of the final siege and capture of ol' buckethead himself. The Glenrowan Tourist Centre even offers a show reconstructing Kelly's last stand. It could be scary for younger kids but our kids enjoyed it (ask at the centre if you're concerned).

- Head to Ballarat to take the kids to **Sovereign Hill**, a huge outdoor museum focused on Victoria's gold-rush history. Go on the underground mine tour or pan for gold. It hosts Winter Wonderlights where all your Christmas in Julys will come at once with European-style street markets, fairy-lit laneways and naughty St Ginger running amok on Main Street. Excite the kids by letting them know it is the site where the world's largest above-ground gold nugget was found. (It was later cashed in and spent at Timezone.) For those missing *Game of Thrones* why not take the tribe to **Kryal Castle**, near Ballarat, where fire breathers, jousting, mystic readers, archery and more await (and where you can always lose the kids in the mediaeval-style maze). In the cooler months you may find us in front of an open fire after catching a feed at the **Tuki Trout Farm** in **Smeaton**, just half an hour north of Ballarat.

- Also not too far from Ballarat is **Bendigo**, where you can take the kids walking the Goldfields. Take a guided tour of **Central Deborah Gold Mine** and venture down beneath Bendigo and deep into its gold-mining history. The kids will love the vintage tram tours too.

- The **Murray River** is the border dividing frenemies Victoria and New South Wales. You can camp along it year-round (you'll find us camping there in the summer months around the Cobram area), ride a paddle steamer along the Murray from Echuca, take an eco-tour or explore the history of the area.

- If you like to pack active-wear on holidays, spend a few days in the **Grampians** for great rock-climbing, bushwalking (the kids will be awestruck by the waterfalls) and anything adventure related. Kids of all ages can go kayaking, rock climbing, abseiling, mountain-biking and more.

- For more adventure, head to Victoria's **Alps**. The alpine region can be fun year-round: ski in winter, bike ride in summer. In winter you might spot us being schooled by our kids on the slopes of **Mount Buller**. It's always fun for kids young and old (Oscar started skiing when he was three). The state's alpine region offers more than just the obvious: go whitewater rafting, kayaking, canoeing, fishing or bushwalking. You'll find many activities in the towns and villages that surround the Alps.

Christmas, Camping and Cricket *(by Pete)*

Should we head up tomorrow or the day after tomorrow? That was the question.

It was that magical week between Christmas and New Years where time becomes largely irrelevant, routines are knocked sideways and watching cricket and eating ham are far more urgent than tending to emails or the garden.

We were going to be camping up on the Murray River – that famous stretch of water that keeps New South Wales at arm's distance from its archrival Victoria. But we were – well, I was – also watching the Boxing Day Test.

The river was waiting and Brij was keen to get moving. Too much stillness makes her anxious. Clearly her father's daughter, she likes to relax for a short period of time before chores begin whispering to her and adventures seduce her from the couch. I, on the other hand, could not be seduced away from the couch for anything, especially during the last two days of the Boxing Day Test.

'You can listen to it on the radio up at the river,' said Brij.

'It's not the same,' said I. 'Anyway, we'll be camping for two weeks. There's no rush. The river isn't going anywhere.'

'Yeah, but I'm bored.'

'Cricket is not boring.'

'But we'll miss out on a good campsite.'

'We always find a site and ... oh, look, the Aussies are reviewing the LBW.'

To cut a medium-length story a tad shorter, after some quality to-ing and fro-ing, cricket won the day. We would head up to the river the day after tomorrow. Sure, I was slightly concerned that every time I said 'the day after tomorrow' I was possibly creating a bad omen triggering a seismic series of weather-based calamities which would usher in a new ice age (apologies for those who have not seen 2004's *The Day After Tomorrow*).

We arrived in the beautiful (and bloody hot in December) town of Cobram once the Aussies had clinched the Test and were pleasantly surprised that we had plenty of excellent campsites to choose from. As relieved as I was, it didn't quite make sense that there were so many premium river sites available at this time of year.

We soon discovered why. Quite a few families had needed to leave after a gastro outbreak caused by, wait for it, a stupid camper depositing the waste from their port-a-loo into the river! On second thought, maybe they weren't stupid, maybe they were just pure evil.

Either way, if we had have arrived a day or two earlier our trip would have been ruined with a potentially chronic case of the squirts.

And the moral of this story? Cricket always wins.

MELBOURNE

The Wurundjeri people of the Kulin nation are the Traditional Owners of the location known as Melbourne.

VOTED THE WORLD'S

most liveable city since approximately 16BC, Melbourne is renowned for having four seasons in one day, which we like to think means it caters for the indoors and outdoors equally well. Its unique culture makes it a fantastic place for families with kids of all ages. Our home city has hosted us many times: we've had staycations for birthday weekends or even just when we have a weekend off from kids' sport but not enough time to travel anywhere else. The city hosts so many shows, festivals and entertainment for kids it's easy to feel like you've been on a holiday in your own backyard. We have joined in on Chinese New Year and danced in the streets with the dragon, we have seen *13-Storey Treehouse* on stage, and we have even taken a gentleman's rowboat down the Yarra River. Melbourne is easy to get around even with a pusher and, well, we just love the people. It's our home.

DID YOU KNOW?

- Melbourne has the highest number of cafes and restaurants per number of people of any city in the world.
- Melbourne's CBD has five of the six tallest buildings in Australia.
- A factory in Port Melbourne is the only place in the world that actually makes Vegemite.

AUSTRALIA

EATING OUT

Melbourne knows how to do food, and most cafes and restaurants are happy to serve anyone. There is always a cultural or food festival on that will offer all sorts of cuisine to entice fussy eaters. Look for pop-up places like the **Winter Village** where you can eat in igloos (well, more like see-through plastic bubbles but it's still fun and interesting, and you can take the kids ice-skating afterwards).

Easey's in Collingwood is a fun place for the kids, where the dining room is three trams on top of a building. Any kid will love the menu – they serve delicious burgers, fries, hotdogs and wings.

The **Sporting Globe** has a number of locations in Melbourne, with Richmond being the city venue. As you'll discover throughout this book, we are a sports-mad family and the kids love it here because they can catch up on whatever sporting game is on and eat wings at the same time. Brij is not a huge fan of it, but will go to watch a Celtics game occasionally. Bear in mind it will be crowded for big games like the Super Bowl.

Donovans on the St Kilda foreshore is a setting to just soak up regardless of weather. It offers a kids' menu, and has a terrace and closed verandah, so there is space to allow kids to move a little. The food is delicious and the walk along the boulevard is fantastic to get those little legs moving. It is nice and close to Luna Park, so if you're making a day of it your day is sorted.

ACCOMMODATION

Melbourne offers accommodation to suit all budgets and all ages. You may want to stay in the CBD for convenience, or further out if you're most interested in daytrips and travelling further afield.

GETTING AROUND

Melbourne is built on a grid and is easy to navigate. Public transport is pretty good too. Kids under four ride free and won't require a Myki card. The city loop tram is free for everyone. Melbourne is one of the few cities that kept its trams, and they are a great way to take the kids around the city – most interstate kids will love the novelty of them.

If you are driving on roads that also cater to trams, don't forget the infamous hook turn: most right-hand turns are done from the left lane, after the light has gone red, meaning you start to turn when the light of the street you are turning into has gone green. Hook turns are always signed, but it does seem to be a rule many people don't know so always keep an eye on the left lane for people preparing to turn right if you're going straight through the intersection. You'll be dreaming of tram bells for weeks.

If you're arriving in or departing from Melbourne by air (at either Tullamarine or Avalon airport), catch the Skybus to various destinations. Children travel free on Skybus when a family pass is purchased.

ATTRACTIONS

- Though Melbourne boasts the impressive **St Patrick's Cathedral**, built in stages between 1858 and 1939, the preferred place of worship for most Melburnians is a cathedral of a slightly different kind. Built in 1853, the **Melbourne Cricket Ground** (also known as the MCG or, to locals, simply 'the G') is one of the world's greatest stadiums. It has hosted everything from the Olympics to a mass delivered by Pope John Paul II (see, it really is a cathedral). The MCG houses the wonderful **National Sporting Museum** featuring historical artefacts, 3D holograms and interactive features. You can take a tour of the MCG, even gaining access to the locker rooms and the spaces usually only available for MCC members. Pete used to work as an usher at the G but we're pretty sure this isn't mentioned on the official tour. When in town, check schedules and catch a game of AFL or see Australia playing cricket in the summer. Kids of all ages can go to the footy and cricket. Half-time at the football is Auskick time, where young kids get a chance to play on the ground. The Boxing Day Test is a classic cricket match, but may be a bit dull for the little ones and it's usually very hot. You might find a one-day or T20 match better for young kids.

- We recently took the kids to **ArtVo** where optical illusions enthral. ArtVo, which is part of the rather divisive Docklands precinct, is a 3D immersive museum where kids and adults are encouraged to interact with the artwork. That's right, touching the artwork is allowed! The friendly staff will guide your kids to position them in the exact pose to make them look like they are actually standing in the jaws of a crocodile, patting a unicorn or even splashing about in a glass of red wine – though that one may be best for the adults.

- When travelling with kids, anything to do with animals is usually a sure-fire winner. The highly regarded **Melbourne Zoo** does twilight concerts in the summer and offers a range of up-close animal experiences.

- **Collingwood Children's Farm** is a unique inner-city farm where the livestock are all hipsters (but it's still worth going). If you like your zoos the way you like your eggs, you can sleep overnight at **Werribee Open Range Zoo**, located 45 minutes outside Melbourne.

- For views of Melbourne, head up the **Eureka Skydeck** or jump aboard the **Melbourne Star Observation Wheel** to see all the sights and lights of this marvellous city.

- Back on solid ground, walk the city's renowned laneways including **Centre Place**, **AC/DC Lane** and **Hosier Lane**, famous for its urban art that our dads call 'bloody graffiti'.

- Explore the city's superb **cafe culture**, especially around Richmond, Fitzroy, Carlton and St Kilda. Most cafes are kid friendly, meaning you can get a babyccino at every place you stop. The only thing that can be hard with little kids is not having much space in the cafe for a pram.

- If you're staying in a self-catered apartment, shop at the **Queen Vic Market** for a classic Melbourne experience and some delicious local goodies. The kids will love the sheer size and energy of this market: get them looking for local versions of their favourite foods. The permanent bookshops and toy stores will be a hit, and look out for what's on, because the market regularly hosts cultural festivals, special book markets, music gigs and food festivals.

- Stroll through Melbourne's gorgeous parks and gardens, in particular the **Royal Botanic Gardens** – take a rug and enjoy a picnic or head to the summertime Moonlight Cinema in the gardens (when there's a child-appropriate film on). Or, for the more active, get the lycra on and run the famous **Tan**, a 3.8km track looping around the Royal Botanic Gardens.

- The kids will scream (in a good way) at St Kilda's **Luna Park** with its old-school carnival rides such as dodgem cars and haunted houses. Before your Luna Park fun, take the kids to one of the fabulous bakeries on St Kilda's **Acland Street**.

- **ScienceWorks** museum is not only fun for kids but will also prevent their brain cells switching to holiday-mode permanently. Our kids particularly loved the **Planetarium**, where they were captivated by the night sky and the fascinating show, especially as it was day-time outside. Worth noting, ScienceWorks is an autism-friendly museum; the website provides a range of 'social stories' to help you prepare your kids for their visit.

- We have been regular visitors to the **Melbourne Museum** over the years and if we had a dollar for every time one of our boys pressed the fart button in the Human Anatomy section, we would have an extra $648 in dollar coins. The museum is great for all ages and is also autism friendly.

- If you want to head out of the city, the kids will love **Healesville Sanctuary**, to the north-east of Melbourne, which has become a must-do for international visitors. From the thrilling free-flight birds of prey display to seeing dingos, wombats and platypus in natural bush enclosures, there's so much to do here. Pack a picnic and tell the kids to find their favourite animals (generally the snakes are a huge hit with our boys!).

- Head north to **Funfields Theme Park** in Whittlesea. With its water slides, go-karts and adrenalin-pumping rides, the place continues to get bigger and bigger and funner and funner becoming a must-do for the kids.

- Drive up to the beautiful **Dandenong Ranges** for a day – have a picnic, let the kids run free at the **Dandenong Ranges Botanic Garden** or go for a ride on century-old steam-train **Puffing Billy** – our kids love hanging out the window waving at people. Every now and then Puffing Billy runs a Day Out with Thomas season where you can meet Thomas the Tank Engine, ride the train and enjoy lots of other family activities – but plan ahead as tickets do sell out.

MORNINGTON PENINSULA

The Bunurong people are the Traditional Custodians of this land.

ABOUT ONE HOUR SOUTH of Melbourne, the Mornington Peninsula, which protects Port Phillip from Bass Strait, was always a favourite beachside holiday spot for Melburnians. Now, with easier access to the city via a newish freeway and bypass, families are moving here to live and simply commuting to the city for work. It's still a favoured holiday destination, so expect crowded roads, shops and beaches all through summer. Renting family-friendly holiday homes is the easiest and the best accommodation option, but there are a number of camping sites too, if tents are your thing. If you're taking public transport, trains stop at Frankston and you can catch a local bus along the bay. A car and passenger ferry can be caught from Queenscliff on the Bellarine Peninsula to Sorrento. For travelling around the peninsula itself, a car is best.

- The entire area gets busy, but especially **Portsea** and **Sorrento** on the peninsula's point. Both have beautiful beaches and Sorrento also has the car and passenger ferry that takes you to **Queenscliff** and the **Bellarine Peninsula**. Consider travelling in the cooler months to avoid the crowds, and don't discount the wild beauty of **Cape Schanck** and **Flinders** on the southern and eastern part of the peninsula.

- We have been visiting the peninsula together for more than 20 years and over the past five the **Enchanted Adventure Garden** at Arthurs Seat has become bigger and better each year. Surf among the trees on its tree-top ropes courses and ziplines, throw yourself down the hill on a tube ride or navigate wonderful mazes both hedged and mirrored.

- Have more fun at the **Big Goose**. Near Moorooduc, this fabulous place offers everything from minigolf, jumping pillows and tyre mazes to tractor rides, snake-handling shows and sheep dogs plying their trade.

- Go on one of the short bushwalks through the **Cape Schanck Lighthouse Reserve** or tour the **Cape Schanck Lighthouse**, a working lighthouse built in 1859. Tours include the museum and climbing the steep, winding staircase within the lighthouse itself (tour times can be limited, so check the website first). Or hike **Bushrangers Bay** to see places unreachable by car. Follow the 2.6km Bushrangers Bay Walking Track from Cape Schanck Lighthouse or get to it via a walk from the Boneo Road carpark. The bay's beautiful beach is surrounded by rocky headlands and basalt cliffs and makes a great bushwalk with older kids.

- Let your kids search for crabs, oysters and baby sharks in the rockpools at **Bridgewater Bay**, marvel at the **Flinders Blowhole** (don't get too close!) and admire nature's very own **London Bridge** in rock formation at Portsea. We've spent many a day just wandering around the rockpools all along the ocean beaches here. Take an esky and bodyboard to the beach, slide down the dunes, ride the waves and throw the frisbee – you'll all be heading home tired, happy and ready for an early night.

- For those keen on military history, **Fort Nepean** formed a crucial part of Victoria's defences from the 1880s to 1945 and you can explore the area's fascinating wartime history. Younger kids will love climbing the gunners.

- The **Arthurs Seat Eagle** is a gondola/chairlift offering panoramic views of the bay. Take some time to explore **Red Hill Market**, held on the first Saturday of the month between September and May, for excellent local produce and gourmet food (feel free to bribe with ice-cream and/or hot jam doughnuts as required).

- Grab an ice-cream and walk along **Rosebud Pier** before a game of minigolf at **Top Fun Rosebud**. We have played this course many, many times and Pete would like it put in print that he crushes the kids every single time (the fact that this sentence made it into print means the kids didn't proofread this book).

- **Safety Beach**, near Dromana, is a great beach for little ones; the water is calm with the only waves being ripples from the ocean liners out in Port Phillip. If you're looking for a more expansive beach, try the other side at **Point Leo**, which is perfect for any family looking to set up an epic game of beach cricket.

- Mornington Peninsula is also a foodie's paradise. There are beautiful olive groves, tantalising strawberry farms, superb wineries and breweries, chocolate stores and **Main Ridge Dairy**, which is the only commercial dairy operating on the Peninsula and will have the right cheese for you whether you like cheese or not!

NEW SOUTH WALES

Australia's premier tourist

destination, New South Wales has so much to offer families. You can't beat Sydney for a fun family holiday – the kids are always entertained and, where Melbourne has trams to get the kids excited, Sydney has boats and lots of them. Sydney is in easy reach of the popular beaches so you could trick yourself into believing you don't really need to go anywhere else. But you must. New South Wales has everything you need for road trips, weekends and adventures. The southern parts of the state, like Merimbula, Batemans Bay and anywhere along the Murray River, have been our camping destinations for years as they are within an easy road trip from Victoria. But we love spending time up north too – we usually fly to Sydney and travel from there with a hire car if moving around. Long weekends and the need for a little more warmth during a Melbourne winter is when Byron Bay gets a visit from us. So, from the south to the north of the state, you'll find something that's just right for your family adventure.

ATTRACTIONS

- There is a reason that once people discover the New South Wales **Central Coast** they keep coming back again and again. With picturesque beaches, scenic waterways and brilliant national parks, the Central Coast has it all going on. The suburb of **Ettalong Beach** is a stand-out for families, with a variety of lakes, beaches, inlets and bays that will satisfy everyone. The beach is calm and easy for the little kids to swim in too, which is a bonus. Excellent boating opportunities abound on the Central Coast. Find a campground or seaside resort and relax for a few days – you won't regret it.

- **Newcastle** is the state's second largest city, where the kids will giggle themselves silly all the way to **Blackbutt Nature Reserve**. Funny or not, the reserve is an excellent place to stop for a picnic – there are adventure playgrounds, bushwalks and a native animal enclosure.

- Just north of Newcastle is the beautiful **Port Stephens**, a perfect spot for a family holiday. With beaches, sand-tobogganing and learn to surf schools on offer, kids will be begging to stay longer.

- Near Port Stephens are the **Stockton Bight Sand Dunes** in the Worimi Conservation Lands at Anna Bay. These are the largest moving coastal dunes in the Southern Hemisphere. There are 4WD, quad-bike and sand-boarding tours. You can take your own 4WD, but you will require a permit. Fishing is allowed. It goes without saying that you should be extremely cautious on quad bikes: children under 16 should not ride them and there are numerous cases of horrific accidents involving quad bikes ridden by both kids and adults.

- If you're on a road trip, keep driving north, stopping off at **Port Macquarie**, where the kids can take a tour of the **Koala Hospital** to see koalas being fed and to learn more about koala conservation. You can even adopt a koala (and, no, you can't take it home). Port Macquarie is also a great whale-watching spot – between May and November check out the migrating whales. Cross your fingers that you see them do a cool flip and splash. Have your camera ready!

- **Ellenborough Falls**, inland from Port Macquarie, has a 30-minute walk to the bottom of the falls through lovely rainforest and it will not disappoint (perhaps avoid the other walk straight to the base of the falls with its 600 steps – not so great for the kids!). The road is steep and windy, and you'll need to check the weight limits if towing a caravan or camper-trailer.

- Australia has long been obsessed with 'big' things and the **Big Banana** in Coffs Harbour sits, or slips, in the top echelon of the country's 'big' things, up there with the Big Merino, the Big Pineapple and the Big Lobster.

- Not far inland from Coffs Harbour, **Ebor Falls** are definitely worth a visit. There's a stunning drop of 100m over two waterfalls and the spectacular rugged gorge has tracks easy enough for smaller children to enjoy.

- The **South Coast** of New South Wales offers just as much as the northern coast. For cool photo opps (and aren't holidays all about photo opps?) get to **Bombo Headland** at **Kiama**. After taking your snaps, head for a surf or swim and take a walk through the unusual dark volcanic rock. Worth noting, it's a dog-friendly beach too.

- Visit the less crowded beaches of **Jervis Bay** for a swim and a spot of whale- and dolphin-watching. If you have time, go on one of the many Jervis Bay cruises available to see these amazing creatures up close (but please be sure to choose an eco-friendly tour that advertises their Eco-Certification). After a relaxing morning there, up the tempo at **Jamberoo Action Park**, a water-based theme park full of crazy rides, or zoom through the trees at **Illawarra Fly Treetop Adventures**, both just over an hour north of the Jervis Bay region.

- If you're keen to pitch a tent on the South Coast and are close to the Victoria border, ever-popular **Merimbula** might be the place for your tribe. With its free campsites and holiday parks you'll love setting up camp here. It also has **Magic Mountain**, a fun adventure and water park (although beware of the Black Hole, an underground waterslide on which an 11-year-old Pete got tumbled resulting in smashed teeth and a broken nose. Fun times!).

- Of course, there's more to New South Wales than just the fabulous coastline. Head inland and take a self-guided tour through the sandstone caves in **Pillaga National Park** near **Coonabarabran**. This is a sacred place for the local Gamilaroi people; to learn even more about the Indigenous history and rock art of the area, book a guided tour (book at the Pillaga Forest Discover Centre in nearby Baradine). Coonabarabran is also home to the **Warrumbungle Observatory**, which is great for night-sky viewing and has a very interesting astronomy presentation.

- Conquer **Mount Kosciuszko** as a family. Not only Australia's highest point, Mount Kosciuszko is part of a wonderful alpine national park. If you want to climb to the top of Australia, start at the Kosciuszko Express Chairlift in Thredbo. It's a 13km return walk. There are also shorter options available to make it more family friendly, especially if you have younger kids, such as the 4km track to Kosciuszko Lookout (this starts at the chairlift too). Remember the mountain will be snowbound in winter so strap on those cross-country skis or snowshoes for the climb.

- Ski **Thredbo** for the longest ski run in Australia. (Skiing holidays are one of our favourite things to do; see p. 32.)

- Visit the spectacular World Heritage–listed **Lord Howe Island**, standing alone in the Tasman Sea 600km east of Port Macquarie. Check QantasLink for flights year-round, unless you have your own yacht – then sail away, skipper. On the island, kids will forget Fortnite ever existed (well, temporarily at least) with bikeriding, kayaking and kite-boarding all available. Add snorkelling at the many splendid beaches and you're on a winner. (You might want to book ahead – the island only accepts 400 visitors at a time.)

SYDNEY

The Gadigal people of the Eora Nation are the Traditional Custodians of the place now called Sydney.

THERE IS A REASON THAT,

on each New Year's Eve, it is footage of fireworks shooting over Sydney Harbour that is beamed around the world, not footage of the fireworks at Melbourne's Federation Square. It is undoubtedly our most iconic postcard-piece of real estate. Framed by the Sydney Harbour Bridge and the Opera House and adorned with yachts, ferries and ocean liners, Sydney Harbour is always breathtaking – with the blue sky as a background you have your social media post without even trying. The weather is generally fantastic and the winters aren't too cold; but, if you're driving prepare yourself to be patient with the traffic (there is never not traffic in Sydney!).

Accommodation

There are plenty of accommodation options for all types of budgets. Hotels are everywhere but not ideal if you have young children. Apartments are easy to find and Darling Harbour, the Rocks and the CBD all have great options. Darling Harbour is close to kid-friendly attractions like Madame Tussauds and the Maritime Museum.

Eating Out

Dining precincts are everywhere in Sydney and some are perfect for eating out with kids. Head to **Spice Alley** with Asian street food and restaurants. Or **Steam Mill Lane** and **Little Hay Street**, both great outdoor dining strips in the Darling Harbour Quarter, just behind Darling Harbour. The **Duke of Clarence** is cosy and just like walking into a pub in England.

Getting Around

Exploring Sydney is easy with the trains, buses and ferries getting you around. Use the Opal Card for all public transport; it will also take you out of the city to the Blue Mountains, Central Coast, Hunter region, Illawarra and Southern Highlands.

Travelling to and from the airport is easy too. The Airport Link train will get you into the city in about 13 minutes and is the fastest way to get to the CBD (trains depart every 15 minutes). Use the Opal Card for tickets. Children aged three and under travel for free, and children four to 15 can travel on a child fare. Head to Ready 2 Go for shuttle transfers and private options from the airport. Taxis are also available.

Did You Know?

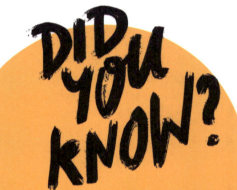

- Sydney Harbour Bridge has a little sibling in Newcastle, England. Named the Tyne Bridge, it looks pretty much identical, just smaller. Sydney has restrained itself from adding another sibling to avoid middle-bridge syndrome.
- The bronze medals for the 2000 Sydney Olympic Games were made from recycled Australian one- and two-cent coins that had been taken out of circulation in 1991. We're not sure if that means they're worth approximately $2.60 each. We suspect not.

ATTRACTIONS

- Before we talk about our favourite things to do with the kids in Sydney, we have to mention the city's must-see attractions. It goes without saying, you must visit the **Sydney Opera House** – see a show, enjoy a meal or just walk around this incredible piece of architecture. Pete has done shows at the country's most famous dwelling and says the best part is entering the Opera House thinking 'I'm about to play the Opera House' and leaving thinking 'Oh my god, I just played the Opera House!' Cruise and eat around **Circular Quay** and **Darling Harbour**, and see the city in 360 degrees at **Sydney Tower Eye**. Climb aboard a submarine or take the VR Antarctica Experience, an immersive virtual reality experience, at the **Australian Maritime Museum**. Re-opening in 2020 after major renovation, the **Australian Museum** is heritage listed and the oldest museum in Australia; it is free for those under 15, family tickets are available and dino-lovers will be happy exploring here. Throw a frisbee in **Hyde Park** or see the heavens at **Sydney Observatory** where day and night tours are available. Nearby is the historic convict precinct of **the Rocks** – walk the cobbled laneways and stop in at one of the historic pubs along the way like **Fortune of War** or the **Lord Nelson Brewery Hotel** (cleverly, they all serve hot chocolates for the kids).

- Take the kids on a **harbour cruise** for lunch, or a family sightseeing tour to get a water perspective of all those amazing harbourside attractions. Or catch a ferry to the beautifully located **Luna Park**, just next to the Harbour Bridge. If Luna Park sounds too dry for your tastes then **Raging Waters Sydney**, the city's biggest water park, might be for you (you'll need to check the website for when the park is open as it's seasonal).

- A cherished family memory will be to climb the **Sydney Harbour Bridge**. Children aged eight and over can climb, as long as they're taller than 102cm. You'll need to follow some rules for the safety of all those on the climb; check out the website for a pre-climb checklist. Fear of heights? There are climb leaders who take on the role of 'facing your fear ambassadors' to help you get through the climb.

- One of the best Sydney attractions for kids is the excellent **Taronga Zoo**, which has beautiful views of the harbour and all the animals you'd expect to see (over 4000 in fact). The zoo cares for many threatened species and the proceeds from the entrance fees go back into conservation efforts, research, the wildlife hospital and breeding programs. See the fabulous shows and interesting keeper talks or take part in the special behind-the-scenes and up-close experiences. There's a tree-tops adventure – Wild Ropes offers courses for both adults and kids – and the Sky Safari cable car, which gives you a sky-high view of some of the animal enclosures and the harbour (it's included as part of your zoo entry fee). And if you're keen, you can all stay overnight in the zoo as part of the Roar and Snore experience, which also includes a night safari – that's something the kids won't forget!

There are some things to know when visiting Taronga Zoo with your children. Shoving a pusher around the zoo's hilly terrain is good for a work-out but probably not the relaxing stroll you may have had in mind. The zoo is on 28 hectares and some paths linking the various levels within the zoo are steep. Pushing a pram up and down is tiring, especially when you've only had four broken hours of sleep with a newborn. Visitors with limited mobility are still able to get around the entire zoo with lifts and ramps located around the site (check the zoo map online). The Sky Safari cable car can also accommodate wheelchairs up to a width of 610mm, and a lift is available to transport guests with disabilities from street level to the lower Sky Safari terminal. Overall, if your kids are up for it Taronga Zoo is a fantastic place to visit.

- A Sydney adventure with a difference is to camp at **Cockatoo Island**. The Aboriginal people of Sydney's coastal region, the Eora people, were likely the first visitors to the island and called it Wareahmah. In the 1800s the island was chosen as a new penal establishment. Convicts were put to work building prison barracks, a military guardhouse and official residences. Today the island is World Heritage listed for historical value, and you can camp overnight. With scenic picnic spots, history tours and two cafes, there's plenty to do. The kids will love the basketball court and large chess board, and there's a free kids' activity book to help them engage with the history of the island (available from the visitor centre). Also on offer are nightly movies at the island cinema – all-age movies show at 7pm and films for adults at 9.15pm. Bring your own tent (4m x 4m each site) or book glamping packages (if camping isn't your thing, other accommodation is available too). There are hot showers and communal kitchens. You can also pre-order barbecue or breakfast packs. BYO food is allowed, but not alcohol (alcohol is available in the licensed cafes). The island is wheelchair accessible. You can get to the island by public ferry, water taxi or kayak.

- Fun Sydney suburbs chock-full of beaches and cafe culture include **Manly**, **Bondi**, **Bronte** and **Avalon** to name but a few. Manly is fun to visit for the beach; our kids especially love the ferry ride there and always manage to convince us to grab an ice-cream before heading back over. Bondi can sometimes get too busy for little ones. We still take the kids there and they have a lot of fun, but we avoid driving there in peak times because we can never find a carpark.

- Two of the best walks in Australia – **Bondi to Bronte walk** and the **Coogi Beach walk** – are suitable for most ages and abilities. They do, however, involve stairs so it may not be suitable for some prams or toddlers.

- Just north of Sydney **Ku-ring-gai Chase National Park** is great for a family picnic, and the kids can run amok cycling, bushwalking and fishing. Happily, it has been listed as a Natural Heritage Place, so it will be preserved for generations to come. While you are in the area, if you have little ones (or more likely older ones) excited about *Home and Away* why not stop and check out the sights of Summer Bay, which is actually **Palm Beach**, just over an hour from the city. You may be lucky enough to catch Alf Stewart at the Surf Club or tucking into one of Pippa's lasagnes at the diner (okay, we haven't seen *Home and Away* in years – do they still serve Pippa's lasagne?).

BLUE MOUNTAINS

The Blue Mountains is within the Country of the Darug and Gundungurra peoples.

AN EASY two-hour drive from Sydney, the Blue Mountains region demands (or at least politely requests) a visit. Bushwalk through the stunning Blue Mountains National Park, admire the spectacular rock formation of the Three Sisters, stop off for lunch at some of the gorgeous country towns such as Leura and Katoomba, or drive to various lookouts to see huge gorges and mammoth waterfalls. There are numerous things to do with kids in the Blue Mountains but two of our favourites are below.

Definitely worth a visit are the Jenolan Caves, an underground system of about 280 caves. Nine or ten of these are usually open to the public and you can explore these spectacular cave formations, and see some very impressive stalactites and stalagmites, on a range of guided and self-guided tours. Download the app for six different self-guided tours of the caves and surrounding bush, including two Aboriginal culture tours. There are also adventure caving tours and an eerie night-time tour (kids need to be ten or older to take part in either of these options), and a very cool Stones and Bones children's tour for kids aged seven to 11. Children aged under six are free and child tickets are available for kids aged six to 17. Parking is free and family passes are available. A wheelchair tour into the first part of the Orient Cave is available but it must be booked in advance.

Our second must-see in the Blue Mountains is Katoomba's Scenic World – whichever way you want to experience the Blue Mountains, you'll find it here. For those with no fear of heights, Scenic Skyway, a glass-floored aerial cable car, suspends you 270m above the ravine floor as it travels 720m from cliff-top to cliff-top offering spectacular views of the Three Sisters and Katoomba Falls. A (slightly) less intense trip can be taken on the Scenic Cableway, another cable car, which descends down into the Jamison Valley and then back up – you'll see more fabulous views of the Three Sisters and Katoomba Falls, as well as Orphan Rock and Mount Solitary. Still after an adrenaline rush? Hop on the Scenic Railway, the world's steepest passenger train-ride, taking you through a cliff-side tunnel to the valley below; its glass roof provides fabulous views and you can angle your seat so it's either extra steep or more reclined (and less scary!). If you and the kids like a calmer pace, wander the Scenic Walkway, an elevated boardwalk that traverses through ancient rainforest for 2.4km (it includes a wheelchair-accessible part).

BYRON BAY

The Traditional Owners are the Bundjalung of Byron Bay Arakwal people.

Byron Bay for a weekend

never feels like enough; even Byron Bay for a week always feels like it should be extended. There is so much to do and see, and so many opportunities to simply relax in Byron Bay. The vibe is an ultra-chilled, time-don't-matter one. An eco-friendly beachside town, Byron Bay has pushed into the big time as a holiday destination for all range of travellers (perhaps to the chagrin of some locals). Plan ahead and book accommodation early as Byron and the surrounding area are very popular.

Byron is a two-hour drive from Brisbane or a nine-hour drive from Sydney (the drive up the Pacific Coast from Sydney to Byron Bay is scenic and rather delightful, though it can be busy in holiday periods). If you are flying, Ballina Airport is the closest and is only 30 minutes south of Byron Bay. It is a small airport, so flights can be limited. Another option is to fly into Coolangatta Airport on the Gold Coast, which is only 40 minutes north of Byron Bay, or fly into Brisbane Airport. These airports all offer shuttles to Byron Bay. We like to hire a car so we can visit other places when staying in Byron Bay (and it's also more convenient with the kids).

- Eco-lodges and eco-resorts are popping up everywhere. The beach is wide and the ocean sparkling; the walk to the **Cape Byron Lighthouse** is a beauty; and, who knows, you might just be lucky enough to bump into a Hemsworth.

- **Main Beach** is patrolled during the school holidays and on weekends. This is a great beach to throw a frisbee with the kids and get surfing. It also gets crowded and it won't be hard to spot the sunburnt backpacker, but stay and listen to people playing their own music and just enjoying beach life. **Belongil Beach** is quieter but is unpatrolled (check the local council website for life-saver patrol times at the southern end). It's a perfect spot for those surfing kids of yours. For younger kids, the walks, playing on the sand and ball sports are fantastic. Be warned: there is a nudist beach at the north end.

- There are a number of **surf schools** catering for all ages, and what better place than Byron Bay to tick learning to surf off your bucket list. For more experienced surfers, **the Pass** can be crammed and can host an aggressive break (which is why it's not suited to beginners). But, Byron's view and cafes are there for everybody to enjoy.

- If your kids have always wanted to run away to join the circus, take them to **Circus Arts Byron Bay**, which offers fun age-specific activities such as flying trapeze classes, balloon twisting and other circus skills. Older kids can try the indoor climbing wall or take a Ninja Warrior class.

- About 2km from the centre of Byron you'll find the **Discovery Parks Water Park** with water slides, fountains, tipping buckets and a child-friendly lagoon. It's actually part of the Byron Bay Holiday and Caravan Park, but anyone can visit the water park (day tickets and family passes available).

- See the local community in action and pick up some delicious produce, local art and craft and artisan food at **Bangalow Market**, 20 minutes from Byron Bay, held on the fourth Sunday of the month.

- Take the kids to **the Farm**, a working farm with the motto 'Grow, Feed, Educate'. About ten minutes from Byron Bay, it has a range of micro-businesses including a nursery, bakery and gelato shop. The kids can check out the animals and you can also take a horseriding tour of the farm (children need to be 12 or over), but if you want to eat at the **Three Blue Ducks** restaurant, you should reserve a table, especially on the weekend.

- Pete has been honoured to be a guest at the **Byron Bay Writers Festival**, which happens in August. Each year, they have a brilliant program featuring over 150 sessions for adults and kids alike.

- If you have the time and the transport, head to **Brunswick Heads**, a 20-minute drive north from Byron. Less busy and more peaceful than Byron, it offers both the beautiful Brunswick River and an ocean beach for good times. The kids will love the **Brunswick Fairy Trail** – pick up the clue sheet from the visitor centre and find the hidden fairy houses around town (all with uplifting messages). Afterwards, take some fish and chips down to **Torakina Beach**, a flat-water beach at the mouth of the river.

- A 30-minute drive through the luscious hinterland is **Crystal Castle**. Enjoy the castle's enchanting Shambhala Gardens, wander the labyrinth, explore the rare crystal displays and giant statues, stand between two towering 5.5m tall smoky quartz geodes, and be awestruck by one of the world's largest amethyst geodes or 'caves', the result of a bubble forming in molten lava over 120 million years ago.

AUSTRALIAN CAPITAL TERRITORY

THE AUSTRALIAN CAPITAL

Territory is Australia's only land-locked state or territory, enclaved as it is within the state of New South Wales. The heart of the action is its capital city, Canberra, also the nation's capital. About 80 per cent of the territory is still bush and Canberra is known as the bush capital, thanks to the surrounding Brindabella Ranges, the many parks and reserves throughout the city and its history: the chosen location for the city was in the bush, set between Melbourne and Sydney to stop the two cities arguing about which one would be the nation's capital after Federation. Design of the city was put up for grabs in an international competition, which was won by American architect Walter Burley Griffin, and Canberra became one of only a few planned major cities in the world (like Washington DC in America and Brasilia in Brazil). Also up for grabs was the new city's name: members of parliament submitted their suggestions in January 1913, which included the, um, interesting Andy Man, Home, Frazer Roo and Watsonia. Thankfully in the end they went with Canberra, which means 'meeting place' and was how the local Ngunnawal people referred to the area.

DID YOU KNOW?

- Advertising and billboards are restricted by law in the streets of Canberra, so you'll only find advertising in bus shelters – this is one of the reasons the place always feels so different from other cities.
- Before 2009 it was legal for the Canberra public to buy fireworks to use in their own celebrations on the Queen's Birthday weekend, leading to many a backyard light-show and singed eyebrow.
- Callister Crescent is a street in Canberra named after the inventor of Vegemite.

CANBERRA

The Traditional Owners of the Canberra area are the Ngunnawal people.

PORN, FIREWORKS AND POLITICIANS –

tired old stereotypes that have well and truly run their course because Canberra has much more to offer and deserves to be in all holidaymakers' considerations. On the practical side, it's easy to drive to from Sydney and Melbourne, and easy to fly to from anywhere else. And it's easy once you're there: no road tolls, relatively little traffic and plenty of places to park. But there are a lot of roundabouts. So many roundabouts. But once you get round you'll need to get about and Canberra is a great place for adventures and indulgence, for culture and art, and for helping the kids brush up on our more recent political and military history. We visited Canberra with the kids over an Easter weekend and didn't have enough time to tick off everything we wanted to do. So, a word of warning, a long weekend may not be enough – take a week if you can and plan out what you all most want to see.

EATING OUT

Canberra offers so many great and kid-friendly dining options. The planned layout of the city has created hubs of cafes and restaurants, especially in the inner-city suburbs of Kingston, Manuka, O'Connor, Braddon and Woden (a bit further out) as well as the city centre itself. You'll be spoilt for choice. Talking spoiling, if, and only if, the kids have behaved treat them to breakfast at **Space Kitchen** (near Woden) where the most colourful breakfast they will ever experience in their lifetime awaits. Oscar and the Unicorn Waffles were a match made in heaven, and we couldn't leave without a couple of Nutella croissants for the road.

ACCOMMODATION

We stayed in the CBD within walking distance of shops and restaurants. Just make sure there is a carpark available if you are hiring a car. We usually opt for apartments so we can do some cooking at home, and mostly have breakfast before we leave for a day of exploring. It's a great way of making sure the kids have had healthy food to start the day and to manage your holiday budget.

GETTING AROUND

Getting around Canberra is easiest with a car. It now has light rail for ease of travel, with a MyWay card (children under five travel free), but if you want to get to various attractions you'll have to change to buses.

ATTRACTIONS

- Why not start by unlocking the secrets of Canberra at the **National Capital Exhibition** (although surely we don't want to know all of Canberra's secrets, do we?). Here you'll find a great introduction to all things Canberra and it's right next door to the Canberra Visitor Centre. It's at Regatta Point, just near Canberra's CBD (which the locals call 'Civic'), and overlooks **Lake Burley Griffin**, the scenic heart of the city. Lake Burley Griffin is as fundamental to Canberra as the Yarra is to Melbourne. Hire a bike or a Segway to ride around the lake's excellent bike paths, explore the parks on the lake's edge or trek through the various lakeside national institutions. You can also hire canoes to explore the quiet waterways.

- If history, art and culture are your thing, then Canberra has you totally covered. Most of its museums, galleries and national institutions are either within walking distance of each other or a short drive away. Up first is **Old Parliament House**, which stares directly at the new Australian Parliament House and is now home to the **Museum of Australian Democracy**. We visited on Easter Sunday with the boys taking on the Easter Egg Hunt. Liam was sceptical about the prospect of diving around looking for eggs with toddlers but it was so much more interesting than that. The boys had to discover answers to Australia's political history as part of the hunt, which meant they had to read and engage with the exhibitions. And then there were chocolate eggs at the end: 17,000 in fact. Walk the gardens or take a guided tour of the historic building any time of year.

- The **Royal Australian Mint**, only ten minutes from Old Parliament House, also offers a treasure hunt, so make sure you grab a 'My Visit to the Mint' booklet at the front desk. This is where the kids can see money getting made, literally, from the viewing points over the factory floor.

- Canberra is also home to the **National Museum of Australia**. In an amazing-looking building on the edge of the lake, the museum tells all range of Australian stories and has heaps of hands-on activities for kids.

- One thing you simply must do is visit the **Australian War Memorial**. It's beautifully curated and respectfully presented, and we were all quite moved by our recent visit. From hand-written notes to reverently restored artefacts, the War Memorial is a national gem and should be visited at least once by all Australians.

- The **National Gallery of Australia** is a stunner and you may get away with strolling through with your kids (though perhaps not at the leisurely pace you would if you were sans children, but better than nothing, right?). The permanent collection is top notch and there are always various temporary exhibitions too; these change often so check the website for what's on when you're in town. The gallery is set on the edge of Lake Burley Griffin – when the kids have had enough inside, take them outside to the lakeside **Sculpture Garden** for a wander and some fresh air.

- Science museums seem to be popping up everywhere, but Canberra's **Questacon:**

the National Science and Technology Centre is one of the best and one of the originals too. Like Timezone for smart kids, Questacon offers kids of all ages interactive challenges, puzzles and brain food. Experience the power of an earthquake (hold on!) in the Awesome Earth exhibit, put life under the microscope in the QLab or feel what it's like to free-fall in the excellent Excite@Q gallery. There's also the Mini Q section, which is aimed at toddlers and children under six.

- It may be illegal not to have a dino-centre in each city and Canberra's **National Dinosaur Museum** won't disappoint with the largest collection of dinosaur and prehistoric fossil material in the country. It's another museum making an effort to be aware of those with autism or a sensory processing disorder; each Tuesday morning between 10am and 12pm is a 'quiet morning' (except in school holidays) when the dinosaur animatronics are switched off. The museum is located in **Gold Creek Village**, about 20 minutes north of Canberra's city centre. Also here is **Cockington Green Gardens**. We've spoken about Australia's obsession with BIG things, but clever Canberra has seen a gap in the market and gone the other way – at Cockington Green Gardens everything is in miniature. Jump aboard the miniature steam-train to explore this miniature world. If the kids are over things in miniature, just a couple of minutes beyond Gold Creek Village is the **Canberra Reptile Zoo** with over 50 species of scaly, slithery creatures to see. Back in inner Canberra you'll find the **National Zoo and Aquarium**.

- If, like us, you and your kids are into sport, visit the **Australian Institute of Sport**, where you can take a tour, maybe spot a champion or two, and test your sporting skills and physical abilities in Sportex, an interactive sports exhibit.

- It's not called the bush capital for nothing, and we recommend making the most of the territory's nature reserves, especially if the kids are completely over museums. In Canberra itself, head to the magical **National Arboretum** where you can set the kids free to run around and burn off their boundless energy among the 44,000 trees. The Arboretum features a free adventure park called the **Pod Playground**, which has huge acorn cubbies, nest swings and banksia pods.

- Just like a roundabout, there is no two ways around it: it can get bloody cold in Canberra but if you get lucky and strike a warm, sunny day (we got three in a row at Easter!) or have rugged up, head to **Stromlo Forest Park** for a bike ride, horseride, walk or picnic. This is one of Canberra's many excellent mountain-biking spots, and is only about ten minutes from the CBD.

- More nature escapes can be found just out of the city. **Tidbinbilla Nature Reserve** is a great place for wildlife spotting, with its emus, koalas and many other species, and is a great spot for a barbecue or picnic (the kids can explore the Nature Discovery Playground). The stunning **Namadgi National Park** features numerous bushwalking and camping options, and has a rich Indigenous history; evidence shows that the Ngunnawal people have lived in the area for over 21,000 years. The most accessible Indigenous rock art in Namadgi can be found at **Yankee Hat**. Take the easy 6km return walk through grasslands (keep an eye out for grey kangaroos) to see the rock art. Respect the Aboriginal heritage and don't touch, damage or disturb any of the paintings or objects.

KID-FREE NIGHT OUT

For a night out, **Ovolo Nishi** (formerly Hotel Hotel) in the city's New Acton precinct is one of the funkier hotels in Australia. It's worth it for the art and architecture alone and the resident **Monster Kitchen and Bar** works for both breakfast and more nocturnal activities. Nearby, **QT** embraces the city's political currency and stylishly weaves it into its fabric with a tongue-in-cheek sense of play. QT's **Capitol Bar and Grill** is a top spot for dinner, then have your waiter point you in the direction of the hotel's **Lucky's Speakeasy** with its DJ pumping tunes – nothing too political here – as you wind down with cocktails and beers. Want to experience Prohibition-era Cuba but don't have a time machine? Head to **Highball Express** to sip rum-based cocktails to a curated DJ set – a perfect finish to your night out in Canberra's CBD.

QUEENSLAND

FOR BRIJ IT'S QUITE SIMPLE: at some point we are moving to Queensland. The Gold Coast, the Sunshine Coast, Port Douglas, Cairns, Brisbane – it doesn't matter, Brij is desperate to enjoy that vitamin D for longer than a two-week getaway. Pete's official response is 'We'll see'.

We've all heard the slogan 'Beautiful one day, perfect the next', and sure we've all been in Queensland when it wasn't so perfect, but my goodness it *is* perfect a lot of the time. With an incredibly diverse range of tourist destinations to visit, from beach to rainforest to outback, you can be forgiven for not even touching the sides in a two-week holiday. In fact, Queensland is the second largest state in Australia after Western Australia, so it would take a while to see it all.

The vast majority of Queensland receives an average of eight to nine hours of sunshine every day. And, with its average of 261 days of sunshine every year, you are almost guaranteed to get plenty of vitamin D on your visit.

Worth mentioning is that most states in Australia have banned holding koalas, but not Queensland, so it remains a popular tourist attraction in the state, particularly for international tourists. Please remember that only trained accredited rangers should be allowed to hold a koala. Koalas are wild animals and have a natural fear of humans and so shouldn't be held for photo opportunities. (This is a cruel blow for visiting tennis players and Hollywood celebrities.)

ATTRACTIONS

- Queensland beaches are some of the best in Australia and one of the main reasons people head to the Sunshine State. If you're after that idyllic beach experience you may want to head to one of our favourite spots, **Great Keppel Island**, famous for its white-sand beaches and baby-blue water. Hop on over to **Airlie Beach** and the Whitsundays and why not follow up with the world-famous **Whitehaven Beach**, on Whitsunday Island, in the heart of the Great Barrier Reef, for some turtle spotting or simply a whole bunch of beautiful bugger-all (if the kids allow it). We love **Main Beach** in **Noosa** after a walk along Hastings Street, and **Four Mile Beach** in Port Douglas. Not all Queensland beaches are swimmable year-round (thanks to stingers and crocs and the occasional cyclone), so check before you book for the best times at the best beaches. The kids love these beaches because they seem to stretch on forever, and there is always something for the kids to do, no matter their age. The towns surrounding towns them have everything you need. It is fairly easy to get to these places, no matter where you are coming from in Australia, which makes travelling with kids that much more relaxing.

- **Cape York Peninsula** is mainland Australia's most northern point and is the largest unspoiled wilderness in northern Australia. You can take a 4WD tour up to the tip if you don't have a 4WD (be prepared for the bumpy roads). Head there when it's the dry season and not too hot and humid. It is remote; it is far away; trips take a lot of planning; and there's a lot of rainforest – this is a trip for true adventurers. You will need to be experienced, highly organised and plan well in advance to ensure you have the right gear if you are going without a tour. Whichever way you do it, it's a trip of a lifetime and the kids won't be disappointed.

- Like most kids, our boys have all been happily obsessed with dinosaurs. Our eldest, Liam, told us he wanted to be a palaeontologist when he was five. If you have budding palaeontologists in your family, head to outback Queensland and follow the **Australian Dinosaur Trail**, which loops between the towns of **Winton**, **Hughenden** and **Richmond**. Some of the oldest dinosaur footprints in the world are found in the area and you can see a large collection of dinosaur fossils at the **Australian Age of Dinosaurs Museum**, as well as explore the museum's fossil-preparation lab, just out of Winton. Only 110km down the road from Winton is **Lark Quarry Dinosaur Trackways**; visit here so the kids can see the fossilised footprints of a stomping stampede of 3300 small dinosaurs, preserved in stone from 95 million years ago (it's thought they were being chased by a bigger, and obviously hungrier, dinosaur). And if the dinosaurs don't get you excited (um, you may want to check for a pulse), Banjo Paterson's famous song 'Waltzing Matilda' was performed for the first time (back in 1895) at Winton's North Gregory Hotel. You can visit the **Waltzing Matilda Centre** in Winton, the only centre in the world dedicated to a song. Surely a 'You're the Voice' Centre needs to open soon!

Spotify GANGgajang and head into sugarcane country around **Childers**, about 45 minutes west from Hervey Bay. The lightning may or may not crack over the cane fields but you can still laugh and think 'this is Australia' while treating yourself to a well-earned locally made **Mammino Gourmet** ice-cream. The **Childers Historical Complex** is a charming interactive, grassroots home to all the things from the 'good ol' days' – let the kids climb the trains, explore the general store and pretend to be students from another century in the old school house. About an hour south of Childers is **Mount Walsh National Park**; visit the park to swim in the beautiful **Utopia rockpools** at Waterfall Creek (a 3km return walk), which will keep everyone cool under that blazing Queensland sun.

Less than an hour north of Childers and arguably most famous for its sugarcane, rum and rum-drinking polar bears, **Bundaberg** is a good place to stop for a couple of days. From the 27-hectare **Botanic Gardens** complete with hidden Japanese garden to the **Basin rockpool** at Bargara where the kids can safely snorkel, Bundaberg has plenty of options to keep kids excited and cool. A few minutes from the Basin is one of Bundaberg's highlights: the turtles at **Mon Repos Conservation Park**. Visit the Mon Repos Turtle Centre, book a night-time turtle encounter or walk along the beach on the lovely Mon Repos Coastal Track. The best time to visit is between November and March when nesting turtles come ashore; if you want to see the adorable baby turtles, hatching usually occurs between January and March. You can also throw a line in at **Woodgate Beach**, enjoy a refreshing ginger beer at the **Bundy Barrel** and walk that sugar hit off with a bushwalk at **Cania Gorge National Park**, just over 200km west of Bundaberg. The national park also offers abundant wildlife so keep your eye out. Or take the kids further west to the rugged **Carnarvon National Park**, a couple of days' drive from Bundaberg, for excellent bushwalking, spectacular scenery and Aboriginal rock art in the stencil style; you can camp in holiday season in the national park and there are good accommodation options just outside the park.

In keeping with Australia's obsession with 'big' things, Queensland has not let the side down. Get your Vitamin C fix with the **Big Orange** in Gayndah (we can only assume the local councillors in Orange, New South Wales, are furious they didn't think of this first). On the Sunshine Coast is the so-daggy-it's-cool **Big Pineapple**, near Woombye, with a pineapple train, tree-top adventure course and heaps of other activities for kids (so it's more than just a big thing and is worth a visit). Road trip around Queensland and you'll also find the **Big Barra** times two (Normanton and Daintree), the **Big Mango** (Bowen), the **Big Captain Cook** (Cairns) and, no surprise, the **Big Cane Toad** (Sarina).

BRISBANE

The Traditional Owners of the land we now call Brisbane are the Turrbal and Jagera peoples.

ANY CITY THAT BRINGS

us Powderfinger, Sandra Sully and Bluey has to have something magical in its waters, doesn't it?

Brisvegas, as it's affectionately known, has plenty to offer, from the first Test of the season at the Gabba to parklands built for picnics on sunny days (of which there are many). Brisbane joins the rest of the country with its burgeoning culinary scene but what sets Brissie apart is the plentiful al-fresco riverside dining options.

Brisbane feels like it has the best bits of its southerly east-coast cousins, with hip Melbourne-esque laneways abuzz with eateries to the swanky playfulness of the Harbour City, yet it somehow feels utterly unique – Brisbane moves to its own beat. And does any other capital city in Australia have better weather than Brisbane?

Okay, Perth and Brissie can toss for it.

If you're staying in Brisbane, the Gold Coast and Sunshine Coast are only an hour's drive away. Hire a car to drive north to the Sunshine Coast (*see* p. 76) or south to the Gold Coast (*see* p. 73).

Accommodation

Brisbane, the Gold Coast and the Sunshine Coast all have an enormous range of accommodation options, from hotels, motels, caravan parks and camping grounds to houses, serviced apartments and beach shacks. You'll easily be able to find something that suits your family and your budget, but do ensure you book ahead in busy periods, especially school holidays and Christmas.

Getting Around

If you don't have a car, Brisbane has a good rail and bus network. Children under four are free, kids aged between five and 14 can ride as a concession ticket (and ride free on weekends if they have an orange child go card). There is a free CityHopper ferry to take you on the river between the city and South Bank and two free bus services, the City Loop and Spring Hill Loop, around the CBD.

On the Sunshine Coast you'll need to catch buses for public transport, so hiring a car is probably the best option, especially if you want to explore the hinterland.

The Gold Coast has light rail, called G-link, that makes it easy to get around, as well as buses and trains to get you further north and south.

If you plan on exploring most of south-east Queensland, it's worth hiring a car. Bear in mind, though, that the M1 between Brisbane and the Gold Coast is renowned for traffic so avoid peak hour (when it becomes a carpark), and if you're coming home from the theme parks at the end of the day, allow at least an extra 30 minutes for your travel time. The Bruce Highway heading north to the Sunshine Coast is also very busy; travel outside peak hour if you can.

ATTRACTIONS

📍 We think Brisbane is the only capital city with a beach right in the centre: **South Bank** boasts a man-made (sorry, person-made) beach along with rockpools and swimming pools – it's a great place to take a dip if you're visiting in summer (really, given the weather in Brisbane and the fact that the beach is patrolled by life guards year-round, you can swim there whatever season you're visiting in!). South Bank offers many more things to do for families: set the kids free on the huge playground, which has a separate toddler zone to ensure the little ones don't get bowled over by over-zealous tweens, or relax with a gelato or a picnic on the grass. Once you've cooled off at the artificial-but-fun beach or had your fill of the playground, wander along the beautiful bougainvillea-covered pathway (grandly called the **South Bank Arbour**) to reach the 60m high **Wheel of Brisbane**. Unlike its Melbourne counterpart, the Brisbane wheel has had a trouble-free history and offers top 360-degree views of Brisvegas. South Bank also has cinemas if you need a rest and some aircon, a range of cafes and restaurants, an enjoyable rainforest walk and a scenic riverside walk. It is easily accessible by train or **CityCat**. The CityCats travel up and down the Brisbane River and are the best way to see the city – stand out the front with the wind in your hair *Titanic*-style or sit inside with the aircon and the commuters.

📍 Brisbane's iconic **Mount Coot-tha** is only about 10km from the city centre. It's a bush haven for locals and a great place for visitors. Mountain-bikers will love exploring the bush tracks and the less coordinated can enjoy a range of bushwalks and take in the views of the city from the summit. There's a cafe and a restaurant, the **Summit Restaurant and Bar**, at the top. There are a number of great picnic and barbecue areas but the most popular are **J.C. Slaughter Falls** and **Simpsons Falls** – they're the kind of places where you can sit back with a barbecue and a glass of wine while the kids catch tadpoles in the creek, old-school style. At the base of the mountain is the **Brisbane Botanic Gardens Mount Coot-tha** (Brisbane also has the **City Botanic Gardens** in the CBD). This is a perfect spot for a picnic and the kids can burn off excess energy at the bush playground. Definitely try the Children's Hide-and-Seek Trail in the gardens (and please let us know if you find the hidden panda). The gardens are also home to the **Thomas Brisbane Planetarium**, which shows excellent space films for kids in the Cosmic Skydome and also features a range of space and astronomy exhibitions, including the very cool Skylore, an exhibition all about Aboriginal and Torres Strait Islander astronomy.

📍 Though **Fortitude Valley** is mostly known as a place to listen to live music and enjoy outdoor bars at night (be aware it can get messy as the night drags on), it's also a good place for a weekend brunch at one of

the many cafes or for lunch in **Chinatown** before taking the kids to the nearby **New Farm Park**, one of Brisbane's oldest and largest parks (CityCats also stop here).

📍 **EatStreet Northshore** markets, in the riverside inner-city suburb of Hamilton, are a great place to go with hungry kids – the markets offer a whole bunch of culinary delights from the **Swedish Candy Bar** and **Japanese Pizza** to **Popper Pete's Popcorn** and **Funky Dragon Dumplings**. There's every type of food from the world over, so you'll easily find something for those hard-to-please eaters. The markets are open on Friday and Saturday from 4pm and Sunday from 12pm. It's not too far from Brisbane's international cruise-ship terminal, so if your kids like big boats keep an eye out for the cruise ships docking.

📍 For high-octane adventure head to **Slideways** in Eagle Farm, ten minutes east of the CBD (and not far from EatStreet Northshore markets), for the pure adrenalin rush of go-karting. The indoor European-style track is a popular one so book ahead. It's best for older kids as there are age and height restrictions, but kids' carts and two-seater carts are coming soon.

📍 Head west to Ipswich (about a 45-minute drive from Brisbane) to visit the **Workshops Rail Museum**, a hands-on science centre and heritage museum aimed fairly and squarely at kids. There are fascinating exhibitions, fun activities, trains to climb on, train simulators and even the Nippers Railway, an adventure playground for young kids with a kid-sized railway (they can pedal along it, stopping at stations and so on). On school holidays you may even be able to catch Thomas the Tank Engine. There's a cafe on-site or you can take your own picnic to have in the grounds.

KID-FREE NIGHT OUT

Brisbane's CBD won't disappoint if you've found a babysitter and left the kids behind. Down by the river at **Eagle Street Pier** you'll have your pick of bars and restaurants, most with beautiful views of the wide Brisbane River. Being the good Melburnians we are, we are drawn to laneways with eateries, and Brisbane doesn't disappoint: visit **Bean**, tucked away just off busy George Street. You'll love this coffee house and bar where local craft beers and boutique small-batch wines await.

The best-kept foodie secret is out: locals and visitors alike love **Burnett Lane** (off Albert Street in the CBD) for its hidden bars, cafes and restaurants. If you want to start your night off with cocktails, we recommend **Death and Taxes** and **Super Whatnot**; follow that up with Korean at **Funny Funny** or Vietnamese at **Pho City**, both also in Burnett Lane.

GOLD COAST

The Yugambeh people are the First people of the land we now call the Gold Coast.

WHEN YOU THINK OF FUN

in the sun most Aussies think of the Gold Coast (perhaps depending on their age and/or relationship status). Once considered cheap and tawdry, the Gold Coast has come a long way, replacing their famed meter-maids with an air of sophistication that can be found in the array of beachside restaurants and bars.

Before you start thinking the Gold Coast has gone all serious and classy, you can relax because FUN is still very much at the centre of its DNA. (Does DNA actually have a centre? Neither of us is particularly science-y, so we'll leave it to you.)

Theme parks loom large on the Gold Coast and, despite being around for decades, most of them continue to evolve, remaining world-class thrill-seeking utopias. These theme parks are a major attraction of the Gold Coast and, travelling with kids, you'll probably be duty bound to visit at least a couple. Embrace the chaos of them – the chances are your kids will remember these days more than any other you share on this family holiday, so be in the moment, let your hair down and get on that rollercoaster! You can take your pick: Dreamworld, WhiteWater World, Movie World, Wet 'n' Wild, Outback Spectacular, Sea World and Paradise Country. Our favourites are Movie World and Wet 'n' Wild. We promise that kids and adults will have a ball. Pete still has fond memories of being picked during the Movie World tour when he was 12 to help create the sound for a famous scene in *Lethal Weapon*. We're not sure it can be counted as his first official acting gig, but he has never forgotten it.

Flick to the USA chapter (see p. 267) for hints and tips about visiting theme parks – these will help you prepare for the Australian parks too. As a starting point, remember to take sunscreen, hats and plenty of water. You can save on theme parks by buying super-saver passes to more than one park (not all parks are available on the super-savers though).

Ethical animal tourism is particularly important to us, and we avoid visiting America's SeaWorld because they capture wild animals to use in their parks (see p. 33). Sea World on the Gold Coast is not affiliated with the American SeaWorld and has different policies on the capture of wild animals. It is good to see that Sea World on the Gold Coast only features dolphins that have been rescued from the wild; however, we still question whether dolphins want to act in shows and swim with humans regardless of their inability to survive in the wild. Dolphins are famous for their 'smile', but that so-called smile is just the configuration of their jaw: are they really happy and content? Visit au.whales.org or orrca.org.au to read more about reasons not to swim with captured dolphins.

- If theme parks aren't quite your style but you want some adventure, head to **GC Wake Park** (just behind Movie World) to try wake-boarding, waterskiing and knee-boarding, or to **iFly Indoor Skydiving** at Surfers Paradise, where it's like you've jumped out of a plane at 14,000 feet (but safer!).

- **Kurrawa Park**, in the heart of Broadbeach, has an all-abilities playground, lifesaving club and beautiful beach. It's easy to get to and excellent to visit with kids of all ages. The beach usually has decent waves for older kids and it's long and wide, so it's perfect for sand play. The playground is full of all things playground and has three main zones – sandcastle, hill and undersea – for the kids to explore. There's plenty of grass to kick a ball around on and good barbecue facilities, so it's a spot-on place for a full day out.

- **Surfers Paradise Beach** might be well known but it's not too busy and it has a perfect beach that stretches on forever. The lifesavers are there to protect the families in the waves, and little kids can play at the water's edge with no trouble. As long as you aren't visiting in schoolies week, the beach is a wonderful place to hang out. It's close to excellent accommodation options and walking distance to **Ripley's Believe It or Not** and ice-cream!

- The **Gold Coast hinterland** is definitely worth exploring when you have kids in tow. The **Glow Worm Cave** at **Tamborine Mountain** is a purpose-built cave so you can see glow worms during the day, and the tour will teach you everything you've ever wanted to know about glow worms. Also at Tamborine Mountain is the exciting **TreeTop Challenge** – experience new heights on the ten ziplines and across various aerial challenges (best for kids over eight), or book in for the epic **Canyon Flyer** zipline adventure. After the adrenalin rush, relax at **Curtis Falls** in **Tamborine National Park**, which offers a range of easy and pram-accessible walks. Swim in the crystal-clear pools, enjoy a picnic and talk about all the fun you had today.

- Also in the hinterland is the beautiful, World Heritage–listed **Lamington National Park**. In the Green Mountains section of the park is **O'Reilly's Rainforest Retreat**, which offers great activities for kids. Stay for a day or for longer, and take the kids on the **Flying Fox Adventure**, a 180m zipline over the rainforest, or the milder **O'Reilly's Treetop Walk**. There's also a birds of prey show and a wildlife encounter show, along with great bushwalking.

KID-FREE NIGHT OUT

On the Gold Coast, head to **Broadbeach** for your adults-only night. Next to the Loose Moose, where lots of people are usually milling around socialising, you'll find the stylish **Roosevelt Lounge**. They'll make cocktails at your table – sit back and enjoy the creativity from the comfort of your leather Chesterfield lounge. We had a top night here recently, and the friendly and extremely knowledgeable staff prepared cocktails so flamboyant we were certain Katy Perry was about to pop out of one.

SUNSHINE COAST

The Gubbi Gubbi people are the First people of the land we now call the Sunshine Coast.

FOR THOSE WHO FIND THE THRILLS

and spills of the Gold Coast a little too taxing, the beautiful Sunshine Coast may be just about perfect for you. The Sunshine Coast moves at a different pace from its party-hard-but-beginning-to settle-down-just-a-bit southern sibling, the Gold Coast. This is no nursing home though. To the contrary, the Sunshine Coast is a vibrant hub and tourist hotspot. If you're after a holiday that perfectly combines relaxation and a healthy dose of activity, the Sunshine Coast may be the ideal fit. It also offers beautiful beaches and wonderful national parks to explore. Stay at one of the many beachside towns for those beach-holiday vibes, but allow at least a day to explore the lush hinterland.

- One of our fave beach spots to visit and stay is Noosa, where the kids will love the beach, the Noosa Chocolate Factory and all the water activities available. The cuisine here is top notch and best enjoyed taking in the sunset – and, because the vibe is relaxed, kids are more than welcome to enjoy the setting sun with a mocktail with you. The much-loved Eumundi Markets aren't far from Noosa and are worth visiting if you're around on a Wednesday or a Saturday.

- Another favourite spot for us is Mooloolaba – stay here if you want a beautiful beach right outside your hotel or apartment window. Mooloolaba has become a busy beachside town but when Brij first started visiting it was just a sleepy little beach place – if only she'd had enough pocket money at 13 to buy one of those blocks of land with beachfront views. Caloundra is another good place to stay, with the calm waters of Golden Beach

great for swimming with young kids. If your kids are older or love surfing, head to **Kings Beach** instead.

- The Sunshine Coast isn't all sand and surf. Hire a car and head up the Blackall Range to the mountain-top towns of **Montville** and **Maleny**. Montville is a scenic spot with lovely cafes and shops (including a fabulous toy shop). Nearby is the beautiful **Kondalilla National Park** – pack a picnic and go for the short bushwalk to the top of Kondalilla Falls, where there's a lovely rockpool (don't forget your togs!). If your kids are up for a harder walk, follow the circuit trail to the bottom of the falls (prepare yourselves for the steep walk back up). Near Maleny is **Gardeners Falls**, which has a range of rockpools great for all ages, including nice shallow ones perfect for toddlers to play in. Also nearby is Maleny's **Mary Cairncross Scenic Reserve**, which has a kid-friendly short bushwalk through remnant rainforest (keep an eye out for the adorable pademelons), an excellent Rainforest Discovery Centre and a spacious picnic area and playground.

- Another good place to explore just inland from the coast is **Glass House Mountains National Park**. The craggy peaks of the Glass House Mountains are volcanic plugs that tower above the surrounding pineapple and strawberry farms. For the Traditional Owners, the Gubbi Gubbi people, the mountains are a family, with Mount Beerwah the mother and the hulking Mount Tibrogargan the father – all the other peaks are their kids.

- Just near Glass House Mountains National Park is the famed **Australia Zoo**. You can easily spend an entire day here – the kids will love seeing the giraffes, zebras and rhinos in the open-range Africa exhibit, the lemurs chilling out in the trees on Bindi's Island and, of course, the many other animals, including meerkats, tigers, otters and a range of native Australian creatures. Plan your visit around the daily crocodile-feeding and birds of prey shows in the Crocoseum. Our kids are huge fans of reptiles and this is a place they just had to see. As a bonus, the zoo has many conservation projects for kids to follow.

FRASER ISLAND

The Butchulla people are the Traditional Owners of K'gari (also known as Fraser Island).

THE WORLD HERITAGE-LISTED

Fraser Island is the world's largest sand island (at 123km long). For anyone who dreams of driving a 4WD along a picture-perfect deserted beach, this is your spot. Let the kids roll down the golden sand dunes, watch the wildlife and explore the exquisite lakes on this incredible island.

Fraser Island has claimed almost as many shipwrecks as Australia has had dodgy referee decisions in various sporting world cups: 23 ships were wrecked between 1856 and 1935. In 1935 the SS *Maheno*, with a small crew on board, was being towed to Osaka (it had been sold to Japan as scrap). It came face to face with the ferocity of a Queensland cyclone and the towline broke. Losing its ride, the *Maheno* eventually crashed ashore. Luckily all eight crew survived, and the rusted ruins of the wreck can still be seen on Fraser's 75 Mile Beach today.

Fraser's beaches are not really safe for swimming, but every year the humpback whales rest and nurse their newborn calves just offshore, so there is much whale-watching to be had (and various eco-tours are available). Fraser gets very busy during the school holidays, so book accommodation and activities early (if you want to go on a bus tour to explore the island, early booking is essential to ensure those who need baby seats are looked after). You can take your own 2WD car over but it can only be used to get to the Kingfisher Bay Resort; off the resort, only 4WD vehicles are allowed on Fraser Island.

For this island you need to be dingo safe, as Fraser is one of the few places you are almost guaranteed to see dingos in the wild. Never feed the dingos, always lock your food cabinets, keep small children within arm's reach, don't let kids of any age run ahead of you (including teenagers), walk in groups, do not run or wave your arms, and camp in fenced-off campsites.

THE TROPICAL NORTH

The Country of the Eastern Kuku Yalanji people extends from Cooktown to Port Douglas, and the Gimuy-walubarra yidi are the Traditional Custodians of Cairns.

THIS MAGICAL part of Queensland is special – it's lucky enough to have two World Heritage–listed areas side by side: the lush rainforests of the Wet Tropics and the stunning Great Barrier Reef. There's so much you could do up here if you had the time and so much we could tell you about, but we're going to focus on our favourite places along this spectacular stretch of Coral Sea coastline: Cairns, Port Douglas and the Daintree. Talking time, a long weekend won't feel like enough but it is possible, even from Melbourne. We know this from personal experience: Brij often suggests a weekend away in sunny Queensland if she gets even just a hint of a few days off from the kids' sports, school commitments and Pete's work. If you're lucky enough to have more than a long weekend, set aside time to drive the Great Tropical Drive from Cairns to Cooktown – a fabulous road trip for the whole family.

It's a 1700km drive to Cairns from Brisbane (yep, it's a big bloody state Queensland). That drive will take around 20 to 23 hours. Remember when driving with kids, you'll need to stop more often and sleep somewhere so break up the trip into a few days (at the very minimum) to keep your sanity (and theirs). Plan the drive ahead of time so you know the best places to stop for the kids (usually somewhere they can run around for a bit, have something to eat and go to the loo). If flying, you will arrive in Cairns. Shuttle buses can take you to Port Douglas, but we think hiring a car is the best plan – there's just so much to see and do but it does involve driving some distance.

This part of tropical Queensland has a pretty warm climate all year round. There are, however, two distinct seasons: the Dry (winter) and the Wet (summer). Winter is dryer and a little cooler than the wet season, which is hot and humid and lasts from November to April. Because the weather is so lovely, you can swim any time. The ideal swimming period is between April and early October. Remember, box jellyfish are around between the months of October and March, so special swimming enclosures are used at popular beaches. Most resorts and some beachside parks have pools so you'll always be able to find somewhere to cool off.

Queensland offers many opportunities to learn about Indigenous history and culture and this area is no different, so make the most of it. **Walkabout Cultural Adventures** (in the Daintree region) and **Mungalla Aboriginal Tours** (in Ingham, about three hours south of Cairns) both offer a range of fascinating experiences and are both Indigenous owned. Or book in for the **Ngadiku Dreamtime Walk** at Mossman Gorge (about 20km north of Port Douglas), where, with an Indigenous guide, you can explore the rainforest via a private track and visit culturally significant sites. As we mentioned earlier in the book, we did this walk and the kids loved it. They learnt about the significance of Aboriginal paint, which they even got to make from ochre, and the bush tea and damper at the end were pretty nice too. You can also explore Mossman Gorge on your own, and there's an excellent visitor centre, the Mossman Gorge Centre, which is an Indigenous ecotourism development with great facilities and a shuttle bus that takes you into the gorge.

Cairns is such a perfect holiday spot that it can be hard to leave – the **Esplanade** has expansive waterfront parklands and a free saltwater lagoon, the **Cairns Aquarium** focuses solely on species from the Wet Tropics and the city offers a great range of kid-friendly cafes. You have to leave the city though, because there's so much else to explore around Cairns (oh and eventually you'll need to go home). Start with a ride on the **Skyrail Rainforest Cableway**, skimming over the top of the World Heritage–listed rainforest for more than 7km and stopping at two rainforest stations on the way: **Red Peak**, where you can wander on the boardwalk or take a ranger-guided tour; and the spectacular **Barron Falls**, where you can admire the view from the Edge Lookout. Skyrail ends in **Kuranda**, a beautiful village on the Barron River and home to the **Kuranda Scenic Railway**, which you can take all the way back to Cairns. Just outside of Cairns is the stunning **Barron Gorge National Park**: book a rafting tour on the Barron River (there are family rafting options for children as young as six) or explore the stunning rainforest on a bushwalk. If you have the time and money, you can find almost any tour on offer in Cairns, so plan ahead.

About an hour south of Cairns, the breathtakingly beautiful **Josephine Falls** has featured in many television commercials over the years. We can happily report back that the TV exposure has not gone to Josephine's head, despite being linked with a bevy of Hollywood A-listers. We are also happy to report that it's a perfect swimming spot – make sure to take a picnic too.

Gorgeous **Port Douglas** is about an hour's drive north from Cairns, along a beautiful scenic coastal drive. Watch the sun rise over the ocean on **Four Mile Beach** – the closest beach to town in Port Douglas. The kids loved the walk up to the Flagstaff Hill Lookout and we all loved its stunning views of the beach and the Coral Sea. It's a fairly easy walk up but if you want to get there in time for the sunrise you can drive up. Walk through the town and pick a place for lunch that offers seafood – the kids' favourite was fish of the day. It's always freshly caught and delicious.

Beyond Port Douglas is the beautiful **Daintree**. Start at the **Daintree Discovery Centre**, which offers much more than information: a rainforest-canopy tower, aerial walkway, boardwalks, an interpretive display centre and a cafe. This is also where you can book the Dreamtime Walk of Mossman Gorge that we've raved about.

Take an eco-friendly tour of the Daintree River (a number of cruise operators offer tours) and spot some crocs in their natural habitat (from a safe distance, of course). Head just north to visit **Cape Tribulation** for rainforest bushwalks and desolate beaches.

- If you've saved your pennies, book a stay at **Lizard Island**, the northernmost island resort in Australia off the coast near Cooktown. It has the most amazing reef to view and will be some of the best snorkelling you've ever done. However, you need to get a private charter flight to get there and it's a luxury resort that only allows children ten years old and over. This would be a once-in-a-lifetime experience. If it's not part of your budget or plans, remember there are all types of excellent options for little and big kids in the Tropical North before you have to think about flying to a remote island: take them exploring the rainforest, rafting the rivers, and, if you really want to get your snorkel on, **river-drift snorkelling**, which is perfect for kids because you simply float along with the river (you do it in the dry season when the rivers are calmer). You can book a river-drift snorkelling tour in Port Douglas.

- Australia's **Great Barrier Reef** is one of the world's seven natural wonders. It is the largest coral reef system and the biggest living structure on the planet, covering 344,400sqkm – it is so large that it can be seen from space. The reef stretches for over 2600km, from Bundaberg in the south to the tip of Cape York. It's composed of almost 3000 individual reef systems, which provide a habitat and refuge for hundreds of different species of marine animals and fish.

- Much of the tourism in the Tropical North is connected to the Great Barrier Reef. The best way to explore this World Heritage site is to focus on the wonderful ecotourism and Indigenous options available to you. More than 70 Aboriginal and Torres Strait Islander Traditional Owner groups have long, continuing relationships with the Great Barrier Reef region and its natural resources and some offer excellent trips and tours that will help you and your family see just how special the reef is. But remember, do not touch the reef or its wildlife or try to take a souvenir home: fines do apply and are enforced. For more information on how you can protect the reef, visit the World Wide Fund for Nature's website: wwf.org.au/what-we-do/oceans/great-barrier-reef.

SAFETY IN THE TROPICAL NORTH

Remember to listen to the locals about swimming spots and be croc-wise. A sentence like 'Be croc-wise' is surely the kind of sentence you only need to hear or read once. Surely. Crocodiles are found in estuaries and on beaches around Tropical North Queensland, and they can also be found in rivers, lagoons and swamps. Always obey crocodile warning signs. Never swim where crocodiles may be present, even if you don't see any signs.

During annual stinger season, beaches may be closed when the buggers are present. Closures remain in place until weather patterns change. Swim between the flags and listen to lifesaver warnings. And, of course, don't swim when beaches are closed. (For more on swimming safety, *see* p. 37.)

WESTERN AUSTRALIA

DID YOU KNOW?

- Space debris from NASA's *Skylab* Space Station was found around Balladonia in Western Australia after it crashed to Earth in 1979. The local council issued NASA with a $400 littering fine, which was later paid by a Californian radio station. True!
- Surveyor General's Corner is the name of the intersection where the Northern Territory and the states of South Australia and Western Australia meet. Access to the area is limited to guided tours and visitors require a special permit in addition to the standard Great Central Road transit permit.
- Mount Augustus, just under 500km east of Carnarvon, is the world's largest rock, at more than twice the size of Uluru. Only one-third of the rock is visible above the surface of the Earth.

IT DOESN'T TAKE

long to feel relaxed in Western Australia. Upon landing in Perth, the world's most isolated city, your shoulders will drop before you even reach your ride at the airport. We don't mind the long flight over to Perth – knowing what you are about to experience makes it all worthwhile. Once you're off the plane and outside, it feels like a completely different city from any on the eastern coast. The beaches and gardens are different – even the air feels different! – and the city itself has benefitted from being further away from other Australian capitals. We experience such welcoming locals every time we visit and if we could we'd spend more time hanging out with them in this fabulous state.

Australia's largest state, Western Australia is as unique as it is huge and presents opportunities for every kind of holiday you have in mind, from beach relaxation and outback exploring to wine-region touring and more. A highlight for us are the beaches – Western Australia has one of the most breathtaking unspoiled coastlines in the world.

ATTRACTIONS

- One thing Western Australia has plenty of is area – as we've said, it's big! And it has areas that are like nothing else in the world – such as the moonscape of the world-famous **Pinnacles Desert** in Nambung National Park. About a two-hour drive north of Perth, the Pinnacles are majestic limestone formations that are up to 30,000 years old. They are part of Western Australia's **Coral Coast** area, which also includes the seaside towns of **Cervantes**, **Jurien Bay** and **Leeman** with their diverse flora and fauna, pristine beaches and the kind of fishing that would make Rex Hunt blush. There are tours to the area from Perth but if you have a car, it's worth spending a few days exploring this unique area and enjoying some downtime with the kids on the beautiful beaches.

- Further north up the stunning coast is the ominously named **Shark Bay**, a World Heritage site with desolate peninsulas, dramatic cliffs and **stromatolites** – ancient microbial 'living fossils' that can be seen in **Hamelin Pool**. Not far from the stromatolites is **Shell Beach**, a 70km beach made up completely of tiny shells – no building sandcastles with the kids here! Visit Shark Bay's much friendlier sounding **Monkey Mia** for an incredible wild dolphin experience. About 200 bottlenose dolphins live in the waters around Monkey Mia, and each day rangers feed the same five adult females. To be part of the dolphin experience, get there early – the first ranger briefing is usually at 7.45am. There is so much more wildlife for the kids to see – keep an eye out for turtles, dugongs, rays and whales. If you want to stay overnight, there's the Monkey Mia Dolphin Resort or a variety of accommodation options at nearby Denham.

- There's so much to see along this part of the Western Australian coastline, but for many people the absolute highlight is the incredible **Ningaloo Reef**. As stunning as the Great Barrier Reef, World Heritage-listed **Ningaloo Marine Park** extends approximately 300km from Red Bluff (near Carnarvon) in the south to Exmouth in the north. Unlike in Queensland, here you can walk straight from the beach on to the reef, which makes it easy to explore with children. **Coral Bay** is a good access point to the reef and is an incredibly chilled-out beachside town, or stay in **Exmouth**, a busier hub and home to the Ningaloo Visitor Centre. So many tours and cruises are available, including the once-in-a-lifetime opportunity to swim with whale sharks (these tours aren't cheap, though), but, with the reef so close to the shore, snorkelling is an easy way for the whole family to see the many marine species and rainbow coral colours of the reef. Just outside of Exmouth is the rugged **Cape Range National Park**, where you'll see amazing wildlife year-round and beautiful wildflowers in winter.

- You can fly from Perth to Exmouth, but if you're road tripping it instead, stop at **Carnarvon**, about four hours north of Denham and the same south of Exmouth, to visit the **Carnarvon Blowholes**. Here the ocean forces water through sea caves and up out of holes in the rocks – a pretty awesome sight. Take a picnic because just a few clicks south is a beautiful small coral bay, perfect for snorkelling with the kids off the white sandy beach.

- Inland from Exmouth (an eight-hour drive where you're guaranteed to hear 'are we there yet?' from the kids about a billion times) is **Karijini National Park** – a unique wilderness of gorges and rockpools that will make you the King and Queen of Instagram for at least a day.

- The south coast of Western Australia is another area of the state chockfull of beaches and stunning landscapes. Visit **Esperance**, a laidback town with a beach lifestyle and arty culture, for excellent beaches and postcard-perfect scenery, along with **Esperance Museum** that the kids will love (it tells the tale of Australia's only recorded pirate, Black Jack Anderson, and also features a display about the crash of space station *Skylab*). **Twilight Beach** is the safest swimming and surfing beach in Esperance, but remember to stay in the patrolled zones. With white sands and clear turquoise water, swimming here is spectacular, and the fishing is good too. A short trip from Esperance is **Cape Le Grand National Park**, great for snorkelling, bushwalking and seeing kangaroos lounging around on the beach. There's a well-equipped campground, so you can set up and stay for as long as you want. The national park's most exquisite beach is **Lucky Bay**, a sheltered bay ideal for swimming, snorkelling, fishing, surfing and launching small boats. It's said to have the whitest sand of any beach in Australia, but that's up for discussion according to Hyams Beach in New South Wales. If you have a 4WD, you can drive it on the beach but be aware of the tidal and sand conditions; check with a ranger before doing so.

- On remote **Middle Island**, 70 nautical miles from Esperance, is **Lake Hillier** (not to be confused with Lake Helliar), a striking pink lake surrounded by a rim of sand and a dense woodland of paperbark and eucalyptus trees. Middle Island was pirate Black Jack Anderson's home and you can take cruises to the island from Esperance.

- Western Australia isn't all sun, sand and turquoise waters – it has inland attractions and charming country towns too. Just outside the town of Hyden, about four hours east of Perth, you'll find the famous **Wave Rock**. This incredible granite cliff looks just like a breaking wave – but in stone, obviously. Eroded by wind for the past 2.7 billion years, Wave Rock is about 100m long and 15m high, and it's worth the trip. Trust us: unlike Big Ben in London, the rock is bigger and more astounding than expected. You can stay overnight in lovely Hyden.

- Don't let the movie turn you off: take an outback tour to **Wolfe Creek Crater** in the Kimberley region (*see* p. 90 for more on the Kimberley). Officially 'discovered' by an aerial survey in 1947 (but known to the local Djaru people for thousands of years), the crater is the second largest meteorite crater in the world. It's believed that an iron meteorite crashed to Earth and exploded about 300,000 years ago – it's thought to have crossed over Australia in five minutes, much quicker than our Melbourne to Perth commute. Enjoy the sightseeing and walking – you can take the 200m return walk to the rim of the crater (it's a steep and rocky climb so not good for younger kids) but you can't climb down into the crater for safety reasons. Take photos but, of course, leave rocks and cultural artefacts as you find them. The crater is in **Wolfe Creek Crater National Park**, about 145km from Halls Creek. You can drive the unsealed road to the national park in a standard 2WD car, but only in the dry season. All access within the park is on foot, and the best time to go is between May and October.

PERTH

The Noongar people are the Traditional Owners of the land we now call Perth.

PERTH MAY BE
the most isolated city in the world but it has weather to die for, gorgeous sandy beaches, a relaxed outdoor scene and the scenic Swan River, which curves through the city, offering lots of opportunities for picnics, play and water activities. Pete always says he feels relaxed whenever he arrives in Perth. Maybe it's the Fremantle Doctor that drops his shoulders or the easy-going locals, but if you want to get away and have some rest and relaxation then Perth may well be the city you're looking for.

EATING OUT

Our main recommendation is to find somewhere close to where you're staying, just so it's easy to get the kids to bed after dinner out. In Perth and Fremantle, you can never go wrong picking the seafood. It's always so good and so fresh!

ACCOMMODATION

As with all capital cities there are plenty of family-friendly accommodation options. Perth is quite spread out and both sides of the river offer plenty to do. The CBD is the best place to stay if you're relying on public transport.

GETTING AROUND

You don't have to have a car in Perth. You can access Fremantle and Cottesloe by public transport and generally the city is well connected. The SmartRider card is used for public transport; children aged four years and younger travel for free. Perth city has a Free Transit Zone for buses and a SmartRider Free Transit Zone for trains. If you plan on heading any further afield, you'll be best to hire a car.

ATTRACTIONS

- The most beautiful inner-city park is situated in Perth. **Kings Park** has many play areas to explore with the kids, along with free guided walks through the gardens, bike hire and the Kokoda Track Memorial Walk. The Family Area is perfect for all ages, with a playground suited to kids under six, an oval for sports and a bike path. A playground for older kids can be found at May Drive Parkland, with forts and an interactive water forest. Saw Avenue Picnic Area was developed with children with disabilities in mind and is a great picnic and play spot. You'll find forts, climbing nets, tunnels and climbing logs. Naturescape Kings Park is where you can immerse yourself in nature and the kids will love exploring, climbing and building throughout.

- Perth's fabulous beaches include **Cottesloe Beach**, one of our favourite beaches in any city, with its beautiful walking trails, soft white sand and great swimming – and it's easy to get to. Grab a bite to eat and a bevvy at the **Cottesloe Beach Hotel** or at **Barchetta** for vegan options and a view you won't forget (it will have you ordering that second glass of pinot gris).

- To make the most of Perth's water opportunities, cruise the **Swan River** on one of the many tours on offer or take a dip at **Mettams Pool**, which is actually a naturally formed ocean lagoon and beach, not a pool, and perfect for swimming and snorkelling with kids.

- Take the kids to Perth's only theme park, **Adventure World**. It has 25 rides and attractions, all set in landscaped gardens, and most have slightly terrifying names like Rampage, Goliath, Kraken and Abyss, which is Perth's only rollercoaster and a massive buzz. It's 25 minutes south from Perth's CBD or 15 from Fremantle, and is accessible by public transport. The park is open from September to April. If you need more thrills, go indoor sky-diving at **iFly Perth**, just across the Swan River from the CBD, or head north to the holiday town of **Lancelin**, just over an hour out of Perth, for a sand-boarding adrenalin rush – rent a sand-board and swoosh down the expansive sand dunes.

- Kids and science buffs, head to **Scitech** in West Perth, a fascinating science centre with a range of interactive exhibits and shows, all with a STEM focus. For more science fun, head an hour north out of Perth to the **Gravity Discovery Centre** at Yeal – explore its hands-on exhibits that focus on space, cosmology and physics; climb the centre's Leaning Tower of Gingin for a new perspective; or spend some time in the Observatory for views of the night sky and a session on Aboriginal astronomy.

- Balance out the science and get your fill of the arts by taking the family to see a kid-friendly show at the stunning **Heath Ledger Theatre** (keep an eye out for Perth Comedy Festival and Fringe World – you may even catch Pete!).

- Animal lovers, **Perth Zoo** is the place to go. In South Perth, the zoo hosts a variety of events for kids like Boo at the Zoo for Halloween, where the kids can dress up and go on a trick-or-treat trail. There are also fantastic school holiday events to look out for. See all the animals you'd expect and 'ride' a zebra (no, not a real zebra, but rather the eight-seater electric vehicle that can take you on an enjoyable guided tour of the zoo).

- The area surrounding Perth has a number of beautiful bushland reserves and national parks that are great to explore with the family. Visit the **John Forrest National Park** in Greenmount, one of Australia's oldest conservation areas and only about 30 minutes east from the city. Choose from easy walks (including a pram-suitable one and a wildflower walk) and a range of more challenging ones. Keep an eye out for the diverse wildlife and enjoy the short walks to the two waterfalls, which flow in winter and spring. Take a picnic or have lunch at the **John Forrest Tavern** right in the middle of the park.

- Another lovely bush escape is **Walunga National Park**, about an hour north-east of Perth. Walk the Aboriginal Heritage Trail with its interpretive signs providing information on the Indigenous history of the area, or follow the Swan River on the popular Syd's Rapids Trail, which takes you to the 'Rapids' area, part of the Avon Descent adventure river race.

- About an hour south-east of Perth is **Serpentine National Park**, with various bushwalking trails and a lovely waterfall. This is a very popular escape for locals and the waterfalls picnic area can get very crowded – arrive early!

- North of Perth and worthy of a full day is **Yanchep National Park**. See the resident koalas by walking the koala boardwalk, watch a didgeridoo and dance performance in the Wangi Mia Meeting Place or explore the mystically named Crystal Cave. Take the Ghost House Walk Trail, a 12.4km loop that is great for older kids. There are campgrounds in the park too; take a swag and camp under the stars. Check the Parks WA website for more.

ROTTNEST ISLAND

Just off the coast of Perth is this idyllic island with its excellent beaches and blue-as-blue ocean. This is the best place for the kids to see quokkas, those unusual marsupials that look like cat-sized kangaroos. In exciting news for quokkas, from 2019 they all officially celebrate their birthday on 15 September – just as the horses party hard on 1 August, quokkas will let their fur down every year on this government-approved celebration day. Thousands of humans made the trek to Rottnest in 2019 for the inaugural birthday bash, which included opportunities for quokka selfies, movie screenings, walking tours and a quokka detective scavenger hunt. It was a huge hit with 80 per cent of the accommodation booked out. This party will no doubt grow each year so it's worth keeping an eye out as it strategically happens during school holidays. Private cars aren't allowed on the island, which makes the place even more peaceful, so plan to explore by bike, two feet or bus. With its coves, beaches and coral reefs, Rottnest is an ideal place for snorkelling, swimming and relaxing. There are also historic buildings to explore and a relaxed family fun park with minigolf, a deckchair cinema, trampolines and an old-school games arcade.

FREMANTLE

This portside city within a city (Fremantle is only half an hour from Perth's CBD) is an excellent spot to spend a couple of days. You'll find plenty to do with the kids, and the relaxed and eclectic feel of the place will make you want to stay longer. It's rich with history and culture (just don't mention their AFL team's complete lack of premierships to the locals).

Fremantle reeks of history, and you can explore the city's heritage in the **Western Australian Maritime Museum** and the fascinating **Western Australian Shipwreck Museum**. Also now history (as it was closed in 1991 for breaches of human rights), **Fremantle Prison** was one of the most notorious punishment gaols and was built by convicts in the 1850s. It was pretty grim stuff and you may be surprised to learn they now offer tours (even for school groups!), including an eerie Tunnel Tour of the labyrinth of tunnels beneath the prison. Also on offer are night-time Torchlight Tours – not for the faint-hearted or toddlers. In 2010 the prison was given World Heritage status for its convict history and its walls have many stories to tell. If it's all too much for the kids, take a break at the prison's Convict Cafe. Western Australia also has a fascinating military history, which you can learn about at the **Army Museum of Western Australia** at the Artillery Barracks in Fremantle, or look to the skies at the **Aviation Heritage Museum**, just 15 minutes from Fremantle.

Fremantle has four main beaches and a family favourite of ours is **Bathers Beach**, which is great for kids with its calm waters. After a paddle, grab a bite to eat at **Bathers Beach House**, literally just a few steps from the sand.

MARGARET RIVER

The Traditional Owners are the Wadandi Noongar people.

WE LOVE Margaret River, part of the lush south-west region of the state and known for its world-class wines, stunning coastal scenery and towering karri forests. It definitely isn't just for wine lovers, though. There are so many family-friendly activities in and around Margaret River, from swimming at **Bunker Bay** in Dunsborough to surfing. We haven't yet mastered the art of surfing in our adulthood so we stick to watching surfers; catch them at Main Break at **Surfers Point, Injidup Beach** and **Yallingup**. You might even be lucky enough to spot dolphins too.

For another fun activity, the Margaret River area has five skate parks. If your kids love skateboarding, check out the recently renovated **Margaret River Skate Park**. Not to forget cycling: there are many cycling trails of varying distances. Some of the mountain-biking trails aren't ideal for kids (unless they are experienced in off-road mountain-biking). For a beginner trail, try part of the **Wadandi Track**, a 30km journey over historic bridges and through farmlands and forests.

Stroll the local **Margaret River Farmers' Markets** on Saturday mornings – a foodie's delight where you can taste and of course buy the tantalising, fresh local produce. Or visit the **Margaret River Fudge Factory** to watch the sweet stuff being made (you'll probably have to buy some for the kids). You can always get the kids lost in **Amaze'n Margaret River**, a half-hectare hedge maze set in beautiful gardens just south of town; it also offers minigolf (check the website as it often closes in winter for garden maintenance).

About 40 minutes north of the town of Margaret River is **Busselton Jetty**, the longest timber jetty in the Southern Hemisphere. You can walk the 1.8km jetty with the kids or catch the miniature train if it's too far for your little ones. At the end of the jetty is the **Underwater Observatory**, where you can watch coral, fish and other fascinating sea creatures from 8m below the ocean's surface.

Half an hour south of the town of Margaret River is **Augusta**, home of **Jewel Cave**, the biggest show cave in Western Australia. It has three huge chambers and kids will be in awe of the towering crystal creations that have formed over thousands of years. Kids under four are free and family passes are available. Just ten minutes south of Augusta is **Cape Leeuwin Lighthouse**. The tallest lighthouse on mainland Australia, it is definitely worth a visit and if it's the right time of year you may be lucky enough to spot whales. Now that's an epic game of I-spy.

THE KIMBERLEY

The Kimberley has many Traditional Custodians, including the Miriuwung Gajerrong, Karajarri, Tjurabalan, Bardi Jawim, Wanjina Wunggur Wilinggin and Rubibi.

This iconic part of Australia

is remote and spectacular – full of dramatic scenery, wild rivers, palm-fringed gorges and incredible rock formations – and definitely worth a visit. It's also home to some of the finest Indigenous rock-art sites in the country. Our travel gurus, Luke and Liz, who we told you about earlier, took six months off to travel around Australia with their kids, Declan and Abby. It was, for all of them, the experience of a lifetime. Judging by the photos alone, the Kimberley looked like one of the absolute highlights of their adventure.

For many of us that kind of trip doesn't seem possible and, to be honest, there's often only a small window of opportunity where all the kids are at the right age for a trip like that – before they grow up and get to the pointy end of their education. But don't despair; there are ways to see this incredible part of the country without taking six months off from normal life.

You only want to head to the Kimberley in the dry season; in the wet season, many of the roads are impassable. Best time to go is between May and October, with July and August the peak times – you'll find campsites and parks crowded, so book ahead. It's best to have a 4WD to explore the Kimberley; although some of the main routes are sealed and okay for a 2WD, many of the sights are on roads best for 4WDs. But you need to be prepared regardless – the distances are long and the fuel and food stops few. Carry extra water and supplies, including fuel and spare tyres. If driving isn't an option for you, there are plenty of family-friendly safaris or tours you can do in the Kimberley. If you are up for a drive, hire a 4WD or a campervan in Broome, which is a good starting point for a Kimberley trip. Allowing about ten days to two weeks for your road trip will let you see much of the Kimberley without having to drive huge distances every day. Check out camplify.com.au for short-term hiring across the country.

📍 **Broome** is a holiday spot with a difference – as well as its stunning beaches, frontier history and bulging boab trees, it reflects a mix of Indigenous, Asian and European cultures. Take a walking tour around town with an Indigenous guide, explore Broome's pearling history or take the kids to Broome's historic **Chinatown** for a meal. The visitor centre has information on the many different types of tours that are available, including whale-watching tours, helicopter flights and 4WD tours. Of course, Broome's most famous tourist attraction is the white sand and turquoise ocean of **Cable Beach** – its shallow waters make it perfect for kids. Wander along the beach, watch the sunset with a glass of something cold, or simply walk forever with the waves lapping at your feet.

- From Broome, take a 4WD tour to the **Dampier Peninsula** and picturesque **Cape Leveque**. Owned and run by the Indigenous Bardi Jawi communities, **Kooljaman** at Cape Leveque offers remote wilderness and incredible Indigenous cultural experiences. You can also take snorkelling, mudcrabbing or fishing tours, or simply relax on the beach.

- The spectacular **Buccaneer Archipelago** is an area of about a thousand islands. Take a scenic flight or helicopter ride over the remote area or book in for a boat cruise to see the ancient geology, waterfalls, rugged cliffs and ancient Indigenous rock-art from water level. Your kids won't forget this trip for a while. Take another flight or cruise to see the incredible **Horizontal Falls** or up the pace and take a jet-boat ride instead so you can tackle the whitewater rapids of the falls, which are created by fast tidal flows churning through a narrow gorge. In the far north of the Kimberley, the twin waterfalls of the stunning **King George Falls** are culturally significant to the Balanggarra people – the falls are the male and female Wunkurr, or rainbow serpents. Cruises, flights and tours for these Kimberley highlights depart from Broome, Derby, Cape Leveque, Kununurra and Wyndham.

- **Derby** is the closest town to the breathtaking gorges of the **Gibb River Road**, one of Australia's most famous and epic 4WD outback tracks that travels almost 700km between Derby and Kununurra. A must-see if you're taking the Gibb River Road is **Windjana Gorge**, a 3.5km long stunning rock formation (actually an ancient eroded coral reef) with walls up to 100m high, carved out by the Lennard River. Take the 3.5km return Gorge Walk or the easier-for-kids Time Walk where you can all play spot-the-fossils in the gorge's limestone walls. Windjana Gorge is also the place to see freshwater crocs in the wild (remember to be croc-wise).

- **Lake Argyle** is an oasis in the Kimberley. The second largest constructed freshwater reservoir in Australia, it offers picnic spots, boat cruises and accommodation. Humans have been thought to live in the area for the past 60,000 years. Just south of Lake Argyle is **Purnululu National Park** where you'll find the **Bungle Bungles**, incredible tiger-striped rock formations, along with ancient Indigenous rock-art galleries and beautiful rockpools. It's accessible by 4WD; tours and flights are available from Kununurra and Lake Argyle or take a week-long safari from Broome.

- The gorgeous four-tier **Mitchell Falls** is remote even by Kimberley standards but it's certainly worth the trek. The Mitchell River has created amazing waterfalls and gorges, and this is a bucket-list spot for outback travellers. It's 4WD only and requires serious planning as you'll travel across the Mitchell Plateau and various creek crossings. The easier option, especially with kids, is to take a scenic flight over the falls. You get the view minus the dust, sweat and tears.

- **El Questro Station and Wilderness Park** lives in the heart of the Kimberley and is a great base to explore from. Experience the exceptional sunsets, rugged landscape and wildlife, and let the kids take part in the El Questro Junior Ranger program, which runs June to August. El Questro Station began as a cattle station and remains a working cattle station to this day. It is the hub of many adventurous activities for the whole family to enjoy, and has a range of accommodation options for different budgets and many tours on offer.

DRIVING TIPS

Western Australia is Australia's biggest state and there are so many truly exceptional trips to do that the hardest decision will be choosing which way to go. Visit westernaustralia.com to see the range of self-drive itineraries that you can follow. Remember, because it's a huge state and driving with kids generally takes longer, it's best to plan ahead, try not to fit in too much and take plenty of breaks. Here are other key things to remember.

- Tell someone of your plans.
- Obtain permits to enter Aboriginal land.
- Know where you will be staying each night.
- Stock up on essentials in bigger towns.
- Have extra water and food at all times.
- When you are walking or climbing, ensure you have the recommended amount of two litres for every hour of activity.
- Have torches and matches.
- Check fire regulations and fire bans before lighting a campfire.
- Get to know the car you're driving before you set off.
- Avoid driving at night; there are too many dangers to consider in the dark.
- Check you have two spare tyres, a good high-lift jack and any other necessary tools.
- Don't rely on mobile service.
- Have a detailed map and know how to read it.
- Be aware that often the roads have soft edges; slow down and move over for trucks with plenty of time.
- Have plenty of fuel and fill up whenever you can.
- If you get into trouble, stay with your vehicle and conserve food and water.
- Be croc-wise.
- All of the caravans you see on the Gibb River Road are off-road caravans (it is a 4WD-only road).
- It is not recommended that you tow your caravan the whole way to Mitchell Falls (also a 4WD-only road).
- Caravans are not allowed in Purnululu National Park.

NORTHERN TERRITORY

THE NORTHERN TERRITORY,

Australia's 'Top End' and 'Red Centre', has a wild frontier feel and yet it's a brilliant place to take kids on a holiday. From the tropical, laidback vibe of Darwin, where we've cooled off in stunning waterholes, to the awe-inspiring Uluru at Australia's red heart, where we've watched the sunrise, the Territory offers experiences we think you won't find anywhere else. It's certainly a trip the kids will never, never forget. Talking never – not that it's all about advertising, but, for us, the Territory has had some of the most memorable ad campaigns: 'You'll never never know if you never never go' was the ad that we remember from the 1990s. Ad campaigns aside, the Northern Territory is truly something special.

The Northern Territory has a very strong Indigenous culture and there are over 40 different Indigenous language groups. The connection to Country is strong across the Indigenous communities and it can be seen in the Territory's art, culture and storytelling. We've spoken previously about the value of Indigenous-led tourism and this is certainly the place to make the most of that.

Because there's so much to see and do in the Territory but it spans such massive distances, we've grouped our suggestions into five main areas: Darwin and surrounds, Kakadu, Katherine, Alice Springs and Uluru.

DID YOU KNOW?

- *NT News*, the local news outlet, is renowned for its irreverent and funny headlines, such as 'Frog struck down by lightning' and 'Why I stuck a cracker up my clacker'.
- The famous Henley-on-Todd Regatta, held each August, consists of a variety of 'boat races' on the bone-dry Todd River bed.
- Daly Waters, with a population of nine, has the country's most pointless set of traffic lights. There isn't another set for 500km.

DARWIN

The Traditional Owners are the Larrakia people and they are prominent members of the local community.

DARWIN IS A COSMOPOLITAN

city – a cultural melting pot, its population is made up of people from more than 60 nationalities and 70 different ethnic backgrounds, and the excellent restaurants and many festivals reflect this diversity. The city is lovely to look at too – wrapped around a natural ocean inlet and home to fabulous beaches, tropical gardens and mangrove forests.

ATTRACTIONS

- With a rich Indigenous culture, Darwin offers much if you want to learn more. Start at **Darwin's Top End Tourism Visitor Centre** in the city centre for information about the Indigenous tours available.

- The weather in Darwin is, as the locals often say, either hot and wet or hot and dry, so you'll want to get in the water. But this is northern Australia so you need to be croc- and stinger-wise. Head to one of the public swimming pools in the city – two good choices with kids are the famed **Wave Lagoon** and the **Recreation Lagoon** at Darwin Waterfront. Swim at beaches in the dry season only, and only if they are patrolled: the most popular is **Mindil Beach**. Patrolled seven days a week in the dry season, Mindil Beach is also the place to come to watch the most spectacular sunsets you've ever seen and it's home to the **Mindil Beach Sunset Market**, where you can eat delicious food, pick up some quality local art and craft and see that sunset all at once (the market operates in the dry season only, from April to October). For pool and water-slide action outside the Darwin CBD, visit two excellent (and free!) water parks in the suburbs: **Palmerston Water Park** and **Leanyer Recreation Park**. Both have water slides (Palmerston has a six-lane racer slide, which the kids will think is pretty awesome), swimming pools, fantastic water playgrounds and paddling pools that are great for the little ones.

- Another water escape is **Lake Alexander** in **East Point Reserve**, which is great for families. Not too far north of the city centre, this reserve is a haven for wildlife (and for locals), and has lovely picnic areas and playgrounds for the kids. The lake itself is seawater but protected from the ocean, so it offers a safer swimming spot in natural surroundings. There are great walking trails through the bush too – get the kids to keep an eye out for the resident wallabies.

- East Point Reserve also forms part of Darwin's fascinating military history (the city was bombed by Japanese forces in 1942) and you'll find the **Darwin Military Museum** here along with the interactive **Defence of Darwin Experience** (family passes are available). Some of the museum's artillery is housed in the original bunker used by the army in World War II. More military history can be seen at the **Royal Flying Doctor Service Museum**'s Bombing of Darwin Harbour exhibit. The museum, situated at Stokes Hill Wharf in the city centre, also has some great interactive, holographic and virtual reality exhibits about the origins and experiences of the Royal Flying Doctor Service, and the kids get to sit in the cockpit of an RFDS plane as a bonus.

- If you want to make the most of Darwin's weather and let the kids run free for a while, head to **George Brown Darwin Botanic Gardens**, just outside the city centre and near Mindil Beach. Surviving both World War II and 1974's devastating Cyclone Tracy, these gardens are an oasis featuring monsoon forests, a rainforest with a

- waterfall, and an Aboriginal plant walk. Enjoy one of the easy kid-friendly walks through the gardens, have a coffee at the cafe (in a heritage-listed church) or head straight for the nature-focused playground, which will be a big hit.

- A five-minute drive from the gardens is the **Museum and Art Gallery Northern Territory**, a cultural highlight in Darwin. As well as exhibitions about Indigenous art, the geological history of the area, and the Territory's native birds and animals, there's an excellent exhibit about Cyclone Tracy and how Darwin had to be rebuilt essentially from scratch.

- For culture of the movie kind, Darwin style, head to the open-air **Deckchair Cinema** on the edge of Darwin Harbour in the city. It runs during the dry season and is a great chance for the kids to be entertained while also looking at the amazing night sky.

- A big part of the Territory's tourism is all about crocodiles. We see this as a complex ethical issue and generally avoid this type of animal tourism. If you do want to get up close to the mighty creatures, you can see them at **Crocosaurus Cove**. If you want to see them in their natural habitat, a better option, you can do that with a tour. There are a few eco-friendly companies in Darwin offering a variety of tours; they will take you about an hour out of Darwin to **Adelaide River**, where you can cruise the river while wild crocodiles leap out of the water to get to food hanging from your boat (tour operators are strictly regulated as to how much and how often they can feed the wild crocs but still, it's not the natural feeding habits of wild crocs).

- **Howard Springs Nature Park**, a 30-minute drive from the city, is a lovely spot for a day out and a swim. It has plenty of wildlife to see, including turtles, barramundi and wallabies, and there's an adventure playground along with a series of constructed wading pools for the kids. Follow the short bushwalk into the rainforest to see the springs that feed the main pool (not safe for swimming), or enjoy a picnic under the lovely trees.

- A popular daytrip from Darwin (less than an hour south), **Berry Springs Nature Park** is the closest waterhole to Darwin and a beautiful spot for lazing about. You can swim from one pool to the next via a creek while admiring the tropical surroundings (pay attention to any warning signs about crocodiles). Make sure the kids have their goggles so they can spot the native fish swimming about. There are walking tracks throughout the park and palm-fringed picnic areas that make it easy to spend a day here.

- A must-do daytrip from Darwin is a visit to the stunning **Litchfield National Park**, an hour and a half south of the city. Come here for spectacular waterfalls and lovely swimming in the natural waterholes (always check with rangers and read any warning signs re crocs, though usually Litchfield is croc-free). You can take any number of bushwalks, including a 90-minute-return walk to **Florence Falls** (you can also drive) where the falls cascade into a gorgeous plunge pool. If you have a 4WD, head to **Tjaynera Falls** or, for 4WD experts, visit the **Lost City**, an incredible series of sandstone outcrops and towers (this is one trip definitely not for 4WD newbies). When you first enter the park, make sure the kids watch for the numerous tall magnetic termite mounds.

KAKADU

The Traditional Owners of Kakadu are the Bininj and Mungguy peoples.

IF YOU WANT

World Heritage–listed wilderness, plunging waterfalls, incredible Indigenous culture and rock art, diverse ecosystems and rugged landscapes, Kakadu National Park is the place to come. We know we keep saying that the kids won't forget their trip to the Territory but they really will never forget a visit to Kakadu.

The best place to start is the Bowali Visitor Centre near the small town of Jabiru, which makes a good base for your Kakadu adventures with its various accommodation options. At the visitor centre you can get help to plan your time in Kakadu, organise walks and tours and buy your park pass (you can also buy the pass online). The centre also has a gallery, cafe and various interpretive displays on Kakadu's landscapes, ecology and habitats so you can really get a sense of how unique this national park is.

There are about 5000 rock-art sites in Kakadu illustrating the complex culture and belief systems of the Indigenous people. Burrungkuy (Nourlangie Rock) is one of the main sites – take the 1.5km Nourlangie Rock Walk to see the ancient art telling stories of Creation Time. Ubirr is another magnificent example of rock art – there's a 1km circuit walk that takes you past the main rock-art galleries and a shorter (but steep) climb to a rocky lookout. This is the place to be at the end of the day to watch sun set over the floodplains. During the dry season there are daily ranger-guided tours of the Ubirr walk – a great way for the kids to understand the ancient nature of Indigenous culture.

The Yellow Water (Ngurrungurrudjba) Billabong and wetland area is an oasis for birdlife, fish and crocodiles, and is an exquisite place to explore. The Indigenous-owned Yellow Water Cruises run river cruises throughout the day, taking you on a journey through the heart of the Kakadu wetlands. Nearby is the Warradjan Aboriginal Cultural Centre with a fascinating exhibit developed by Kakadu's Traditional Owners; often there are also talks and artist workshops here.

Kakadu is known for its waterfalls – don't miss Maguk (Barramundi Gorge), which is one of the best waterfalls in Kakadu and flows year-round (accessible by 4WD); the beautiful Gunlom Falls; the giant Jim Jim Falls (huge at 200m high; accessible by 4WD only); and the stunning Twin Falls Gorge (also accessible by 4WD only, but there is a boat shuttle service up the river to the falls). There are a couple of lovely walks around Gunlom Falls and to the Gunlom Falls Plunge Pool (some are steep so if you have little kids check out your options before you start, but the short walk to the plunge pool is usually fine for kids and strollers).

If it's in your budget, a scenic flight over Kakadu is a once-in-a-lifetime experience worth doing – you'll see inaccessible waterfalls, huge sandstone formations and wetland wilderness.

KATHERINE

Katherine sits within the traditional lands of the Jawoyn, Dagoman and Wardaman peoples.

THE TOWN of Katherine, about a 3.5-hour drive south of Darwin, is the gateway to the spectacular gorges at nearby **Nitmiluk National Park**, but there are things to do in town too. The **Katherine Visitor Centre** is a good place to start to find out what's on in town. Learn more about Indigenous culture and art at **Top Didj Cultural Experience** or feed the kids damper (and possibly kangaroo or camel) at **Marksie's Stockman's Camp Tucker Night**. You can also explore the town's Indigenous art galleries and art centres. One of the best ways to buy Indigenous art is to purchase it ethically from Indigenous-owned art centres and galleries. In Katherine, you'll find great art at **Mimi Aboriginal Art and Craft**, an Indigenous-owned, not-for-profit art centre. For more on buying Indigenous art ethically, see indigenousartcode.org/how-to-buy-ethically.

Also in town is **Katherine Hot Springs Reserve**, natural thermal springs on the edge of the Katherine River. With the water an average temperature of 25–30 degrees Celsius and shady picnic areas, this is definitely a place for relaxation (but in the dry season only). For more hot-springs action, head an hour or so south of Katherine to **Mataranka**, where you can swim in the warm, turquoise water at **Mataranka Thermal Pool** and **Bitter Springs**, both in **Elsey National Park**.

On the way to Mataranka, stop at **Cutta Cutta Caves Nature Park**, just 25 minutes from Katherine. Take a one-hour guided tour of the Cutta Cutta Caves; the kids can look out for the various bats and (harmless) tree snakes that live in the caves, as well as impressive stalactites and stalagmites.

Of course, the main highlight of the area is the magnificent **Nitmiluk National Park**, with awe-inspiring gorges carved by the Katherine River over millions of years. The national park is owned by the Jawoyn people and the **Nitmiluk Centre** is a great place to learn more about their culture and history and the significance of the area. The best way to explore the gorge (really a 13-gorge system) is to hire a canoe and use your own paddle-power to find hidden waterfalls and ancient rock art. If canoes aren't your thing (or your children are under six years old), take a relaxing cruise up the gorge instead – various cruises are available. You can swim between sheer cliffs and find sandy freshwater beaches (observe all warning signs). Or splurge on a helicopter ride to get an incredible bird's-eye view of this majestic landscape. Camping is available in the park, but you'll need to book ahead.

ALICE SPRINGS

The Traditional Owners of Alice Springs are the Central Arrernte people.

THIS BUZZING town, with its striking red earth and expansive blue sky, is a great base for when you're exploring the Red Centre. Often simply called 'the Alice', the town is set on the usually dry Todd River and is home to some great things to do.

For kids (and adults too), Alice Springs Desert Park is a major highlight. Just out of town at the base of the West MacDonnell Ranges, the park encourages you to wander through its three habitats – desert rivers, woodland and sand country – and learn about the complex eco-system that is the desert, from its plants and wildlife to the role of Indigenous people and their culture. There's an excellent free-flight birds of prey show and fascinating talks and guided walks. See dingos, bilbies, thorny devils and barking spiders among the wide range of mammals, reptiles and birds that live in the park. Stay late to go on the nocturnal tour, spotlighting animals inside a large predator-proof enclosure. In the Desert Rivers section there's a nature-play and discovery path for kids too. There's a cafe, a playground and lots of shady picnic and barbecue areas, and if your little ones are tired strollers are available to use free of charge. All up, definitely worth a visit.

To get a good sense of Alice, drive or walk up Anzac Hill, the most visited landmark in Alice Springs, for 360-degree views of the town and the MacDonnell Ranges. It was originally dedicated to members of the armed services from World War I but is now a memorial to all who have served to defend Australia.

If the kids are interested to see how school works in the outback, take them to Alice Springs School of the Air Visitor Centre for fascinating displays and presentations about 'the largest classroom in the world'.

In town you'll also find the Araluen Cultural Precinct, the home of a number of the Alice's cultural attractions. Visit the precinct's Museum of Central Australia and the Central Australian Museum of Aviation, and spend time at the excellent Araluen Arts Centre.

For kids seriously into trucks and wheels, the National Road Transport Hall of Fame is the place to go. For trainspotters, the small Old Ghan Heritage Railway and Museum is just next door. Both are about 10km out of town so you'll need a car.

There is so much worth exploring outside of Alice. Visit the striking gorges of Tjoritja–West MacDonnell Ranges National Park, particularly Ormiston Gorge (135km from Alice Springs) with its beautiful waterhole providing year-round swimming. In the national park you'll also find Ellery Creek Big Hole and Simpsons Gap, both with picnic and barbecue facilities and easy stroller access (Simpsons Gap also has a visitor centre).

ULURU

The Traditional Owners are the Anangu people.

THIS COLOSSAL ROCK

at Australia's heart is surely the country's most recognisable natural landmark. Around 400,000 visitors arrive each year to stand in awe before it. In **Uluru–Kata Tjuta National Park**, which is owned and managed by the Anangu people, the rock rises 358m above the surrounding desert, dwarfing the arid landscape (it's estimated that Uluru extends up to 5 or 6km beneath the ground). The distance around the base of the rock is almost 10km and the **Uluru Base Walk** takes about three and a half hours. There are a number of much shorter walks that are great to do with kids, and all take you up close to the incredible monolith where you'll see ancient rock-art sites, gorgeous waterholes and incredible crevices and gullies caused by erosion over millions of years. If you prefer two wheels to two feet, hire bikes and ride around the base of the rock. Ensure you are carrying sufficient water at all times.

Ever since 1985 when the Anangu people were recognised as the Traditional Owners after decades of campaigning, people have been encouraged not to climb Uluru because of its sacred spiritual significance to the Anangu. Finally the climb was officially closed in October 2019.

In the national park, make the **Cultural Centre** your first port of call to get a visitor guide and chat to rangers. You can actually easily spend a couple of hours here learning about Uluru and the culture and language of the Anangu people. The centre also has galleries, displays, various shops and a cafe. You can also hire bikes here.

The composition of the rock means that the colours of Uluru shift during the day, making sunrise and sunset a photographer's dream. If you have early risers or night owls, make the effort to take in a sunset or sunrise but plan ahead. Everyone will have the same idea so you need to get to your favoured spot early (take some activities, like a deck of cards, for the wait).

A stunning art installation is on show at Uluru (just outside of the national park) until December 2020. Entitled *Field of Lights* or *Tili Wiru Tjuta Nyakutjaku* (meaning 'looking at lots of beautiful lights' in local Pitjantjatjara), the installation by artist Bruce Munro features 50,000 solar-powered lights covering the landscape on a grand scale. (Unfortunately prams and strollers are not permitted at the exhibition site.)

The other reason people flock to the Red Centre is to visit **Kata Tjuta**, otherwise known as the Olgas. About 50km west of Uluru, these amazing domed rocks (about 36 in all) tower above the surrounding landscape and glow red at sunset (the tallest domes reach 546m). There are a couple of lookouts offering extra-special views, and a number of walks: the Valley of the Winds walks can be challenging with some rocky sections (the longest walk takes three to four hours); the best one to do with young kids is the **Walpa Gorge Walk**, a gentle one-hour-return trip into a peaceful gorge. It can get so hot out here that some of the walks are closed when the temperature goes over 36 degrees Celsius. Remember to carry sufficient water and sun protection.

The tourist resort of **Yulara** is the place to stay when you visit Uluru and Kata Tjuta. There are six accommodation options to suit all budgets and lots of tours and activities are run from here.

TRAVELLING IN THE TERRITORY

Throughout the Territory, the heat can be intense, so make sure you're always prepared with extra water supplies, sun-protective clothes, hats and sunscreen. It's best to explore and see the sights in the early morning or late afternoon. Of course, rising early is not a teenager's favourite thing to do on holiday (or ever, let's be honest), but it's definitely wise to get out sightseeing before the heat gets too much for you all. As hot as the day can be, the night can get quite cold in the desert. Ensure you have adequate clothing and bedding for the cooler nights.

For kids (and adults) who may get easily annoyed by flies, consider getting a classic cork hat to wear. The flies are persistent most of the time (not just in summer), and you'll most likely be wrapping T-shirts around you head if you don't have one of those iconic bush hats. Of course, we probably all laugh at the typical Australia cork-hat look – but, hey, who's the one laughing in the end?

Please remember that any body of water in the Northern Territory may contain large and potentially dangerous crocodiles. *Always* observe safety and warning signs, listen to rangers and be croc-wise. Other than crocs, you may be lucky to see other native wildlife: never disturb animals and insects, and never feed native wildlife.

There are many Indigenous sacred sites in the Territory. Respect any advice or recommendations from the Traditional Owners and never touch or take cultural items.

If you're driving, it is very important to plan your trip through the Northern Territory as there are large distances between accommodation, fuel and food stops. Before you depart on your adventure, make sure you are organised: check the weather, roads, general information and updates on where you will be travelling. Let people know where you will be going and when you are planning to be back. Plan every detail, work out what equipment and supplies you might need in an emergency and if driving make sure your vehicle is suitable for the conditions. Before you head off check northernterritory.com for safety and useful information.

If you want to visit or drive through Aboriginal land in the Northern Territory, you must have a permit. So, get organised and make sure applying for a permit is part of your itinerary planning. Permits can usually be bought online, but check with local visitor centres for more information.

SOUTH AUSTRALIA

DID YOU KNOW?

- The world's first IVF triplets were born in South Australia.
- Tumby Bay is where Peter Brinkworth invented chicken salt, which is God's gift to chips.
- Rural South Australia is home to stunning painted silos, art at a massive scale and a craze still spreading through the countryside – keep an eye out on your road trip.

AUSTRALIAN COMICS HAVE

used Adelaide as a punch line for decades now (perhaps because inserting Hobart or Canberra feels too easy) but let it be known that South Australia is thriving and Adelaide is absolutely brilliant and beginning to get the credit it deserves. From the renowned wine country within arm's reach of the city to the excellent food culture in Adelaide – and let's not forget some world-class beaches – the festival state has a huge variety of exciting places to see, things to do and beaches to swim at.

ATTRACTIONS

- Visit the **Eyre Peninsula**, sitting between Adelaide and the Great Australian Bight, and considered part of the famed Nullarbor Plain road trip. It's most known for its incredible beaches, but you'll also find great food, excellent wine and abundant wildlife. Enjoy fresh oysters at **Coffin Bay** and swim with dolphins and sea lions (or cage-dive with sharks if you're game) at **Port Lincoln**. There are a couple of wild national parks, **Coffin Bay National Park** and **Lincoln National Park**, on the peninsula and some great beachside camping. On the western edge of the peninsula, stop at beautiful **Greenly Beach** for a swim and a play in the sand. Further along the coastline near **Elliston** you'll find **Talia Caves**, huge caverns carved into the granite cliffs by the mighty ocean. You can start from Port Augusta, about three hours north of Adelaide, and then head down through Whyalla on to the peninsula and explore it clockwise. Regardless of where you start, make sure you stop as often as you can at the many beaches and gorgeous fishing towns along the way.

- Feel like driving 860km from Adelaide to see a pink lake? Hell no! But if you are in **Ceduna** after a trip along the Eyre Peninsula, keep driving for just over an hour to **Lake MacDonnell**, a stunning pink lake and a great holiday photo opportunity. The lake's high salt levels make it the perfect home for salt-loving algae – it's the algae that give it the striking pink hues. If photos are your thing, the dirt road that separates the pink lake from a neighbouring blue-green lake makes a stunning Insta-worthy shot. On the way to the lake, you'll pass through Penong where the kids will be astounded by the many windmills scattered across the wheat fields (they're actually now called the **Penong Windmill Museum**). If you're visiting between July and October, head just over an hour further west to **Fowlers Bay** and take the kids on a whale-watching cruise to see the magnificent southern right and humpback whales.

- Everyone will enjoy some fun in **Clare Valley** – the kids will get busy at the **Mintaro Maze** and the **Model Engineers miniature railway**, and the adults will love visiting the many cellar doors, from Grosset, Pikes and Sevenhill to something a little more niche like Mr Mick Cellar Door or, Pete's favourite, Mad Bastard Wines. The Clare Valley is regarded as the home of Australian riesling (there's even a walking and cycling path called the Riesling Trail) and is just under two hours north from Adelaide.

- We can never get enough of South Australia's beaches and **Yorke Peninsula** has some of the best along its 700km of coastline. Think pristine water and stunning white sand and historic lighthouses; you can surf, swim, eat and enjoy the very laidback feel of the many seaside holiday towns. Take the kids to **Moonta Bay** for its fun beachside water park or to **Port Vincent** for putt putt golf right next to the beach.

- More South Australian highlights are the **Flinders Ranges** and the incredible geological formation of **Wilpena Pound** in **Ikara–Flinders Ranges National Park**. There's a resort and camping ground at the small township of Wilpena, which is about a five-hour drive from Adelaide. We haven't yet taken the kids to the Flinders Ranges but it is definitely on the list.

ADELAIDE

The Traditional Owners of Adelaide and surrounds are the Kaurna people.

ADELAIDE FOLK

have been trying to shift away from the City of Churches tag for a while now. And they're doing a great job of creating a reputation for being a centre of excitement, particularly if you arrive in March when they have about 70 festivals in a month and a half. Okay, maybe that's a slight exaggeration, but Mad March is nuts with world-class festivals such as the beloved Adelaide Fringe Festival, renowned world music festival WOMADelaide, the Adelaide Cabaret Festival, the Adelaide Festival (somehow different to the Fringe) and, to top it all off, the Supercars come to town. Add to this the Crows and the Power kicking off their AFL campaigns and you have a city going off like a frog in a sock.

EATING OUT

If you have gone for your morning run or if you want to treat the kids, try one of the many dessert bars Adelaide has to offer, like **St Louis House of Fine Ice-cream and Dessert**. Delicious!

ACCOMMODATION

As with other major cities, you're spoilt for choice here in terms of accommodation options. It's about what works for you and your family and where you want to be. We like being within walking distance of attractions in the CBD but there are good options near the beaches too.

GETTING AROUND

Travelling around Adelaide on public transport is easy with the MetroCARD visitor pass; this allows three days of unlimited travel. The passes are available at the airport, train stations and the information centre in the city. Children under five travel free.

Electric scooters (through two operators, Beam and Ride) are a popular way to get around Adelaide, but you need to be at least 18 years of age and they are geo-fenced so they can be used only in the CBD.

Driving is easy in Adelaide – the roads are wide and well designed and there is plenty of parking, but during big festival times it does get busy. A car is definitely the best option for exploring outside the city.

ATTRACTIONS

- Speaking of frogs, South Aussie–owned **Haigh's Chocolates** and their famous chocolate frogs will make everyone happy. Drop into their store on Beehive Corner in the city's famous Rundle Mall and load up, or head to the factory just south of the city centre for a tour, which is best for kids over five (booking required). You must also get a photo of the iconic silver balls in **Rundle Mall**, Adelaide's shopping heart. We don't know exactly why, but you do. Brij spent 40 minutes trying to get a 20-cent coin to stay on the top ball and never succeeded. Let us know if you do!

- Nearby, **Adelaide Central Market** is the place to stock up on delicious fresh produce and gourmet food products, especially handy if you're staying in a self-catered place. In the school holidays, look for food trails, cooking classes and free art workshops, all for the kids.

- In the city's cultural precinct, just near Rundle Mall, the **South Australian Museum** is worth a visit, especially for its kid-focused Discovery Centre. Just next door is the **Art Gallery of South Australia**, so you can get your culture fix in one go. **MOD**, the science museum at the University of South Australia, is a great museum for seeing science and technology in action. The interactive exhibitions are aimed at people aged between 15 and 25. Those under 15 will still find MOD interesting but may need some guidance.

- Adelaide's city centre is surrounded by the beautiful **Adelaide Park Lands** where you'll always find green space for the kids to run around. Off Glen Osmond Road in the parks south of the CBD, you'll find both **Marshmallow Park**, a fully fenced interactive play space for the little ones that includes sand, hill and water play, and **Oxbow Playspace**, which has been revamped with input from parents of children with disabilities. With nature-filled play spaces, lots of climbing and interactive play all to be found here, it's definitely worth taking some time out for a play in the park. (It's also just near the Haigh's Chocolate factory so combine the two!)

- Pete can't drive past putt putt without pulling over and in Adelaide it's available in the city centre at **Holey Moley Golf Club**. The kids will love the putt putt holes with Happy Gilmore and Flintstone themes.

- Not only will you find golf in the CBD but also **TreeClimb Adelaide**, Australia's first inner-city aerial adventure park. In Kurrangga Park in the Park Lands, it has over 70 obstacles and offers the Grand Course for adults and kids taller than 135cm, and three courses for little ones over 100cm.

- Take on the **Adelaide Oval Roof Climb** (not great for people who don't like heights obviously). Kids eight and over, and taller than 120cm, can do the climb too. Since its redevelopment, the **Adelaide Oval** has become one of the must-visit sporting venues in Australia. Catch the Adelaide Crows or sworn enemy Port Adelaide take on their rivals (or each other in the always fiercely contested Showdown) or watch Australia's cricket team play a night Test.

- Adelaide is fringed by beaches, with some only 20 minutes from the CBD. A favourite beach of Brij's is **Glenelg Beach**, and it is probably the most popular with families because of its wide beach and gentle waves. There's a huge foreshore playground that you'll struggle to get the kids away from and a jetty to wander along. Also for the kids is the **Beachhouse**, an indoor amusement park with waterslides and dodgems just across from the beach. There's enough here for adults too: **Jetty Road** is Glenelg's beachside precinct and has great shopping, good food and a cinema, and **Marina Pier** has excellent cafes and restaurants.

- Another golden standout is **Henley Beach**, 20 minutes west of the CBD. This is what holidaying at a beachside town looked like when we were growing up – promenades lined with fish and chip shops and ice-creameries.

- **Port Noarlunga** is a small seaside village only 45 minutes from the city. It's perfect for kids who love bodyboarding and surfing, yet the surf is usually gentle enough for little kids too. There's a safe swimming area and patrolled beach, and you can snorkel around the beautiful **Port Noarlunga Reef**.

- Adelaide is not immune to Australia's BIG thing obsession and many locals claim it all started with the **Big Scotsman**. Standing at 5m, Scotty is the gatekeeper for Scotty's Motel and has been since 1963. Other big things in South Australia include the **Big Lobster** in Kingston and the **Big Wine Bottle** at Wirra Wirra Winery in McLaren Vale. The most interesting one for kids will be the **Big Rocking Horse** at Gumeracha (about 45 minutes from the city in the Adelaide Hills), mainly because it also includes a **Toy Factory**. Kids can climb the rocking horse and get a certificate or spend their pocket money on handmade toys in the Toy Factory shop.

- About 30 minutes from Adelaide (or 30 minutes south from the Toy Factory is **Hahndorf**, which is the oldest surviving German settlement in Australia and totally wunderbar. Enjoy strawberry picking and graze on a platter of local gourmet produce at **Beerenberg Farm** and then head three minutes down the road to **Hahndorf Farm Barn** for a picnic or pony ride and to meet lots of farm animals.

- Just 15 minutes from Hahndorf or 30 minutes south-east from Adelaide is the **Steamranger Heritage Railway**, which offers steam-train rides the kids will love. The trains depart at various times and points (usually from Mount Barker and Goolwa stations), so check the website.

FESTIVAL STATE

South Australia is known for its festivals, so keep them in mind when you plan your holiday. The best one for kids is definitely **DreamBIG Children's Festival**, held biennially in May (the next one is in 2021). Others include:

- Crush Festival, in the Adelaide Hills – January
- Laneway Festival, music in Port Adelaide – February
- Fringe Festival, with plenty of things to do for the kids – February–March
- WOMADelaide, with world music and a kids' zone – March
- Mount Gambier Fringe Festival – March
- Barossa Vintage Festival – April
- History Festival, hundreds of events held state-wide – May
- Adelaide Fashion Festival – October
- OzAsia Festival, with a diverse arts program from across Asia – October–November

KID-FREE NIGHT OUT

We can totally recommend Hardy's Verandah Restaurant and the Arthur Waterhouse Lounge (both part of boutique hotel Mount Lofty House in the Adelaide Hills) for a magnificent and romantic dinner just for the two of you. Perched on a hill, Mount Lofty House was built in 1852 – ask your waiter for the fascinating history of the home. We did actually take our kids here recently and the staff were brilliant with them, so it could work with the tribe too.

If you want to spend the evening in the CBD, the Tasting Room at East End Cellars is a perfect place to begin or end your night, with hard-to-find bottles of wine in their extensive cellars and on their wine list – and we highly recommend their famous charcuterie boards. You don't even have to leave this part of the city centre; after East End Cellars you can stroll to its neighbouring joints Mother Vine and NOLA (with an amazing range of whisky), or explore the nearby artisan hub of Ebenezer Place with the Belgian Beer Cafe for a more raucous evening.

KANGAROO ISLAND

The Traditional Owners of Kangaroo Island are the Ngarrindjeri, Ramindjeri, Narrunga and Kaurna people.

JUST OFF the state's Fleurieu Peninsula, Kangaroo Island is a fabulous spot to spend a few days exploring with the family. Almost half the island was affected by the devastating fires of the 2019–2020 summer. Tourists are encouraged to keep visiting to help the island and its communities recover.

This extremely accessible island is easy for families to visit (fly from Adelaide or catch a ferry from Cape Jervis on the Fleurieu Peninsula). **Kingscote** is the biggest town on the island and makes a good base – you can go on daytrips from here.

Nearly half the island is either bush or national park, making it an incredibly scenic place to explore. And wildlife is everywhere on Kangaroo Island, from koalas, kangaroos and wallabies to seals, sea lions and penguins – see penguins on a guided tour at **Penneshaw**.

Vivonne Bay is the only safe harbour on the south coast of Kangaroo Island and is the base for crayfishing boats when in season. It's also home to the most pristine, beautiful beach – have a picnic or barbecue or fresh fish and chips at the beach or next to the town's jetty.

The family will love **Seal Bay Conservation Park**, on the island's south coast, and its wild sea lion colony; you can take a guided tour on the beach to see the sea lions up close or follow the self-guided tour on the boardwalk (but you won't get as close to these amazing animals as you will on the guided tour). Visit **Little Sahara**, also at Seal Bay, to sand-board down massive sand dunes (hire boards and toboggans at Vivonne Bay).

Further to the west of the island is **Flinders Chase National Park** with the incredible **Remarkable Rocks**, precariously balanced granite boulders – their unusual shapes have been caused by erosion over millions of years.

Kangaroo Island is not only home to an incredible range of Australian wildlife, it is also one of the world's oldest sanctuaries for Ligurian bees (you can see the bees and taste some of their honey at **Clifford's Honey Farm** at Haines).

MOUNT GAMBIER

The Boandik people are the Traditional Owners of Mount Gambier

SOUTH AUSTRALIA'S

second biggest town and just near the Victorian border, Mount Gambier is lucky enough to sit at the base of an extinct volcano, which is why the area is wonderfully full of caves, craters and lakes. The must-see highlight of the area is **Blue Lake**. Situated in a gorgeous volcanic landscape, Blue Lake inhabits one of the extinct volcanic craters and, no surprise given its name, turns an intense cobalt-blue colour from about late November through to March each year, before reverting back to its normal subdued blue. The colour change is believed to have something to do with the change in the lake's water temperature and how that affects the lake's chemical properties, but really it is still considered a mystery (some locals even say it has something to do with bunyips ... go figure).

Walk the lovely 3.6km circuit trail around the edge of the lake. It's mostly flat and there are viewing platforms so you can stop to enjoy the views. Guided tours are available too, and there's even a tour available that takes you down an old well shaft in a glass lift to see the lake up close (it involves about 14 stairs and a 200m walk so possibly not the best for toddlers and strollers).

Also right in town is **Umpherston Sinkhole**. Known as the Sunken Garden, it was once a cave and when the top collapsed the sinkhole was created. Mother Nature did her thing and thus the topsoil formed the perfect environment for the garden oasis you see today. You can walk down into the 30m deep sinkhole along platforms behind lush green vines. Don't forget to get a view from the top too, and keep an eye out for the large colony of resident possums that always come out at dusk.

Under the city is a labyrinth of (mostly flooded) limestone caves. One you can tour is **Engelbrecht Cave**. It has an interesting history: people in town used to dump their rubbish down a natural well that actually led to the cave. The cave was sealed in the 1940s but in 1979 the local Lions Club decided to restore it and, once about 400 tonnes of rubbish was removed, this beautiful cave was open to the public. You can explore its two caverns and underground lake on a guided tour.

Just over an hour north from Mount Gambier is **Naracoorte Caves National Park**, South Australia's only World Heritage site. The caves have acted as an animal trap for the past 500,000 years and preserve an incredible fossil record from that time period. There is a World Heritage Walking Trail (and other walks) at the caves and also a pricey but fabulous behind-the-scenes tour that includes a visit to the fossil lab.

TASMANIA

The Traditional Owners of
Tasmania are the Palawa people.

FOR MANY MAINLAND

Aussies, Tasmania occupies a 'we'll get there when we're older' mentality. We urge you to reconsider. Even after a hectic start to our Tasmanian adventure (we almost missed our flight to Hobart), the anxiety wore off quickly as the kids happily began to explore this fun-filled island. Yes, Tasmania is quaint and charming and will never be described as a thriving metropolis, but it offers so much more, particularly for families. This intriguing island at the edge of the world is full of World Heritage areas, fascinating history and endless family-friendly activities.

While Tasmania isn't known for its scorching summers it's also not quite as freezing cold in winter as those in the north may have you believe (lucky for us because we forgot our winter coats). Yes, snow does fall in various places across the state in winter, but Hobart's day-time temperatures can hover around 12 to 13 degrees Celsius making it a great place to get some adventure done. Rainfall does vary dramatically across the island. Hobart is Australia's second driest capital city (after Adelaide) but has the most rainy days of any capital (must be a lot of drizzle). The west coast has a higher annual rainfall and thus beautiful lush rainforests to show for it.

Tasmania is full of history but you'll also find it easy to get into adventure here, particularly because of all the fabulous wilderness areas, and this makes it a great place to visit with children. Try caving, kayaking, rock climbing, bushwalking, surfing, hang-gliding and mountain-biking. The kids loved every bit of our holiday, whether it was searching for blowholes on wild beaches or walking through mountain forests, and they were even happy to take on some of the more confronting exhibits at MONA. Oh and back to the history – Tasmania also has the best ghost tours in Australia!

ATTRACTIONS

- The best known of Tasmania's convict heritage sites is the haunting **Port Arthur**, well worth the 90-minute drive from Hobart. This World Heritage–listed convict prison on the Tasman Peninsula was Australia's most infamous penal settlement, with more than 12,000 convicts shipped here between the 1830s and 1870s. Once called 'Hell on Earth', it is now a collection of heritage buildings and ruins set on eerily beautiful grounds. Port Arthur is suitable for children – pick up a 'Hidden Stories' Activity Book when you buy your tickets as this will help them understand the place's history and is a great way to make your visit more interactive. If you have toddlers, pack a pram as the Port Arthur site is quite large (you can also hire prams there). Tickets cover entry over two days and include a guided introductory walking tour and a harbour cruise, as well as access to the historic buildings and ruins. Hang around until night to take the very cool **Port Arthur Ghost Tour** – by lantern light you'll hear stories of Port Arthur's mysteries. Although there is no age limit, the ghost tour is not advised for very young children, sensitive kids or those prone to nightmares. And if your children disrupt the tour you will be asked to leave … spoooooky.

- On the way to or from Port Arthur, stop to enjoy some of the Tasman Peninsula's stunning natural wonders such as the **Blowhole**, **Devil's Kitchen**, **Pirate Bay Lookout** and the crazy **Tessellated Pavement** at **Eaglehawk Neck** (this thin piece of land, joining the Tasman Peninsula to the rest of Tasmania, used to be guarded by dogs to ensure convicts couldn't escape from Port Arthur).

- After our Port Arthur visit, we also stopped at the **Tasmanian Devil Unzoo**, not a typo but rather the world's first intentional unzoo, a 'revolutionary project' that aims to both educate and excite the conservationist in visitors as well as allowing animals to live as freely as possible in their natural habitats. The kids loved seeing animals in a more natural environment, and learning about the efforts to save the Tassie Devil.

- The big natural drawcard in Tasmania is of course **Cradle Mountain** – if you close your eyes and think of Tasmania there is a fair chance images of Cradle Mountain will appear. Located in **Cradle Mountain–Lake St Clair National Park**, part of the Tasmanian Wilderness World Heritage Area that covers around 20 per cent of Tasmania, Cradle Mountain is Tassie at its most splendid. You can spend a day exploring this wild place with its ancient rainforests and rugged mountains – it's a 1.5-hour drive from Devonport or 2.5 hours from Launceston. Or stay in any of the various accommodation options nearby and take a few days. As well as the untouched wilderness, there's lots to do: abseiling, bushwalking, rafting and canyoning are all great options. Canyon tours include the Lost World Canyon trip, which is suitable for kids aged eight and over – a really fun way to experience the wilderness.

- Wilderness abounds in Tasmania and in the north-west part of the state you'll find the stunning **Dip Falls**, a two-tier waterfall with unique rock formations near Mawbanna. If you're on a road trip or staying in the beautiful far north-west town of Stanley, then it's worth having a look at the falls – they are among the best in Tasmania. There's a short kid-friendly walk to the top of the falls and you also have lush forest to explore. Take an extra few minutes to walk a kilometre or so beyond the falls carpark to the **Big Tree**, a huge tree with a 17m circumference, funnily enough found in Big Tree Reserve. What a coincidence!

- Also in the north of Tasmania is **Launceston**, Tasmania's second largest city and a great place to stay for a few days. At the head of the Tamar River, the city has a vibrant food and arts scene and bucketloads of history. Just a brisk 15-minute walk (or two-minute drive) from the city centre you'll find the wilderness of **Cataract Gorge**, a huge rock chasm with the South Esk River flowing through it. Follow the cliff-side path from the historic Kings Bridge or enjoy one of the other walking trails. Hop on the **Gorge Scenic Chairlift** to fly (very, very slowly) over the gorge, explore the beautiful gardens or have lunch at the cafe. If you're there late in the day, look for the peacocks and wallabies as they usually come out at dusk.

- For the best kid-friendly walks not far from Launceston (about 20 minutes to be exact), try **Hollybank Forest Reserve**, with its lovely picnic spots, walks and bike trails. If the walks are too tame for your adventurous kids, within the reserve is **Hollybank Wilderness Adventures** with ziplines, ropes courses and mountain-biking. For another reserve not too far from Launceston (about an hour away), visit **Fern Glade Reserve** in Burnie – a natural bush reserve along the Emu River. Stroll among the lush ferns and enjoy a barbecue while taking in the amazing birds and wildlife. Extra points for the first to spot a platypus on your way around. For more wildlife stay in **Burnie** to see the colony of little penguins on the foreshore.

- If the kids have had enough wilderness, take them to **Tasmazia**, about half an hour south of Devonport (and not too far from Cradle Mountain). You can't help but have fun at this popular theme park. Lose and (hopefully) find yourselves in the Great Maze, one of the world's largest botanical mazes, and then get lost in one of the other excellent mazes (perhaps the Cage or the Confusion Maze). Or walk among the crazies at Tasmazia's **Village of Lower Crackpot**, a whimsical model village with lightly 'politically incorrect' signage. There's a cafe too, and it's also a working lavender farm. Our guess is that Tasmazia will be a hit with your entire family.

HOBART

The Traditional Owners of the Hobart area are the Muwinina people, one of the Palawa network of clans.

HOBART, the Tasmanian capital, was founded in 1804 on the River Derwent. The river was one of Australia's finest deep-water ports, so the settlement quickly grew into a major port. You can't escape the city's early history as you wander the streets, and why would you want to – it's part of Hobart's appeal. Hobart doesn't feel too busy, unless you're at the Salamanca Market, and it's a beautiful city that is perfectly situated around the docks. We stayed in the CBD and could walk to the market, dock area, parks and shops.

EATING OUT

As with all major cities, Hobart offers a wide range of food options for families. You can't go wrong with seafood here – fresh fish and chips will have the kids happy.

ACCOMMODATION

From Hobart to Launceston to the smaller towns, staying in Tasmania is easy with all types of accommodation available to families of all sizes. We prefer to find a place with a kitchen and some sort of lounge to crash at the end of a big day of adventure – that way the kids can be tucked up in bed in a separate room while we relax. Even though there are plenty of options available around the state, you will need to plan ahead because the whole state can get busy with holidaymakers. You definitely want to make sure you have beds booked in if hitting the road, and if you're hiring a car or van make sure that's booked in ahead of time too.

GETTING AROUND

To get around Hobart, there is a bus service, otherwise cycle or walk. Children under five travel free on the public transport system. If you want to do daytrips, a car is the easiest option, and parking and navigating the streets are easy.

To get around the entire state, campervans and caravans are a popular option. There are plenty of good places to park and most roads into the national parks are sealed so campervans are allowed to enter. Rest stops on the side of the roads are easy to find, but phone service is not always available, so take a map or download your maps before leaving home. Check out discovertasmania.com.au for fantastic self-drive itineraries across the state. You can also break them down to kilometres, helping you get the most out of the time you have.

ATTRACTIONS

- To get a big-picture view of this beautiful city, start by heading up **kunanji/Mount Wellington**, the striking mountain that towers over Hobart. It's only 20 minutes from the city and is part of **Wellington Park**, which has a wide range of walking trails and gorgeous picnic spots. You can ride, walk or drive to the summit – at the top take in the spectacular views from the Pinnacle lookout and observation deck.

- **Salamanca Market** on the waterfront is a large vibrant outdoor market. It's open every Saturday and many consider it Australia's best market. With lots of local produce, arts and collectibles, the market offers so much to see and do (and eat and buy) that the kids will definitely find this fun. And it will give weary legs both old and young a chance to rest. Even if you're not visiting on a Saturday for the markets, take the kids for a walk along **Hobart's waterfront** and enjoy fish and chips while watching the boats come in – it's a seafood-lover's dream.

- **Tasmanian Museum and Art Gallery** is a fascinating place showcasing Tasmanian art, culture and history. It's a great place to visit with kids – they even have a 'Kids in Museums Manifesto' to guide their approach – and there are a range of hands-on activities and interesting exhibitions for families.

- If you want something more cutting edge, you can't go past the world-renowned **MONA**, the **Museum of Old and New Art**. The museum itself has plenty to entertain the kids, like the poo-making machine (yes, it smells) and various fascinating interactive art works. It's set in beautiful surrounds and there's art outside too, so you can spend time in the fresh air with the kids if they tire of walking inside. Controversial and adult-themed works of art are displayed, so speak to staff about what's suitable for children. Staff throughout the museum can inform you along the way and, if it's not for your family, simply keep moving. You can get to MONA by car or bus but for the full MONA experience the best way is via the river on a MONA ferry, which departs the city from Brooke Street Pier (there are many steps once you get to MONA's pier, so keep this in mind if you have a pram).

- The **Royal Tasmanian Botanic Gardens** is a great place for a picnic and an easy run-around space for little kids – they'll also love the winding paths of the Lily Pond Garden. Look for the Japanese Garden, the Conservatory and the Community Food Garden too. It's set on the edge of the River Derwent, so it can get a bit cool – rug up! If you all have the energy, you can walk from the city to the gardens; it's about 2.5km or 25 minutes.

- If it's not too cold, head to **Seven Mile Beach**, 15km east of the city. It's Hobart's closest surf beach and is a safe beach for kids to swim (waves are usually pretty small). It's close to holiday parks and resorts so it's a good spot to stay if you want to avoid the bright lights of Hobart.

Located a half-hour drive from Hobart is the gorgeous town of **Richmond** offering a historic feel with numerous heritage buildings and **Old Hobart Town**, which depicts 1820s Hobart life – wander the streets of the model village to see exactly what Hobart would have looked like back in the day (but this version is smaller, obviously). Take a horse-drawn carriage to the **Richmond Gaol**, built in 1825, to experience the pitfalls of convict life. Nearby is the **Peter Rabbit Garden**, the only licensed Beatrix Potter Peter Rabbit garden outside the United Kingdom. It's good for younger kids and Peter Rabbit fans – the garden isn't huge but the shop has everything you could ever want related to Peter Rabbit. It's set in a winery, **Riversdale Estate**, with views over the Coal River, so, you know, win-win for parents. If your kids are too old for Peter Rabbit, try Richmond's **Pooseum**, a museum dedicated to, um, poo – how can you resist when the slogan is 'Where talking about poo is not taboo'?

KID-FREE NIGHT OUT

You won't find it the robust wharf full of sailors that it once was, but Hobart's **Salamanca Place** will give you what you are looking for – busy on weekends, there are enough bars and restaurants to suit your taste. If catching a flick on date night is your go, then head to the historic **State Cinema**; as well as the usual theatres it has something special – a rooftop cinema and bar in the summer months (it still gets cold – it's Hobart after all – so wear something warm). In the warmer months **Preacher Bar** at Battery Point offers a hipster-cool beer-garden vibe. If you enjoy checking out fossils while you sip (and we mean actual prehistoric fossils not mouthy barflies), go straight to **Evolve Spirits Bar** underneath the MACq 01 Hotel where you can see 37 different fossils displayed in glass cabinets. The bespoke gin and whisky revolution shows no signs of slowing down and the petite hole-in-the-wall **Gold Bar** could be what you're looking for – it stocks spirits from every Tasmanian distillery and the skilled bartenders make unforgettable cocktails.

FREYCINET NATIONAL PARK

The Traditional Owners are the Palawa people.

A must-see on your Tasmanian holiday is Freycinet National Park along the state's east coast. Founded in 1916, it was named after French navigator Louis de Freycinet and is an impossibly beautiful collection of sapphire-blue bays, rugged headlands and pristine beaches. The jagged pink-granite formations of the **Hazards** rise above the small town of **Coles Bay** on the edge of the national park, which thankfully does not have a Coles in sight but rather a more old-school Coles Bay General Store and Post Office. The pink tint of the mountains is caused by iron impurities in the granite. Of all the bays and beaches in the area, **Wineglass Bay** is the one everyone raves about – it's ranked as one of the ten best beaches in the world. Take the one-hour walk up to the **Wineglass Bay Lookout** (there are some steep bits so perhaps don't fill your wine glass all the way to the top) and, with kids who like longer walks, continue on from the lookout down to the bay itself (about a three-hour-return walk). Humpback whales, bottlenose dolphins and southern right whales can be seen in Wineglass Bay, which they use for calving, feeding or simply enjoying a pinot gris.

The national park offers a variety of walks for all abilities, including to the fabulously named **Friendly Beaches**, **Little Gravelly Beach** and **Sleepy Bay**. There are also heaps of tours and cruises available in the area. Hire a kayak at Coles Bay to take the kids out on the beautiful water – keep an eye out for dolphins. Or devour some fresh seafood (including fine oysters) at **Freycinet Marine Farm** – enjoy it on the deck or order takeaway (you can also take a tour of the farm).

The abundant wildlife of the area also makes it a great place to visit with the family. Kids can keep an eye out for echidnas, quolls, wallabies and an incredible range of birds. At dusk you might also see wombats and the occasional Tasmanian devil. These carnivorous marsupials were once very common in Freycinet National Park, but the population has suffered because of the infectious Devil Facial Tumour Disease.

There is much evidence of a rich Indigenous culture and history in the area, and **shell middens** can be seen at Hazards Beach and the Friendly Beaches.

Funnily, considering the Freycinet Peninsula is named after a Frenchman, the temperatures in Freycinet National Park are very similar to those in France, and it has more than 300 sunny days each year. Obviously summer is a lovely time to visit but it can get super busy, so consider going in the shoulder-season months of October/November or March/April.

Camping is available at various sites, but it's so popular over the summer period that you can only book via a ballot system (ballots are drawn in August; see parks.tas.gov.au for more). Just outside the park there's accommodation ranging from eco-retreats and luxury lodges to beach shacks and holiday cottages in Coles Bay. Also in Coles Bay is family-friendly Big4 Iluka on Freycinet Holiday Park. It has cabins that sleep up to six people and a playground for little ones.

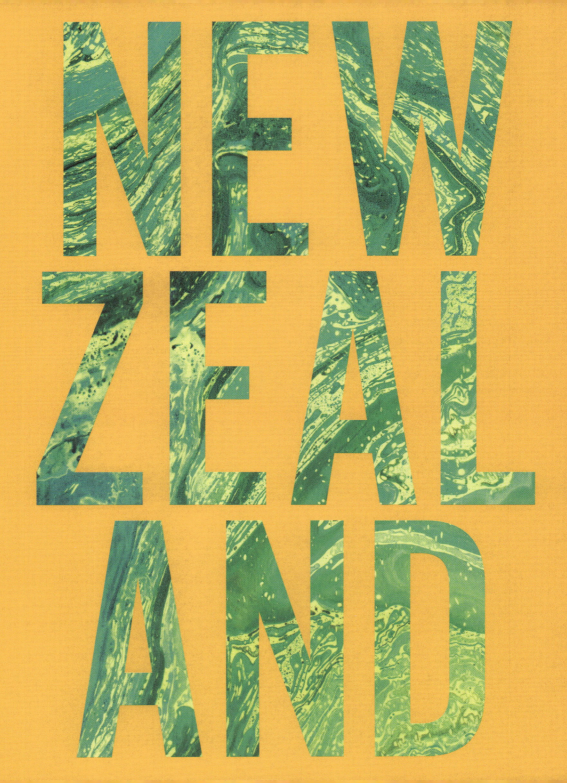

IF YOU HAVE EVER BEEN TO NEW ZEALAND OR HAVE BEEN FORTUNATE ENOUGH TO KNOW A HANDFUL OF KIWIS, YOU'LL KNOW THAT HAVING A PRIME MINISTER LIKE JACINDA ARDERN MAKES PERFECT SENSE.

New Zealand Prime Minister Ardern is also a perfect representation of the land of the long white cloud – progressive, clever, inclusive, warm, friendly and fun. Pete has been appearing on New Zealand TV and touring there for over a decade and always says he hasn't met a Kiwi he hasn't liked (although to be fair he hasn't met them all!). And on top of the local folk being generally awesome, New Zealand may just be the most photogenic country on Earth. It's so stunningly beautiful it wouldn't surprise us if Mother Nature was herself a Kiwi. New Zealand sits over two of the Earth's tectonic plates and has underground volcanic activity too, all of which creates some striking landscapes, huge mountains and delightful natural hot pools. The country also has incredible wildlife, such as its famous flightless bird, the kiwi – kind of the Nokia 3210 of birds.

Because New Zealand is not the biggest country and is fairly easy to get around, we've grouped this chapter into North Island and South Island. Within the two islands, the north and south, you can fit in quite a bit, but don't stretch yourself too thin – some places you'll want to spend more time as there is an abundance of outdoor activities for all abilities and ages. After all, this is the country that decided jumping from a great height head first with a stretchy rope tied around your ankles was a fun idea. To help plan your trip, visit newzealand.com for the official tourist guide to New Zealand; they have a great array of recommended itineraries based on the time you have available and your interests, whether it be adventure, volcanos or *Lord of the Rings*.

New Zealand is a great first trip 'overseas' for kids – they get to experience a different culture (there is a wide range of wonderful Māori cultural activities) and landscape without having to sit in a plane for 24 hours. And New Zealanders are generally incredibly friendly when you're travelling with children. We have found the Kiwis to be so proud of their country that of course they want to show it off, so ask around for the best local things to do, see and eat.

GETTING AROUND

Railway travel is an option, and it's a great way to sit back, relax and enjoy the scenery. You can travel through national parks, across volcanic landscapes, over river valleys, past alpine areas and along rugged coastlines. Get a Scenic Rail Pass, which allows unlimited travel on the long-distance passenger trains, including the Interislander Ferry from Wellington on the North Island to Picton on the South Island, meeting trains at both ports.

ACCOMMODATION

The key for travelling to New Zealand is to book your accommodation well in advance as it's such a popular travel destination for people with kids that accommodation does book out, especially family suites in peak holiday periods.

If you've been saving up, book into one of the luxury lodges available across the country, which are great for a big family or two families. Some come with personal chef and private pools.

If hitting the road is on the cards, renting a car and booking accommodation is easy, but campervans and motorhomes are very popular in New Zealand. Camping on wheels makes for a memorable trip – you can travel to places in your own time without having to worry about finding beds and the kids will be talking about the trip for years to come. Download the CamperMate app to find campsites, toilets, dump points and plenty of other information to help you on your way around. Remember driving with kids will require more stops, mainly to keep the driver's sanity from constant 'I need to go to the toilet' and 'I'm hungry' chants from the kids in the back. Load up on healthy snacks and always have dinner planned for arrival day. You won't want to be driving around looking for a supermarket at the end of a long day.

DID YOU KNOW?

- The Māori name for New Zealand is Aotearoa, which means the land of the long white cloud, although whenever we have been there we have failed to spot the one, continuous white cloud.
- The kea, a bird native to New Zealand, is the world's only alpine parrot. Smart and cheeky, it is known for pulling windscreen wipers off cars and other 'funny' habits.
- The longest place name in the world belongs to Taumatawhakatangihangakoauauotamateaturipukakapikimaunga-horonukupokaiwhenuakitanatahu, a hill in Hawkes Bay on the North Island. Good luck if you are asked to spell that in a Spelling Bee contest.
- Gisborne is the first city in the world to see the sunrise because it is just 496.3km away from the International Date Line. They can humblebrag about it but everybody else is still asleep.
- Baldwin Street, in Dunedin, was the world's steepest street until it was outdone in 2019 by an unpronounceable street in Wales. Check it out and then avoid!
- The emblem for the Royal New Zealand Air Force is the kiwi – a flightless bird. (The kiwi obviously didn't mention this in its job interview.)

WELLINGTON
NORTH ISLAND

NEW ZEALAND'S CAPITAL,

Wellington is the southernmost capital city in the world. It's a great place to fly into to begin your New Zealand holiday. This vibrant compact capital city, tucked down the bottom of the North Island, has lots of things to see and do, amazing culture and beautiful cuisine – and, of course, glorious Kiwi nature and magnificent landscapes. Spend a couple of days in the city before either heading north to explore the North Island or catching the ferry across to the South Island.

One of the favourite attractions for kids in Wellington is **Te Papa Tongarewa**, which may or may not mean 'tell Papa about Tongarewa' (it actually means 'Container of Treasures'). Te Papa is the national museum and has excellent interactive kid-friendly activities. It's also arguably the best place to gain an understanding and appreciation of Māori culture (outside of an All Blacks game, of course). Its six floors of treasures tell New Zealand's story. General admission is free, but charges apply to some exhibitions and activities.

Another fun thing to do with the kids is to ride on the historic **Wellington Cable Car**, which takes you on a five-minute journey from the city centre up to

Kelburn Lookout with views out over the city. At the top of the cable-car ride, you can easily walk to the **Botanic Gardens**, the **Cable Car Museum**, and **Space Place** at Carter Observatory.

Absolutely worth a visit is **Zealandia**, an urban eco-sanctuary not far from Wellington's CBD (you can get a free shuttle to Zealandia from Kelburn Lookout after you've enjoyed your cable-car ride, and also from outside the city's i-SITE Visitor Centre, or drive, or catch a bus). Zealandia has some of the country's rarest wildlife in its fully fenced, 500-hectare wilderness sanctuary; you can explore the place on your own or join a guided tour. Zealandia's main focus is conservation and kids can research its 500-year plan to return the land to its pre-settlement state.

Another popular attraction for kids is **Wellington Zoo** – it's small and a bit hilly but has a wide range of animals and a sense of history (it was New Zealand's first zoo when it opened in 1906). Oscar's favourite animal is the giraffe and the good news is this zoo has giraffes! In fact, Sunny the giraffe arrived from Australia in May 2019 joining aunty and niece duo Zahara and Zuri. (Personally, Pete would have liked it if the Aussie giraffe was named Trev.)

Visit **Frank Kitts Park**, more fun for the younger ones as they swoosh down the famous lighthouse slide. Here you'll find the **Wellington Underground Market**. Open every Saturday it's a great place to buy local art, freshly cooked food or simply some colourful socks!

AUCKLAND
NORTH ISLAND

TĀMAKI MAKAURAU, as it's culturally known, is an amazing and vibrant city with over 200 ethnic groups living here. This harbourside city offers spectacular water views and it's also known as the City of Sails, so it's a boat-lover's paradise. A good way to get to know the city is to go on a guided or self-guided bike tour of the city – popular paths include the **Auckland waterfront** and **Tamaki Drive Promenade** (bike hire is available at numerous places in the city).

Another great way to get a sense of Auckland is to head to **Sky Tower** – the 328m high tower offers spectacular views. If that's a little sedate for you, try the tower's outdoor **SkyWalk** or, if you dare, **SkyJump**, where you're wired up and then leap off the building, falling 192m straight down (kids under ten can't do either of these activities). Brij chickened out of SkyJump at the last minute and you can't blame her!

In Auckland you're never too far from wild beaches and rugged mountains. But if you don't have the time or inclination to head up to actual mountains, then **Snowplanet** offers a way more convenient option especially for kids. Just 20 minutes outside the city, this indoor snow recreation park presents heaps of room for skiing, snowboarding, snow-tubing and games year-round. The kids are going to have a ball, trust us. Open late, with night-time activities for all ages, Snowplanet changes its terrain weekly so there are always new challenges. Kids who need ski lessons can get them, but you need to book in for these. There is also a restaurant with a fireplace to sit back and enjoy après dinner.

For another kid-focused attraction, **Rainbow's End** is your theme park fun in Auckland. It offers more than 20 rides and attractions for everyone in the family with plenty of thrill rides for older kids. It also has Kidz Kingdom for kids under eight.

If your little ones love animals, **Butterfly Creek** is a privately owned animal attraction with animal exhibits, a butterfly house, playground, dinosaur park and train.

Like any major city, Auckland has good museums that offer interesting activities for younger visitors too. Visit **Auckland War Memorial Museum** – despite the name, it is not a museum solely focused on war, though it has excellent war memorial galleries. It's often referred to simply as Auckland Museum and its collections focus on New Zealand history, culture and natural history, along with Māori culture. Apart from the various exhibitions and activity programs, the museum often puts on kid-friendly events; check the website for what's on.

Another good museum in Auckland is **MOTAT**, the **Museum of Transport and Technology**. It's the country's largest transport, technology and social history museum. Spread over 16 hectares, this huge museum is chockfull of interactive exhibits for kids to get involved in and is a great way to discover more about New Zealand's many achievements.

Auckland is surrounded by beautiful wild spots and nature is never far away. Visit the city's amazing regional parks and waterfalls like **Mauku Waterfall**, 40 minutes south of the city. About the same amount of time east of Auckland is **Waitakere Ranges Regional Park** with great walking trails, lush rainforest and black-sand beaches. Before you head into any natural area, be sure your walk won't be doing any damage to the environment – as the bushwalking saying goes: take only photos, leave only footprints.

For nature in the city, visit the beautiful **Cornwall Park**, which is centred around the volcanic cone **One Tree Hill**. Since 2000, it's actually been no-tree hill following a chainsaw attack on the lone pine tree by a Māori activist who, years later, expressed regret for the nature of his protest. Standing on its peak still, though, is an obelisk unveiled in 1948 and a statue of a Māori warrior – the obelisk, marking the grave of a European settler, is dedicated to the Māori people. Cornwall Park has perfect picnic spots and a farm too.

Our boys have never watched *The Lord of the Rings* or *The Hobbit* but they somehow know the films were made among the magnificent landscapes of New Zealand. If you have fans in your family, about two hours south of Auckland is **Hobbiton**, the set for the Hobbit village used in all six films. Set on a still-working farm, Hobbiton is in the middle of the Waikato region. Tours last for two hours; you will need to pre-book as it is a popular place and tours book out early.

Take a ferry from Auckland to **Rangitoto Island**, an incredible volcanic cone. It's New Zealand's youngest volcanic cone, rising unexpectedly from the ocean after a volcanic eruption only 600 years ago. It is easily accessible and great for families. Explore the caves and old World War II bunkers on the trail to the summit. There are outstanding views of lush forests, lava fields to explore and basalt rock paths to follow. A great family day out and about.

Over 170km west from Auckland is **Hot Water Beach**. This place is like no other. At low tide, the sand is hot under your feet and you can dip your feet into hot water. Either dig your own hole to lounge in, or reap the benefits of the toil of others and find a pre-dug hole and enjoy. You can only experience the hot sand at low tide so work your plans around that timing. There is plenty of parking; check the signs for pay and park, and road parking is free. Remember, this is still a stretch of ocean that has dangerous rips. It is patrolled on weekends but always swim between the flags. Watch children and take precautions as with any other beach.

KID-FREE NIGHT OUT

What we love about a big city is being able to get a meal late at night after a big day travelling around. **Dr Rudi's Rooftop Brewing Co.** has a late-night menu, plenty of alcoholic and non-alcoholic beverages and fun cocktails. Brij has a soft spot for heading out in Auckland without the kids: being asked for ID at age 31 to prove she was over 18 is a terrific start to the night!

ELSEWHERE ON THE NORTH ISLAND

- About three and a half hours south of Auckland, **Rotorua** in the stunning volcanic Bay of Plenty region is the spot to go for hot pools, bubbling mud and shooting geysers. It's also a great place for families with so many activities, from lake cruises, glow-worm tours and kayaking to jet-boating and whitewater rafting for the more adventurous. **Hell's Gate**, with its clouds of steam and Māori myths, is one of the most active geothermal reserves in New Zealand and features **Kakahi Falls**, the largest hot waterfall in the Southern Hemisphere, and the country's only outdoor mud bath (you pay for entry). On the must-visit list is **Kerosene Creek**, which, despite sounding like an ecological disaster, is where a cool stream meets hot springs. Still in Rotorua, learn more about the Māori culture at **Te Puia** and watch **Pōhutu Geyser** erupt. You could easily spend a day in the stunning **Whakarewarewa Forest**, also known as the Redwoods. Its bushwalking trails, ziplines, canopy tours, a 500m long tree walk and excellent mountain-biking mean you'll easily have enough to do with the kids here.

- The northernmost region of the North Island is called, unsurprisingly, **Northland**. Subtropical and with a mild climate, it's also known as 'The Winterless North'. The region has enormous cultural significance, magnificent kauri forests and idyllic beaches. Head to **Cape Reinga** where you can swim and sand-board on **Ninety Mile Beach**. Time your visit for the incredible sunsets – you will be in awe at the beauty of nature. And, believe us, the kids will want to sand-board all day it's that much fun, so you'll probably still be around at sunset!

- Along the east coast of the northern region is the **Bay of Islands**, which is made up of over 140 subtropical atolls. It's the perfect place for a family holiday – think snorkelling, paddling, kayaking, swimming, dolphin-watching and more in calm waters. With so much to do, we'd recommend heading to **Adventure Forest** near Whangarei for the kids, with circuits for all ages and abilities and challenges like the wire traverse, tight ropes, swings and flying foxes. Visit the unusual '**hole in the rock**' formation on rugged **Motu Kōkako** (Piercy Island); boat tours actually take you through the hole in the rock. See more of the beautiful Bay of Islands by foot – there are many excellent trails you can take, with quite a few being kid friendly and many that follow the stunning coastline. Try a Cape to Cove hike or bike ride from Bay of Islands to **Hokianga Harbour**, to see lush New Zealand forest, suspension bridges, waterfalls, streams and more.

- The Bay of Islands has great historical significance – it was here at **Waitangi** that the Treaty of Waitangi was signed in 1840. New Zealand's founding document, it was an agreement signed between the British Crown and about 540 Māori chiefs. The best place to introduce the kids to this history and the country's incredible Māori culture is at **Waitangi Treaty Grounds** in the heart of the Bay of Islands. With the Museum of Waitangi, cultural performances, the Treaty House, a Māori carving studio and so much more, it's a wonderful place to explore – you can take a guided tour or wander through the attractions and grounds yourself. An hour or so south of Waitangi, Whangarei is also an excellent place for Māori cultural experiences, with a range on offer.

CHRISTCHURCH
SOUTH ISLAND

THE LARGEST CITY

on the South Island, Christchurch, in the Canterbury region, is renowned for its history and heritage buildings, and yet it has a strikingly modern feel too. This is partly because the earthquake-susceptible city has had to rebuild a number of times, especially after the 2011 earthquake that hit the city and surrounding suburbs hard – tragically 185 people were killed. The city has bounced back though, with urban regeneration and renewed community connection. One of the initiatives is **Gap Filler**, a public art and activity program to fill the vacant spaces left behind after the earthquakes. One of the city's faves is **Dance-O-Mat** on Gloucester Street – using an old laundromat washing machine, $2 and an app, you can have music and lights for half an hour and dance to your heart's content. Another great Gap Filler initiative is **Super Street Arcade** on Tuam Street. You need two people to play the oversized game, one controlling the giant joystick and the other stamping on the pleasingly oversized buttons.

Christchurch has some great activities for kids and many of them are in the city centre. First up, take a tour of the inner city on the **heritage tram**, where, if you have a day pass, you can hop on and off throughout the city and get to various attractions. Kids will love to create all things LEGO and DUPLO at **Imagination Station**, created to encourage creative play, on the first floor of Tūranga, the city's central library. For more play, head to **Margaret Mahy Family Playground**. In the city centre, this great all-ages park for kids has big slides, a flying fox, a water-play area, a climbing net and other fun obstacles. The playground is at the end of **Rauora Park**, which is a great place to go if your kids are missing their sport – play a game of basketball or table tennis, or bike/scooter over the **East Frame pump track** (another Gap Filler project).

Snaking through the city centre is the **Avon River**, and you can hire bikes to ride along it or hire a paddle-boat or kayak at the historic **Antigua Boat Sheds**. If you don't feel like doing it yourself, go punting on the river – you can sit back and relax while someone else pushes you along the scenic river. Also in the city centre is the **Christchurch Botanic Gardens**, a lovely spot for a stroll through beautiful gardens.

For a touching experience, head to **Quake City** in the city centre. This museum tells the stories of the 2010 and 2011 Canterbury region earthquakes – the aftermath, the experiences of survivors, the incredible emergency service responders and the community's resilience.

About 20 minutes away from the city centre and next to the international airport is the fascinating **International Antarctic Centre**. It's one of the most popular tourist attractions in Christchurch and you can see why – you can go on a 15-minute off-road field trip that mimics driving across Antarctica (best for kids five and over), experience an Antarctic storm in the Storm Dome, cuddle huskies and see penguins among many other things. It's not cheap but it's worth it, and children under five are free.

Finish off your Christchurch explorations with a ride on the **Christchurch Gondola**, a cable-car that travels from the Heathcote Valley to the top of Mount Cavendish, only 20 minutes from the city centre. You'll see just how stunning this South Island city really is.

QUEENSTOWN
SOUTH ISLAND

If adventure is your thing,

Queenstown is your place. It is the adventure capital of New Zealand – the first-ever commercial bungy jump company started here – and you will most likely find whatever adrenalin rush you're after in this picturesque town. It's set on the edge of Lake Wakatipu with the majestic Remarkables mountain range as a backdrop – you can explore this area or just take in the views. For kid-friendly activities at a gentle pace, enjoy a cruise on the lake or take the Skyline Gondola to the top of Bob's Peak (kids under five are free). Of course, being Queenstown, you don't have to simply rest and enjoy the cafe at the top of the gondola ride; you can go on the fast-paced luge track for a wild ride before hopping back on the gondola.

Take your pick of adventure activities: paragliding, heli-skiing, jet-boating snowboarding, ziplines, whitewater rafting, hang-gliding, skydiving, bungy jumping and more. Queenstown has the highest bungy jump in New Zealand with the Nevis Bungy; the same company also offers the Nevis Swing and the Nevis Catapault. The Shotover River is home to numerous activities too. You can go on the Shotover Canyon Swing, Shotover Jet boat and Shotover Canyon Fox (a 445m zipline across Shotover Canyon). Whatever adrenalin buzz floats your boat you will find it in Queenstown.

For a different type of adventure, visit Middle Earth – the Queenstown region is where a large chunk of *Lord of the Rings* was filmed. You can take a number of *Lord of the Rings* themed tours, including a helicopter tour and a horseriding tour – it really depends on your time and budget (and how obsessed your kids are).

One of the country's most popular destinations is in this region. Five hours away from Queenstown by road, Milford Sound is a stunning fiord, carved by glaciers and surrounded by huge peaks. You can fly, 4WD tour or horseride to Milford Sound, or even walk there – it's the end point of the famed 53km Milford Track. This open-sea inlet lined with sheer rock faces should be named one of the most beautiful places on Earth.

WANAKA
SOUTH ISLAND

WANAKA, NOT TO BE CONFUSED

with Wakanda, which is, of course, in Africa (well, in Marvel's Africa), is a relaxed place to visit, with great cafes and restaurants. At the base of mountainous alps, it sits on the edge of picturesque Lake Wanaka and is the gateway to Mount Aspiring National Park. It's a very popular ski resort in winter and an adventure hub in summer, but has a more chilled-out feel than the bigger Queenstown, which is only an hour away.

It's a top place to visit with the kids, especially those who love an adventure or two. There's great mountain-biking, hiking, paragliding, abseiling, canyoning and climbing, and, with a beautiful lake at its doorstep, Wanaka also has water-skiing, sailing, fishing and wakeboarding. Or you can go horseriding and, in winter, skiing and snowboarding. You get the picture – there's a lot you can do!

It's not only adventure activities on offer here, though. The kids will love Puzzling World, Wanaka's 'Wonderful World of Weirdness', with its 3D maze (it's not just one level), Leaning Tower of Wanaka and numerous illusion rooms. Dinosaur Park is a playground in the centre of town, known for its dinosaur slide. Another great park to explore is Wanaka Station Park, which used to be part of an old sheep station. A highlight for kids might be the National Transport and Toy Museum, with hundreds of vehicles (including planes) and thousands of toys to see, plus both indoor and outdoor play areas.

Wanaka may not be a huge town but it has the largest virtual reality experience in the Southern Hemisphere, or so say the people at Realm VR. It is a pretty awesome virtual reality experience, and you can play a wide range of VR games and even climb Mount Everest. It's not recommended for kids under seven and those between seven and 12 will need to be supervised.

See recycling in action at Wanaka Wastebusters, a recycling and reuse centre where you can shop sustainably and see the recycling team do their thing. Or, for a different pace, head to Wanaka Lavender Farm to wander through the purple fields, talk to the farm animals and enjoy lavender ice-cream.

Of course, Wanaka is also home to a hashtag – #thatwanakatree – and photos of the curved willow standing alone in Lake Wanaka abound on social media. The associated popularity has damaged the tree, with people trying to climb it even though it's in the lake. If you really are keen to snap a pic of it, expect crowds.

ELSEWHERE ON THE SOUTH ISLAND

📍 At the top of the South Island, the **Marlborough region** is renowned for its wineries and particularly its sauvignon blanc, but you probably don't want to spend your holiday dragging the kids from one winery to the next. That's okay, because even if you're not doing the wineries it's still a fabulous region to visit. You can take scenic cruises around the **Marlborough Sounds**; its islands are safe havens for wildlife and you can cruise to **Motuara Island** or, near Picton, **Kaipupu Wildlife Sanctuary**. Walk the trails of the region, including **Snout Track**, also near Picton, which takes you up to the **Queen Charlotte View Lookout** – from the carpark it's about a three-hour-return walk, but it's shorter than doing the 70km Queen Charlotte Track! For more natural beauty, explore Pelorus Bridge Scenic Reserve, another site featured in *The Hobbit* films.

See World War I and II history in memorials dotted throughout the region and by visiting the **Omaka Aviation Heritage Centre** in Blenheim. And for some play time, wander the kid-friendly **Picton Foreshore** with its playground, water-play area, model train and sandy beach.

📍 At the opposite end of the South Island is **Dunedin**, or Ōtepoti. Known as a university town – it's home to the University of Otago – Dunedin is a party town at times, mainly because its students, like students all around the world, do like to party (couch burning in Dunedin is a favourite pastime). However, this is a great place to visit – it has a strong Māori and Scottish heritage and curves around a beautiful harbour. It has all the beautiful nature and picturesque views you will have come to expect from New Zealand, and it's an excellent spot for cycling and mountain-biking, hiking and spotting wildlife – visit **Orokonui Ecosanctuary** just outside of Dunedin to see some of New Zealand's rare creatures. The city has stunning beaches nearby; **St Clair Beach** has great surf while **Brighton Beach** is in a more sheltered bay and is a little more kid friendly. Dunedin is a quirky, creative city and it's worth following its **Street Art Trail** featuring 25 vibrant artworks (go on a guided tour or get a map from the Dunedin i-SITE Visitor Centre). For a bit of Scotland in New Zealand, visit **Larnach Castle**. The country's only castle was built in 1871 and has been beautifully restored. You can explore the castle, wander its beautiful gardens and even stay overnight in accommodation in the grounds.

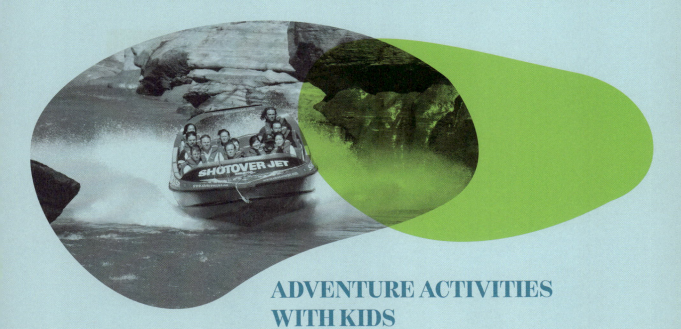

ADVENTURE ACTIVITIES WITH KIDS

As soon as your first child is born you become very aware of how much things hurt. You try not to get worried when they face-plant the coffee table while dancing along to the Wiggles and you want to protect them from absolutely everything. We found it hard to let the kids walk along high brick walls and jump from the top level at the playground, but we knew it was all about letting them have a go and manage (sensible) risk themselves. Of course, we always watched with bated breath! The same goes for activities that have the fear factor or are adrenalin pumping. All adventure activities in New Zealand will have an age guide, and common sense must prevail – like, would a three-year-old really like to bungy jump even if the guide says a three-year-old can? We always look for companies that pride themselves on safety, companies that make sure their equipment is well looked after and offer enough training and assistance and double-check everything before the activity starts. If you do the same, while you'll still watch with bated breath, you will have ticked the boxes. Oscar has recently mentioned he wants to skydive at 12. Brij is still thinking about it … we'll keep you posted.

BALI IS LIKE A CHEESE TOASTIE ON A SUNDAY: EASY, COMFORTING AND INEXPENSIVE. YOU JUST KNOW IT'S GOING TO BE WHAT YOU NEED.

Aussies have been lapping it up in Bali for years. It's a beautiful Indonesian island that caters for both party-goers and families. It also has a fascinating history and a vibrant culture that has been strongly influenced by Hinduism.

The island is small enough to do some fantastic daytrips (we mention a couple on page 135). Choose the area you would most like to stay and head out from there.

Of course, Bali does have some animal attractions you may want to avoid for ethical reasons. Where an animal, such as a snake or monkey, is a tourist attraction it is usually treated very poorly and trained through punishment. Teach your child not to pay the animal's keeper, pose with animals or ride animals when holidaying in Bali.

With that said, Bali has so much more to offer than Bintang singlets and fake Rolexes. So, time to get into it with some of the island's best holiday regions, sights and activities!

ATTRACTIONS

📍 **Kuta**, **Legian** and **Seminyak** are three popular regions next to each other. It's cheaper to stay in Kuta, but there are plenty of accommodation options for all budgets in these areas. Here you'll find great nightlife, shopping and restaurants, but it is often crowded and, depending on the time of year, chockfull of Aussie sporting teams on rowdy end-of-season trips. It can be kid-friendly though: the **Hard Rock Hotel** in Kuta has a foam party for families as well as kids' clubs – basically, between the Roxity Kids Club, Lullaby Playroom and Tabu Teens Club the kids will be well and truly catered for. The Hard Rock Hotel also has an awesome water park with slides so the kids will love it. For another water park, head to Kuta's **Waterbom Bali**, which will be a huge hit with the kids and adults. Set in lush tropical gardens, it has water slides and pools for everyone. Little ones can splash about in the toddler pools while adults kick back on the plentiful sun lounges.

📍 **Nusa Dua** is great for families, mainly because it's a little further away from the action of Kuta (there is a free shuttle to the malls so everything is still within reach). It's the place to be for a relaxing holiday with huge pools and great beaches. The **Laguna Resort and Spa** here is excellent as is **Club Med Bali**, which has all-inclusive meals, open bar, watersports and kids' club (for ages four to 17).

📍 **Ubud** is a touch more boutique and a little less touristy, and has lots of sightseeing like rice fields, temples, the stunning **Tegenungan Waterfall**, health resorts, yoga retreats, biking and markets.

📍 **Sanur** has calmer waters making it better for younger kids. It's not far from the airport and Kuta, and it's easy to hire a bike to ride around exploring. Try the **Byrdhouse Beach Club** as it has a playground and toddler-friendly pool and, if the kids are up for it, you can find kid yoga classes.

- Each of the above regions has great accommodation options. Of course, a private villa with your own staff, pool, chef and security is pretty hard to beat when thinking about a relaxing holiday. With villas, there are many options to choose from, starting with four people and up to groups or families. There are also resort options, which are great if you want to stay somewhere with a kids' club.

- When you're not getting massages, pedicures and braids, you can venture around Bali for all things **watersports** – you'll find everything here, from paddle-boarding, wake-boarding and kite-surfing to banana-boating, sea walking and jet-packs or fly-boarding. Make sure you choose a reputable company for the more adventurous activities, particularly with the kids. A few years ago, one of our friends decided to go parasailing on a beautiful Bali beach. Something went wrong – either he wasn't harnessed correctly or the boat didn't take off fast enough as he was lifting off from the sand – and he went up in the air then landed back down on his head with a thud. He was very lucky to escape with no injuries. We can laugh about it now, but it always makes us think about the risks we tend to take when on holidays. Remember, your passport doesn't make you bulletproof!

- To give the kids insight into Bali beyond the tourist centres, go to the cliff-top **Uluwatu Temple**, thought to be around a thousand years old. The kids will love spying on the monkeys (macaques) who are free to roam. Definitely resist the urge to feed them and ensure the kids know not to get too close (the monkeys have been known to climb up people to get sunglasses, cameras and caps). Don't take food or any loose items with you, take off any hanging jewellery and keep your bags well and truly zipped up.

- If you have time for daytrips away from where you're staying, consider hiring a private car and driver to take you around the island. Pick out your desired destinations and get a local's perspective. Visit markets, temples, beach clubs and all the attractions in your time. Or catch a boat to visit some of the nearby islands. Head to the chillaxed island of **Nusa Lembongan** for beautiful white-sand beaches – hang out at **Dream Beach** (the name says it all). Or try **Blue Lagoon** in **Nusa Ceningan**, although posting pics from here may get you unfollowed by friends back home shivering through winter. If one beach isn't enough, there are tour operators who will take you island-hopping for the day.

- There are many other things to do with kids on this beautiful island. Take some time to venture away from the beach to:

  - go river-rafting on the Ayung River near Ubud or on the Telaga Waja River for something more challenging
  - visit Toya Bungkah, Kintamani, for hot springs and cool-water pools
  - learn to surf at Rip Curl School of Surf in Legian near Kuta
  - shop for souvenirs from local artists
  - go on a bike tour
  - visit the stunning Nungnung Waterfall, about an hour from Ubud.

KID-FREE NIGHT OUT

Chilling out beachside with tapas on the menu and signature cocktails delivered to your seats screams adults' time. **El Kabron** is pretty cool; it's open until 10pm and is a spectacular place to enjoy the sunset, sit by the infinity pool overlooking the Indian Ocean or try the Spanish-inspired restaurant for amazing food. It's a 30-minute drive south from Seminyak and you'll need to organise your own transport. While ride-share options can drop you off, only taxis can take you home.

Missing the footy back home? The **Bamboo Bar** in Kuta has just what you are looking for. The bar is Australian owned and operated and you will be sure to catch live sports here in a friendly atmosphere.

ISLAND RESORTS

Oh, sweet resort holidays. Where books get read, poolside drinks are sipped and kids play to their hearts' content knowing there are no stuffy, boring old museums they're going to be dragged along to.

Dip those toes in turquoise sparkling waters, snorkel in the coral wonderlands, get a massage and eat incredibly delicious tropical cuisine. When the kids are young, some places offer day-time nannies; when they get a bit older there are all-day kids' clubs. If sun, fun and easy is what you're after, it's all to be discovered on a tropical island.

Most resorts will have deals, such as book for a number of nights and get one night free, or combined food and beverage packages or upgrades. Check the resort websites for the latest packages they offer.

Like any tropical location, there are illnesses to be aware of, from malaria to gastro. Check with your doctor to see if you require any immunisations for the country you are visiting as some diseases can be serious, even fatal. Make sure you pack the first-aid kit, mozzie repellent, sunscreen, hats and sun-safe shirts. It's all fun until someone gets sunburnt and they can't go out in the sun for the rest of the trip. When Pete's mate Kieran was 13, he fell asleep on an inflatable lilo in a hotel pool in Hawaii. Silly bloke didn't slip, slop, slap and had to fly home red raw and sore in a middle seat.

FIJI CONSISTS OF MORE THAN 300 ISLANDS WITH BEAUTIFUL LANDSCAPES, LAGOONS, PALM-LINED BEACHES AND COLOURFUL CORAL REEFS.

This South Pacific nation has a rich culture and heritage that is visible throughout the country. Viti Levu is the largest of Fiji's islands and is home to the capital, Suva. Most flights arrive and depart from the Nadi International Airport on the western side of Viti Levu.

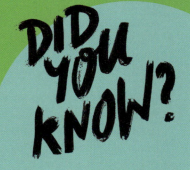

- The island of Taveuni is the place where you can be in two days at once. The International Date Line crosses Taveuni so there are two time zones. This will mess with the kids' minds in a very cute way.
- In Fiji, the village chief is the only one allowed to wear a hat. Earlier we mentioned putting on a hat to avoid sunburn, but if you're visiting a village take it off as it is considered an insult to the chief. As is wearing your shoes in a bure (hut), so hat and shoes off. Might be best to play it safe and just get nude!

ATTRACTIONS

- Viti Levu has plenty of big resorts and all offer great options for kids, including nannies and kids' clubs. If you want to head off Viti Levu, there are many other islands to choose from, many with resorts. Depending on your budget you can get anything you desire: private pools, all-inclusive beachfront bures and more. We share our favourite resorts but first we touch on what else you can do on **Viti Levu** when the kids' clubs, pools and water activities have had a fair run and you're ready for a change of scenery.

- The kids will love easy daytrips exploring Fiji's mountains, small villages and rainforests. We can recommend a couple of off-resort trips worth doing. First, visit **Kula WILD Adventure Park**, which is about 90 minutes from Nadi. It's the biggest family fun park in Fiji and has adventure activities, nature trails and wildlife enclosures – it's a great spot to see native Fijian animal species. And **Kila Eco Adventure Park**, about 22km from Suva, is a great place for thrills, with Fiji's longest zipline, a giant swing, ropes courses and abseiling.

- Fiji's highest mountain is **Mount Tomanivi**, an extinct volcano in northern Viti Levu. You can hike to the summit (from the village of Navai), but it's a challenging walk that can take between four and six hours return. We recommend a guide and perhaps saving it for another time if you have young kids and if you're not all experienced bushwalkers.

- If you're staying near **Suva**, head to the festive **Suva Markets** to pick up some local produce (there'll be fruit there the kids will never have seen), have a fresh pineapple juice and get a feel for the Fijian way of life. Other things you might want to do away from the beach and your resort are:
  - shop at Port Denarau
  - watch a traditional fire show
  - eat lovo, a feast of meat and vegetables cooked in the ground
  - book an authentic village tour
  - go hiking
  - watch the sunrise.

Now, to the resorts! Here are some of our favourite Fijian resorts.

- **Jean-Michel Cousteau resort** on Savusavu is about an hour from Nadi or Suva airports and is a sustainable resort with eco-friendly services. We visited here when Liam and Aidan were young and *mostly* happy to be at the Bula Bula Club for part of the day. Be aware there is a no-kids-allowed pool and area, and they do enforce it. The family pool has a 20m slide. Kids will enjoy the kids' club and the educational parts that go with it. Children under six are assigned their own nanny, and the kids' and teens' clubs run from 8.30am to 9pm. All à la carte meals and afternoon tea, bottled non-alcoholic beverages, specialty teas and espresso coffees are inclusive.

- **Kokomo Private Island** is accessible by sea plane. This is a great place to consider if you've been following the Barefoot Investor and put some holiday money aside. With the all-inclusive meals and nanny service, pools, tennis, sailing, beach games, watersports and a kids' club, everyone will be happy here. As an added bonus you can drive the kids mad by singing the Beach Boy's classic 'Kokomo' all day long with improvised rap interludes. Accommodation consists of beachfront villas or luxury residences. Travel by boat for a nearby trek to a stunning waterfall, head out on a glass-bottom boat or go harder on the banana floatable.

📍 **Malolo Island resort** is a great place for families with teenagers; the family bure is spacious enough for those growing limbs. They offer a wet-weather program for everyone, because sometimes when it rains it pours and you'll want to find something else to do. Along with all the typical watersports and activities Fijian resorts offer, there is Khail's Club, an air-conditioned lounge for teenagers aged between 13 and 18, with table tennis and other games, huge bean-bag lounges, satellite TV and free wifi. The little ones won't miss out. They can have fun in Tia's Treehouse, with a seven-day program focusing on different themes – four- to 12-year-olds will love it here. Children under four will need a nanny or parent to participate.

📍 **Outrigger Fiji Beach resort** on the coral coast of Viti Levu offers a teens' club for those 13 and over (for a fee). Activities include spear-making, sand-dune adventures, Tavuni Hill Fort tour, Bebe Hill hike and Enchanted Pool hike.

📍 **Cloud 9** is not a resort but a fun must-do – a two-level floating bar and pizzeria, where kids are welcome and you can even jump off the pontoon into the crystal-blue water. It's about a ten-minute fast boat from Plantation Island resort and Musket Cove resort. You can get there from other resorts too; just ask your concierge for details.

📍 **Plantation Island resort** on Malolo LaiLai Island is only ten minutes by air from Nadi International Airport. It has kids' and teens' clubs, watersports (of course), cooking lessons and tours to name just a little of what's on offer. Children under 16 stay for free when sharing the same room as the parents. The water park on-site has an age restriction: it's for kids aged between five and 16. Teenagers will have fun in the teenage club (12–16) with sports like water polo and fun activities like minigolf.

📍 **Shangri-La Fijian resort** on Yanuca Island has a sea-sports centre. Kids aged between two and 12 eat free; the water park is for ages seven and up. It will take about 50 minutes to get here from Nadi International Airport, and you can organise a transfer with the hotel for a fee.

📍 **Six Senses Fiji** on Malolo Island will treat you well. With your own lap pool and absolutely everything watersports available, and even an outdoor cinema, you can very much enjoy this holiday. Kids are well looked after with the kids' club and under fours have a complimentary nanny from 9am to 5pm. You can learn to surf, paddle-board, Hobie Cat and more. Breakfast is included and children under five eat free.

📍 **Vomo resort** on Vomo Island is 15 minutes from Nadi International Airport via helicopter and approximately 75 minutes via sea transfers. All meals, non-alcoholic beverages, wifi, daily laundry service, non-motorised watersports and use of the golf course, gym and tennis court are included, along with a weekly Fijian cultural show and Fijian Lovo feast on Thursday nights. The resort has a kids' village, which is a fantastic place for the kids to hang. Kids aged four and over can play at the kids' village without parents from 9am to 9pm with some breaks for lunch and bath time. Children under four require parent or baby-butler supervision. The kids' village has a dedicated chef and activities such as drumming lessons. Children over ten can try the PADI Discover Scuba Diving course.

Oscar's Day Not To Be Remembered
(By Pete)

There's no denying it. Fiji is popular with Aussie families because it can be done cheaply and because Fijians love your kids even more than you do. Yep, I know you love your kids – we all love our kids – but Fijians love them even more!

We were excited to be back in Fiji and keen to have some Pete and Brij time. Now, I don't mean that to sound like we were looking for romance. Really we were just longing for some time when we didn't have the kids clinging onto us, swinging from our forearms, surrounding us like a slips cordon while we were on the loo, asking 'What are we having for lunch?', 'When is lunch?', 'Can I sleep in the other bed tonight?' ... as fellow parents I'm sure you understand.

Admittedly this was more of an issue for Brij, whose visits to the toilet had begun to resemble a media conference full of junior cadets. For some reason, the boys were less keen on circling the crapper when Dad was sitting on the throne.

So one fine, sunny Fijian day we decided Liam and Aidan could spend the afternoon at the Bula Bula Club, which I think translates as the Hello Hello Club. For Oscar, still a bub, we hired a babysitter, a local woman named Kelera who, we think, had somewhere between eight and 32 kids of her own, judging from her expertise.

Kelera had a smile as wide as Luna Park and a laugh as infectious as the common cold. She was delightful and clearly loved kids, tussling Oscar's white blonde hair, pinching his rosy cheeks and tickling his pot tummy, giggling all the while.

Secure in the knowledge that Oscar could not be in better hands (including possibly ours) we set off for a relaxing kid-free afternoon. After walking along the beach and enjoying a cheeky beer or two by the pool, we decided that kayaking would be a fun thing to do.

We thought we'd paddle for twenty minutes one way, turn around and paddle twenty minutes the other, and that way we'd be back at the time we'd told Kelera. The problem with this is when we paddled for the first twenty minutes we were paddling with the tide. Our oars cut through the water like hot knives through butter.

'We are killing this!' I remember boasting.

'Olympics here we come!' Brij may or may not have screamed triumphantly.

Then, after a PB-setting twenty minutes, we turned around. Suddenly we weren't slicing butter with hot knives but rather paddling with hammers through honey. It was taking much longer, and much more effort, than we had anticipated. We had forgotten to factor in paddling against the tide on the way back.

At long last we made it back to the beach and rushed to our room, which, to our shock, was empty. 'Oscar!' Brij might have shouted. Then we remembered that Kelera had said she might take Oscar for a short stroll. Lo and behold, before we could say 'bula bula', in walked a beaming Kelera and a happy Oscar.

'We had the best day,' announced Kelera proudly. 'We took the bus, we went to my village, my family all love Oscar!'

'I'm sorry, you what?!' I think we both said at the same time.

It turned out that the little stroll involved a bus and a new family! Oscar has no memory of this but we can only imagine how many times his little cheeks were pinched, his hair tussled and his belly tickled.

We loved Kelera and were very grateful for the day she gave Oscar but, with that said, you may want to check how far the babysitter is planning on strolling with your bub ... and set some limits.

SINGAPORE

CLEAN FREAKS AND GERMAPHOBES, DO WE HAVE THE PLACE FOR YOU!

Singapore, an island city off southern Malaysia, is a city, island and country, and is possibly the cleanest city, island and country in the world. If the Tidy Town campaign played out on a global scale then Singapore would be the Roger Federer of Tidy Towns (they have a ban on chewing gum!). It also has a year-round summer, which helps with packing the suitcase too.

With its fascinating history, multicultural population and vibrant culture, it's a great place to take the kids, either on a stopover or as a destination. It's hard to pinpoint our favourite thing about Singapore because visiting there is always a pleasure. The people are fantastic and friendly, and eateries such as hawker centres and food courts are everywhere – you'll find some of the most delicious food at very cheap prices. One of the best things about Singapore is that it's oh so easy to explore with kids. Getting to subway platforms or finding a share ride with car seats is easy, visiting attractions and learning about local cultures is fun, and the locals love kids and sometimes hand out small gifts to the little ones. A week here just won't feel long enough.

GETTING AROUND

Get your Singapore Tourist Pass (STP) and select your desired length of time (one to three days) for unlimited travel on buses and trains. Upgrade to the Plus Pass to get offers on dining, shopping and entertainment around the city. You will find these cards at ticket offices and automatic kiosks. Trains are the best way to get around, but like any big city there will be crowds at peak times so plan to avoid this if you have little kids.

Some ride share companies have booster-seat bookings available; look at GrabFamily, which advertises booster and car seats for kids aged between one and seven, and also offer cars for six passengers. For taxis you'll need to have your own booster and car seats.

EATING OUT

Head to **Chinatown** for delicious food. Our favourite place to hang out and eat is at one of Chinatown's **hawker centres**. You won't have much trouble finding one as they are everywhere. Choose a food stall that is busy – this is one instance where Brij doesn't mind queuing, because the food is nearly always amazing. And for the best street barbecue and satay, go to **Lau Pa Sat satay street** at 18 Raffles Quay. The street closes to traffic from 7pm until late every night – take a seat anywhere and then go and select your satay. You can also order other dishes from people walking around with menus and find the bar waitress for drinks.

ACCOMMODATION

On Sentosa Island you'll find classic resort hotels with waterslides. These hotels are close to the adventure-park activities kids love. Having said that, we actually prefer to stay on the mainland and commute to Sentosa as there is so much to do in Singapore that getting from Sentosa and back every day will become a bit annoying. If you want city action, Downtown is the area to stay. The city skyline is magnificent and this is where the world-famous Marina Bay Sands Hotel is located. You'll find plenty of family friendly accommodation from Orchard Road all the way to Marina Bay.

ATTRACTIONS

- Kids will love the many kid-friendly attractions the city has to offer, from theme parks to gardens, towers, history and delicious food. Head down to **Orchard Street** where this shopping strip offers luxury retail and lots of kid-friendly activities. Let your kids go silly at **Amazonia**, an indoor playground where they can climb the walls with slides, navigate mazes and run across bridges (for kids aged between three and 12).

- For more shopping, go to **Chinatown** and **Little India**. In Little India you'll find one of our favourites, the **Mustafa Centre**, which is the best for bargains and souvenir shops. Here the kids will find something great to take back to the classroom.

- Beside the shopping and eating, **Chinatown** is a great place to visit with the kids because it's full of history. Learn about the Samsui women, immigrants from China who did hard labour in construction. Or take a walking tour because the streets have many stories to tell; look for a free or self-guided walking tour or get a local tour guide to show you around. Include a visit to the **Chinatown Heritage Centre**, where you'll hear the fascinating stories of the people who made the difficult journey to call Singapore home.

- The **Singapore Botanic Gardens**, just nearby, are fun to explore and offer a peaceful escape from the city's buzz. This tropical garden is Singapore's first World Heritage site, listed in 2015, and was first established in 1858 on an old plantation. You can take a tour to see the exquisite gardens or let the kids run free in the excellent Children's Garden, which features nature play areas, a suspension bridge, streams, treehouses, a farm and a forest.

- Keep the nature experiences coming at **Gardens by the Bay**. Wander through the beautiful Floral Dome or the mystical Cloud Forest, or walk the 22m high Skywalk through the constructed Supertree Grove. The Cloud Forest was our favourite: it hosts a 35m mountain with the world's tallest indoor waterfall and you can follow a path that weaves in and around the mountain. It's also a great place to cool down on those hot humid Singaporean days. The whole family can get involved in doing a garden make-over design activity here – pick and choose your favourite bits and design your dream-home garden. Save exploring the Children's Garden for last, as the kids won't want to leave – it has a water park and playgrounds geared to different ages. There are also options for behind-the-scenes tours and a little garden cruiser tour that will save little legs from getting too tired. There's so much to see – make sure you pace yourself to see all the sections you want to and remember to pack the swimmers for the Children's Garden. If you're visiting in the evening, stay around for the Garden Rhapsody show in the Supertree Grove – the 50m tall 'supertrees' are illuminated in a blast of

colours (the show starts around 7.45pm – check the program). Just magical.

- For a free and amazing view of the city skyline, head to the **Marina Barrage**, just near the Gardens by the Bay. This reservoir facility is a great example of Singapore's desire to become a greener country; not only does the facility store water and control floods, it also has a fantastic green rooftop, which is a great place to take the family for a picnic, to fly a kite or to simply enjoy the views. It's open 24 hours a day, every day of the week.

- The nearby **Marina Bay Sands** offers accommodation, shopping, restaurants, the ArtScience Museum and a theatre, with stage shows suitable for kids. And at the end of it all, head up 57 storeys to the Skypark Observation Deck for absolutely amazing views of this wonderful city.

- **Singapore Zoo** is much more than just a zoo – it often hosts wonderful shows and events – and has 11 zones representing different wildlife habitats around the world. We suggest planning your visit ahead of time to make the most of it, especially with kids. Jump on the website and use the handy planning tool to map out a great day taking in all the animals and attractions. Plan extra fun bits regularly to keep the kids' legs motivated, as there will be lots of walking involved. You can also explore the park by tram. The high-ropes course and the water-play area in the Rainforest Kidzworld section will keep the kids happy, and you can give your own legs a rest. For something a bit different the zoo has Night Safari, a spectacular night-time wildlife park featuring nocturnal animals. You will need to book ahead for tours and tickets, and remember when planning your visit that it will take around 40 minutes by car to reach the zoo from the city.

- **Singapore Wake Park** is a cable-ski park – go here to get your heart rate up! This place will impress older kids and teens in particular, although kids over six can participate. With experiences for complete beginners and up, step outside your comfort zone and have some family fun.

- Indulging in a Singapore Sling at the historic **Raffles Long Bar** is a highlight, so head there with a plan in mind for something the kids can do at the table while you soak in the wonderful atmosphere and the cocktails. You'll see the Raffles name around Singapore a lot – Sir Stamford Raffles founded modern Singapore in 1819 – and the Singapore Sling was created by a Raffles bartender back in 1915. The Raffles Hotel is a beautiful building and the Long Bar is a popular place to visit, so if you see a queue, it's quite likely you'll be there quite a while waiting for a seat. Because Brij isn't a huge fan of queues, we decided to head to the **Fullerton Bay Hotel** instead for a Singapore Sling. It may not have as much history as the Raffles version but the hotel also offers a Sydney Sling, which is a mocktail version and will keep the kids happy. If you skipped lunch, the afternoon tea at the hotel's Landing Point restaurant is delicious.

- Singapore is diverse and welcoming, and you'll find many temples to visit, such as **Thian Hock Keng Temple**, **Buddha Tooth Relic Temple** and, our favourite, **Sri Mariamman Temple**, the oldest Hindu temple in Singapore. Located in Chinatown, it has an unmissable elaborate entrance. You are welcome to enter, and can involve yourself with prayer or blessings if you would like, but remember to remove your shoes before entering.

- Take a long walk and soak in some nature at **Southern Ridges**, a 10km stretch of green space joining five different parks. It's a good chance for kids to reconnect with nature or to use up excess energy. If you want to walk the entire ridges trail, it's long (10km), but it has a bunch of bridges and pathways through different gardens that will keep you interested, and there are shorter options available too.

- At **Haw Par Villa**, not far from the Southern Ridges, the kids will have a lot of fun checking out the interesting statues that fill the park. Check the website for park events, such as Dia De Muertos Fiesta, the Mexican Day of the Dead celebration that includes piñatas and face-painting. Entry into the park is free, but you'll need to buy tickets for some of the events. Aw Boon Haw, the man who invented Tiger Balm, created the park's eclectic outdoor gallery in 1937 to showcase Chinese history and it's filled with monuments dedicated to him and his family.

- A perfect daytrip from Singapore is **Sentosa Island**. Known as 'Singapore's Playground', this place has something for everyone – an aquarium, an adventure park, beaches, water parks ... the list goes on. Sit down with the family and have a 'choose your own adventure' day, with each family member choosing a place to visit. Make sure you visit the Merlion, though – this climbable 'guardian of prosperity' has a great story the kids will love. The Megazip and Megaclimb are also great fun (check online for ticket deals) and we recommend getting more than one ride on the zipline. For a little skydiving fun, iFly is here and is a great way to pretend you really went skydiving. Getting to the island is easy: a taxi is relatively cheap and you pay just a small fee to enter at the island's entrance. You can also take the Sentosa Express from Harbour Front Station or catch the cable car. You can explore Sentosa all day without even heading to a theme park, so plan your day before you visit, and look for ticket deals online before you go.

- Jump on a ten-minute ferry ride to the island of **Pulau Ubin** for a daytrip to an authentic village. Hire a bike once you're there and head off on an adventure. You can also hike, kayak and even camp on the island. Stroll along the boardwalk at the island's Chek Jawa Wetlands and wander around the granite quarries of the past (please remember they are not safe for swimming in).

KID-FREE NIGHT OUT

Avoid the crowds (and in some cases the cover charges) of rooftop bars and visit the secret bars Singapore has to offer. The speakeasy trend is alive and well here with bars like **Employees Only** and **Operation Dagger** offering innovative cocktails and excellent service. Half the fun is actually finding the places. Or try **Orchard Road** where the strip is packed with bars, lounges and even nightclubs. Just off Orchard Road is **Emerald Hill Road**, which is less busy and has interesting historic buildings that will happily house you for the night out. Lastly, all the five-star hotels have some pretty wonderful cocktail bars now; check out the **Grand Hyatt** during happy hour.

THAILAND IS A POPULAR AND AFFORDABLE FAMILY HOLIDAY DESTINATION.

You can train or fly to various destinations within the country easily enough, enjoying city, jungle and beach life all on the one holiday.

Most people think of the beaches when they think of Thailand and for good reason – the beaches are spectacular. The most popular islands with great beaches are **Phuket**, **Koh Samui** and **Koh Phi Phi**. Some of the most beautiful beaches include **Maya Bay** on Phi Phi, which featured in the book *The Beach* and then in the Leonardo DiCaprio movie that followed. **Freedom Beach** on Phuket has soft white sand with a backdrop of jungle and hills. The lovely **Sunrise Beach** is also on Phuket. The island of **Koh Phangan** is becoming more popular and its beautifully secluded **Bottle Beach** is only accessible by boat. The island is largely made up of granite and lush tropical jungle and, with its white-sand beaches, including the stunning **Haad Yao**, and over 20 dive sites, it is a quiet tropical paradise.

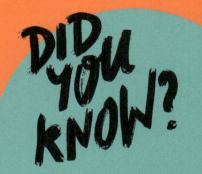

DID YOU KNOW?

- Bird's nest soup is considered a cure-all in Thailand. Tiny birds build nests made only from their saliva high in caves along the ocean; the nests are then gathered after the babies have left. This delicacy will cost you a bit of money so consider who in your family will be daring enough to take it on. We actually wouldn't recommend trying it regardless of the price, because the welfare of the birds and the workers collecting the nests can be compromised. And remember, there is always ice-cream to be found somewhere.
- The waterfall-climbing cave fish, also known as the cave angel fish, can walk on land. Protected by the Thai government, this fish with no eyes climbs waterfalls and is only found in a few caves. Surely a Marvel superhero waiting to happen.

ATTRACTIONS

- Thailand is more than Bangkok and beach islands. Consider visiting **Chiang Mai** when planning your trip to Thailand. This beautiful city, set in the mountains of northern Thailand, is home to stunning temples along with Wiang Kum Kam (an ancient city from the 8th century) and some of the best street food you'll find. It's almost a nine-hour drive from Bangkok, or you can fly or take the train. There's also a lot here to interest kids. Go on the incredible **Chiang Mai Night Safari**, explore the jungle on an eco-friendly adventure trek, get your extreme-sports buzz at the **Chiang Mai X-Centre** and wander the **canopy walk** in the **Queen Sirikit Botanical Garden**. Chiang Mai also has the **Elephant Jungle Sanctuary**, home to over 60 formerly mistreated elephants from the logging and tourism industries. You can visit to see the elephants, who are now free to enjoy their lives and date whoever they like!

- **Phuket** is a fun island to visit with kids. It has the upside-down house of **Baan Teelanka Baan** in Phuket town – search for a way out in the escape room by solving the riddles. Learn to surf at **Surf House Flow Rider** in Kata Beach, or go scooting down waterslides and relax in pools and float in tubes at **Splash Jungle Water Park**. If that's not enough activity to wear out the kids, try Zorbing (sphering) at **Rollerball**.

- **Koh Samui** is a great island with lots of things for families to do. **Chaweng** is its most popular beach with some smaller waves, and there are a variety of shops and restaurants. Chaweng also has **Aquapark**, a water park with a water trampoline and huge floats. **Pink Elephant Samui** is another water park on the island, with big water slides, kids' lagoons, an adults-only jacuzzi area and food on-site. For a calmer playtime and shallow water, the little kids will love **Mae Nam Beach**.

THAI RESORTS

Thailand is a great place for resort holidays. Here are some top family-friendly resorts.

Centara Grand Beach resort in Phuket is right on Karon Beach. Along with all the watersports you'll want, there is a kids' club and a teens' club. The resort has two lagoon pools, a water park and Thai kickboxing lessons (so you can work off those cocktails).

Intercontinental Koh Samui resort has two kids' clubs, nannies and babysitter services. There are seven pools to try out here, with a toddler pool attached. Teenagers will enjoy the Thai kickboxing classes.

Katathani Phuket Beach resort has four kids' pools, two water springs and a water slide. The resort has character rooms, which will delight the kids after a big day at the kids' club. Teenagers might prefer to stay somewhere closer to the action, though.

Movenpick Resort Phuket caters for the little kids very well, with high chairs, pushers, kids' cutlery, portable baby baths and more. Little Birds Club will entertain kids aged four to 12 as well as provide activities the whole family can do together. The main swimming pool has a water slide and water activities daily. This resort is only ten minutes from Patong Beach.

Outrigger Laguna Phuket Beach resort has a 55m water slide in the kids' pool. Koh Kids Club is for ages four to 12 and has a fun daily activity program. There is a babysitting service available for under fours and a games room for the older kids.

BANGKOK

IF YOU HAVE THE TIME,

explore the colourful, bustling, enchanting city of Bangkok, which welcomes more visitors than *any* other city in the world. Considering you will probably be flying in or out of the Thai capital city, ensure there are days spare on either end of your holiday to check out this sprawling metropolis. From temples and palaces to museums and parks, the city has much to offer – and, good lord, don't forget the shopping, both at markets and in climate-controlled mega-malls that feel as big as cities themselves. Another highlight of this great city is the nightlife – just don't go too *Hangover 3* on us. If you wake up with face tattoos or Mike Tyson's tiger in your hotel room, that's on you! Nightlife or not, this is a fascinating place to explore with kids.

Definitely visit the impressive **Grand Palace**, which was built in 1782. The wows will keep coming here from the shiny gold spires and stunning architecture to an ancient emerald Buddha. For older kids, download the map before you visit, get them a highlighter and have them test their navigation and mapping skills by highlighting the route as you walk. There is a strict dress-code here (no tank tops, no thongs or sandals – you'll need socks if you're wearing sandals); if needed you can hire clothes to cover up. Just near the Grand Palace is **Wat Pho** or the Temple of the Reclining Buddha. The 46m long Buddha is covered in gold leaf. Spectacular.

- A **Floating Market tour** with the family will be a day to remember. Get some inside info from a local as to which tour offers the best experience and then head out early. Take a guide with you if you want to learn more – or if you want the kids' questions directed to someone else!
- Other kid-friendly attractions include **KidZania**, where the kids can role-play the real world, and **Snowtown** – no, nothing to do with the infamous South Australian town, but an indoor themed village of artificial snow.
- It's hard to resist the shopping in Bangkok (make sure the kids have some spending money too). For high-end shopping go to **Siam Paragon**. For a wonderful Thai experience, head to **Chatuchak Weekend Market**. With more than 8000 stalls, this market is one of the largest in the world.
- For other classic Bangkok experiences that are good for kids:
  - see a traditional puppet show (check it's one that is suitable for kids)
  - take a boat down the Chao Phraya River
  - eat at Chinatown.
- If you have the time and energy for a daytrip, visit **Kanchanaburi**, about 150km west of Bangkok. It's a wonderful escape from the pace of Bangkok and is famous for its World War II history. The **Burma Railway** runs through the region and historical sites are everywhere including the **Kanchanaburi War Cemetery**, the **Death Railway Museum** and the famous **Bridge 277**, or **Bridge over River Kwai**, made famous in the movie *Kramer vs Kramer* (or was it *Bridge over the River Kwai*? Note to self: fact-check later.). As with any serious content, speak to your children first about what the history of the area involves. In Kanchanaburi you'll also see stunning natural beauty in **Sai Yok National Park** and may be lucky enough to spot some wild elephants, tigers or deer.

KID-FREE NIGHT OUT

Bangkok has so many rooftop bars – your hotel may just have the best one and, with a city skyline that lights up like a Christmas tree, it's worth heading up to take it all in. But if you want to leave your hotel, venture out to the **Skybar** at Lebua State Tower, where the *Hangover* boys hung out. It gets pretty packed with young professionals so you may be standing while enjoying your cocktail. But it is 63 storeys up and the view is undeniably breathtaking.

VIET NAM

VIETNAM IS A COUNTRY OF BEAUTIFUL CONTRASTS.

Dive into one of its incredible bustling micro-cities with all the modern perks and then drive to the edge of town to find elderly women working rice paddies with an ox in tow. Amazing landscapes, incredibly friendly locals, spectacular food – Vietnam absolutely deserves your consideration for a family holiday.

We visited Vietnam pre-kids and have been itching to get back there with the crew. On that first visit we were confronted with a temple that was said to inspire fertility. We ran through it as quickly as possible but, lo and behold, nine months later, Liam was born. Coincidence? Possibly, but a very happy one!

Our personal preference when travelling in Vietnam is to start in either Hanoi or Ho Chi Minh City and visit everything you have time for in between. Fly into one city and out of the other. You will need to take overnight trains or domestic flights to major cities. Domestic flights are cheap enough for families and probably a better option. Private cars are available for shorter trips or city tours, or book a family tour of the whole country.

Vietnam is quite large, so allow at least ten days to two weeks for your holiday if possible, but be prepared not to see everything. There are some great things to see either in cities or not far from them, but some sights will be a long car or train ride away. Plan the trip so you get plenty of rest time for the kids.

Vietnam is a multi-ethnic country with 54 ethnic groups recognised by the government. Each ethnic group has its own language and culture, so good luck learning all of those for your two-week tour!

Accommodation

You'll find it pretty easy to organise your accommodation in Vietnam, from connecting rooms in hotels, apartments or family rooms in resorts. The kids will love a homestay experience too, and there are many reputable homestay companies that can help with your family holiday.

In Hanoi, Somerset Grand Hanoi has a good range of accommodation and spacious apartments (small apartments usually have several rooms). In Hoi An, Four Seasons Resort is great – we love a hotel that gives kids toiletries. It's pricey but if you're looking to splurge this is a good one. In Nha Trang, you can stay at Vinpearl Resort. In Hue, La Residence Hue Hotel and Spa is good. Two hours from Ho Chi Minh City, Ho Tram Beach Boutique Resort and Spa is right on the beach and has private villas with their own plunge pools.

Attractions

Visit the many **night markets** in the bigger cities to see Vietnam life up close.

Vietnam is a country of **festivals**, so check out which festivals will be on when you visit, such as the **Lunar New Year**, the **Mid Autumn Festival**, the **Perfume Festival** or the **Hoi An Lantern Festival**.

For an unforgettable and authentic experience, consider a **homestay** with hill tribe families.

Visit **Phu Quoc island** for its beautiful **Long Beach** with luxurious beachfront resorts and restaurants, its traditional villages and its World Heritage–listed national park. A flight from Ho Chi Minh City takes about an hour.

For some adventure, sand-board at the **sand dunes of Mui Ne** and visit **Mui Ne Beach** for watersports and rock-free waters.

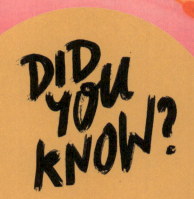

Did You Know?

- There are eight World Heritage sites in Vietnam: five cultural sites, two natural ones and one mixed one. And we're pretty sure they have at least one McDonald's.
- Vietnam's flag consists of a golden star with five points to represent farmers, workers, intellectuals, young people and soldiers. The red background pays tribute to the blood shed during the wars.
- Vietnam is home to water puppetry, an art form that began in the 11th century and one that, we assume, goes nuts on *Vietnam's Got Talent*.

HANOI

THE MOMENT you arrive you'll get a sense of how busy Hanoi is – this is actually the one and only place where Brij has experienced culture shock. We aren't sure why exactly because 45 minutes later she was walking the same busy streets in search of lunch. Despite those busy streets, the city is absolutely delightful, with small temples everywhere, narrow lanes, street food to enjoy, and the Old Quarter for shopping. The kids will be fascinated by the maze of streets and the different world in front of them – it's almost like they can play a real-life game of Frogger to get across the road.

For some Vietnamese culture, take the kids to the **Thang Long Water Puppets Theatre**. This art form was created centuries ago when the rice paddies flooded and the villagers needed entertainment. The show is relatively short, lasting around an hour, and offered at various times of the day. Book tickets ahead to get close to the front.

Hanoi has some incredible museums and one of the most interesting is the **Vietnam Museum of Ethnology**, which tells the stories of Vietnam's many ethnic groups and has something for everyone. Older children will enjoy the artefacts and meaning behind this museum that celebrates diversity. For your little kids, the outdoor area has huts on display representing various ways of living in Vietnam's history.

You'll struggle to eat better food while sitting on plastic furniture or possibly a milk crate than in Vietnam. Check out **Bia Hoi Junction** in Hanoi or try some local cooking classes with the kids.

Interested in getting into the wilderness? **Tac Bac Waterfalls** offer a hike through the forest and a swim in the rock pools. The natural hot springs are in **Ba Vi National Park**, which is about an hour and a half west of Hanoi. The kids will love a boat ride through the caves of **Ninh Binh**, about two hours south of Hanoi.

About 170km east of Hanoi is the beautiful **Halong Bay**. You've all seen the stunning pictures – the steep rise in tourism over the years has taken its toll on the bay but it is still an absolutely incredible sight. The World Heritage-listed bay has over 1600 limestone islands. If you're feeling fit enough, take the kids kayaking to really soak up the bay's beauty. Otherwise, jump aboard a boat and cruise Halong Bay with a little luxury. Some of the cruises offer kayaking so you can even have your rice paddy and eat it too! Some cruise companies have family cabins and specific family tours available.

DA NANG

ON THE
coast in central Vietnam, Da Nang was a French colonial port and is still an important port city for Vietnam today.

My Khe Beach and **Non Nuoc Beach** are perfect for a beach day out in Da Nang. Attack the hills at **Marble Mountains**; you can climb the stairs to the top but it's not ideal for younger children. Kids of all ages will enjoy **Asia Park Da Nang Amusement Park**.

Da Nang is home to the **Dragon Bridge**, the longest bridge in Vietnam – and as a bonus it's designed like a dragon. You could keep it a surprise – imagine the kids' faces as you drive over it! Time your visit to see the scheduled fire and water display for a real highlight. Everyone loves a dragon, and the display can be enjoyed from cafe locations along the water's edge or even from a boat if you're wanting to experience it from the water.

Head to **Phap Lam Pagoda** and get the kids to be the photographers for the visit. Then download a postcard app (Touchnote is good and easy to use) so they can send Buddha postcards home – the pagoda's golden laughing Buddha would make a great postcard and you'll get some time to enjoy the peaceful surrounds.

HOI AN

THIS COSMOPOLITAN
town is a fabulous place to visit and will be heaven for foodies.

Visit **An Bang Beach** for the day – it's great for swimming and paddle-boarding and there are a few resorts too. The kids will love a unique ride in a basket boat, or take them crabbing.

Got a wedding coming up and it's been a while since you busted out that suit or dress? Get tailor-made clothes in Hoi An – you can get them back in 24 hours. A suit or a special dress will require several fittings and can take up to five days, but you can get casual items quickly. It is totally worth it.

NHA TRANG

IN SOUTHERN VIETNAM,

Nha Trang is a beachside city sometimes referred to as the Riviera of the South China Sea. It is *very* easy to relax here.

Thap Ba Spa is a mineral mud spa and hot springs where the kids are welcome, finally. It's an experience that will leave everyone in the family with silky soft skin. The age limit is two and above, and it is not recommended for pregnant women.

A morning visit to **Nha Trang Beach** is a must. Head to one of the popular safe swimming sections and enjoy some fun in the sun. **Hon Chong Beach** is great for relaxing and the kids can explore along the rocks and white-sand beaches.

The huge and high **Vinpearl Cable Car** and the **Vinpearl Amusement Park** are going to capture the eye of the kids big and small. The cable-car travels over water from Nha Trang to Hon Tre Island where the amusement park is.

HUE

THIS HISTORIC

city in central Vietnam was once the imperial capital and is home to the World Heritage–listed **Imperial City** with its Royal Palace and hundreds of monuments and temples. You can tour the Imperial City and its ruins. Getting a child-friendly tour guide will enhance the experience and bring the place to life with fascinating stories.

Head to **Dong Ba Market** to experience an open-air market and all its colours, smells and vibrancy.

About three hours from Hue are **Son Doong Cave**, thought to be the largest natural cave in the world and around 400 million years old, and **Paradise Cave**, both in **Phong Nha-ke Bang National Park**. It would be amazing to explore Son Doong Cave but there's a waiting list of about two years, so you'll need to be patient (and pretty cashed up). And while there are other caves to visit, most of them have a minimum visitor age of ten. Your family may prefer to take a private national park tour, where you can see kid-friendly caves, zipline, kayak and more.

HO CHI MINH CITY

HO CHI MINH CITY, also known as Saigon, is a city famous for the crucial role it played in the Vietnam War. It is the hub of Vietnam for business and has a very prominent history. It is a popular tourist destination for everyone, especially families who can get a lot out of this amazing city.

The **Cu Chi Tunnels** run under the city and were used during the Vietnam War. They are a popular and fascinating tourist attraction and a great place to learn about Vietnam's past. Older children will really gain a deep insight into the war and the country's history, but perhaps talk to your younger kids first about what the tunnels were used for and what the tour might involve.

To experience the city like a local, visit **Cholon (Binh Tay market)** in the centre of Vietnam's largest Chinatown district. It has a range of foods from many regions across Vietnam. You'll find crafts, materials and little items to take home, but mostly it is a great way to experience the local lifestyle. With plenty of food on offer, get there early and grab some breakfast.

For some kid-focused fun, visit **Suoi Tien Cultural Theme Park** with rides to suit the whole family. It is themed to tell the history of Vietnam so you get a great sense of the country and its history while exploring the park. **Dam Sen Water Park** is another good spot to visit; its slides and pools make it a great place for cooling off on those warm days.

Do a **cyclo tour** of the city, especially as some of the riders will offer history and facts about the city as you ride along. Or try a **Mekong Delta river cruise**, where the kids will learn how important the river has been over the centuries.

If you have time for a daytrip from Ho Chi Minh City, treat the family to a private tour to **Ben Tre**, a journey along the Mekong Delta to a beautiful town. Catch the boat through the maze of waterways, seeing the different islands along the way. The kids will love trying the coconut candy.

A bit more than a daytrip but another fascinating experience for the kids would be to do a **homestay** on the Mekong Delta and immerse the family in a different way of life. This would be an experience to remember.

KID-FREE NIGHT OUT

In Ho Chi Minh City, **Pham Ngu Lao Street** in District 1 has alleys and laneways to meander around. You'll find a variety of restaurants, bars, cafes and souvenir shops. Check out some street vendors, enjoy some live music and find cheap drinks at the small pubs. For drinks on a rooftop with history, head to **Saigon Saigon** on the top of Caravelle Saigon, where war correspondents would meet and swap war stories over beers with a view. There are areas of the bar that are private and romantic.

JA
PAN

JAPAN RATES PRETTY HIGHLY AS A DESTINATION THAT CATERS FOR BOTH ADULTS AND KIDS ALIKE, AND THE FACT THAT IT DOESN'T HAVE A SPECIFIC TOURIST SEASON IS AN ADDED FEATURE.

Yep, Japan just does not switch off. The summer is sweltering, the winter is crisp and the cherry blossoms in spring bring people to Japan in a manner the band the Cherry Blossoms could only dream of.

We had heard about the famous Japanese hospitality and, lo and behold, the first time we emerged from the subway and unfolded our map (with four suitcases and three tired children), we were approached by a kind businessman who pointed us in the direction of our hotel – which was the exact opposite direction of where we were heading. Admittedly this only happened a couple more times during our two and a half weeks in Japan, but we like to think we equipped ourselves quickly and appeared less lost and desperate with each passing day.

DID YOU KNOW?

- Japanese farmers grow square watermelons for ease of stacking and storage – we too find that the most important thing we look for in our watermelon is functionality.
- The average delay for a Japanese train is just 18 seconds, which, sadly, drastically cuts down the number of excuses you can use for being late to work.
- Japan consists of over 6500 islands and is home to over 126 million people, so if one in every three of those people could buy this book that would be awesome.
- A department store in Kawasaki has the world's shortest escalator consisting of five stairs. It may also be the world's most pointless escalator.
- Baseball is Japan's most popular spectator sport.

For travelling with kids, Japan is without a doubt one of the easiest non-English-speaking countries we have visited. The country is so clean – take it from the germaphobe in the family, you will notice this immediately. It's astounding how clean Japan is given the number of people in its big cities and the fact there appear to be no bins around! The country also runs very efficiently. It has an unusual combination of pragmatism and straight out weird and wonderful.

Traditional Japanese accommodation is perfect for families; a tatami room in a ryokan (a traditional inn) has plenty of space and can be a new experience for kids. Regardless of age, your kids will love the lights, bizarre theatres, cafes and the picturesque ancient towns. And if your kids (or you …) love to sing, find yourself a karaoke parlour; settle in and Rock the Casbah or whatever karaoke classic you want to belt out. Many karaoke places welcome kids and many have songs in English. This is where Brij will belt out 'What's up' from 4 Non Blondes and Pete goes all bogan with 'Livin' on a Prayer' Bon Jovi style.

Nervous travellers may like to hear that Japan has the lowest crime rate in the world, so go with peace of mind. Of course, don't walk around with your wallet dangling out of your back pocket but fanny packs aren't required here.

Accommodation

Throughout Japan, if you are staying in a hotel with a pool, check the hotel's rules on swimming. Some will cost Yen to use but if you're a member of the hotel's group this cost may be waived. Some hotel pools don't allow children, which is not fun if you have children. Follow any rules given for the pool and cover up tattoos. (Dane Swan, if you're reading this, you may need to wear a full-body Thorpedo suit.)

Eating Out

Ramen is king in Japan and we had the best ramen in Hiroshima at **Ichiran Hiroshima Hondori Ekimae**. You order your ramen at a vending machine, then walk through to a slender booth with small bamboo draw curtains in front of you. You slide your ticket from the machine through to a mysterious hand that appears and literally a minute or two later you have your noodles and a cold beer or soft drink. Possibly the best fast food we've ever had!

None of us had experienced the food **okonomiyaki** before. A Japanese savoury pancake invented during World War II, it is sometimes referred to as Japanese pizza. The best place to try these is an actual 'food theme park' called **Okonomi-mura** at 5-13 Shintenchi in Naka-ku, Hiroshima. Here you'll find 24 tiny okonomiyaki restaurants each fitting only six to ten people. The chefs cook in front of you teppanyaki-style however you like it, which is where the name comes from (okonomi means 'how you like'). Toppings often include cabbage, cheese, green onion, meats and various seafood. These can vary around the country but our first and favourite will always be from Hiroshima.

GETTING TO JAPAN

Tokyo has two major airports: Haneda International and Narita International. Make sure you're aware of which one you are arriving in, especially if you have organised a car service or shuttle to escort you to your hotel.

Haneda is our preferred airport as it is closer to central Tokyo (about 25 minutes) and therefore quicker and cheaper to get to than Narita (over an hour). However, direct flights from your capital city may take you to Narita and we always prefer a direct flight, because less transit time with kids means a better start in the arrival destination. It's also worth being aware that you may arrive in one airport and fly out of the other. We had a near travel-crisis when we arrived at Haneda to find the Qantas check-in desk conspicuously empty. The flight board backed up our fears with no flight to Sydney showing up, and a quick check of our ticket confirmed it. Yep, we were at the wrong f&*%$@g airport. If it wasn't for the helpful woman (with the heels taller than a German stein) at the airport helpdesk who sprang into action and had us loaded onto the bus that runs between the two airports, we would have been not quite Banged Up Abroad but more Kicking Ourselves Abroad. That bus takes about an hour and 15 minutes.

GETTING AROUND

Purchase a Japan Rail (JR) Pass before leaving Australia (a travel agent can organise this for you). Choose from 7-, 14- or 21-day passes; you can get adult and child passes.

Once in Japan you need to validate your exchange order to receive your JR Pass, then you can book your train travel or travel on any local JR lines. You will need to show your passport as the pass is only available to temporary visitors. You fill in a quick application form and it's done – it's that easy. The JR Pass allows you unlimited travel on the entire national JR network including high-speed (shinkansen) train lines, which are incredible. Visit japanrailpass.net for a guide on how to collect your pass and how to reserve seats, along with tips for Japan and guidelines for the pass. Book your shinkansen seats at the ticket counter; we always did this a few days before because we knew where and when we were heading next.

There are great subway maps you can download for all of the cities you are visiting; we still like getting a paper version from the stations as it just makes it easier (and the kids can help out).

Getting around while breastfeeding was not something we had to consider as our boys were well and truly off the breast, but we are aware that the Japanese tend not to feed in public. The change and feeding rooms are so clean, mothers probably feel more comfortable feeding there than the hard bench outside. However, people who have fed in public just used a breastfeeding cover and it wasn't a problem.

ATTRACTIONS

- When kids think of Japan they most often think of ninjas! **Nagano** has the **Togakure Ninja Museum** (also called the Togakure Ninpo Museum) and a kids' **Ninja Village** to encourage your own little ninja. The museum will take you through the history of ninjas and ninja skills dating back to the 12th century. The building itself doesn't look too spectacular but the kids will especially love **Ninja House**, a maze of rooms, secret doors and contraptions that they need to get through. For a fee you can try throwing a star (shuriken) at the throwing range. The Ninja Village is set within a forest, consisting of obstacle courses and jungle gyms so everyone can pretend they are in ninja training. There will be snow in Nagano in winter so be prepared with the right clothes (as a bonus, the kids will love the snow monkeys).

- **Okinawa** is a group of islands off the southern point of Japan. The Okinawa region has a beautiful history and culture, and also crystal-clear waters at its beaches. The main (and largest) island is **Okinawa Island**: you'll need to fly to Okinawa or catch an express ferry from Kagoshima to Naha. **Bios no Oka**, an incredible Japanese garden and park, has a huge jungle playground and tram rides (and you can hire strollers at no cost). Although you can get regular ice-cream, try one of the fascinating desserts on offer at the garden's restaurant. Go canoeing and explore nature in **Yanbaru**, a mountainous region in the northern part of the island with tropical forests and gorgeous waterfalls. Learn about the island's royal history at historic **Shuri Castle**, and the kids can take part in some traditional crafts. And, like all other cities in Japan, you'll find good shopping in **Naha**.

SKIING IN JAPAN

Japan is known for the best powder skiing in the world, which means when you stack it on the slopes it shouldn't hurt quite as much as it does on Australian snowfields. Of course, you don't need to be a skier to spend time in Japan during winter – there are plenty of other things to do. If there are non-skiers in the group, look for resorts that have more options, such as onsens or being near snow monkeys, castles and quaint villages. Regardless of where you stay, the people are friendly, the food is incredible, the landscape is picturesque and the culture is wonderful.

Hokkaido is the second largest, most northern of the four main islands in Japan. The Hokkaido area has constant good snow, and is about a four-hour shinkansen ride to its capital, Sapporo, from Tokyo. Direct flights to Sapporo from some capital cities in Australia are available over the ski season. It is particularly well known for its dry, fluffy powder snow. There are many places to choose from, so it's always a good idea to go with what suits your family and the ages of your kids over the quantity or difficulty of runs. Here are three of the best areas in the Hokkaido region for skiing on your Japanese holiday.

- The most popular with Australians is **Niseko**, which is family friendly. English is widely spoken, which makes it easy too. There are tree-skiing routes, beginner runs, constant snow and deep powder, so it suits all abilities. Door-to-door transfers from Sapporo or the airport are available with lots of accommodation options. There is a great village vibe and a vibrant nightlife. It gets pretty busy over Christmas and January, so you will need to be organised and book early.

- **Furano** is another large destination ski resort and is known for long groomed runs and being very family friendly. It also makes a great base to visit other nearby ski areas. You'll find good amenities and services at the resort, and the town of Furano is nearby. The resort caters well to English-speaking guests and has nine lifts and 24 courses with runs for beginners through to advanced.

- **Rusutsu** has incredible powder and tree skiing, and is generally not as crowded as Niseko – even on weekends you're unlikely to see lift lines. The lifts are good: 18 lifts with four gondolas and six fast quad chairs. It has ski-in, ski-out accommodation and heaps of facilities. There's also a Japanese kitsch feel with a singing tree and Disney features, and great snow-tubing, snow biking and more

- Beyond the Hokkaido region, you'll find great skiing in the **Japanese Alps** near Nagano. The village of **Hakuba** in the Alps is big on skiing, with 128 courses and five resorts, all of which offer different things. Most of them are family friendly. Hakuba has more bluebird days (a beautiful day after snowfall) than some of northern resorts, and has good nightlife. **Nozawa Onsen** has a more authentic town, and there are lots of onsens (hot springs) to soak in after a big day on the slopes.

TOKYO

Japan is more than just Tokyo

but it's certainly a great place to start! Loud, colourful and chaotic, Tokyo makes absolutely no apologies – and nor should it. It is the vibrant capital of a country that has given so much to the world, added splashes of colour to places we had deemed 'colourful enough' and is in most part an absolute joyous city to visit.

It's easy to think you are drifting through an electronic crèche when you make your way through Tokyo's JR (Japan Rail) line, and it's hard to stop your head from spinning as you wander through the city. Billboards are digital and every ad seems aimed at an eight-year-old to the point where you're not sure if the anime owl with the cartoon bubble is trying to sell you toothpaste or inform you of a terror hotline.

Eating Out

Tokyo has some outstanding sushi and ramen; try places without English menus (though perhaps quickly get on Google Translate before being served to get exactly what you want). Tokyo also has some amazing French and Italian restaurants, so don't feel bad having something that is not typically Japanese here.

Accommodation

Shinjuku and Ginza are in the heart of it all, and Shinbuya and Asakusa are great places to stay too, but if you stay near a train line the whole city is easily accessible anyway. We stayed in hotels but needed two rooms and in Japan it was almost impossible to find connecting rooms. For a family bigger than four, it can be a bit harder to work out, but you can find some large twin rooms that also have a sofa bed. Share accommodation is available in Tokyo and, while small, you'll get everyone in at least.

Getting Around

Your tourist JR Pass isn't part of the other lines like Tokyo Metro and Toei Subway, so you'll need to purchase extra tickets for them. A Tokyo Metro 24-hour ticket will get you around the city unlimited for one day.

ATTRACTIONS

- If you like the idea of your kids paying for your next overseas holiday, then it may be worth booking the little ones into **KidZania** where they learn how to work for money, become leaders and be part of a society. Sure it sounds a bit like school, but it's way more fun because you get to earn sweet KidZos, the official currency of KidZania (we believe KidZos are now officially worth more than Bitcoin), and the other really cool thing … no gender pay gap! In KidZania, girls and boys can become pilots, journalists, dentists, scientists, athletes, chefs and more (comedian is not on offer because that quite obviously cannot be learned … *cough*). Over 60 pavilions are available and parents can watch on from various viewing decks, but are not allowed on the floor. The floor is strictly kids only!

- **Tokyo Disneyland**, the first Disneyland to be built outside the United States, will give the kids their theme park fix, and it's only about a 15-minute train trip from Tokyo Station. It has all the theme lands you'd expect and is so much fun – the kids will love this Disneyland.

- The United States may be the undisputed home of baseball, having hosted every World Series since 1903, but Japan surely takes the silver medal for their love of America's national pastime. The best place to check out all the action is **Tokyo Dome**, the home of the Yomiuri Giants. Built in 1988, Tokyo Dome is easy to get to, well priced, clean and fun, making Tokyo Dome *the* place to catch a home run … and a hotdog. The atmosphere is electric and more amped than in the United States. Drums get banged, songs get sung and banners unfurl. Petite Japanese women carry kegs on their backs and work tirelessly to deliver beer and whisky to your seat with a smile. The concession stands offer Japanese food, such as bento boxes. Of course, it would be sacrilegious not to offer hamburgers and hotdogs at the baseball. They kindly oblige.

- Every great city has a tall building you can go up and look out from. In Tokyo there are a few, but **Skytree** is a stand out and, at 643m tall, it doesn't disappoint. Skytree offers views of this huge city that sprawls as far as the eye can see. Go at night to enjoy all the pretty lights.

- For a more kid-focused observation deck, head to **Sky Circus**, or Sunshine 60 as it used to be called. You'll get fabulous views but it also has interactive virtual reality attractions for the kids. They can be shot out of a cannon or swing high through the sky – well, not literally, but by virtual reality the kids will seriously feel like they are.

- Kids love robots. Adults love restaurants. Put them together and what do you get? The **Robot Restaurant** is a little snapshot of modern Japan. Walk through the little weird and plenty wonderful restaurant, which is less a restaurant and more of a catwalk that showcases a parade of robots (to loud music, pyrotechnics and smoke machines) being jumped all over by bikini-clad women in a fight to the fictitious death. Including the Robot Restaurant in this book is quasi-controversial as reviews were a little mixed among the Helliars. You are squeezed into your seat (you wouldn't want to be sumo-sized) and it can be hot (Brij did use the term 'firetrap' at one point). We skipped the 'restaurant' element of the evening and just enjoyed the show. Firetrap or no firetrap, the Robot Restaurant is fun, colourful and chaotic – a bit like Tokyo itself.

- You may like to call the **Ueno Zoological Gardens** a 'zoo' for short and we are pretty confident it'll catch on, because, ahh, that's what it is. Ueno is Japan's oldest zoo and in June 2017 it welcomed a brand new panda cub, Xiangxiang (Pete nominated the name 'Gary'). She's a toddler panda now but, if you get there quick enough, Xiangxiang may still have that new panda cub smell.

- If you love your zoos a little less cagey and more open then check out **Tama Zoological Park**. Set in a 52-hectare park, Tama Zoo has three separate ecological areas covering Africa, Asia and – drumroll please – Australia! It also has an **Insectarium** that will make your skin crawl all the way back to your hotel but that your kids will love. Soothe yourself by visiting the more majestic and way more respectful butterflies in the aptly titled **Butterfly House**. It's about one hour from central Tokyo by train, so make a day of it. Kids under 12 are free.

- For another nature spot, visit **Inokashira Park** in Kichijoji. Ride a swan boat (you can hire pedal boats that look like swans) or visit the park's aquarium, small zoo and **Ghilbi Museum**, which showcases the animation, art and technology of Studio Ghilbi (think *Spirited Away* among other films). There's something for everyone at this park – you will all be able to enjoy your time here.

- More than just about eating, the **Ramen Museum** is a museum of a different kind; it's a museum about the very popular Japanese noodle dish. On the first floor you can experience the history of ramen, but on the two basement floors you'll explore some of the streets and houses of Shitamachi, the Old Town of Tokyo when ramen was first becoming more popular. You can try different ramen from different parts of Japan (we suggest choosing mini ramen to ensure you don't overdo it). Our favourite part was purchasing tickets for the meals at the vending machine in front of the restaurants. It may take a second or two to grasp the very simple system, but it's a bit of fun, especially for the kids.

- For one of those family experiences you'll all remember, get a **fish pedicure**, where tiny toothless fish nibble away at the dead skin on your feet. Fun for the whole family, or just a little bit weird and funny, but you won't forget it. Choose a reputable spa and enjoy it for as long as you can. Your feet will feel like silk at the end.

- We love a place with a funny name and Tokyo's **Piss Alley** is right up there next to Takeshita Street. Actually called Omoide Yokocho (or Memory Alley), its nickname came from the time after World War II when toilets weren't easily available. Nowadays it's a cute little alley jam-packed with fabulous food stalls, restaurants and bars, and, thankfully, you'll find clean restrooms. Piss Alley is at the west gate of Shinjuku Station. Not too far away there really is a **Takeshita Street**, where teenagers will love the shopping. The street itself and its side streets have so many trendy shops, boutiques, second-hand clothes, fast food and food stands, you have to go check it out, take a photo, have some overly sugary dessert and enjoy the experience. It's only a minute or two away from one of the biggest shrines in Tokyo, **Meiji Jingu** in Yoyogi Park.

- If the kids need a play, visit **Asobono**, one of Tokyo's largest indoor play centres, in Tokyo Dome City. It's a heap of fun, with ball pits, slides, trampolines and climbing walls; there's even a play area set aside for children under two. It's a great rainy day place to keep the little ones busy.

- For a classic Japanese bathing experience, head to **Oedo-onsen-Monogatari**. This is a great place to take kids; so many baths have different rules where you might not be able to take kids, but this one has a family onsen. People with tattoos can't use the facilities here; this is etiquette in most onsens, but you can find some that are tattoo friendly. Also worth noting is that babies are allowed but toddlers who aren't potty trained must be in an adjacent pool.

- For insight into another Japanese tradition (and the country's national sport), watch **sumo wrestlers** train. The sumo tournaments may not be on when you are in town, but if the unique sport takes your interest you can watch sumo wrestlers train at their stables in the morning. The Japan Sumo Association website has a list of stables; find one that allows tourists to watch.

- An oh-so-Japanese thing that the kids will love are Tokyo's **pet cafes** – where one person's OH&S concern is another person's coffee-and-animal-cuddles time. Yes, long before we knew turtles could provide emotional support on an Airbus, they were providing companionship in cafes across Japan. You'll find cafes with owls, rabbits, chihuahuas, unsonic hedgehogs, snakes and even micro pigs. Oh and of course cats, who we're pretty sure are there simply for the free feed.

- A daytrip from Tokyo is much easier than some other parts of the world because of their incredibly reliable shinkansen, or fast trains. Tokyo won't bore you, but if you find you have a spare day, visit **LEGOLAND Japan**, about a two-hour train ride away. The park is small and especially suits kids under ten, but bigger kids who love LEGO will have a ball too. Or head to **Mount Fuji**, Japan's highest mountain, also about two hours away. Either hike or just look at this breathtakingly beautiful mountain (it's actually a volcano) and the picturesque lakes surrounding it. It makes for a great day out at a very different pace from Tokyo.

KYOTO

ONCE THE CAPITAL OF JAPAN,

Kyoto is a beautiful historic city, known for avoiding the atomic bomb in World War II; it was taken off the American military's target list because of its cultural history and value.

Kyoto has many beautiful temples, and with so much history you could spend days and days visiting them. However, when you're travelling with kids, consider that they won't want to visit every single one (nor every castle and palace you can visit). Choose your favourite, the quieter the better, and you will get more out of that one visit than visiting the temples with many tourists. Importantly, remember to *wear socks* with your shoes: in many temples you're asked to remove your shoes and wear the slippers provided. Socks or no socks those well-worn slippers are going on your feet. It happened to Brij – we have a video of her trying to float in the air.

As well as its peaceful temples, Kyoto offers many attractions that kids will enjoy. Plus it's a spectacularly green city, with lots of places for kids to run and play.

ATTRACTIONS

- For train lovers young and old, **Kyoto Rail Museum** covers everything train related. The kids will love riding the steam train and checking out display trains like the shinkansen. There are also model trains and a roundhouse.

- Visit the **Fushimi-Inari-Taisha Shrine**, dedicated to rice and sake, with its seemingly unending path of torii, or Shinto shrine gates. These orange gates (over 5000 of them) will captivate everyone. Hike to the top of the mountain with the kids and enjoy the surrounds.

- Those ninja-loving kids (aged six and above) will get a kick out of the **Samurai and Ninja Museum** with family-friendly ninja displays and experiences. You can also buy authentic and replica swords. Check out the ninja lessons offered daily.

- Kyoto's **Kamo River** has many parks and paths along its banks and it's the perfect place to see cherry blossoms in spring. Near the Imadegawa-dori bridge in Demachiyanagi, the river features wonderful **turtle stepping stones**. The kids will love playing on them and using the turtles to cross the river – it's an enchanting place to play.

- **Gion** is a lovely area to dine in – find a place that overlooks the canals. It's a big district: the most popular area is Hanami-koji Street, and try Shirakawa Area, which runs along the canal. We found it a little confusing with our maps and asked a taxi driver for help. We had walked completely the wrong way, which was in the direction of Gion's geisha district. By this stage the kids were used to us leading them the wrong way by accident. Remember, it's all part of travelling.

- **Maruyama-koen Park** will become the most crowded park for cherry blossom viewing in spring, but you can watch the school of carp and turtles in the pond any season. It's a beautiful place to rest those weary legs. And we are talking about parents here, although in Japan we did have tired little children at the end of every day.

- The most entertaining temple for children is **Kiyomizu-dera Temple**. At the temple's **Otowa Waterfall** the water is divided into three separate streams, and visitors can use cups attached to long poles to drink from them. Each stream's water is said to have a different benefit, such as longevity, success at school and a fortunate love-life. A tip for those who want it all: drinking from all three streams is considered greedy. After the temple make your way around to Sannen-zaka and Ninen-zaka to explore the teahouses, souvenirs and restaurants of these quaint lanes.

- **Nishiki Market** is in downtown Kyoto and has a great atmosphere. The food market has lots of fun Japanese items to check out, which can make it really interesting. It does get busy though, so stick together like white rice.

175 JAPAN

Respect goes both ways! Oscar and new friend in Nara Park.

📍 Out of Kyoto (about half an hour away) but worth visiting is **Arashiyama – The Bamboo Forest**. Walk down the paths among towering bamboo – it is incredible. On the same day you can do the **Sagano Scenic Railway** (or the Romantic Train). Old and slow, it's a bit like a bullet train in super slow-mo (think more Puffing Billy than shinkansen), but it's certainly a lovely trip. Once we got off at the other end it was admittedly a little confusing; the lack of directions and English signage didn't help. We ended up catching an old horse and cart (the horse may or may not have been wearing a sleep apnea mask) to the **Hozugawa River Cruise** on which we pleasantly floated back to Kyoto. To this day we have no idea if that was what we were supposed to do. Regardless, it was a lovely day.

📍 In **Nara**, about an hour out of Kyoto, go to **Nara Park** to feed the wild deer – the deer even bow to say thank you. The park is an open park, so the deer are free, but they know which side their bread is buttered on. Afterwards sanitise your hands, walk the shopping strips and buy some Japanese souvenirs.

📍 Slightly further out of Kyoto is the scenic city of **Kobe**. You could spend the whole day here just in its busy Chinatown. Take a walking tour in the historic sake district in the Nada area where they have been brewing sake for hundreds of years.

📍 About two hours away from Kobe, the pretty city of **Okayama** has a beautiful castle and magnificent gardens to explore. The city's **Korakuen Garden** is ranked one of the three best landscaped gardens in Japan and makes a lovely spot for a wander.

KID-FREE NIGHT OUT

Japanese people are so delightfully helpful and want to make your experience of their town or city spectacular. So, for up-to-date places that are great for a romantic dinner, ask your concierge, taxi driver or sales person, and you may find yourself the perfect local, tourist-free place for a night out without kids. Or head to the **Gion** or **Pontocho** districts, which are filled with bars, restaurants, hostess clubs, karaoke clubs and geisha teahouses. Take your pick. If you want a bar without the nightclub, go to **In the Moon** bar in Gion – it has outdoor seating, great cocktails and a fantastic view. And for something different try **Gear Theatre**, a non-verbal performance with impressive stage effects. It is certainly something to remember. (If you want to do this with the kids, every first and third Saturday of the month the theatre offers a matinee show for all ages over three.)

OSAKA

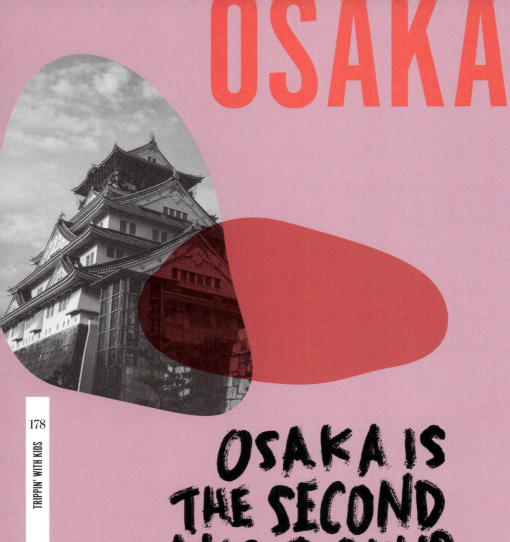

Osaka is the second most popular

prefecture in Japan after Tokyo. It is known for its passion for food, the vibrant lights of Shinsaibashi and its culture – music, theatres, museums and cinemas are found throughout the city. But it's not all about the party – unwinding in a family onsen is a must-do even if the kids think it's a bit weird (they'll get used to it). Kids are adored in Japan and Osaka offers so many fun, sensory, visual, outdoor and indoor activities that they won't want to leave.

ATTRACTIONS

- One of the big-ticket items in Osaka is undoubtedly **Universal Studios**. Many of the attractions, such as the Harry Potter, Minions and Jurassic Park ones, mirror Universal's bigger cousin in Los Angeles. We raced with the crowd at the start of the day to get on the new Harry Potter Ride. Brij gets motion sickness but still managed to get through without being sick, and the kids and Pete loved it. By the end of the day it wasn't just the kids who were tired and very happy; Mum and Dad were dragging their little toes too. The Japanese love their theme parks and watching the crowd's excitement before the gates open is fun in itself.

- **Kaiyukan Aquarium** is one of the best aquariums in the world. Get there early, because it can get busy. From a vast array of fish to manta rays and even two whale sharks, it's a great place to explore and the kids will love their time here.

- **Osaka Castle** is quite simply one of the most stunning castles in Japan. Built in 1583 by the order of Hideyoshi Toyotomi, one of the most famous unifying warlords of Japanese history, the castle is surrounded by a maze of other smaller buildings, gates and a moat, along with beautiful gardens.

- Check out the theatre and entertainment district **Dotonbori**. It's full of tourists but you're a tourist so jump on in and see what all the fuss is about. Eat in or grab some street food, from Kobe beef to Japanese cheesecake. If you really love your cheesecake, check out **Pablo** where you'll have your cheesecake baked exactly to your taste, just like ordering a steak! The district has plenty of crazy photo opportunities with 3D lobsters and squids protruding from the front of restaurants. The alleyways are lined with small to tiny bars. And if the kids are a bit tired and sick of walking, take in the colour and madness of Dotonbori with a **Tonbori River cruise** in a boat the colour of a New York taxi.

- **Kids Plaza Osaka** was the very first museum in Japan dedicated to children's education. The fifth floor, wonderfully referred to as the Let's Try floor, is often a favourite as the kids can be hands-on with all the activities – they can even create electricity among all the other fun stuff.

- If you missed the Giants at Tokyo Dome, you can check out the Hanshin Tigers at the **Hanshin Koshien Stadium**.

- To get a bird's-eye view of the city, head to the brilliantly designed **Umeda Sky Building**. This architecture of the highest order features an observation deck called **Kuchu Teien** (Floating Garden).

- Osaka has great shopping: want to dress in Japanese street fashion (dads, know your strengths)? Check out **American Mura** (American Village) for edgy boutiques, cafes and restaurants. For a different feel, **Shitennoji Temple** hosts a huge outdoor flea market two days a month.

HIROSHIMA

You go to Hiroshima because

you know what happened there on that horrible, unimaginable day on 6 August 1945 when American planes dropped an atomic bomb on this lively and energetic city. You go to pay your respects for those who disappeared from the face of the Earth that day and for those who somehow carried on afterwards. But you leave with a feeling of hope and a sense that Hiroshima is not purely defined by its tragic past. Slowly but surely, Hiroshima is out of the shadow of its heart-rending history and looking forward to a much brighter future.

Today you'll find a city of nearly 1.2 million people with a strong economy, which reformed on the back of a bustling manufacturing industry, a city where culinary delights can be found in unexpected places and beauty seen around almost every corner – it's a very special place to visit.

Of course, the World War II bombing still looms large over Hiroshima but the community has reclaimed the narrative. Though largely destroyed by the bomb, the **Hiroshima Peace Memorial** (Genbaku Dome) was the only structure left standing when the bomb first exploded (it was a promotional hall). The fact that it's standing today, preserved in exactly the same state as it was after the bomb, says a lot about the Japanese people. It is World Heritage listed for Universal Value and has become a powerful symbol for the need to eliminate nuclear weapons.

Hiroshima is a place you will want to share with your kids. Depending on their age and understanding of World War II they will get a sense of how it affected the city, how strength and courage rose from such a horrific event. The kids will love the city – it's quieter than Osaka and Tokyo by a lot, but it's still big enough to do lots of exploring.

ATTRACTIONS

- **Hiroshima Peace Memorial Park** and the **Hiroshima Peace Memorial Museum** are amazing memorials to the people who were affected by the bombing of Hiroshima. There are some parts that you may want to move smaller children through quickly, especially if they are very sensitive, as you'll see stories of children and families who were torn apart on that day. However, the museum is done in such a beautiful way that it does emphasise the importance of peace in this world. The **Children's Peace Monument** features a statue of a young girl and a crane with the quote: 'This is our cry. This is our prayer. Peace in the world.' This monument was created around the true story of a young girl called Sadako who was two when the bomb was dropped. At about the age of ten she fell ill with radiation-induced leukemia. She folded origami cranes daily to wish for good health and a world without nuclear weapons (according to Japanese legend, if you fold 1000 cranes your wish will be granted). Sadly she didn't survive but her legacy lives on through the millions of cranes sent daily to the park as a symbol of peace from all over the world.

- Only a kilometre or so from Peace Memorial Park, **Hiroshima Castle** is worth a visit. It's a fortress surrounded by a moat and a park. Though completely destroyed by the bomb, the castle was rebuilt to replicate the original. The gardens are fun for the kids to explore. For more gardens nearby, head to **Shukkeien Garden**, a formal Japanese garden in the heart of the city.

- The **Hiroshima Children's Museum**, located in the City Children's Library, is a place for the kids to laugh and play while interacting with science and technology exhibits. Complete with a planetarium, it's great for kids of all ages.

- Car lovers will be interested to know that the Mazda car originated in Hiroshima. Explore the history of Mazda since the 1920s in the **Mazda Museum**, complete with an assembly line.

- Make sure you create time to visit **Miyajima**, a small island in Hiroshima Bay. Use your JR Pass to catch the ferry to the island and spend the day there sightseeing. Climb or take a cable-car to **Mount Misen** to see the surrounding areas, the floating shrine of **Itsukushima**, the giant torii gate and the Buddhist temple. With its World Heritage sites, temples, deer, food and nature, you will be happy exploring the island all day.

UNITED KINGDOM

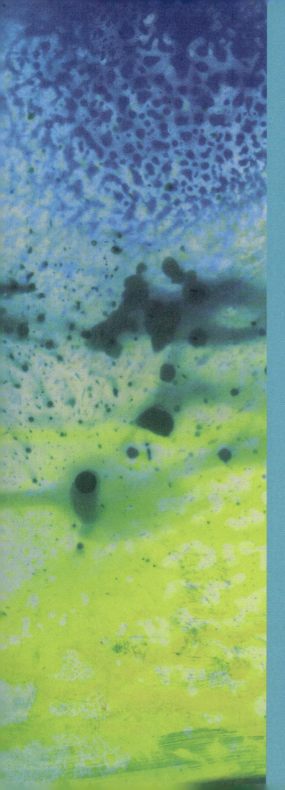

YOU CAN EXPLORE THE UNITED KINGDOM IN ONE TRIP, OR FOCUS ON A SINGLE COUNTRY, ESPECIALLY AS EACH COUNTRY DOES HAVE PLENTY TO OFFER FAMILIES JUST ON ITS OWN.

If you do make it one trip, heading to London, Belfast, Edinburgh and Ireland's Dublin will be an incredible tour of the history of knights and royalty; Celtic, Viking and Roman settlements; regal palaces; idyllic countryside; and extraordinary towns. You can book a family tour to assist with the travelling or jump on trains, boats and planes and hire cars.

ENGLAND

OL' BLIGHTY,

the empire's home base, the place where royalty reigns – all of the above. England presents lush green fields, quaint country towns, historic buildings and a stack of neatly stacked stones that may have been put there by aliens.

With a fascinating history spanning thousands of years, England has been an archaeologist's jackpot. From the ancient finds of prehistoric England and the treasures of the Roman era to its rich mediaeval castles and Victorian-era buildings, the country's history is writ large across the landscape – basically it's like one huge history lesson for the kids, but a really fun one that you can all do together.

England is pretty small (apparently two Englands could fit in Victoria) so you can get lots done either by travelling around or by using London as a base for daytrips. Great daytrips include visiting the famous baths of, well, Bath (about two and a half hours from London) or the ancient Stonehenge (about two hours). Of course, if sport is your thing then there are plenty of options, from English Premier League to cricket in the summer. Just be prepared for those 28-degree summer scorchers that wreak havoc on this famous old city.

England is great for kids. It's easy to get around, they can help navigate as there is no language barrier, and what kid doesn't love Harry Potter, Paddington Bear, Robin Hood, Noddy, Winnie-the-Pooh and Thomas the Tank Engine – all of which originated here. (Watch some of these classics with your kids before heading over.) England will entertain the kids no end and they'll never forget the fun quirky adventures you'll no doubt have.

DID YOU KNOW?

- The annual cheese-rolling competition near Gloucester attracts people from all over the world. The person to cross the finish line first wins the cheese they chased down the hill (and some wine and crackers, we hope).
- Modern British law still includes historic oddities. It's against the law to enter the houses of parliament in a suit of armour; to fire a cannon within 300 yards of a home; to carry a plank along a pavement; and to jump the queue when buying a ticket for the Tube. Please know this before travelling to England and adjust your plans accordingly.
- English people consume more tea per capita than anyone else in the world, meaning they probably have more toilet breaks per capita than anyone else in the world.
- England was part of the shortest war in history, against Zanzibar in 1896. Zanzibar surrendered after just 38 minutes (which is still longer than some English Ashes innings in the 1990s).
- The official residence of the Queen, Windsor Castle is the largest occupied castle in the world. Most of its occupants are corgis.

ATTRACTIONS

- The beautiful town of **Bath** is home to the renowned **Roman Baths**. See how the Romans lived (and washed and relaxed) in this incredible historic site. The springs that attracted the Romans almost 2000 years ago still flow into the Baths, and you can walk through the site to see the heated rooms and plunge pool, the great bath, the sacred springs and ruins of the temple. Taste the famous spa water and throw a coin into the plunge pool, and as the kids walk across the worn stones through the Baths remind them that they are walking where, 2000 years ago, Romans walked. Download the free children's app before you go.

- **Stonehenge** is a famous prehistoric monument and one of the ancient wonders of the world. Stand and stare at this incredible stone circle and enjoy trying to work out how and why this phenomenon came to exist in 3000 BCE (our guess is drunk uni students). You can also explore other elements of the surrounding prehistoric landscape, such as barrows and postholes. The visitor centre is great and outside there are reconstructions of Neolithic houses. It gets seriously busy so you need to pre-book your timed entry tickets, which cover the fascinating visitor centre and shuttle buses to the stones too. Tours run from major nearby towns such as Bath and Salisbury, and you can also daytrip from London.

- After visiting Stonehenge, head to nearby **Salisbury** to see the **Salisbury Cathedral**, which has the tallest spire in all of the United Kingdom and is home to one of the few remaining copies of the **Magna Carta**, which was written in 1215.

- In **Cornwall** you'll find the popular **Eden Project**, a global garden that aims to promote a sustainable future for all. The landscaped worlds cover three different biomes in a futuristic collection of greenhouses, with plants collected from many diverse climates and environments. You'll find so much for the kids to do here. Walk the **Rainforest Canopy Walkway** or explore the many themed play areas. The 660m long **SkyWire** will have kids all juiced up as they zipline above the Eden Project. If adventure is your thing, there's also a 360 swing and a giant swing, aerial trekking, a 'leap of faith' drop and more. The Eden Project also offers seasonal special events aimed at kids. The whole place is stroller friendly and there are free 'land trains' to take you down the hill to the site (and back up at the end of the day).

- Your kids will fall in love with **BeWILDerwood**, an outdoor adventure park near Hoveton in Norfolk. In the park's 20 hectares of whimsical woodland, the kids can climb trees and rope bridges, play in treehouses, fly on ziplines, wander the paths, get lost in the maze and enjoy storytelling and puppet shows featuring BeWILDerwood's enchanting characters.

- Visit the beautiful riverside city of **Cambridge**. Its rich history is evident down every street, and its University of Cambridge is one of the oldest universities in the English-speaking world. You'll be walking in the steps of alumni such as Isaac Newton and Charles Darwin as you

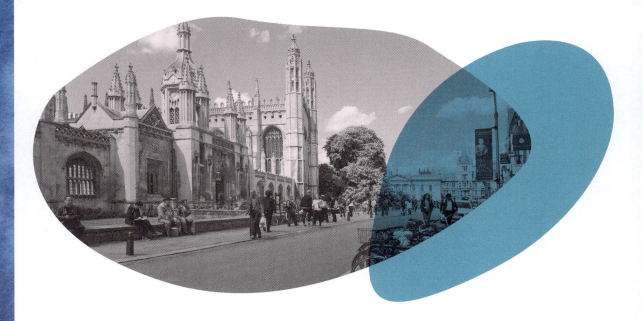

explore the stunning university grounds. The university has museums, historic buildings and collections that are open to the public throughout the year. Walk the self-guided Cambridge Treasurer Hunt Trail to check out all the sights in town or, if you need to put your feet up, go punting on the River Cam (there are many tours available).

Head to **York** in north-east England to visit the **Jorvik Viking Centre**, a museum and discovery centre brilliantly depicting Viking life. The centre is on the actual site of a Viking village, only uncovered in the 1970s, and you can see some of the excavations as well as travel in a 'time capsule' back to the 10th-century Viking village. Check the centre's website for family activities.

For a fun theme park experience, visit **Drayton Manor Theme Park**, near Tamworth in Staffordshire. It's the home of **Thomas Land**, for those kids keen to hang out with Thomas the Tank Engine and his friends. If your older kids are rolling their eyes at the thought, don't worry – Drayton Manor will have them entertained with rollercoasters and all the usual theme park fun, along with an open-plan zoo.

We know you're in the England section, but we have to recommend a spot in North Wales. **Llandudno** is a lovely seaside village – well, it's actually the largest holiday resort in Wales but it still feels like a lovely seaside village. There are puppet shows on the promenade, amusements at the 19th-century pier, which is the longest in Wales, and a beautiful white-sand beach. It's also home to the **Great Orme Bronze Age Mines** where you can wander ancient tunnels, and the historic **Great Orme Tramway**, which you can catch to the headland's summit.

LONDON
ENGLAND

ART, CULTURE,
a cracking comedy scene, museums and year-round world-class sport – it's little wonder some Aussies never come back from their gap year in London. It's also a wonderful place to bring the kids for a holiday because London has so many kid-friendly activities, and many are free. Oh and did we hear somebody say Harry Potter?

Soaked in history from mediaeval knights to the Beatles' Abbey Road, London's landmarks, while not quite as grandiose as those in Paris, are something to behold. Big Ben, the Tower of London and that joint where the Queen lives, teamed with the more contemporary additions such as the Tate Modern, the Sky Garden and the Shard make for a compelling skyline without the city ever becoming a sterile concrete jungle.

Accommodation

It's not easy to pinpoint one great area to stay in London as it's quite spread out and all the areas are easily visited via the well-run Tube (mind the gap though – you'll hear this announcement a million times on the Tube). West End is central and has plenty of hotels, places to eat and good access to Tube stations. Book your accommodation early so you get the good family rooms. Otherwise look for centrally located serviced apartments if you're staying longer than a few days.

Eating Out

There is a huge range of options and you will always be able to stumble on a place that does good fish and chips. For traditional fare, look for bangers and mash, shepherd and cottage pies, Yorkshire pudding and roasts at taverns and pubs all over.

Getting Around

Travelling long distance around England is really easy on trains. The BritRail Pass needs to be purchased before you arrive in the United Kingdom. All members of the family over five require their own pass; under fives travel free. Choose the BritRail Consecutive Pass if you have set days and the BritRail Flexi Pass for flexible days. It can be used anywhere in England, Wales and Scotland, but for London you'll need a separate card.

For travelling around London, buy a London Travel Card for the number of days you are there. This will also get you discounts on some of the main attractions. Children aged between zero and ten do not need their own ticket as long as they are accompanied by a ticket-holding adult (just ask a member of staff at the station to let you through the ticket barriers). Avoid getting the Tube during peak times when it's crowded. Look for family tickets to the big attractions for some good savings.

ATTRACTIONS

- If you have a Harry Potter fan in the family, your first stop should be the **Harry Potter Warner Bros Studio Tour**. You'll get to explore the film set and be transported to the Great Hall, Diagon Alley and the Forbidden Forest. Best of all you can ride the Hogwarts Express from Platform 9¾. You'll also get to see props and costumes from the films, and learn how the film-makers were able to bring all those magical creatures to life with special effects. You can even buy your own wand (parents, be prepared: there are three different shops on the studio tour). You have to pre-purchase your tickets online so plan ahead. Check wbstudiotour.co.uk for seasonal tours and events (they even occasionally have dinners in the Great Hall).

- If you need a break from the hustle and bustle, head to **Richmond Park**, just near Wimbledon, to enjoy some space, stretch the legs, top up on fresh air and get a nature fix. This 500-year-old park is home to deer herds, which are wonderful to watch, and has great views of London. And, for the adults, it's always nice after the park to head to one of the many fabulous pubs or cafes in Richmond.

- Like New York's Broadway, London's **West End** offers plays and musicals for both adults and kids, from *The Lion King* and *Aladdin* to Australia's very own Tim Minchin's brilliant production of *Matilda*. Parents can save *Book of Mormon* for the kid-free night!

- The ginormous **London Eye** on the South Bank of the River Thames is a great way to get an up-high view of London. Book tickets online to save some cash and to combine the Eye with other popular places such as the Dungeon and Madame Tussauds.

- The **Churchill War Rooms** give kids the opportunity to see firsthand where Churchill and his cabinet worked and lived during World War II and how they won the war. You will feel like you have stepped back in time to 1945 in the underground bunker headquarters beneath the streets of Westminster.

- World Heritage–listed **Westminster Abbey** has been around for over a thousand years and has been there for pivotal moments in England's history. There are often family events and there's also a self-guided family trail. Pack a picnic and enjoy it in the College Garden or the Cloisters.

- Visit **Buckingham Palace** so the kids can see the daily **Changing of the Guard Ceremony**. Or head to the **Dismounting Ceremony** daily at 4pm outside the Horse Guards building (facing Whitehall). Kids will be fascinated by the ritual and fanfare of it all.

- One of the best free attractions in London, the **British Museum** chronicles human history, art and culture and has family visits covered. There are activity trails, treasure hunts, a list of the best 12 objects to see with children, art materials and family challenges. Or pick up one of the museum's free gallery backpacks full of activities to give kids a focus. Backpacks are themed and age-specific, but only available on certain days, so check online and plan your visit accordingly.

- London's **Borough Market** is a renowned spot for fresh produce, breads, cheeses, seafood and just soaking up the London atmosphere (note that it's super busy on Saturdays).

- **Shakespeare's Globe** is a performing arts venue along the river. It always has a variety of plays on, and also offers tours, including the **Globe Theatre Family Tour**, which is the perfect way to introduce the kids to Shakespeare's London and the plays he created. Check the website for what's on when you're visiting.

- Visit the **Tower of London**, a historic castle-fortress on the River Thames, to see the sparkling **Crown Jewels** and have a go at shooting arrows (in the **Armoury in Action experience**). There are a number of excellent tours included as part of your entrance ticket; take the **Yeoman Warder tour** to see the **Traitors' Gate**, where famous Tudor prisoners entered. The website lists upcoming special events, such as ceremonies, and it also has interactive storytelling for children of all ages – it's definitely worth exploring before your visit.

- For a darker side of London history, visit the **London Dungeon** to get transported back in time and have some fear-inducing experiences. The dungeon is popular with children and adults alike (but if you think it might be too scary for your kids, check out the information online and make the call before you give them nightmares). Book online and reserve a time slot to save yourself time and money.

- For a daytrip from London, take the kids to **Hever Castle**, an elegant 13th-century castle in

DID YOU KNOW?

- London hasn't always had the same name. In the past it has been called Londonium, Ludenwic and Ludenburg.
- Big Ben is not actually the name of the clock, it is the name of the bell that is inside the clock. Word of warning: Big Ben isn't as big as you think he is.
- For the breakfast cereal lovers of the world, there are actual cereal cafes in London. With so many varieties on offer we think the glittery rainbow of Unicorn Poop might be the one to taste-test.

189

UNITED KINGDOM

Kent about an hour and a half south of the city. They'll love the castle's gardens with its various mazes, including a water maze. There's also a playground, a boating lake and model houses to find through 50 hectares. The kids can take lessons in archery, paint their own shield and in summer there's jousting to watch and an open-air cinema to enjoy.

Under two hours from London, **Brighton** is a great seaside town for families and a lovely daytrip. Brighton's **Royal Pavilion** has been restored to its glory days as it was when King George used it as his seaside pleasure palace. Wander through each elaborate room and then have lunch at the **Pavilion Gardens Cafe** and go shopping in the **Lanes district** in the city's historic quarter. **Brighton Palace Pier** is always a highlight for kids thanks to its dome arcade and fun rides. **Brighton Beach** is a beach with a difference for Aussie kids, given that it's a pebble beach, not a sandy beach. Go for a ride on the **Volks Electric Railway** that runs towards the marina or head to **British Airways i360**, the world's tallest moving observation tower, with views over the city.

Just over an hour's drive from Brighton, the pretty town of **Rye** is worth a visit. It is picture perfect, with its cobbled lanes, cute historic houses and hill-top position. Meander down the street and choose a lunch spot – given the seaside is right there, it's a great place to order seafood. The kids will love the old-style sweet shop for dessert. Make sure to spend some time at the **Rye Castle Museum** because the exhibitions, replica swords, armour, helmets and costumes will appeal to children of all ages.

KID-FREE NIGHT OUT

An English pub is a good choice if you have a night out; it won't be hard to find one as they are on almost every corner. (Remember pubs close at 11pm so you might want to find a bar to head to after.) In London make it a proper English night out at a pub with some real history, such as Ye Olde Cheshire Cheese where Mark Twain, Alfred Tennyson and Charles Dickens were said to be regulars or the Spaniards Inn, which features in Charles Dickens' *The Pickwick Papers* and Bram Stoker's *Dracula*. The Lamb and Flag in Covent Garden had the nickname 'Bucket of Blood' in the early 19th century because it hosted bare-knuckle prize fights – it's much nicer now. And Cittie of Yorke is charming, with its wooden booths and fireplace; the basement has its own bar and there's a beer garden hidden out the back. For a wide range of bars and restaurants you can't go past the Soho, South Kensington and Mayfair districts.

SCOTLAND

Did You Know?

- Scotland's love of history and legends makes it no surprise that the unicorn is its national animal (no joke), narrowly beating the Tooth Fairy for the title.
- Scotland has the highest hedge in the world: the Meikleour Beech Hedge is over 30m high.
- There is a town called Dull in Scotland, which is home to fewer than 100 people, and doesn't have much to entertain the children. It is believed the name may come from an old Gaelic word meaning 'meadow'. Or it could simply come from the contemporary English word meaning 'dull'.
- Inchconnachan Island in Loch Lomond is home to around 60 wallabies – an eccentric local introduced the marsupial to the area in the 1940s. Heading over? Take them Vegemite and Tim Tams.
- The *Encyclopaedia Britannica* originated in Scotland in 1768, the bright idea of two Scotsmen. We'll leave it to you to explain to your kids what *Encyclopaedia Britannica* was. Perhaps start with, 'Before there was Google …'

Oh, the Scottish Highlands

where the fog across a loch is like a filter from God. Pete fondly remembers a bus trip he took from Glasgow to the tiny west-coast town of Inveraray while listening to Paul Kelly's 'Wintercoat' on his Walkman and being mesmerised by the beauty of Scotland. And if you think the rolling green hills are eye-wateringly stunning, wait until you try Scotland's single malt whisky.

The Scottish people are famously friendly even when they sound famously angry (it's the red hair gene we think). It's a compact country, which makes it easy to traverse, especially with kids. You may think haggis when you think Scottish cuisine (which may cause you to vomit into your own mouth) but do not fret – there is world-class fare here to enjoy, particularly the freshly caught seafood or beef from a paddock down the street from your table.

Scotland is a country of such natural beauty you'll feel a real desire to reconnect with the natural world around you. And who knows, you may just come home a fan of poetry (beginning with Robbie Burns, of course).

The magical land of Scotland is a wonderful place for kids to visit. Search for an answer to the mystery of Loch Ness, check out the stone castles and crumbing forts, learn about Scottish clans and be in awe of the majestic landscapes. Of course, the weather in Scotland can be unpredictable, so be prepared to encounter rain. In the countryside, the roads are narrow so getting from place to place can take longer than you expect – planning the trip beforehand and allowing extra time will be important with the kids.

ATTRACTIONS

- For stunning views of the wild Scottish West Highlands and the chance for the kids to pretend they're Harry Potter, take a ride on the **Jacobite Steam Train**, which travels over the famous **Glenfinnan Viaduct**, a location that was featured in the Harry Potter films.

- Visit **Inverness** on the north-east coast for some old-school mystery at **Loch Ness**. The kids can keep an eye out for the **Loch Ness Monster** (aka Nessie) and decide whether the monster is in fact a living dinosaur or a myth. You can take a cruise on Loch Ness for a closer chance to see Nessie and, if that doesn't happen, the cruise will provide a great vantage point to see **Urquhart Castle**. Spend time walking the nearby **Abriachan Forest Trails** to see Scottish wildlife. While in Inverness, also visit **Fort George**, the **Highlanders Museum** and **Nairn Beach** for dolphin-watching.

- Scotland is known for its islands. Take a ferry ride or boat tour to an island or three. With a range of services and so many magnificent islands, it's a great way to explore the stunning countryside of Scotland's more remote areas.

- **Fingal's Cave** is a unique sea cave on the uninhabited island of Staffa off Scotland's west coast. This natural wonder can be visited inside on calmer days, when you can even go ashore and play on the rocks. The National Trust for Scotland owns the cave as part of the Staffa National Nature Reserve. There are a number of boat tours to the island; some visit other islands as well so you could make a full day of it. Children under five are free on some tours.

- Visit the beautiful (and very popular) **Isle of Skye**, for rugged landscapes, prehistoric history, abundant wildlife and mediaeval castles. Also on Skye, the **Staffin Dinosaur Museum** gives the kids a chance to see dinosaur fossils and footprints (they offer tours to the hard-to-find Staffin dinosaur footprints). It's also an example of a childhood dream come true: Dugald Ross established the museum when he was just a teenager. That'll inspire any budding palaeontologists in your family.

EDINBURGH

SCOTLAND

ONCE GIVEN

the nickname 'Athens of the North', Edinburgh is one of Europe's true beauties (well, it's technically still European at the time of writing), surrounded by rocky, rolling hills and a constantly whispering ocean. Edinburgh's mediaeval dwellings remind you of its incredible past and at the same time the city's modern energy welcomes you to the now. The cobblestone streets lined with shops, restaurants and bars make it feel like a little country town, but this unique city is far from country. Its vibrant atmosphere takes a giant leap during all the festivals it offers, and the locals seem to love it just as much as the tourists.

Arrive for our favourite festival, the Fringe festival, in July/August and the buzz of fireworks and world-class (and some not-so-world-class) street performers will have you feeling you're exactly where you're meant to be. There are plenty of shows for the kids to attend and they can even try their hand at some juggling.

Edinburgh can be a kids' wonderland – most things to see and do are kid friendly. With plenty of parks and events throughout the year, kids will love this city. The narrow lanes and cobblestone streets lead to all sorts of wonderful and hidden places.

EATING OUT

For food, you have to introduce the kids to a traditional meal and there are plenty to choose from: neeps and tatties, cock-a-leekie, stovies and the all-time favourite haggis. For dessert try the Dundee cake. A popular place to visit is **Cafe St Honore** where the menu changes regularly to reflect the seasons.

ACCOMMODATION

Brij would recommend staying somewhere in the Old Town (it's her favourite area) for the historic mediaeval feel, but you will be surrounded by those beautiful cobblestone streets, which are not so pusher friendly. Staying in New Town will most likely be an easier choice because it offers good access to transport options, shops, places to eat and tourist attractions, and so it's perfect for families.

GETTING AROUND

You will do a lot of walking. It's fairly easy to get to all the attractions on foot, but the little ones will get tired so jump on a bus when you need to. You can get a daily family ticket for two adults and up to three children for use on trams and Lothian buses.

ATTRACTIONS

- The **National Museum of Scotland** has a life-sized skeleton cast of a *Tyrannosaurus rex* and if that doesn't get the kids going, put them on the human hamster wheel and see how much energy they burn. Race a Formula One car in the racing simulator (for kids over 137cm tall). Or get robots to spell your name, go on dino digs, dress in historical clothes, bring a Chinese dragon to life and more. (Please note that if you bring a Chinese dragon back to life you will need to declare this on your Customs form when you return to Australia.)

- **Camera Obscura and World of Illusions** is a major tourist attraction in Edinburgh's Old Town. There are six floors of amazing effects, like the World of Illusions, with its Magic Gallery, along with Eye Spy Edinburgh and Bewilderworld, the biggest illusion, which is best kept for last. With the Camera Obscura show and rooftop views, the world of puzzles, special effects, games and interactive attractions, this place will have the kids entertained for hours.

- The central figure of the Royal Arms of Scotland is the unicorn. Get the kids to see how many unicorns they can find as they explore Edinburgh – there are many! (Here are a couple of clues to get you started: a gatepost at the **Palace of Holyroodhouse**, the **National War Museum** and **St Margaret's Chapel** at Edinburgh Castle.)

- Even if you're not hunting unicorns, **Edinburgh Castle** is a must-visit. Join a 30-minute tour that's included in the ticket price and hear stories that will definitely keep the kids interested. The castle hosts performances and concerts, so check your dates to see if you can catch one.

- Stretch your legs climbing **Arthur's Seat**, an extinct volcano in beautiful **Holyrood Park**, and be rewarded with stunning views.

- Only half an hour from the centre of Edinburgh is the **Bo'ness and Kinneil Railway**, a wonderful heritage train trip. Enjoy the on-train afternoon tea while watching the world go past. Kids will love the Day Out with Thomas special events – check the website for dates.

- Discover what mediaeval battles were really like (minus the blood) with the 3D technology at the **Battle of Bannockburn Visitor Centre**, just under an hour west of the city centre. Kids can experience their own mediaeval battle and discover the history of those battles. Be prepared: they'll become their own versions of Braveheart!

- For more battle fun, visit the impressive **Stirling Castle**, just ten minutes north of the Battle of Bannockburn Visitor Centre. The castle offers family tours particularly catering to children aged five to 12, but even without going on a family tour you'll find much to interest the little ones. All the vaults have interactive exhibitions and the **Queen Anne Garden** is a lovely place to play.

BELFAST
NORTHERN IRELAND

While part of the United Kingdom, Northern Ireland is a stunning part of the Irish countryside and, after decades of political instability and violence, Belfast is now a great place to visit.

EATING OUT

Belfast has many award-winning restaurants and food markets to try. **St George's Market** is one to get to on Friday, Saturday and Sunday. For something a little cute for the kids we suggest trying **Fratelli Belfast**, where the kids can enjoy their own (affordable) three-course kids' menu.

ACCOMMODATION

Family rooms are available in most Belfast hotels. As with Dublin, the city centre is our choice of where to stay because it has plenty of shopping and attractions and is close to St George's Market.

GETTING AROUND

Belfast has a bus and train network, and you can get a Belfast Visitor Pass offering unlimited travel and discounts to some attractions. Children up to the age of five travel free and children under 16 can get a concession ticket.

ATTRACTIONS

- Belfast has a flourishing cultural scene and a vibrant nightlife, particularly the hip bars in the historic **Cathedral Quarter**. It has also become something of a festival city with two highlights being the **Belfast International Film Festival** and the **Belfast International Arts Festival**, which is getting bigger and better each time and is now one of the biggest festivals of its kind within the United Kingdom and Ireland. And because it's such a kid-friendly city, it even has the **Belfast Children's Festival** each March.

- With its rich history and culture, Belfast offers much for families. Much-loved author C.S. Lewis was born here and there's a self-guided **C.S. Lewis Trail** through the city. Have a *Lion, Witch and Wardrobe* celebration, watch the movie or read the book, and then head to **C.S. Lewis Square**, the sculpture park that celebrates the author (and is part of the trail). The kids will love spotting the seven sculptures inspired by the magical land of Narnia, and it's an impressive example of public art. They are lit up at night, so if you enjoy a night stroll this could be fun too.

- You may not know that the *Titanic* was built in the Belfast shipyards, and you can discover more about the tragic ship's history at **Titanic Belfast**, one of the most popular places to visit in the city. It's a fascinating experience for all. With special effects and interactive galleries, this place will have the whole family engaged and learning about history. There are options for tours and combined tickets online.

- For something a little more modern, **W5 Discovery and Science Centre** is sure to be a favourite with the kids, with experiences ranging from climbing to virtual reality to medical labs – you could spend days here. There are special events on weekends and holidays and the website allows you to build your own itinerary. There are areas for picnics, so you can pack lunch, or alternatively visit the centre cafe or head out of the centre for lunch and return after.

- The first Northern Ireland site given World Heritage listing, the **Giant's Causeway** is an impressive natural phenomenon so worth visiting (it's just over an hour from Belfast). This astounding system of basalt columns looks like giant stepping stones and was created thanks to volcanic activity about 50 to 60 million years ago. You can visit the Causeway for free, though you'll have a bit of a walk; advertised ticket prices apply only to the visitor centre and its parking. There are a number of walking trails, cliff-top views and a walk down to the Causeway itself. It's okay to visit here with toddlers – you just may be better off not venturing too far out. The kids will definitely love climbing over the rocks and playing on the different formations.

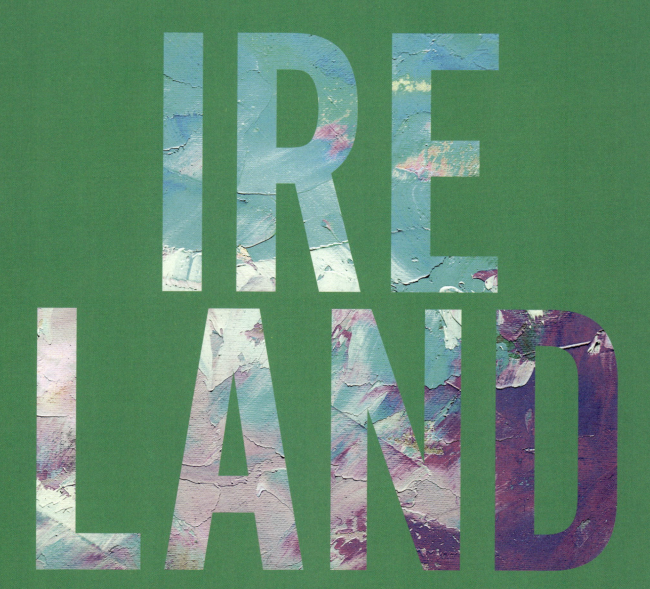

GREEN ROLLING HILLS AS FAR AS THE EYE CAN SEE, BREATHTAKING COASTLINES AND *REAL* IRISH PUBS THAT ARE AS COSY AS THEY CAN BE ROLLICKING – IRELAND IS A COUNTRY HELD CLOSE IN MANY HEARTS.

And it's hard to think of a people more loved than the Irish. Yes, many of them become more Irish the further away they get from their Gaelic shores, but to shoot the breeze with an Irishman or Irishwoman in Ireland is to know you are winning at life.

DID YOU KNOW?

- Sean's Bar in Athlone is the oldest pub in Ireland dating back to 900 CE. Under new management since 1376.
- Ireland is the only nation to have won Eurovision seven times and the only one to have won it three times in a row. Now that is important history right there!
- Halloween actually comes from the ancient Gaelic festival of Samhain, where people would light bonfires and dress up to ward off ghosts. Known as All Hallows Eve, it was the day before All Saints Day and marked the end of summer and the harvest, and the beginning of winter. Yes, Halloween: made in Ireland, marketed in the US of A.
- St Patrick wasn't actually born in Ireland but you may not want to go on about that too much!

Pete once hitch-hiked from Dublin down through the south coast and back up to Galway before catching the bus back to Dublin. He fondly recalls being picked up by Jimmy Flannigan, a man in his fifties with rosy red cheeks. All Pete wanted to speak about was Irish history and politics, all Jimmy wanted to know were the latest plot-lines in *Neighbours* and *Home and Away*.

Ireland has a fascinating and ancient history and spectacular natural beauty. It is, no surprise, an island, separated from Great Britain mainly by the wild Irish Sea. Ireland is a republic, a stand-alone country not part of the United Kingdom as such, except for Northern Ireland, which remains a country or region of the United Kingdom and covers about one-sixth of the Irish island. It's definitely worth visiting Northern Ireland too, and we mention some of our highlights on p. 205.

Ireland is a fantastic place for kids. While our kids enjoyed the scenery and craic with the locals they were most captivated by eating simple dough balls: a small round ball of pizza dough baked in the oven. It's typical that the Irish can make something so simple just so tasty (mashed potato, anyone?). It's so easy to drive everywhere, which allows you to slow down and plan a trip at a more relaxed pace that will suit the children. There is music everywhere – the kids will love the music and the entertainers themselves. Walking the streets is pretty easy in the cities with pusher-friendly footpaths, and the Irish are absolutely wonderful people ... *to be sure*. They are welcoming and family friendly. Trust us, once you visit Ireland it will keep calling you back for the rest of your life.

GETTING AROUND

Ireland is easy to get around but you won't be able to do everything, so plan your trip well beforehand. The highways will get you from destination to destination pretty quickly but you'll miss a lot of the magic in between.

Hiring a car is the best option when getting around Ireland. It is full of beautiful towns and landscapes. If you're heading to Northern Ireland, check with your car rental company about whether you are allowed to drive your car across the border without a fee.

To get around Dublin, buy a Dublin Pass; it will give you discounts to over 30 different attractions, with fast-track entries and guidebooks too. The Leap Visitor Card will save you on public transport, and you can choose the number of days you want (children under five are free).

EATING OUT

The pubs in Ireland are for telling stories, listening to music and enjoying the craic (the atmosphere). They are about having a good time and great conversation, not just drinking. Children under 15 are allowed into pubs if with an adult, but they will need to leave by 9pm.

Dublin has a variety of food markets the kids will love to explore. Try the **Temple Bar food market** on weekends or the **Irish Village market** at lunchtime on Wednesday, Thursday and Friday.

ACCOMMODATION

Years ago, Brij was fortunate enough to stay with a family in a small Irish country town for a week. The Irish are that nice, taking in backpacking Australians; it might, however, be a stretch to get the whole family in. All throughout Ireland B&B accommodation is available. Hostels are usually clean and affordable and some even have family rooms. There are some castles that offer accommodation, and you'll find lodges in country towns. Our pick for family travel would be self-catering apartments and houses.

In Dublin you'll notice the hotels are a bit pricey, but there are more affordable B&Bs and guesthouses. South City Centre around Trinity College is near many attractions. The city centre is where we stay because it's close to main attractions and also many pubs, so we can easily pop in for good old-fashioned Irish music. Many hotels in the city centre will have family rooms.

ATTRACTIONS

- A drive around Ireland's countryside is a must-do. One of the most beautiful is the **Ring of Kerry**, a gorgeous drive that loops around County Kerry's Iveragh Peninsula. You'll see magnificent Atlantic Ocean views, stunning landscapes, seaside towns and ancient ruins – and there are numerous pubs on the way. To drive the circuit itself only takes three and a half hours without stopping, but that would be no fun. When backpacking around Ireland, Brij did the opposite to Pete and picked up a hitchhiker who wanted to get out once he realised he was in a car with three girls on the way to the Ring of Kerry, which he had done the day before, and that they weren't going to talk about *Neighbours* or *Home and Away*.

- Take some time to visit the historic and vibrant town of **Killarney**, which is a great starting point for the Ring of Kerry. Visit **Muckross Traditional Farms** to make your own butter and see what farming in Ireland used to be like; there's also an old schoolhouse the kids can peer in. Killarney and its surrounding region offer so much to do: go for a waterfall walk (**Derrycunnihy Falls** is beautiful and great for kids, but not stroller friendly), find the hidden ruin of **Parkavonear Castle**, go on a fairy quest on the **Irish Fairy Trails** (see irishfairytrails.com for more), and let the kids have a play at **Port Road Playground**, just inside **Killarney National Park**. Also in the national park is the (supposedly haunted) 15th-century **Ross Castle**.

- **County Clare** is another gorgeous county in Ireland (aren't they all?). In Clare, visit the breathtaking **Cliffs of Moher**, an incredibly popular and heavily photographed wild landscape. Get here in the early morning or late afternoon when it's less busy. The lookout provides spectacular views and has a fence built with slabs of rock; kids are safe but, like anywhere, keep hold of your little ones, especially if they like to climb. Look out for signs warning you about unsupervised areas. It may not be ideal to take younger kids here but access is allowed.

- The city of **Galway**, in **County Galway**, has plenty of playgrounds and typically fun things for the kids to do. Take some time to wander the streets, go shopping and grab some food in one of the excellent cafes (the city has a fabulous food culture). Visit a festival or the popular **Galway Farmers' Market**, or explore the mediaeval part of old Galway such as the **Spanish Arch**. The seaside suburb of Salthill has the 2km long **Salthill Promenade** – it's the perfect place for a stroll followed by delicious fish and chips.

DUBLIN

Is Dublin the jewel

in Europe's crown? No. Is it the most beautiful city in Ireland? Probably not. But what it lacks in sheer beauty it more than makes up for with soul and humour. For a community that has seen tough economic times, Dubliners have never lost their knack for seeing the brighter side of life while at the same time acknowledging they don't exactly have it all. But then again they don't need it all because they live in Dublin, which is, according to many locals, 'the greatest city in the world!' Not only is Dublin home to many of Ireland's famous musicians, including the Dubliners, Sinead O'Connor and U2, but also it has the **National Leprechaun Museum of Ireland**.

One of the friendliest cities in Europe, Dublin will be perfect for the little ones. Full of music, happiness and attractions, it's on the money for a fun-filled city holiday.

ATTRACTIONS

- Download the **Dublin Discovery Trails app**, and explore the city yourself with this great variety of self-guided themed walks. The family can learn about different sides to the history of Dublin, from the Vikings to the Easter Rising. Walk in the footsteps of rebels, take the streets filled with parks and castles, or take the north side and learn about the cultural and sporting history of the city. Our favourite trail is the Real Dublin one – take the alleyways and winding streets ending at the famous Temple Bar.

- If you have some Irish heritage, visit **EPIC: the Irish Emigration Museum** to learn about the many people who have left the Irish shores over the years. You may find Brij's grandfather Jack Murphy.

- Perhaps surprisingly, exploring **Trinity College** with kids is very interesting. The college was created in 1592, which makes for a fascinating history. The grounds can be used for lounging and picnics; you can see the Book of Kells, a 9th-century illuminated manuscript; and you can tour the Long Room Library that houses over 200,000 of Trinity's oldest books and some of the oldest harps.

- If the weather is unkind, **Dublinia** is a top option. It's a great display of Dublin's Viking and mediaeval history and has interactive sections for the kids. The Dublinia website has an online learning platform, which may be good to do with your kids before or after your visit.

- Most kids can't go past a zoo, and we're sure you'll find **Dublin Zoo** no different. First opened in 1831, it has a big conservation focus and is popular with locals and tourists. With a full program of talks to choose from throughout the day, plan your visit to include the shows you want to see. The Dublin Zoo website has an animal cam link where you can get a little sneak peek at some of the animals – fun to do in the lead-up to your visit. Over the winter months it has Wild Lights, a magical night-time spectacular (wear warm clothes!).

- The **Guinness Storehouse** doesn't scream children's museum, but the history of the brewery is actually very interesting. The experience is family friendly especially if you focus on the historical advertising, interactive displays, culture and tradition.

- For a lovely daytrip from Dublin, visit **Cork** and take a trip to the **Blarney Castle and Gardens**, which are home to the **Blarney Stone**, and give your kids the gift of eloquence – or the gift of the gab as it may be referred to. There's nothing like a story to bring history to life and the Blarney Castle and Gardens have plenty. It's a three-hour drive so you may want to make a night of it and stay nearby before heading back to Dublin the next day.

KID-FREE NIGHT OUT

If you don't need to tick off a visit to the **Temple Bar** and the crowds it brings, try the **Brazen Head**, the oldest pub in Dublin. It has great food – good old hearty dishes. Dublin isn't just about fun-named pubs; there are plenty of fine-dining restaurants, like the **Greenhouse**, to try out. If you can't decide among the many, try **Eatyard**, a street-food pop-up market with a variety of cuisines to enjoy under twinkling lights.

Meander through the Temple Bar district, and head to **Love Land**. This alley at Crampton Court is a tribute to love – stroll along reading the tiles with quotes of love found and lost.

WE SAY THIS UNASHAMEDLY: WE COMPLETELY ADORE PARIS AND THE WHOLE DAMN COUNTRY.

Like most who visit and fall for this old romantic, we swooned at French culture, we marvelled at the world's finest cuisine, we forgot ourselves as we floated down to the local bakery to grab a French stick and morning pastries.

France offers absolutely everything a kid could love about holidays: beaches, iconic parks, museums, history, rivers and canals, the best food and a Disneyland. The French are absolutely lovely people; despite a common comment from travellers that the locals are rude, we found this to be completely wrong. The French love children – they may expect them to be a little quieter in a museum or on a train, but they are very accommodating and helpful.

We've started this chapter with Paris, then we move on to some of the fabulous regions of France worth visiting. We should say that not all roads lead to Paris. If you're driving, don't exit the freeway at the first sign to Paris like we did as we left Charles de Gaulle airport. Pete panicked a little as visions of us forever circling the Arc de Triomphe roundabout swirled in his head. It was 2012 and, thanks to sat-nav not being readily available, we ended up driving 190km away from our destination. On the bright side, we did enjoy a night in the delightful town of Rouen, which we would have otherwise not seen. Pete claims that as a win.

Thanks to the world falling in love with French chic, you'll find France both alien and strangely familiar. From the picturesque countryside hosting some of the best and most famous vineyards in the world to the sassy street markets; from the outward-seated bistros where coffee lovers and people watchers gather to the art and attitude of one of the world's most adored countries; from the miraculous Mont-Saint-Michel to the beaches of the South; you'll be utterly enchanted and helplessly seduced. As we have been and continue to be. Essentially, in your lifetime, if you can, you simply must visit France.

Where do you board the Yoplait hot-air balloon?
Où montez-vous dans la montgolfière Yoplait?

Why aren't these French poodles speaking French?
Pourquoi ces caniches français ne parlent-ils pas français?

Seriously, how don't you people get fat?
Sérieusement, comment vous ne devenez pas gros?

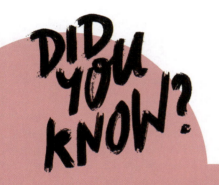

- During World War I, artists painted vehicles and equipment to blend into the background making the French Army the first to use camouflage. It also eventually became fashionable. So French.
- It was a Frenchman, Nicolas Appert, who came up with the idea of canning foods, using sealed glass containers and placing them in boiling water. In tribute, he was buried the same way. Or not.
- The oldest person in the world according to the Guinness Book of World Records is a French woman who lived to be 122 years and 164 days old, but didn't look a day over 118 years and 122 days. We really need to get one of those French diet books.
- There are hundreds of different types of French cheese and, with the many varieties of each one, it's thought there are over 1000 different types of French cheese available. How don't the French have an obesity problem exactly?

PARIS

IT'S HARD TO IMAGINE more icons gathered in any one city outside of New York's Met Gala. Unlike the style celebs and Kardashians of today, though, these Parisian icons have been around way longer and will survive the test of time. (This is not a dig at the Kardashians per se – these icons will outlive us all!)

EATING OUT

Finding good food is very easy – often we'd grab a baguette and some cheese and deli foods for lunch and keep on going. Restaurants don't have a problem with kids; if they don't have a kids' menu they will usually offer to adjust a dish to suit those tiny tummies. Usually you can't go wrong ordering the *bœuf à la bourguignon* (beef burgundy) or the *coq au vin* (chicken with wine) for dinner, but the *soupe à l'oignon* (French onion soup) will also be absolutely divine. The French do a great *steak frites* (steak and hot chips) if you're feeling homesick. The kids loved the food but their favourite meal was always dessert. Go simple and popular with the *crème brûlèe*. And, oh, you must try a *soufflè* if it's on the menu – it is likely to be mouth-watering. Sweet soufflès are always good but try a savoury soufflè too; Brij tried a pizza soufflè and it was amazing. Our main tip for eating in Paris is to head away from the touristy areas and look for places frequented by locals. The smaller the place, the more likely an amazing experience will be waiting for you.

Be prepared for some cultural differences – for example, shop hours are different and not many places are open on Sunday or between 12pm and 2pm on weekdays. We even noticed the supermarket was closed!

Getting Around

We always stay in apartments in Paris. It doesn't matter where but closer to the Seine means you'll be able to walk to more attractions and parks. We recommend making sure you have a patisserie, deli, supermarket, park and metro stop nearby when looking for a place to call home for a bit. Getting up in the morning and walking to the bakery for fresh croissants and pastries for breakfast is our idea of Paris living. Outside Paris, look for homestays or B&Bs because meeting local people adds to the experience and, as a bonus, they will often recommend things to see and where to go for great food.

Accommodation

It's easy to take in the Paris sights that you can't or don't want to walk to by using public transport. The hop-on hop-off boats along the River Seine are a scenic way to get around, and the city's buses are a great way to get to those touristy places but will take you longer. The Paris Metro subway system is absolutely the best way to get around and it's easy to navigate. Some stations may not have access for pushers all the way to the platforms – the best option with a stroller is to use one of those quick fold-up umbrella strollers, perfect for when the stairs are endless and the peak times are coming.

Europe's busiest railway station – and one of the oldest in the world – is Paris Gare du Nord. More than 190 million passengers go through the station each year. Sadly, your Myki or Opal card will not work here. There are a number of ticket options, though – you can buy single tickets, day passes or multi-day passes, pre-loaded cards or discounted books of ten tickets (including reduced fare tickets for children aged between four and nine). Children under three travel for free. Pick up a map of the metro system or download one. You may need to refer to it several times a day or more.

There are plenty of taxis and ride-share companies if you need to be above ground, but the metro system is so good you don't really need to use anything else. Perhaps just get a taxi to take you around the Arc De Triomphe roundabout if only to see how this crazy, chaotic roundabout works.

Playing nice in Nice

ATTRACTIONS

- The **Eiffel Tower** dominates the Paris skyline, the hulking **Arc de Triomphe** stands like security detail for the dazzling **Champs-Élysées** and the recently fire-devastated **Notre-Dame Cathedral** sits wounded (but is being reconstructed) along the famous **Seine**. It's hard not to think that Paris is the greatest city in the world. A city that has given so much to the globe. Can you imagine a world without French wine? Champagne? Cheese? Pastries? Fashion? Yoplait? And that's before you walk into the art mecca that is the **Louvre**.

  And then, of course, there is the shopping. The kids loved wandering the streets in search of toy stores, lolly shops and the best crêpes and croissants. This was until they discovered a shop window filled with taxidermied rats (it was at a pest control store), and then it seemed there were taxidermied things to be found *everywhere* (we're not sure why these were more captivating than lolly shops but they were!).

- We've been to Paris a couple of times because we just can't seem to keep away. On a visit to celebrate our tenth wedding anniversary, we placed a love-lock (next to tens of thousands of others) on the well-known **Pont des Arts**, a bridge crossing the Seine. But in 2015 it was brutally removed and heartlessly thrown away. Well, really, all the love-locks were cut off and discarded because the weight of the locks was causing serious damage to the bridge's structure (it's estimated that *one million* locks were removed – that's a whole lotta love). We still love each other despite the lack of our lock on a bridge in the most romantic city in the world.

  Regardless of the romance and the fact that it's generally a safe place to visit, Paris does have a variety of scams aimed at tourists, such as the gold-ring scam, the signing-a-petition scam, the cup-and-ball scam or the friendship-bracelets scam. Don't be fooled by the gypsies along the river, like Pete was, when they tell you they've found your ring, give it to you and then demand money. Lucky for Pete the police were down the road and the gypsies ran. The best approach is to not look too much like tourists, stay aware of your surroundings (not always easy when you're trying to manage the kids too) and just not engage with any scammers (don't be afraid to be rude).

  Most importantly when exploring Paris, take a moment each day to simply remind yourself (and the kids) that *you are in Paris.* It's just so different from Australia and such a wonderful experience for the whole family. There are so many things to do; here are just a few of our favourites.

- One of the most iconic monuments in the world, the **Eiffel Tower** is definitely one to visit. Climbing it is worth it as you'll get spectacular views of the city – the only thing you'll have to get through are the queues. Book your tickets online and pay a little more for 'skip the line' passes and also maybe a guided tour. If you can, wait for the sparkling lights at night when the entire tower is lit up – the lights are so pretty and probably worth the tired ones on your shoulder. We don't recommend eating at the restaurant – it isn't the best culinary experience Paris has to offer and the service ... well, it's a tourist attraction so don't expect much. To go up the tower, kids under four are free and there are options to use the lift or stairs or a combo, so choose based on your family's level of love (and ability) for stairs.

- The Eiffel Tower is set in the beautiful **Champ de Mars** park so, if you can, spend time in the park before or after your visit to the tower; with a beautiful carousel, green lawns, pathways, colourful flower gardens and shady places, it's the perfect Parisian setting to watch your kids have fun.

- A bit weird and wacky, the **Musée de la Magie**, or Museum of Magic, in the 4th arrondissement is full of fascinating artefacts from the history of magic and illusion. Its seven rooms feature all sorts of magicians' items, from magic wands to secret boxes, spanning from the 18th century to now. Look out for the shows on offer: they will be in French but you don't need the words to enjoy the shows, which are great for both kids and adults.

- **Parc des Buttes-Chaumont**, in the 19th arrondissement, is filled with grottos, waterfalls, paths, bridges and an artificial lake. Built on old quarries, the park has some good hills: the hike up and the roll down is a terrific experience for kids on a beautiful Parisian day. Relax with a picnic or explore the park: find its most famous feature, the **Temple de la Sibylle** (a smaller version of Italy's Temple of Vesta). If you want more green space, visit the more formal and popular **Jardin du Luxembourg**, or Luxembourg Gardens, in the 6th arrondissement, with its puppet shows, pony rides and famous carousel. The playground in the gardens is perfect for kids wanting to jump, run and climb.

- The **Louvre Museum** in Paris is consistently the most visited museum in the world. Over nine million visitors go through its doors annually. It goes without saying that you need to go there at least once, but the Louvre with kids can seem daunting – and we all know the fine arts scene doesn't really love sticky fingers and kids running around. With that said, it's still possible to enjoy this amazing museum on a family holiday. We suggest you skip the guided tours and don't even think about the recorded headphone tours, which are just nightmares in silence. Although the Louvre is a must-see museum it is seriously MASSIVE! It's also crowded – if you want to get a peek at the *Mona Lisa* in her glass case you will need to have very patient kids. We reckon that allowing kids to skip parts of a museum (so you all avoid exhaustion) will help make them want to visit other museums in the future, and that's a good thing. So, plan your visit and know which areas will interest you the most, and this way everyone will enjoy it. Book your tickets online before you go and, except for Fridays, you can use the Porte des Lions entrance to avoid the queues at the Pyramid entrance. Look for ways to entertain the kids, like a treasure hunt for information or word-finds and pictures they need to check off. In our experience, you will get about two hours here from most kids before things pass the point of no return. If your kids will be interested in a few museums (and we strongly suggest going to a couple as the kids will have a good time) then look at getting the Paris Museum Pass. As well as the Louvre, it gives you entry to **Musée d'Orsay**, the **Arc de Triomphe**, the **Pantheon** and about 60 other museums (perhaps don't aim to visit all 60 ...) and it can also allow you to skip the queues.

- **Sacré-Coeur**, located in **Montmartre**, a former artists' village, stands at the highest point in Paris and can be seen on the Parisian skyline from many points in the city. The area of Montmartre itself is completely charming and is that 'classic Paris' seen in so many movies. The kids can catch the little train of Montmartre and meander through the cobblestone streets. Visit **Espace Dalí**, or the Dali Museum, in Montmartre. A museum with over 300 of Salvador Dalí's works of art, it will hold the attention of your little ones because of the fun nature of Dalí's art (melting clocks, anyone?). Around the gorgeous Montmartre streets, go looking for the family's favourite street art, and find an artist to paint your portrait.

- **Notre-Dame** is a mediaeval Catholic cathedral on the Île de la Cité. With beautiful French Gothic architecture, this world-famous cathedral is over 850 years old and took about 200 years to complete. It survived the French Revolution, World War I and World War II, and somehow still stands after the devastating fire in 2019. Within months of the fire, the French Parliament passed a law that the cathedral was to be rebuilt exactly as it was before the fire. It is closed to visitors but you can take the kids for a walk around this incredible monument.

- Think of Paris and you think of food (well, we do). **Kids' cooking classes** are going to be a win-win – you might get a night off from cooking or perhaps be delivered croissants in bed and the kids are going to be entertained. Sign them up – there are many classes on offer around the city – and enjoy a quiet coffee, or all join in and learn some French culinary skills together.

- For a wonderful daytrip, **Disneyland Paris**, originally Euro Disney, is a fabulous choice for families. It's about 40km east of Paris and actually includes two parks: **Disneyland Park** and **Walt Disney Studios Park**. Theme parks are a great way to see how adventurous your kids might be. Will they be brave enough to take on the Star Wars Hyperspace Mountain? Or how about the Phantom Manor (which is a French Haunted House)? Liam had worked up the courage to go on the Indiana Jones et le Temple du Peril ride only for it to be closed when we got there – disappointing! In terms of the practicalities, there are a few ways to get there and a few things to consider. The park itself opens to general admission at 10am, but if you are taking a planned shuttle from the city, you will be meeting your bus around 8am. Or you can catch the train, which takes about 35 minutes. You'll want to spend all day here (like all the other Disney parks) so if you want to do Walt Disney Studios Park as well, consider staying in one of the hotels in or near the park. You'll all want to make the most of your time here so spend some time on the website to work out what you most want to do – this will help you to plan your day well. If using a shuttle to get to and from the park, make sure you are where you need to be when you need to be there. Pete nearly missed the shuttle back because young Aidan insisted on having a plastic Halloween jack-o'-lantern, which, in fairness, we had promised him earlier. After a few quick dashes and some zig-zagging, Pete and Aidan just made it back to the bus and a slightly stressed Brij, who was pleading with the bus driver not to drive away without the whole family on board. A close call.

PARIS DEGUSTATION: A WARNING
(BY PETE)

Celebrity chef Matt Moran kindly gave us a suggestion for a fancy night of dining when we were in Paris: Alain Ducasse au Plaza Athénée in the 8th arrondissement.

Alain Ducasse is a living French legend with 21 Michelin stars. His restaurants are dotted around the world, from Paris and London to New York, Hong Kong, Tokyo and Beirut to name just a few.

The photos on the restaurant's website showed Paris at its most decadent – chandeliers adorned with Swarovski crystals, spacious tabling, and silverware from the Christofle Museum. If you were shooting a movie set in a fancy French restaurant, you'd shoot it here. It was recently ranked the 16th best restaurant in the world.

Understandably, we were giddy with excitement when we secured a reservation. We booked the babysitter until 1am – this was our one night to be adults in Paris, the City of Love. Dinner at one of the best restaurants in the world then we'd see where the night took us. We spoke of hitting a Parisian jazz club, something we never did back home in our regular, domestic lives.

One part Europhile. Two parts wanker.

We put on our best threads and headed to the 8th. Excited, nervous, hungry.

Shown to our table by the maître d', we were then accosted by a further six waiters. One kindly pulled out our seats, the next poured water, another offered drink menus. I seem to recollect being given a back massage at some point but I may be mistaken.

We felt very fancy, very grown up and a long way from La Porchetta.

Then came the fateful moment when the Frenchest of French waiters asked: *Would you like the degustation menu?*

He asked it in a way to suggest that if we didn't want the degustation then he, along with the chef, the staff, the fellow diners and the great Alain Ducasse himself, would be aghast.

We looked at each other with wavering confidence and simply nodded. With that the French Waiter of the Year snapped his fingers and half-a-dozen waiters whizzed around us. We had taken on degustation menus before with varying degrees of success. Brij eats less than me, and she's guilty of having eyes bigger than her stomach.

'It's okay,' I assure her, 'we'll just take it slow.'

The first course arrives and it's something teeny-weeny. From memory it could have been an anchovy on mini-toast.

'May have to go to Macca's on the way home,' I smugly quip.

About eight courses in and we are doing okay. The wine is liquid gold, the food is every bit as good as you'd hope for it to be. But then it happened.

The chicken. That yellow sauce.

It looks like the least fanciest of all the fancy things we had eaten. A chicken breast with a custard-yellow sauce drizzled over it. Everything had been so small, so delicate and perfectly sized. This. This seems big. And we are eight courses in. I look at Brij. The look on her face suggests she's in trouble.

'Take your time,' I whisper, trying not to let the fancy French staff know that suddenly we are flustered and out of our league.

Brij takes tiny bites, cutting up small pieces just like she had cut up steak for Oscar the day before.

'I might just go to the bathroom,' she says before excusing herself.

Upon her return, she nods that everything's okay, before I similarly excuse myself and head to the gents. I remember sitting in the cubicle *on* the toilet seat, not actually using the toilet, just sitting there taking a breather. Loosening my belt.

'Dig deep,' I tell myself, 'dig deep.'

We somehow get through the meal. The waiters remain fancy but completely understanding. I feel they've seen this before: out-of-towners taking on the great Alain Ducasse.

As we wrap up this epic dinner we talk about which jazz clubs we'll hit.

'We have the babysitter until 1am. We are in the most romantic city in the world!' We rub our stomachs to find some relief. A tummy gurgles – it's hard to say whose tummy it is. We decide it's best to head home.

It's 9.25pm.

If you head to Paris, if you can afford it and if you can get a reservation, we highly recommend the Alain Ducasse experience, but discuss before you go: 'Are we up for degustation?'

Because if you're not prepared, the chicken will get ya!

Lock it in! Brij and Pete just after padlocking their love to a bridge in Paris.

NORMANDY

SITUATED in northern France, the Normandy region is renowned for its mediaeval history, the D-Day landings in World War II and, importantly, inventing Camembert cheese. And it's a great area to explore with kids. There are so many cultural and sporting activities, water parks, water sports, boat trips, all-ages beach clubs and mazes, but what is truly wonderful about Normandy isn't just kid entertainment – it's that *all* the sights will interest kids.

Visit the iconic and World Heritage–listed **Mont-Saint-Michel**, the mediaeval island monastery; the pretty harbour town of **Honfleur**; the cultural and vibrant **Rouen** (worthy of a detour as we can attest); the striking white cliffs at **Étretat**; and the many sights, museums and memorials of the **D-Day beaches**. If you have any artists in the family, take them to the birthplace of Impressionism at Claude Monet's home and garden in **Giverny** and the Museum of Modern Art in **Le Havre**.

TOULOUSE

THIS VIBRANT, COLOURFUL city is great for families to explore: take a walking tour or tour the canals to see what this beautiful and historic place has to offer.

Do the moonwalk at the **Toulouse Cité de l'espace** or City of Space. This space museum is popular with young and old, especially budding astronauts. You can see real spacesuits, moon rocks and spacecraft replicas, try the moonwalk simulator, explore the many interactive exhibits and buy souvenirs; there is also a 'little astronaut's corner' where the wee ones can play space games.

Head to Toulouse's idyllic **Jardin des Plantes**, the Garden of Plants, and you'll be spoilt for choice. Wander through the beautiful gardens, let the kids frolic on the lush green lawns and the excellent playground, and admire the historic statues and fountains. Very close by is the **Muséum de Toulouse**, a natural history museum, with lots of exhibits for kids. Plan your visit to the gardens and the museum well and allow plenty of time.

CÔTE D'AZUR

THE FRENCH RIVIERA

is absolutely awesome for families and you don't need to own a $300 million super yacht to enjoy it. The best time to visit would be just before or after peak season when you can enjoy all the restaurants, beaches and weather without the crowds. Also, as a bonus, some accommodation places will have great discounts and incentives to entice you.

Our favourite place to stay is in **Villefranche-sur-Mer**. Near the French–Italian border, it is tucked away between Monaco and Nice. The cobblestone streets are filled with wonderful cafes offering unbelievable food – it is a charming town with just-as-charming locals. We think your kids will love all the beachside towns of the south of France. There are sandy beaches to be found, but it's worth noting that the beach in Nice is rocky. It's a new experience and in our opinion requires strong ankles. But it's well worth a trip.

Villages des Fouls or Village of Fools is an amusement park in Villeneuve-Loubet where you can go crazy and play the fool as much as you like. Done a little differently, the park offers games at every turn, with go-karts, mazes, tree climbs and heaps of other things; there are water activities too so bring swimmers or a change of clothes for the kids. All ages will have fun here and admission for under threes is free, with family tickets available too. And just nearby is **Le Bois des Lutins**, an adventure park where the kids can do tree climbs, play with wooden games, go in an underground troll cave and look around for the hidden fairies, elves and pixies.

You can hire bikes and scooters or even rollerblades to enjoy the path along the **Promenade des Anglais** in Nice.

BURGUNDY

A DAYTRIP to **Beaune** is totally worth it, believe us. You may think this incredible wine town won't be great for kids – and to be honest we didn't go there for the kid attractions on offer – but this beautiful town is situated among some of the most picturesque countryside you will ever see. Just walking around town, stopping at parks, buying local produce and seeing what's in the centre square (sometimes there's a carousel) will have the kids entertained (and tired) by the end of the day.

Staying in **Dijon** is a great idea for families, and parents who love their wine. First of all, buy some mustard: for not many euros you will pick up some of the best Dijon mustard you have ever tasted. Dijon is a charming city filled with incredible Renaissance and mediaeval buildings. Do the **Rallye Mômes**, where the kids hunt for the city's points of interest using a log book to mark out their discoveries as you all stroll through the historic streets. Another fun exploring trail is the **Owl's Trail** or le Parcours de la Chouette. Download the Owl's Trail app or pick up the booklet at the tourist office and take the route to discover old Dijon – the trail covers 22 sites but there are a couple of loop options too. Each site is marked by a golden owl, the lucky charm of Dijon, and the kids will love hunting for the next owl plaque. It's an easy walk and will take about an hour, unless you stop at a cafe for a break. Don't forget to stop at the famous statuette stone, the **Owl of Notre Dame de Dijon**, which has been granting wishes to those who reach up and touch its face for three centuries (but make sure it's with your left hand!). If you have a chance to look into it before you go, the church and owl have a fascinating history.

FRENCH ALPS

YOU MAY NOT CONSIDER the **French Alps** a destination if you are not planning a skiing holiday, but even in summer there are some great things to do in the area with the kids. **Chamonix** is located at the base of **Mont Blanc**, the highest peak in the Alps. From Chamonix-Town, you can take a cable-car to the summit of **Aiguille du Midi**, and from there you can hop on the **Panoramic Mont Blanc cable-car**, the highest cable-car in the world. This is the closest you can get to Mont Blanc without climbing the massive peak. The cable-cars run any time of year (other lifts and tramways are available too) but do depend on the weather.

A visit to scenic **Annecy** will back up its picture-perfect reputation. There are stunning views of **Lake Annecy** from everywhere in town – the sparkling lake is meant to be the cleanest in Europe. Canals wind through the town and the colourful historic houses with flowers on windowsills and balconies are delightful. And for you adventurous ones, the options are endless with rafting, canyoning, mountain climbing, caving, glacier walking, ziplines and more all within the Annecy basin, and great water activities on the lake. The little ones will love the quaint minigolf course and lakeside beaches.

SKIING IN FRANCE

Of the skiing destinations in Europe, France isn't the cheapest option but it's also not the most expensive – Switzerland can take that badge of honour. But regardless of your skiing likes or dislikes, the French resorts in winter are just so lovely. You don't even need to ski to have a good time: Brij loves a trip to the day spa as a ski-free-day treat, but as a family we have always enjoyed investigating each resort's extra activities. And kids and snow photograph so well – you'll always have wonderful reminders of your holiday. If you are thinking of a French skiing holiday, here are two of our favourite places.

Avoriaz
This purpose-built, car-free resort is not only beautiful but also very family friendly. It offers a children's village and the Burton Kids Parkway, a snowpark designed especially for younger children to teach them the rules of using a snowpark in a fun way. They will learn how to jump, balance and fall. The resort offers free ski passes for under fives too. Visit in summer for great mountain-biking and trekking and, of course, beautiful alpine views.

Val Thorens
This stunning place could be considered the best ski resort in Europe. With more than 600km of slopes and 140 lifts, it is one of the largest ski areas in the world. It's perfect for all levels of skiers and snowboarders and ticks all the boxes: lessons, excellent ski runs, delicious food, entertainment, rest and adventure. They even offer a huge range of snow activities beyond skiing, such as paragliding, sledge trains, mountain-biking on snow, snow mobiles and snow trikes – you can even go to a yoga class on the snow if that's your thing. Val Thorens has various accommodation options available, from apartments to hotels. If you've been saving your pennies, check out Hotel Pashmina le Refuge with ski-to-door access, a luxurious wellness centre and two restaurants, one of which is Michelin starred.

Livin' on the edge...

COLLINGWOOD VERSUS FRANCE
(BY PETE)

On a late September Saturday afternoon Brij and I sat in shell-shocked silence surrounded by 100,016 people also shocked into an eerie stillness. It was like a hundred thousand people had just been told there would be no dinner tonight.

We had just watched the 2010 AFL Grand Final between our beloved Collingwood Magpies and the St Kilda Saints – a drawn grand final for only the third time in history. We could barely look at each other, let alone know what to say.

The grand final would be replayed the following Saturday. We had airline tickets booked for France ... on Wednesday.

I think it was Sunday night when I floated an idea past Brij: 'How about we put our trip back a week?' The look I received was the kind of look you may expect if you asked your fiancée, 'How about we get married in tracksuit pants?'

It was fair enough, and I wasn't expecting an affirmative response. Brij had spent months planning our trip, meticulously plotting our itinerary and making sure we got from point A to point B on time.

We were due to arrive in France and head north to Normandy and the beautiful harbour town of Honfleur. I was nervous that we wouldn't find anywhere showing the AFL Grand Final in Normandy (keep in mind this was pretty much before apps and live streaming).

'They're still hung up on World War II,' I proclaimed.

On Monday Brij came to me with a proposition. We could forgo our trip to the Loire Valley, our second destination, and head somewhere else to watch the grand final. I quickly suggested London where I knew heaps of Aussie pubs would show the game live. Brij wasn't keen on London.

'Dublin?' she proposed.

To her proposal, I replied, 'I do!' Or was it 'yes'? I forget, but we were definitely going to watch the Pies *hopefully* win the premiership from Ireland.

We ended up at the Woolshed Baa and Grill in Dublin – a sports pub catering for homesick Aussies and Kiwis. We found a corner booth, let a jet-lagged little Oscar sleep and Liam and Aidan eat fries, and watched the mighty Pies claim our 15th flag. Praise the Lord!

The lesson: sometimes you need to be flexible with your plans (and maybe don't book to leave on holiday until two weeks after the Granny!).

As a nice little postscript, a couple of years later I surprised Brij by taking her to the Loire Valley for our ten-year wedding anniversary and, I must admit, it's a much better place to visit without the kids!

In Dublin and the 'Pies have just become Flagpies!

ITALY HOLDS A SPECIAL PLACE IN SO MANY HEARTS AROUND THE WORLD.

Italians have given so much to the world – their history, art, cuisine, wine and passion for using their hands in conversation. From Leonardo da Vinci's *The Last Supper* to Michelangelo's Sistine Chapel (which Pete grew up thinking was Michelangelo's Sixteenth Chapel), Italy leads the world in art history and it is not hard to see why this beautiful country has inspired so many great artists.

Italy's landscape offers bountiful diversity with the glacial lakes of the Alps, the Amalfi coastline, the canals of Venice and the vineyards of Lake Como where the Clooneys will be more than happy to have a Nespresso ready and waiting for you.

The best part of travelling with kids in Italy is the people. Italians make travelling with kids much easier because they are so welcoming. In big cities they may seem less helpful and, like any city, you also have to work around stairs, narrow sidewalks and crowds. But the kids will have a ball everywhere in Italy and, depending on the length of time you have, they will get to experience so many different aspects of it. Italy does look small but to get from north to south can take over ten hours, so if you are limited to a week set up in a city and take daytrips.

As with most places, visiting in the off-peak seasons will be much easier with kids. If you are travelling in peak season, remember there will be crowds everywhere, especially at the big tourist attractions, and the heat can be a bit much for the kids if you are having busy days. Keep in mind that opening hours will be different from home: shops, museums and parks close in the early afternoon. Don't pack a big pram – the narrow cobblestone streets will be enough to make you want to dump it.

You may have moments of being overwhelmed, but your trip will be wonderful. Italy will grab you by the heart, hug you and kiss your cheeks a thousand times over. Metaphorically. Probably.

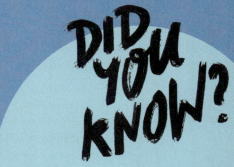

DID YOU KNOW?

- In the Abruzzo region, there is a fountain that flows red wine 24 hours a day. It was set up to quench the thirst of pilgrims in the area. Anyone can drink from it, which is both the best and worst thing about it.
- The first thermometer was made by Italian inventor Santorio Santorio in 1612. He originally named it a Thermometer Thermometer until it was shortened to simply Thermometer.
- At Genoa's airport, the security liquid limit of 100ml has been relaxed for pesto. Pesto is Genoa's specialty, so grab a pot or two and you can travel with it in your hand luggage if you donate to a children's charity and get the appropriate sticker.

ATTRACTIONS

- Italy is full of wonderful sights, recognisable the world over: **St Mark's Square** in Venice, the **Leaning Tower of Pisa** and the **Milan Cathedral** are just three. And then there are all the beautiful towns to visit. There's so much to do, and you'll have your must-sees we're sure, but here are some not so obvious things to do on your trip.

- Eat **tagliatelle al ragu**, the world's best spaghetti Bolognese, which originated in Bologna. Fair warning: it will be so good, the kids may not want to eat your version ever again.

- Go **truffle hunting** in Piedmont – you can actually do a walking tour with the dogs that find the truffles.

- Visit the **Egyptian Museum** in Turin. Full of mummies and excellent displays, it is family friendly unless an ancient tomb is disturbed, then you're screwed!

- Take a **gondola ride** in Venice. For a cheaper version take a traghetto, a less fancy gondola, which will take you across the Grand Canal and to eight different spots. It's a much shorter but cheaper gondola experience. And kids under six are usually free.

- Visit the finest chocolatier in Venice, **VizioVirtù Cioccolateria**, for guided tastings and hot chocolate to die for. Also in Venice, a company called **Macaco Tour** offers fabulous **scavenger hunts** for kids along with family games and other tours created especially for children. These tours are a great way for them to discover this beautiful city. The company also offers them in Rome and Verona.

- Walk or cycle along the walls of the beautiful Tuscan city of **Lucca**.

- Also in the beautiful region of Tuscany and half an hour or so from Florence is **Pratolino** – go there to meet the Gentle Giant, the **Colossus of the Apennines**, by 16th-century sculptor Giambologna. Guarding the pond in beautiful gardens, the 10m high Colossus isn't just a statue, he's also a building. There are chambers inside his body, and even a fireplace in his head that makes him look like he should be in a headache commercial. When the fire used to be lit, smoke would come out of his nose. The park itself is stunning and a lovely place to spend some time.

- For a different experience, visit **Leolandia**, a theme park for families in **Milan**. Its miniature Italy is a great way to understand more about some of the country's iconic buildings and their significance. There are also fun rides, splash parks and an educational farm too. For more thrills head to **EuroPark Milano**, not too far from Leolandia. It has both scary rides and gentle rides, along with games for all ages. But you don't have to go to the amusement park to enjoy the area as just next to EuroPark Milano is **Idroscalo Park** and its scenic lake. Take your pick of some fun family activities – go kayaking with the kids or enjoy some horseriding.

- The kids will be fascinated by the World Heritage sites in the **Puglia** region, the heel of Italy's boot. The favourite one for most children is the town of **Alberobello**, with its **trulli** – the trulli are unusual whitewashed limestone houses with pointy or conical roofs that make the town look like a village for gnomes. They are using a prehistoric building technique and some date from the 14th century.

ROME

STEEPED IN HISTORY,

Rome, more so than any other city in the world, has maintained so much of its past for all to see. We're not just talking about relics and artefacts in a museum but actual centuries-old buildings that dominate the city, from the Colosseum, the Pantheon and the Roman Forum to St Peter's Basilica in the Vatican.

Even if you're not a museum kind of family, Rome may be the city to encourage at least a little sampling. Michelangelo, Raphael, Leonardo and Donatello are all here – just trick the kids by telling them you're all off to see the Ninja Turtles.

Sitting on the same site of Ancient Rome, thousands of years old, Rome is full of life – the kids will love this city and not just for the gelato and pizza, although they will both feature prominently, trust us. The Colosseum, with its cages for leopards, bears, lions and elephants used in battles; the puppet theatres; boat rides on the Tiber River; treasure hunts, like finding the giant foot of the Egyptian goddess Isis – this city is primed for inquisitive young minds.

Couple Rome's rich history with some of the best food and wine in the world (and, remember, that food includes gelato) and you have a family holiday that will hit every mark.

DID YOU KNOW?

- Tourists throw around $4700 of change into the Trevi Fountain daily; it is collected and donated to charity. As opposed to the Trevor Fountain in Australia where all the money goes to Trevor's chain-smoking addiction.
- Rome has 280 fountains and more than 900 churches.
- It is believed that more than a million wild animals were killed and 500,000 people lost their lives during the battles at the Colosseum. It's *way* more family friendly these days.
- In Ancient Rome the luxury dish of flamingo tongue was a delicacy. They also loved a sauce called garum, made from fish intestines and blood. Reckon we'll stick with the capricciosa, thanks.

EATING OUT

Pizza and pasta will be on the list of must-eats for sure – even Brij, who's not a huge pizza fan, was impressed. Bowls of pasta are a manageable size and Italians use local in-season produce, so the food is always delicious. Go for a walk to find some good local cuisine, staying away from the tourist-clogged restaurants. As eating dinner late is the norm, the kids might be tired enough to give you a sleep in.

ACCOMMODATION

The beauty with Rome is you'll find a delightful piazza just around the corner from wherever you are staying. Rome is an ideal city to just walk around and get lost in. The area of Trastevere is a great place for families; it's not as touristy as the Spanish Steps so you'll find more affordable accommodation and places to eat. It's a little further to walk to all the attractions but when in Rome. This area can be a little more lively at night than the historical centre, such as Centro Storico, though this is another great area for families where you can find apartments in hotel-style buildings. It's also close to day-time activities and is quiet at night.

GETTING AROUND

The easiest way to get around Rome is on foot. The metro isn't a large network but does have stops at main attractions; buses are the way to go if you want to move around the whole city on public transport. If you're heading out of town, jump on the trains as they have express options to other cities making a night stop-over very easy. As you'll mostly be walking if staying in the city centre you probably won't be needing to catch public transport, but if you need a bus to get to town, get a three-day tourist pass or Roma Pass that offers discounts to attractions as well. Some public monuments and museums are free to those under 18 and children under ten travel free on public transport. Take note that many museums, churches and attractions will require shoulders to be covered and skirts or shorts to be at least knee length.

HOW DO YOU SAY THAT?

Don't do what Brij does and get your Italian mixed up with your French (thankfully the Italians thought it was funny). Try these instead:

Can you please stop pinching my child's cheeks?!
Per favour, potresti smettere di pizzicare le guance di mio figlio?

Just double-checking they don't kill anyone at the Colosseum anymore?
Vorrei verificare che non uccidono più nessuno al Colosseo?

We are having a kid-free night out – where is the bunga bunga party?
Abbiamo una serafa fuori senza bambini, dov'è la festa di bunga bunga?

ATTRACTIONS

- Start with a **hop-on hop-off bus tour** as it's a great way for everyone to get a feel for the city. If your kids are old enough, do the after-dark tour, as Rome sparkles at night.

- The kids are going to love the idea of the **Mouth of Truth**. While there are many theories of its origins, the legend surrounding the stone carving was that if you were to stick your hand inside the mouth and tell a lie, it would be bitten off. You'll find it on the outside wall of the portico of the **Santa Maria in Cosmedin church**.

- Visit the **Colosseum** on a guided family tour. We found it the best way to explore this huge amphitheatre, which is almost 2000 years old. You won't have to wait in line, and it means you can experience this ancient icon with a little more info aimed towards the kids. They can also be a gladiator and go to gladiator school for the day – just remember what they do in gladiator school echoes for eternity.

- The **Catacombs of Rome**, ancient burial places under the city, go for hundreds of kilometres beneath Rome's busy streets. You can explore them with an organised tour (there are kid-friendly ones available too); it's a great and often moving experience for older kids, but don't wander off from your guide or you'll get lost. The kids can pretend to be Indiana Jones as they explore this oldest and longest underground tunnel network in the world.

- The sprawling **Roman Forum** is a collection of Roman ruins – it was actually the political and social heart of Ancient Rome. Looking at old broken things can get a little confusing or boring for kids, but these 2000-year-old ruins are still worth exploring. Teens will have fun exploring on a Segway tour; for little kids, try a family-oriented tour, avoid taking a pusher and take plenty of water on warm days.

- The ancient **Pantheon** has so much history and is such an amazing place to visit. The hole (*oculos*) is there by design so when it rains, the rain comes in – the kids can find all the draining holes. Once you have visited this famous attraction, wander the small square, the **Piazza della Rotunda**, outside the Pantheon with its fountain and interesting obelisk, or visit the old-fashioned toy shop **Bartolucci**, a five-minute walk from the Pantheon (it's on Via dei Pastini). It's not about technology here; rather, it's full of colourful wooden toys like Pinocchios, planes and rocking horses.

- Famed **Trevi Fountain** is Rome's largest fountain and the oldest water source in the city. Find some facts about the fountain before visiting and get the kids to look for all the answers as well as where they can fill up their water bottles with fresh water.

- The **Spanish Steps** are to be climbed and photographed, but be prepared: you'll be doing it alongside hundreds of other tourists. Not only a must-see, it's a great meeting place (just don't sit on the steps – that was banned in 2019). The kids will love to run up to the top like an Italian Rocky Balboa (actually he *was* Italian, but you know what we mean!) to see all the souvenirs, caricaturists and artists up there.

- Visit **Vatican City**, often simply called the Vatican, a city-state surrounded by Rome. Home to the Pope, art and architecture, it may seem on the surface to be not very kid friendly or kid interesting ('Hey kids, we're on holiday! Let's go to Church City!'), but it is certainly something you should see. Crowds are vast as there are always lots of tours happening, so it's a good idea to be well prepared and to have planned your visit beforehand. Pre-book your tickets online to save time and choose one of the family-focused tours – these will have experiences to keep all of the kids interested.

- Head to **Explora**, a fabulous children's museum where history and science come together. This one is definitely for the kids, so take a break from sightseeing and enjoy some play. A couple of hours here will have everyone feeling better and perhaps ready to dive into more Roman history.

- Everyone wants to go to the gorgeous **Amalfi Coast**. It is possible to do it as a (long and likely tiring) daytrip from Rome but you'll want to stick with one place only, such as **Sorrento**, **Positano** or **Amalfi**, especially if you want to hit the beach, wander the streets and enjoy the views over lunch. It's a two-hour train ride from Rome to Naples and then it will take approximately an hour and 20 minutes to get to the Amalfi Coast by car. If you don't mind where you go but you want a beach, pay a day fee for a private beach – you'll get a dressing room, bathroom facilities and lounge chairs. If you can plan it, it's better to organise accommodation in Naples or on the coast if your budget allows so you can have a relaxed day or two on this unforgettable part of the Italian coastline. An easier daytrip is **Sperlonga** – it's almost two hours from Rome and has beautiful clean sand and water, and it's lovely walking around the quaint town. **Ostia Lido** is much closer to Rome (about 40 minutes from the city) and clean enough for you to enjoy the water, but it has only a few public beach areas. **Santa Marinella** is approximately an hour from the city and has clean beaches, bars, restaurants and shops to enjoy.

KID-FREE NIGHT OUT

Heading out for dinner about 9.30 or 10pm is normal – we find having a late lunch or afternoon snack helps with lasting until this time. Be prepared to be squished into the wine bars, follow the locals and enjoy what Italians do very well: eat fabulous food and drink great wine. Try **Cul De Sac** with 1500 wines to decide on (get a recommendation from your waiter). Try to get on the patio of **Enoteca Bulzoni**, or enjoy the home-style food of **Enoteca Corsi** and grab a takeaway bottle from the wine store on the other side for later. Lap up the atmosphere in **Il Goccetto**, a local favourite where the crowd spills out onto the street. Or spend some time lining up without the kids to get the best pizza in Rome: try **Pizzarium**, **La Gatta Mangiona** and **Sora Margherita** to name just a few.

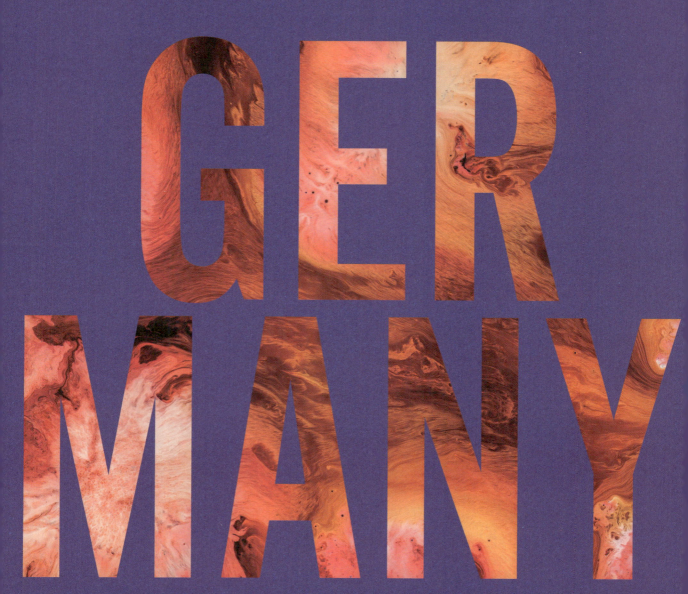

WHEN WE WERE GROWING UP, SO MUCH OF WHAT WE KNEW OF GERMANY WAS ABOUT ITS DARK PAST,

but as the country itself moves on it has struck an impressive balance of acknowledging that past but looking to the future.

From remnants of the Berlin Wall and the still-standing Checkpoint Charlie (now outside a McDonald's) to the utterly sobering experiences of Dachau, the first concentration camp opened by the Nazis in 1933, Germany has some hard-hitting to-dos for history buffs. But again, it is also a country that is thoroughly modern and, as far as right now goes, Germany, with cities like Berlin, is on the cutting edge of fashion, live culture, architecture and art.

Germany may not have the wrought iron or limestone icons that Paris has, but it can claim to have made its mark on the world with its citizens: from Einstein to Marx (Karl not Richard), from Johann Sebastian Bach to David Hasselhoff, Germany has contributed much to culture, philosophy and the arts – and, of course, to the sandy beaches of California.

It is also a country whose landscape offers fantastic diversity for its size. With its gothic forested hills including the famous Black Forest, its river valleys of the Rhine and Danube, and its real-life snow-globe imagery of Neuschwanstein Castle (the mountaintop castle that inspired Disney's *Sleeping Beauty*), Germany is full of delights from border to border.

The kids will love Germany. It's like a life-size version of all the fairytales they've ever heard, which makes sense as Germany is the birthplace of the Brothers Grimm – the tykes will be writing their own tales before you can say Hansel and Gretel. Germans are organised, honest and straight to the point, which makes travelling with kids very easy. You know what to do and what not to do very early on. Even though they are honest,

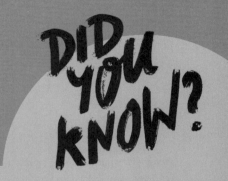

DID YOU KNOW?

- The currywurst served with spicy sauce is a cult classic.
- It was a German who first made book printing a thing when Johannes Gutenberg invented the printing press ... lucky for us.
- Germany is the traditional home of the Christmas Markets, and its markets are considered the best out of all the European countries, with a long tradition dating back to the 1300s.
- Hamburgers actually originated in Germany – you probably should visit Hamburg for one.
- Because it is a basic human instinct to be free, prisoners in Germany have the right to escape jail without punishment. They just can't damage property or inflict injury on anyone when doing so, as that is punishable.

they aren't rude or lacking in kindness; we found the locals very welcoming to kids and so many places you'll visit offer the chance for kids to enjoy the best parts of childhood. Many attractions are free to those under 18, and you can pretty much assume anyone under five is free. Family tickets are available at most places, including on public transport. Many factories have tours. Why would you want to tour factories, you ask? Well, think factories that make the best of all things German: chocolate, cars, candy and beer of course.

EATING OUT

Across Germany, as long as the kids eat meat, you'll have no problems getting them a sausage and bread for any meal. We once ordered a meat platter for two that could have fed ten. Meat is available everywhere – by the end of our trip we were ordering the kids vegetable soup just so they had some greens.

In Berlin, we had a lovely dining experience with the kids at **Entrecote**, a French brassiere not far from Checkpoint Charlie. The food was so nice, the staff so friendly and the environment so cosy and pleasant we went back again. Recommended.

GETTING AROUND

Taking the train is the best way to get around Germany as a whole. There's free travel for kids under 15 if they are registered on an adult ticket, and children under six don't need to register. The fast trains have compartments suited for young children and it's a fun, relaxing, easy way to get around.

In Berlin, public transport is very convenient; there is always a public transport stop within a radius of 500m. Get a Berlin Welcome Card: it offers unlimited travel with the public transport system in certain zones, mainly city, surrounding areas and airport. Travel for three and under is free, while children aged between six and 14 travel with the adult cardholder. The Welcome Card also offers 50 per cent discounts at many sights and attractions.

ACCOMMODATION

Throughout Germany we found it best to stay in guest houses and apartments. They are more easily available and generally cheaper than interconnecting hotel rooms.

We recommend staying in the Mitte neighbourhood in Berlin. It's close to many attractions, good food, shops and transport options, and it's easy to get around with a pusher if you need to.

ATTRACTIONS

- Drive the **Fairy Tale Road**, a winding route through Germany inspired by the work and lives of the Brothers Grimm. You can re-create the fairytales by taking a hike in the Little Red Riding Hood forest, visiting the castle of Sleeping Beauty and climbing Rapunzel's Tower. On the trail you can also visit the **Museum of the Brothers Grimm** in Steinau. Approximately 50 towns along the route offer family-friendly fairytale-themed attractions from concerts and markets to puppet shows. The easiest way is to drive and begin just outside of Frankfurt.

- Theme parks are well represented in Germany, with **Europa-Park** being the most visited and the largest – it was also named the world's best amusement park in 2019, so it's definitely worth a visit. Europa-Park is on the French, Swiss and German border and can be easily accessed from a few airports surrounding the town of Rust via the park's shuttle service. **Heide Park** is home to the only dive coaster in Germany; it's easy to get to by train from Hamburg, Hanover or Bremen. An all-rounder like **Phantasialand** has all ages and all thrills covered (the Cologne/Bonn international airport is the closest airport). And **LEGOLAND** can be found between Munich and Stuttgart and is easy to get to via their shuttle service from Günzburg Station. If you have read our Denmark chapter, you'll know we *love* LEGOLANDs. Stay in themed cottages, explore the LEGO world and enjoy fun LEGO-themed events.

- If your kids would love the idea of staying in an actual castle, drive **Castle Road**, or Burgenstraße, in southern Germany and see over 70 castles. On this incredibly scenic route, you'll see a 1000-year-old castle where you can actually spend a night (talk about fairytales), fascinating museums, mediaeval towns and picturesque ruins. The entire drive will take about three to four days to complete, starting in Mannheim and leading all the way to Prague. The closest airport is Nuremburg.

HOW DO YOU SAY THAT?

Where is David Hasselhoff's holiday house?
Wo ist das Ferienhaus von David Hasselhoff?

Are there any vegetarian options that *don't* contain meat?
Gibt es vegetarische Optionen, die kein Fleisch enthalten?

I'm just not sure if I would actually wear this lederhosen back home …
Ich bin mir nur nicht sicher, ob ich diese Lederhose zu Hause tragen würde …

A DARK HISTORY

We researched at lot about whether to take the kids to concentration camps and Holocaust museums. As the experience is very emotional, we wanted to make sure the reasons we were taking our kids to these places were the right ones. The conclusion we came to was to leave the concentration camps out of our trip. We read a lot of information, forums, articles and Holocaust websites and the same story stood out: young children visiting the concentration camps don't understand what actually happened in these places. Children laughing, playing on memorials and running around would actually be upsetting for other visitors. We knew our children would be respectful and not intentionally make it a playground but, at the end of the day, they are kids – they play, they laugh, they cry, they scream – and we just felt that this wasn't a place for them at this time in their young lives. We have, however, taken them to many memorials, museums and places of rest over the world, such as the Oskar Schindler Factory in Poland, and used these visits as an opportunity to talk about the horrible events that have taken place and the importance of peace and how we need to love everyone. Children are welcome to visit concentration camps with their parents but be mindful that most of the content and programs are recommended for children 13 and above.

Where Schindler's list was typed, Oskar Schindler Factory museum

BERLIN

BASED ON THE AMOUNT

of World War II documentaries we'd consumed over the years, it has always been hard not to think of Berlin as war-torn. Strategically bombed by the Allies in the 1940s, the city was almost completely destroyed, which meant one hell of a rebuild. This means that the Berlin of today is an extremely modern city with trailblazing architecture and a vibrancy that few European cities can match – though you can still see the occasional World War II ruin, such as the Kaiser Wilhelm Memorial Church.

We visited Berlin in 2012 and have been plotting our return ever since. Berlin is a great city for kids; because so much of it had to be rebuilt after the war, it's now incredibly efficient and very easy to get around. It has terrific children-friendly places everywhere, from restaurants to playgrounds, and the streets are filled with excellent street art that makes just getting where you want to go interesting. The public transport system is so easy to navigate too. Oh, and you should know before you go, Berlin is a party town so you may want to enquire about that babysitter ASAP. Berliners are a people who know the value of freedom and they don't intend to waste any time on time wasting.

DID YOU KNOW?

- Berlin has more bridges than Venice.
- The city's oldest pub, Zur Letzten Instanz, is almost 400 years old. Thankfully the dress code has evolved over that time.
- There are over 250 weekly markets that occur across Berlin's urban area so remember your re-useable shopping bags!
- The International Berlin Beer Festival is the longest beer garden in the world at 2.2km. Does that count as a marathon?

ATTRACTIONS

- We've mentioned how much thought we gave to where we took the kids in Berlin with regard to the city's war history, and we're sure you'll want to do the same. The **Jewish Museum Berlin** is an age-appropriate museum to help educate children on the Holocaust and the history of Jews in Germany. The museum has child-friendly exhibits and a new Children's Museum.

- For a change of pace, visit **Berlin Zoo**, Germany's oldest and most popular zoo, and one of the most visited zoos in the world. The zoo is set on 33 hectares and features nearly 20,000 animals from over 1300 species. If the kids get tired of looking at the wildlife, there's also a petting zoo and an adventure playground.

- Close to the centre of the city, **Tiergarten Park** is a lush green park that is a perfect escape when you need some nature. It is massive, covering more than 200 hectares, and used to be the royal hunting grounds. Take a ball to play on the grass, go bikeriding, skate, or walk around looking for the memorials and cultural sites – it also borders the **Brandenburg Gate**. After your exploring, find the beer garden and cafe by the lake – you'll be ready for it! For kid-focused fun, hunt out the six playgrounds in the park.

- A more recently created green space is the park at **Gleisdreieck**, which used to be a railway hub and industrial area. Head there for lunch on the grass and a relaxing play for the kids. Enjoy the open spaces and see why this park has won awards. There is something here for everyone, from rose gardens to nature play and more.

- Berlin has many brilliant museums but the stand-out is the **National History Museum** – it's definitely worth a few hours of your time. With the largest mounted dinosaur in the world, fossils and skeletons, your dinosaur-loving kids will be in awe at this museum. Exhibitions cover the Earth, solar system, animals, minerals and so much more (the museum has over 30 million items in its collection) and they are so well done that the kids will be fascinated. Check the website for current events and exhibitions. Children under five are free.

- Another popular museum is Berlin's **Labyrinth Kinder Museum**, an excellent and interactive museum for children (up to 12). This is the place for your kids to let their curiosity run wild. There are no shoes allowed so remember to pack socks or slippers and check online for opening times as they can vary.

- If games and tech are more your thing or your kids are budding programmers, visit the **Computer Spiele Museum**, a museum about video and computer games. You can learn about the history of gaming, see some serious geek action and play with classic computer games such as Space Invaders. Go on Sunday for a tour in English.

- If you're looking for a great daytrip from Berlin, visit **Tropical Islands**, the largest water park in Europe and only about 50 minutes south of Berlin. We know it seems crazy to have a water park in wintery Europe but this isn't like most water parks. Open year-round and built in an enormous former airship hangar, it's the world's biggest indoor rainforest complete with real-life flamingos. The indoor complex has a sandy beach, slides and lounges, and even a cocktail bar for parents.

KID-FREE NIGHT OUT

If you're nocturnally adventurous and love techno as much as Berlin does, then head to Berghain and Watergate, two of the best clubs in the world. We suggest doing your research before you hit the line at Berghain as there is a good chance you won't be let in. Find out when the line is at its quietest; dress to suit the club, but make sure you look and feel comfortable (apparently the main bouncer doesn't like pastels and boat shoes so avoid looking like you just stepped off a dinner cruise on River Spree); attempt to speak German; get to know the music; and don't rock up noticeably drunk.

But if you're after a night out with a little more quiet time, then Simon-Dach-Straße will be your scene. It has plenty of restaurants, bars and cafes where you can relax and chat about your day, and it's not too party oriented. Here you'll find a diverse crowd and delicious world cuisine. Weserstraße has a bit more to offer: you can party, shop, eat, relax and enjoy the view of the Landwehr Canal.

HUGO'S HAS A DRESS CODE *(BY PETE)*

We organised a babysitter in Berlin because we had heard so much about the city's nightlife and restaurant scene and we were keen to get amongst it.

Nothing too hardcore, punk or techno – a nice cocktail lounge and a fancy restaurant were more our speed. Let the twenty-somethings jump over each other for Berghain, the impossible-to-get-into nightclub in a power station.

Hugo's, a Michelin-starred restaurant with the best panoramic views of Berlin, obviously appealed to us. We booked and got in – win! I enquired about the dress code and was told smart casual but no jeans or trainers.

Now, normally this would be fine but when you are backpacking with your three kids and plan to have maybe one or two 'fancy' dinners over the month, you're not packing a pair of brogues and slacks. Brij certainly didn't have a dress rolled up between her toiletries and the Dry Nights.

The thought of arriving at Hugo's underdressed was mortifying. We didn't want to let down our homeland. Bogans abroad? No, not on our watch. So, we decided to spend the afternoon op-shopping our way around Berlin.

What an afternoon it was, a great way to see parts of the city we never would have seen if we weren't on the lookout for cheap but seemingly classy enough clobber. There may have been a couple of whingy kids but nothing we couldn't handle.

We wound up in a store called Made in Berlin where we found a tweed jacket and black shoes for me – sure, I may have passed for a divorced librarian on a first date, but it would have to do. Brij found herself a flowing green dress and matching handbag. We were set. The only thing that was missing was a 1980s movie shopping montage.

With the right accessorising with jewellery from home, Brij looked beautiful and I looked like a man who knew the ins and outs of the Dewey Decimal system and often ate toast over the sink alone in his apartment.

Once the babysitter arrived, we took off into the Berlin night. We enjoyed pre-dinner drinks at a lovely little bar near Hugo's before ascending the Intercontinental to the 14th floor, feeling lightly buzzed – not just from the martinis but because we had done it. We had found some sophisticated *enough* garments to avoid judgement from the chic German waiting staff at one of the most refined restaurants in Berlin.

If the friendly maître d' judged our thrifty threads we couldn't tell. We were kindly shown to our table. We had done it. The views were spectacular. The space refined. Our outfits elegant.

We had barely been offered sparkling or still before the next guests arrived. You wouldn't believe it: six American tourists all dressed in matching parachute tracksuits. Tops and bottoms. Matching! Parachute! Were they planning on base-jumping out of the 14th floor? The friendly maître d' kindly showed them to their table.

We looked at each other in disbelief. Didn't matter. We'd had the better day. And boy do we laugh about that moment to this very day.

MUNICH

MUNICH IS

a fascinating city that somehow balances its historical traditions with all things new and cutting edge. Before we get into our top Munich attractions we have to mention another fairytale castle just nearby. Under two hours from Munich, visit **Neuschwanstein Castle**, or Schloss Neuschwanstein. One of Germany's most recognisable icons, the castle was built in 1800s as a palace for reclusive King Ludwig II. Neuschwanstein looks like a real Cinderella castle and, located in the Bavarian Alps, it has the stunning scenery to match. You can tour the castle with visits to the throne room, grotto and conservatory and even the singers' hall. We say it's a Cinderella castle but, in fact, Disney's *Sleeping Beauty* castle was modelled on Neuschwanstein. Be careful during the peak times (July to September) as tickets are limited each day and can sell out fast, and the queue can be long. You can reserve tickets online, but you'll want to get there early and have something to entertain the kids while you wait. Guided tours are the only way to explore the castle, and it's worth noting that you can't take prams or bulky objects into the castle.

In Munich itself, spend a day at the **Nymphenburg Palace** for some history, boat rides (in summertime) and stunning gardens. There's even a dedicated museum section all about carriages that will have any fairytale fan dreaming. The expansive park-setting is perfect for a stroll if you all need a bit of fresh air.

The **BMW Welt** and **BMW Museum** are impressive even if you're not car crazy. There are children-focused activities and family days during holiday periods and if you're wanting to experience some driving luxury, driving experiences are available. That's going to impress the big kids!

Did you dream of **Oktoberfest** in your twenties and never quite make it? It is quite okay to take kids to this famous beer festival – and Munich is its home. There are rides, concerts, parades and opportunities for them to learn about Bavarian culture, history and food. If you head into a beer tent, children under six must leave by 8pm. If you're not visiting at Oktoberfest time, never fear – there are numerous beer halls around the city, the most famous of which is **Hofbräuhaus**.

Munich is a bike-friendly city and cycling through the city is a perfect way to see the sites. There are many tours and bike-hire options, but one of the most popular is **Mike's Bike Tours**, which has bikes for all the family, including babies and toddlers, and a variety of tour and hiring options.

DEN
MARK

IF IT'S GOOD ENOUGH FOR PRINCESS MARY THEN IT'S GOOD ENOUGH FOR YOU!

When Mary walked into the Slip Inn in Sydney on that now famous night she chose her prince wisely. Denmark is a Scandinavian country full of happy, contented people who have managed to formalise the notion of cosiness through *hygge*, a uniquely Danish custom that celebrates togetherness and contentment. We experienced hygge during a visit to Brij's Danish cousins in 2012 and it was like a warm embrace. Certainly as the eyes of the world look more towards screens and away from each other, we could all use a little hygge in our lives.

If Princess Mary's story seems like a magical fairytale, you shouldn't be surprised – fairytales loom large in Denmark thanks to the legacy of Hans Christian Andersen, 19th-century author of childhood classics such as *The Little Mermaid*, *Thumbelina*, *The Little Matchstick Girl* and *The Ugly Duckling*. It's certainly a fairytale country – villages with colourful houses, spectacular historic castles, ancient forests and wild beaches. The country's official name is the Kingdom of Denmark and its territories include Greenland and the Faroe Islands. Denmark has always been a sea-faring nation too – after all, this is where Vikings came from.

And we have to mention the bikes: the Danes love their bikes. Four out of ten people own a car in Denmark; *nine* out of ten own a bike. You'll get very used to seeing families getting around with their kids in cargo bikes. It's a very family-friendly place, and if LEGOLAND doesn't scream how great Denmark is for kids you'll have plenty more to entice them with. It is packed with kid-friendly gems all over, from its Viking history, thrilling amusement parks and royal family to its Shakespearean castles and friendly capital Copenhagen.

Denmark is a bit more expensive than some other European countries, but it's such a great place to visit that it's worth it. It's easy to plan a holiday too: the super helpful and friendly website visitdenmark.com has an A to Z of all the things you may need to know before you go. Things like the Smiley Scheme, introduced by the Danish Food Authority to tell customers if a cafe or restaurant serves good or bad food. See, even their rating system is polite. It also helps that many Danes speak some English and are usually always willing to help.

That's the thing – the Danes are so friendly and happy you'll be completely stumped as to how such dark and gritty TV dramas as *The Killing*, *The Bridge* and *Borgen* could possibly come from their cheery minds. Progressive, charming and inclusive, the Danes will be thrilled you've visited. And so will you.

- Denmark is the best place to ride bikes because it's flat. In fact, the tallest mountain is just over 170m tall. Even we'll ride to that summit.
- The Danish language doesn't have a word for 'please'. That's just how polite they are, they can simply gesture pleasantries and it works.

ATTRACTIONS

📍 Okay, it goes without saying (but we're saying it anyway) that the hands-down best attraction for kids has to be **LEGOLAND** in **Billund**. LEGO's target ages for the park are children aged between two and 12 years old but, let's be honest, adults will love it just as much, and if your teenagers have any interest in LEGO, fun rides or food they will be entertained just fine too. Even though there may not be as many thrill rides as Disneyland, everything is actually awesome and, you know, LEGO! Download the LEGOLAND app and start planning your visit with all the app's useful info and times for shows and rides. There's even a LEGOLAND hotel so you can stay overnight ... or forever (though it is pretty pricey; Billund has other accommodation options too). You can get from Copenhagen to Billund by public transport in around four hours or by car in about three. *See* p. 248 to read Pete's take on LEGOLAND.

📍 **Billund** has more LEGO than just LEGOLAND (as if that wasn't enough); if you are organised enough and book in before the tour sells out, you can tour the **LEGO Factory**. Those lucky LEGO lovers will get access to exclusive experiences such as seeing the moulding process. In town is also **LEGO House**, a massive building filled with 25 million bricks ready for some interactive fun – with six different play zones your kids will never want to leave.

📍 But there is more to the place than colourful plastic blocks. Take in the sights of Billund by cycling its paths: you can hire anything you need, like cargo bikes for little kids or small bikes for those able to go on their own, and helmets come free. Billund has beautiful natural surrounds too: go fishing, take walks, canoe, golf or visit the parks and pack a picnic. There are also a number of attractions within easy reach of Billund. If you pick up a Be Happy Pass for free, you'll receive VIP experiences, gifts and discounts around Billund and other attractions. (You can get the digital pass online once you are in Denmark.)

📍 Billund's **Lalandia Aquadome** doesn't stop all year – even when it's snowing you can take to the slides at this tropical water park where the sky is always blue. **Givskud Zoo**, about 25 minutes north-east of Billund, has a dinosaur exhibition, an African savannah, various habitats, a climbing tower and hands-on playgrounds including an Ice Age Camp, a Dino Camp and a Teepee Camp. The kids will enjoy stepping back in time at **Karensminde Agricultural**

Museum, 20 minutes west of Billund, where they get a chance to milk a cow, collect eggs or shear a sheep. Go on a wagon ride, make wooden toys and help in the kitchen.

- If you have time to explore more of this wonderful country, travel to the **North Jutland** region, as this unique and stunning area will blow you away. Race to see the iconic landmark **Rubjerg Knude**, a famous lighthouse on the edge of the dunes, facing the winds and waves of the icy North Sea. Battling against the forces of nature and under threat from erosion, it is expected to crash into the ocean before 2023.

- Further north, **Grenen**, Denmark's most northern point, is where you'll see the colliding seas, a 4km long sandbar where the Skagerrak and Kattegat seas come together. Put one foot in each sea but leave it at that – the currents are strong so there is no swimming. The nearby town of **Skagen** is worth a visit too.

- In southern Denmark, explore **Odense**, the home town of Hans Christian Andersen. Famous for his fairytales, Andersen must have been inspired by this quaint place. Visit the tiny yellow house he was born in, the **Fairytale Garden** (also called the Hans Christian Andersen Garden) where you will find his statue, and the 12m high mural of his face, painted by a street artist on Bangs Boder. Kids can create their own fairytales as they wander the cobblestone streets of this historic town.

- Only half an hour or so south of Odense, **Egeskov Castle** is the best preserved castle in Europe, and it even has a moat. Its grounds are not only spectacular but also the perfect spot for the kids to run around, climb among the trees in the **Play Forest** or explore the mazes nearby. The castle itself hosts the most amazing doll house, **Titania's Palace**; it is on display but your little ones won't be able to play with this incredible dollhouse, which took 15 years to complete and has more than 3000 components.

COPENHAGEN

BIKES, OH SO MANY BIKES.

No city in the world has incorporated bikes into its culture better than Copenhagen. Cyclists are everywhere and yet not in the way (although, when Brij drove into Copenhagen from the airport she was petrified she was going to take a dozen of them out). Bike lanes are plentiful and you can ride the Bicycle Snake, a bikes-only bridge across the harbour. Copenhagen locals love their food and we're not just talking about Copenhagen Ice Cream stores here – the city has 15 Michelin-starred restaurants so if you have an eye on a night out without the kids while on tour, Copenhagen may be the best place to do it! If you're looking for something less fancy and more 'street' then head to **Reffen**, which was once an industrial area but is now a food market where cuisine from all around the globe is sold from shipping containers.

It already sounds good and we haven't even got to the famous Viking culture or Danish-designed furniture. Oh and Copenhagen is particularly great for kids – the wide open spaces of this nature-filled city invite kids of all ages to explore, play and run. In this wonderful city, your kids will feel welcome to be exactly who they want to be.

EATING OUT

We assume you won't want to take the kids to all the Michelin-starred restaurants Copenhagen has to offer, but, never fear, in this city you'll find something to suit everyone's tastes. All the restaurants will welcome kids and provide high chairs when needed, and you'll find everything from burgers to pizza if that's what you're after. But, get the kids to try out some local cuisine: head to **Torvehallerne Food Hall** for a variety of traditional foods, or **Bio Mio** for organic Scandi food.

ACCOMMODATION

Nyhavn is the popular neighbourhood and canal where you'll find a great restaurant culture and trendy vibe. You can also take boat tours from here. Christianshavn is a more residential neighbourhood and offers easy access to all the sights. It is quieter yet still close to the city centre.

GETTING AROUND

Across Denmark, some of the road and bridge tolls will be expensive if you're driving; consider the various train options to save money. As we were covering more of Denmark and then heading onto Berlin we opted to hire a car. Copenhagen is a really friendly city to visit and it's easy to get around, with 400km of bike paths. If biking gets too much, jump on the metro: it will take you everywhere you need to go.

ATTRACTIONS

- **Bakken Deer Park** isn't just a park for deer, it's an amusement park that's over 400 years old. Surrounded by woodland, it's full of children's amusements, restaurants, and pubs and bars that entertain with live music. Because it has historic value you will only see independent shop owners and stalls here. Enjoy the rollercoasters, roaming deer and smaller rides for the younger ones. Just don't scream too loudly on the rides or you'll startle the deer! Entry is free.

- For more outdoor adventure, the **Nature Playground**, Denmark's largest natural playground, has 17 themed gardens to explore, including an orchard, a rose garden, a garden catering for people with disabilities, and a kitchen garden. Look for the climbing ropes, footbridges and towers. The kids will love exploring here at any age. And afterwards you can all gorge on famous Danish hotdogs.

- Just a short drive from Copenhagen centre, take the kids on a treasure hunt to find the **Six Forgotten Giants**, incredible massive troll sculptures by artist Thomas Dambu. Made from scrap wood and with the help of volunteers, the trolls are part of Dambu's project to get art outside and remind people of how beautiful nature can be. The sculptures contribute to Dambu's ongoing work of, as he describes it, 'the great story of the little people and the giant trolls'. The six giant trolls are in regions around Copenhagen.

- Take a **boat ride** on the canals in Copenhagen – because it's an old harbour town and maritime city this is a great way to take it all in, and there's something special about being on the water. **Nyhaven Harbour** is the most famous of Copenhagen's waterways and there are loads of options, from romantic gondolas (perhaps not so great with the kids in tow) to being a captain of your own hired solar picnic boat, which the kids will love.

- The **National Museum of Denmark** is like a time machine – with a children's museum that prides itself on having no 'do not touch' signs, it's a great place to learn together about history. There are loads of exhibitions and, true to the goal of making it family friendly, they have installed 'boredom buttons' throughout the museum where boredom will be busted! There is a lunch room and garden where you can enjoy your own packed lunch or a restaurant if you feel like letting someone else prepare your meals.

- Opened in 1843, **Tivoli Gardens** is the Luna Park of Copenhagen and is the second oldest operating amusement park in the world. The oldest, by the way, is the much harder to pronounce Dyrehavsbakken in Klampenborg, which is also in Denmark. It is said Walt Disney, who visited Tivoli on occasion, found inspiration here for his very own amusement park (which you may have heard of). Enjoy the modern virtual reality thrills of the Demon or the nostalgic rattle of the wooden rollercoaster, which is one of only seven remaining rollercoasters in the world with a 'brakeman' on board. There is a full day of fun to be had at this Danish institution. Traditionally closed for the colder months, Tivoli's gates are now open year-round.

- Fairytale perfect and built by King Christian IV in the early 17th century, **Rosenborg Castle** is a beautifully preserved monument to Danish history. From the tapestries on its walls depicting the bloody battles between Denmark and Sweden to the life-sized silver lions guarding the Knights Hall, the castle will give you a great sense of Danish history. You can also check out the Royal Jewels here. Guided tours are available or cruise around at your own pace, and then enjoy lunch in one of surrounding parks.

- For a change of pace, take the kids to the **Experimentarium**, a completely interactive science museum. Battle a 3D evil virus in the Immune Game, test your grey matter in the Puzzler and get a 360-degree view of the Sound and Copenhagen via the maritime exhibition the Wave. The Sound is the English name for the strait that forms the border between Denmark and Sweden.

- From Copenhagen, take a daytrip to the **Viking Museum** in Roskilde, 30 minutes west of the capital. There are so many activities here to keep everyone in the family engaged – from taking a Viking boat ride to having a go at Viking crafts (some are age-restricted to children over eight, though) and seeing replica tools in action. The museum allows you to bring your own food, so pack a picnic and enjoy the picnic tables or throw in a rug and sit on the grassed area.

- Another excellent daytrip from the capital is a visit to **Frederiksborg Castle**, just over 30 minutes north of Copenhagen. This castle has been fully restored and features stunning formal gardens and interactive activities for kids, including a picture trail to follow through the castle. If you go in summer months, which is peak time, staff are dressed in Renaissance dress. Guided tours are also available.

KID-FREE NIGHT OUT

In keeping with the Danish way of life, take your loved one to a place where you'll experience hygge for real. As it doesn't require a specific place, time or person to achieve, you can seek it in many of the pretty awesome places in Copenhagen.

Get into **Ruby** for delightful cocktails and typical gorgeous interiors – this bar is in an old townhouse built in 1740. **Liakoeb** has three floors and a courtyard so there's plenty of space to enjoy their interesting and sometimes weird cocktails. **Ørstted Ølbar** is a fun, fully stocked bar with a foosball table and dartboard. **Duck and Cover** is all mid-century Danish design cool and it has equally cool drinks. **Andy's Bar** in the city centre is your classic local pub, and it serves until 6am, but we are pretty sure you would have relieved the babysitter by then!

LEGOLAND
(BY PETE)

Over a decade ago I overheard Brij make a flippant remark to our then five-year-old son Liam: 'When you turn ten, we'll take you to LEGOLAND in Denmark.' I was a little surprised at the grandiose nature of the statement but we've all been guilty of over-promising to our children to encourage better behaviour, so I didn't think too much more of it.

Imagine my surprise then when, five years later, we decided to plan a European getaway and I discovered that apparently, rather than Italy, which was on top of my list, our itinerary simply had to revolve around a visit to Denmark.

'Why Denmark?' I inquired. Had I somehow forgotten we were related to Princess Mary? I didn't remember getting an invitation to the wedding.

'Because LEGOLAND is in Denmark, silly,' came Brij's reply in a tone that suggested there had been a weekly family meeting discussing this plan for the past five years that I had completely forgotten about. How had this throwaway line five years ago manifested itself into a concrete promise?

One thing I couldn't deny was our eldest son's complete dedication and unwavering passion for those tiny coloured blocks. Liam had written to LEGO HQ in Denmark when he was seven asking what he needed to do to one day work for LEGO. Impressively, they replied to his email the next morning giving him genuine and considered advice as to how to achieve his dream of being employed by LEGO. Who was I to stand in the way of my kid's dreams?

To say our boys were excited in the lead-up to our LEGOLAND adventure would be an understatement. If a modern-day Dr Frankenstein had offered Liam, Aidan and Oscar the chance to have their human heads replaced with yellow plastic ones with painted-on faces, I would have been left with three boys with clip-on hair and semicircles for hands.

First things first, the LEGOLAND Hotel is on the pricey side. Later on in our travels we would stay in a large apartment in Krakow perched above a cafe overlooking the Main Market Square; we stayed in a three-bedroom apartment with a rooftop terrace in Prague; and we stayed in similar places in Berlin, Budapest and Vienna. LEGOLAND was more expensive than all of them by a significant amount. The rooms are pretty basic (if you don't get in on time and book a themed room) but adorned with nice little LEGO touches such as LEGO-patterned carpet and doona covers. The boys were thrilled to discover a small LEGO gift for each of them. Nothing, I should note, for the parents, which made my decision to swipe the LEGOLAND bottle opener from the mini-bar a little easier on the conscience.

With all that said, the key to the LEGOLAND Hotel, the secret to its sheer awesomeness, is this: the kids rule the roost. Kids are encouraged to be kids and are free to run around and explore. Around every corner are giant tubs full of LEGO just waiting for a child's imagination to bring them to life. I have never been so relaxed with so many kids, including mine, running amok around me, and I'm pretty sure I'll never be lucky enough to experience that feeling ever again.

The LEGOLAND theme park itself does not disappoint. We visited in autumn and got a good pleasantly crisp, sunny day. Liam and Aidan displayed an ability to adapt to European driving conditions by obtaining their LEGO licence at LEGO traffic school, and little Oscar journeyed around on the LEGO train wide-eyed and happy.

As much as LEGOLAND primarily caters for the kids there are also enough thrills for the adults. We got lucky with a new marquee ride, the Polar X-plorer, opening only days before we arrived. It's a fast, smooth rollercoaster ride that passes real penguins and finishes with a drop, which, like most rides, teases you more in the anticipation than scares you with the drop itself. With that said, I screamed like a little kid and I am grateful my boys have either forgotten or are too embarrassed to mention it to me.

Possibly the best thing about LEGOLAND, and admittedly this may have to do with the timing of our visit, are the short queues. The longest we waited to get on a ride was ten minutes and we only did that once. Countless times we jumped off a ride and ran back to the entrance and got back on almost immediately.

One piece of advice: leave the gift shop until the end of the day. Once the boys spotted it, wild LEGO horses couldn't have kept them from galloping in. We wasted an hour in there with *most* of the LEGO already available in Australia or soon to be released.

So, it's true, while my Italian dream of wine and pasta in Cinque Terre is still alive in my mind (where most parents' dreams remain), LEGOLAND indeed won me over. The look of unadulterated exhilaration as Liam ran through the gates, Aidan's unflinching glee after surviving the Polar X-plorer, Oscar's amazement that he didn't get in trouble for self-serving himself more ice-cream than he could possibly eat – yep, it was all completely worth it.

Now I'm off to promise Liam we'll take him to the Guinness Factory when he turns 18.

EASTERN EUROPE

IN THIS CHAPTER WE FOCUS ON PRAGUE IN THE CZECH REPUBLIC, KRAKOW IN POLAND AND BUDAPEST IN HUNGARY.

We travelled to these places in one trip, and did daytrips from each city to see a little more of each country. With little kids, and even big ones, you'll want to eliminate too much time in transit (there's only so many stickers to play with or puppet shows you can perform). When we researched how to get around this part of Europe, the train that travelled Prague–Krakow–Budapest–Vienna was a great, easy way to travel across countries (this included catching two overnight trains). Of course, each country has so much to offer – if you have the time, spending weeks in each one would be very enjoyable. But if you, like many Australians, are heading to Europe with three weeks' holiday or less and want to visit as many countries as possible, consider focusing on key cities and taking a train trip like this.

PRAGUE
CZECH REPUBLIC

IF YOU LIKE

your toys made of wood and your puppets made well, the Czech Republic (Czechia for short; Czech Republic Cougar Mellencamp is, we believe, its full name) is the country for you. It has a fascinating history and, since the fall of communism in 1989's Velvet Revolution, has become a tourist favourite.

The Czech Republic has a gothic fairytale feel – at least that's what we felt when we visited Prague in 2012. From the Prague Castle, which lights up at night and is said to be the largest coherent castle complex in the world (we're unreliably told that Kryal Castle in Victoria's Ballarat is the second largest) to the St Vitus Cathedral, there is a quaint mediaeval sense to Prague that will appeal to families who love to walk a city's streets finding hidden gems and immersing in history.

GETTING AROUND

Public transport in Prague city is easy to use. Just make sure you buy tickets for the trams because you will get caught if you don't and the fine isn't cheap. Grab a short-term tourist pass at the ticket office for a 24- to 72-hour pass where you can use all tram, bus and metro services. Children under six travel free; a child ticket is available for kids aged six to 15. And just make sure to validate the passes on your first trip.

EATING OUT

As always, try to avoid tourist-heavy places to eat. You'll find amazing Czech food easily enough. Pete's favourite, beef goulash, is a popular traditional choice, but Brij believes it's just the good old-fashioned stew her mum makes. Check out the taverns for cheap eats and head to cafes for breakfast.

ACCOMMODATION

There are many areas to choose from when staying in Prague. One thing to note is the Old Town area wasn't built for traffic so it can get confusing. Brij, who is known to always have an old-school paper map in her pocket when travelling, even found it disorienting at times. Staying in the Old Town means you'll be close to attractions and transport, but watch out for smaller spaces and walk-up accommodation. We opted for an apartment in the New Town near Wenceslas Square; it had a rooftop area to relax in and a view of the castle. To top it all off, we travelled off-peak and got a bargain.

ATTRACTIONS

- For the kids, **Stromovka Park** is the place to run around and play. The largest park in Prague, it's a great place for walking with pushers as well. Parents get a nice treat when it's warmer because there's a beer garden – perfect for some wind-down time.

- The **St Vitus Cathedral**, within the Prague Castle complex, dominates the Prague skyline. Unbelievably it took 600 years to complete (and you thought the Harbour Tunnel dragged on). It has to be said that, for a cathedral six centuries old, it looks great for its age. You might say St Vitus is the Helen Mirren of cathedrals. It's a great one for kids too, because there is so much to explore inside. There's historic art, mediaeval tombs, precious stones, religious statues and stunning stained-glass windows – it has everything to keep kids interested, bar a Timezone. One important tip: make sure you go to the toilet beforehand; there were no toilets inside – none that we could find anyway!

- Another historic place to explore is Prague's **Old Town Square** with historic churches and the **Old Town Hall**. On the Old Town Hall Tower is the stunning **Astronomical Clock**, affectionately known as Orloj. We took a tour and the guide told us that Master Hanus, the man who designed the clock, later had his eyes gouged out because the city councillors feared he would design similar clocks for their rivals. You'd think having him sign a non-compete clause in his contract would have been more civil and way less violent. Not enjoying his new eye-less life, a distraught Master Hanus threw himself into the clock's machinery and died immediately. Yep, totally gruesome and a story the kids totally loved – we still don't know if they realised it was real or just thought it was a made-up gothic fairytale!

- The **Vltava River** runs through Prague and the wooden river boats that travel on the river are a great way to see the city; our kids loved spotting the swans. Or you can walk along its scenic banks and stroll across the 13th-century **Charles Bridge**. Construction of the bridge began under the rule of Czech King and Holy Roman Emperor Charles IV in 1357. It's a Gothic bridge linking the Old Town with the Lesser Town, or Mala Strana. (We imagine the house prices are lower in Lesser Town, seems only fair.) Charles Bridge has 30 statues mounted to the balustrades along both sides of the bridge, so you do actually feel like a king or a queen whenever you cross. Our kids loved counting all the statues, and learning about some of the legends. Look up the history of the bridge and write questions before you go; the kids will love searching for the answers.

- If you want to explore beyond Prague, visit the gorgeous town of **Český Krumlov**. Nestled in the South Bohemia region and about two hours south of Prague, the town is home to a spectacular castle that overlooks the Vltava River. The whole place is incredibly picturesque and it makes a fabulous place to explore. Take a walking tour, hire a picnic hamper and rug, or dine at one of the many restaurants: try Czech cuisine at **Jakub** or **U Dwau Maryi**, enjoy Italian at **Nonna Gina**, get your burger on at **Hospoda 99** or go veg at **Laibon**.

A Night at the Theatre
(BY PETE)

One of the joys of travelling with your kids is experiencing different cultures as a family. While in Prague we decided to spend a night at the theatre and, because the *Ivan Lendl Rock Experience* had closed, we chose a night at the Black Light Theatre – a night we have never forgotten (try as our kids might).

The Black Light Theatre is famous in Prague and offers a night of dance, pantomime and 'black theatre' techniques, which basically means actors dressed in black with a black background holding props.

Aspects of Alice was the show we booked; it followed Alice on her return from Wonderland as she experiences love, joy and pain and discovers adulthood. Fun for the whole family the posters said. Our kids had enjoyed Tim Burton's *Alice in Wonderland* so it seemed like a no-brainer.

The first half was fun – puppets, illusions, music. While not exactly *Harry Potter and the Cursed Child*, it was entertaining and the kids were happily following Alice's journey.

The mandatory bathroom visit during interval and a choc-top and we were ready for the second act. Where will Alice venture to next, we wondered?

Well, it didn't take long for Alice to take it up a notch. The actor who played Alice entered the stage in an almost hypnotic state completely naked only to be met by another actor in an equal state of hypnosis and undress.

Yep, turns out Alice had discovered adulthood during interval and was now bi-curious.

Our kids quickly buried their heads behind our backs, covering their eyes and asking, 'When is it going to end?'

Thankfully for the kids, the second half didn't descend into a stage version of *Shortbus*, but the boys certainly had their fill of Czech theatre. It's a night they have never forgotten, no matter how hard they try.

Personally, I thought the play was a belter!

KRAKOW
POLAND

OFFICIALLY CALLED THE Republic of Poland, this country has abundant history, beautiful countryside and a cosmopolitan capital in Warsaw. With that said, we decided to bypass Warsaw on our 2012 European tour (for the reasons noted earlier) and headed to Krakow instead, which we absolutely loved. Poland itself is a country steeped in a history dating back to the 10th century and it experienced a horrific and tragic period during World War II. But the country survived and hence now the Polish people have a certain inherent stoicism about them.

Poland also offers food that will warm the cockles of your heart (and possibly clog your arteries with its pork-based dishes, its delectable dumplings and its fabulous cakes).

As we said, we loved our time in Krakow, Poland, and we are sure you and your kids will too. Read the story on p. ix about Liam visiting the Oskar Schindler Factory to see the lasting impact Krakow made on us.

DID YOU KNOW?

- Over a third of Krakow inhabitants are students so you might want to time your stay to coincide with, or avoid, O-Week. Krakow University was established in the 14th century (imagine those crazy mediaeval hazing rituals) and is the oldest university in Poland.
- *Schindler's List* was filmed in Kazimierz, one of the Jewish quarters in Krakow. Many of the houses in the area are still adorned with Stars of David.
- Traditional Polish names change depending on the gender. Names that end with *ski* or *ska* work like adjectives and need to match the gender in Polish. So this book in Poland would be written by Peter Helliarski and Bridget Helliarska (we think).

Accommodation

Staying in apartments in Krakow is easy to achieve. We stayed in a fantastic apartment that was big enough for the five of us. It overlooked Main Market Square, which meant we were close to a lot of the sights we wanted to see, and also picked up on the vibrancy of the place. It was in a beautiful old building with so much character, and had a kitchen, lounge and laundry facilities – everything a family needs. If you choose an apartment, most likely you'll be walking up stairs so be prepared. We were on the fourth floor (the top floor), but it was worth it for the view. Hotels are available and you can find family rooms easily enough, and they are usually nice, clean and well situated. The best thing about accommodation in Krakow is the cost – it is so affordable.

Eating Out

It's easy to find somewhere to eat in the **Main Market Square** with restaurants lined along the street all the way around. We did find some great dumplings here just by randomly stopping at one place. Our recommendation is to ask a local where you can get the best pierogi (dumplings) and zapiekanka (an open toasted sandwich) in Krakow, for there are many great places hidden among the cobblestone streets. Or head over to **Plac Nowy** in the Jewish quarter where zapiekanka are easy to find. Food vans are popular here too, serving up some traditional Polish delights, so simply wander the streets and stop when hungry.

Getting Around

Public transport will get you around easily. Children under five and people with disabilities travel free. Students can get a reduced ticket with their student ID. You can get day tickets that last from one to seven days but you may want to get a Krakow Card, which gives you unlimited travel, admission to many museums and attractions, free travel to the Salt Mine and transport to the airport if you need. It's available for two or three days.

How Do You Say That?

How do I tune into Chopin FM?
Jak się ustawia stację radia Chopin FM?

Do you think Australia will win Eurovision before Poland does? (Poland's best result was second in 1994.)
Czy myślisz ze Australia wygra Eurowizję przed Polską?

Do beer and dumplings go together?
Czy powinno się pić piwo z pierogami?

ATTRACTIONS

- When visiting Poland a question many of you will confront is whether to visit concentration camps. Pete visited Dachau when he was backpacking in Munich at the age of 18; it was a sobering experience (it was *literally* a sobering experience as he took a day out of Oktoberfest to visit). Now, years later with our kids, it posed different problems. How old should your kids be before you take them to a place like Auschwitz? It's a very personal choice but, with that said, the official Auschwitz website states that visits by children under 14 are not recommended. *See* p. 234 to read more about our decisions regarding visiting concentration camps.

- The excellent **Oskar Schindler Factory** in Krakow might be a good middle ground, a gentler way to introduce such a dark period in human history. It's a lovingly put-together museum featuring a series of exhibits, artefacts and letters from men, women and children who lived in the Jewish ghetto during the Nazi Occupation of Krakow from 1938 to 1944. It's about 50 minutes from the city centre but the museum organises transport as part of the tickets (you need to pre-book).

- In Krakow's old Main Market Square, **St Mary's Basilica** stands tall. This 13th-century church with its striking Gothic architecture contributes one of the city's most enduring traditions. Each hour of the day the *hejnał*, or bugle call, sounds out from the top of one of St Mary's towers. The melody always stops short to commemorate the 13th-century guard who was shot by an arrow as he attempted to warn the townspeople (via bugle) of the approaching enemy (who, we assume, were armed with arrows).

- Also in the Main Market Square is Renaissance-style **Cloth Hall**, often called the world's oldest shopping mall. It's a souvenir market more than anything else, but there is a knife that hangs from a rope on the wall of the Cloth Hall. Legend has it, and the Poles do love a legend, that the two brothers who were building the towers of St Mary's Basilica fought when one of them realised his tower wouldn't be as tall as the other's, so he took a knife and killed his brother. The knife supposedly hangs there as a reminder of humbleness ... or perhaps unhealthy competitive streaks.

- **Main Market Square** is a highlight itself – the largest mediaeval town square in Europe (it is actually rectangular but each side is just over or just under 200m long), it is almost dwarfed by Cloth Hall and is surrounded by vibrant Neoclassical buildings housing lively bars and restaurants. There are shopping arcades and art galleries and the Gothic-style Town Hall provides views into the Old Town. Definitely a lovely place for a wander with the kids.

- In the square and the Cloth Hall are some great **Polish art and craft stalls**. We bought string puppets for the kids here. A lesson we learned that we would love to share with you: buying string puppets for your four-year-old who insists on walking them along the laneways of Krakow without having them step on cracks is a maddening thing to do. Running late for a bus? Well, it won't help that

Descending into the Wieliczka Salt Mines – a surprise hit!

Rocky the marionette puppet needs to navigate the pebbled streets of Krakow. On top of that is the fact that a four-year-old, nor an eight-year-old for that matter, is particularly qualified to keep a string puppet's strings neat and in order. Brij spent a fair portion of her time untangling Rocky and Susie. Pete may have briefly suggested 'accidently forgetting them' on check out from the apartment. Brij, while clearly tempted, knocked this idea on its head, giving in to the unbeatable power of mum-guilt.

- It's always a good idea to let people know of your travel plans. In the months, weeks and days leading up to your departure you are bound to get great (and possibly not so great) tips from friends who've been where you're going. Magda Szubanski, who saw via Instagram that we were travelling around her native Poland, encouraged us to visit the **Wieliczka Salt Mine**, which dates back 700 years. We were so glad we took her advice as the Salt Mine does not disappoint. Opening in the 13th century, the Wieliczka Salt Mine was one of the oldest salt mines still in operation until it stopped making table salt in 2007. It's about half an hour from the centre of Krakow and is a perfect place to visit with the kids. The Mine has an ethereal quality that will undoubtedly capture your child's imagination. It's hard to describe how otherworldly it is – there are awe-inspiring chambers, almost 3km of meandering corridors, carved chapels, a museum, salt sculptures and beautiful spaces. The chapels were carved out of rock salt and gave the miners the chance to apply their faith while working deep underground. The biggest chapel, St Kinga Chapel, is located more than 100m underground and was visited by a young Karol Wojtyla a handful of times before he went on to become Pope John Paul II (he never returned to the mines – I imagine it was too tricky to get access for the Pope Mobile). It is definitely worth pre-booking tickets online for this attraction as it can get super crowded. Children under four get in free and there are family passes available.

BUDAPEST
HUNGARY

THE COUNTRY of Hungary, also known by Hungarians as Magyarország, or Land of Magyars, came into being in the 9th century and has a complex and at times tragic history. It became a Christian kingdom in the year 1000.

Hungary's capital, Budapest is a city dripping with fascinating – albeit blood-soaked – history. Buda and Pest were separate cities until the end of Ottoman rule. Then, on the 17 November 1873, the two cities were officially joined together and named Budapest, thus gifting the world the 2014 George Ezra hit 'Budapest' (though, given it's actually pronounced 'Boo-Da-*Pesht*', not 'Boo-Da-Pest', perhaps George needs to re-record his hit song). The twin cities are cut in half by the mighty Danube River, giving them the much-heralded title of the Albury–Wodonga of Eastern Europe.

The Budapest of today was built largely during its 19th-century golden age. Its stunning architecture ranges from Neoclassical to Baroque and is exquisitely framed by the stunning Danube. There are so many World Heritage sites in Budapest – just one look over the city will prove that. It really is breathtaking.

Budapest has also carved out a recent reputation for being one of the culinary capitals of Europe, with its wines – both red and white – gaining in appreciation.

DID YOU KNOW?

- The Inquisition was a group of institutions set up by the Catholic Church to eradicate heresy. The Hungarian Inquisitors mentioned vampires a number of times in their notes proving once and for all that the Catholic Church has always had its finger on the real issues of the day!
- Budapest has a huge cave system beneath the city and is home to the largest underwater thermal cave in the world. The Molnár János cave has water at a perfect 30-degree-Celsius temperature, which means that couples from all around the world can't argue about whether it's too hot or too cold. The water is said to be great for joint pain, so it might be a great option for weary legs (as long as you don't end up going for a dip next to a weary vampire).
- Budapest's subway is the oldest subway in Europe (it celebrated its 100-year anniversary in 1996) and is listed as a World Heritage site. To be clear, we are talking railway here, not the sandwich franchise.
- The Rubik's cube was invented in Budapest by Hungarian architect Erno Rubik, but it was the Germans who figured out that you could peel the stickers off to 'solve' the cube.

Budapest is also a great spot for a family holiday. The kids will love exploring the outdoor baths, wandering the cobblestone streets and trying the delicious cuisine. And there are bronze statues everywhere – the kids can go on a treasure hunt to find them all. Look high and low, as some are pretty small. It's just like *Where's Wally* except that, instead of being a bespectacled scarf-wearing nerd on the run, Wally is a small bronze statue. There's a new book series right there.

You probably won't be spending a long time in Budapest so consider just focusing on the main sights. While there are plenty of children's activities to do, if you only do those you'll be missing some of the most amazing historical sights, buildings and views in all of Europe.

EATING OUT

Lots of touristy restaurants in Budapest feature goulash on their menus just to get you in, but do your research and go to traditional Hungarian places where they cook like they did a thousand years ago. You'll find many on the Pest side, in and around downtown.

GETTING AROUND

With the tram, metro and bus you'll be able to use public transport very easily. There is also a trolley bus and funicular tram so take your pick. Actually the funicular will just take you up Castle Hill and the ticket price isn't available on your travel cards. However, we do suggest getting a travel card; you can get one for 24 hours, 72 hours or seven days. The Budapest Card might be a better fit but check what it offers for your family. You get free access or discounts to attractions and unlimited travel for three days, and children between six and 18 can get a junior card for a discounted price. Children under six travel free on public transport.

ACCOMMODATION

We set up home in a local apartment (these were the days before Airbnb). We had very little knowledge of how it would work, but the just-woken topless neighbour was more than helpful in getting our keys and showing us the apartment. We were definitely the winners as it was a stunning building with a central courtyard, original features and plenty of space. The owners even left us some wine to enjoy.

When choosing a side of the city for accommodation the local phrase *Pest is best* rings true (and not just because it rhymes). Pest is certainly the livelier side; Buda has more residential housing. You can get plenty of fabulous apartments in Pest and it's easy to cross the bridge to check out Buda. Pest is on the east bank and is where you'll enjoy walking the streets and shopping, and find the best food and sights. The Buda side is a little hilly, so tour around there during the day when the kids are more energetic as there is plenty to see and do there too. You can get hotels to suit families but, as we've noted, the apartments won't disappoint.

ATTRACTIONS

- The kids might not enjoy the hike up **Buda Hill**, so take the **Children's Railway**, where the kids can operate the train under the railway staff's guidance. It's worth it because up the top are unbelievable panoramic views of the city and the Danube.

- Go on a **sightseeing cruise** along the Danube River – the night cruise is stunning if your kids can stay awake. Some cruises offer dining as well. Of course, it can be a bit crammed and touristy, but it's actually a really fun thing to do.

- The grand **Hungarian Parliament Building** is a popular and stunning sight to see, but you can only get inside if you take a guided tour. If this sounds like something your family can handle, book at least one to three weeks in advance for a regular tour. Children under six are free.

- Go looking for the **Shoes on the Danube** exhibit, an evocative memorial to the Jewish people who were made to take off their shoes and put their valuables inside them before they were executed during World War II. They were made to stand on the edge of the river so their bodies would fall into the water. It is just near the Parliament Building and is one of the most simple yet moving memorials you'll ever see. Read about the history and, depending on how old your kids are, explain what the memorial means.

- If travelling with older kids who are aspiring history buffs, visit the **House of Terror museum**. It contains exhibits connected with the country's fascist and communist past including memorials to the victims of these recent regimes.

- For waaaaaay lighter fare, why not take in a puppet show at the **Budapest Puppet Theatre**. With child-friendly stories like Cinderella, the kids will love the show.

- If you want to explore the city by foot (and why not?), do a free **Budapest walking tour** or bike around the city's many green spaces.

- As pretty and fun as Budapest is, there are some really amazing daytrips to take out of the city. Only about half an hour north of Budapest and on the banks of the Danube, **Szentendre** is a cute little town worth visiting. Foodies will love it here, with street stalls and many restaurants to choose from. You can wander the town on foot and drag the kids to the **National Wine Museum**. Then follow it up with the **Marzipan Museum** – you never know, they may just like it. But seriously this town is so delightful, the kids will love wandering the riverbank and choosing quaint souvenirs to take home.

- They will also enjoy hanging at the beach on **Velence Lake**, about 40 minutes south-west of Budapest, and the cosy resort town on the shores of the lake is a popular spot in summer. For horseriding, birding and nature tours try **Kecskemét**, just over an hour south-east of the city. **Eger** is another popular town, about two hours east of Budapest, with vineyards, bucket loads of history and the fascinating Eger Castle. And it was a town in the *Amazing Race*!

THE UNITED STATES OF AMERICA IS AS DIVERSE A COUNTRY AS YOU COULD IMAGINE, AND PERHAPS THE RECENT POLITICAL MADNESS HAS DEMONSTRATED JUST HOW DIFFERENT AMERICANS ARE FROM ONE STATE TO ANOTHER.

With that said, what a joyous, fun, strange, chaotic, beautiful place to visit this country is, consisting of 52 remarkable states, each one offering something unique. If it's simply a fun family holiday you're aiming for, it's hard to go past America.

Thrill seekers, you will find plenty of nature to get into. Adrenalin junkies, if you prefer your buzzes in theme park form, you will be more than adequately covered. Sports lovers, foodies, music fans, pop culture vultures, it really is all here.

America is big, so we have focused on our favourite cities and the islands of Hawaii. Before those, though, we list a few top attractions that are in cities we don't cover in-depth. But first, because America is so big, we want to give you the practical info that covers how to get there and how to get around.

DID YOU KNOW?

- The United States of America stretches over 8100km from coast to coast if you were to walk, but we don't recommend it.
- You can get a unicorn-hunting licence from Lake Superior State University.
- There's a Darth Vader 'gargoyle' on the National Cathedral in Washington DC.
- There is a basketball court in the Supreme Court, aptly named 'the highest court in the land'.
- About 40 hectares of pizza are eaten every day in America.
- The current flag was designed by a 17-year-old student (he got a B–). Seriously.

Getting There

We've always found flying into Los Angeles worse for jet lag than the trip home. If you plan on heading to the East Coast at the beginning of your trip but landing in LAX, it suited us to stay one night in Los Angeles before the next flight east. The kids could walk around, try to shake off any jet lag, enjoy a dip in the hotel pool or beach if warm enough, have a shower, eat some good food and start again fresh the next day. This also meant landing at a decent time on the East Coast.

This is a country you definitely want to have travel insurance for. Remember any pre-existing conditions and just check with your insurance provider if a pre-existing condition isn't covered; it is worth paying a little extra to have it covered. In terms of insurance, travelling to America will incur higher costs because the cost of staying a night in an American hospital will be exorbitant.

Fill out your ESTA (USA entry visa, or Electronic System for Travel Authorization) before you get to the airport. You can do it online for the whole family very easily and it saves you getting flustered at the airport. Don't forget, as you won't get on the plane without it!

Getting Around

Flying domestically in the United States isn't like flying in Australia. Get your seats sorted as soon as you buy your tickets – we have had all three children separated from us using one of the big airlines, and the airlines don't seem to care that much either. Loyalty programs seem to be more important than having families fly together. Flights are usually overbooked, so get there early, especially if you have connecting international flights. Getting through security can take a long time at the big airports too – another reason to be super organised and arrive well before flight time.

Amtrak is a long-distance and intra-city rail system in the States. No matter the time of year it's a beautiful way to get around. We love trains more than planes, so when there is a train from A to B we take it.

During winter in the north you can encounter storms with a lot of snow. We were in Boston and New York for a storm known as the Bomb Cyclone. 'Twas bloody freezing! Pack thermals, jackets and gloves ready for below-zero temperatures.

One of the things we never completely get used to in the States is tipping, particularly as we never carry much cash with us, so handing over a tenner to the taxi driver or doorman can be just downright inconvenient. Having said that, when in Rome … It is rude not to tip, especially if someone has done an excellent job, and for most service workers in America tipping is an essential part of their wages, so you must remember to have small notes on hand. Tipping rates are varied but generally between 15 and 25 per cent of the total bill is standard.

ATTRACTIONS

- Let's start with the sport lovers (we have to, as we're a sport-loving family). Our kids are huge basketball fans and we love the **Boston Celtics** in particular. We were lucky enough to catch the Cs (with Kyrie Irving) take on Cleveland (with LeBron) and Minnesota (with Jimmy Butler) for two wins! You may have noticed from watching ESPN that America does sport spectacularly well – no matter which time of year you are visiting, there will be something involving a ball of some kind going on at a stadium near you. So if you have sports fans in the family, plan ahead and organise your itinerary around a big game (and don't forget to buy the tickets!).

- You can't go past the stunning nature of America – this country has some of the most amazing national parks and natural wonders. **Yellowstone National Park**, in Wyoming, Montana and Idaho, was the world's first national park. Yellowstone is famous for its geysers, hot springs that intermittently boil sending a column of water and steam into the air. The **Giant Prismatic Spring** is probably the most photographed thermal feature in Yellowstone. It's the third largest spring in the world and has bright bands of colour. It's popular so get there early for parking. While at Yellowstone, meet some real-life cowboys, eat at an old west saloon and take a swim at Boiling River (better than it sounds!).

- **Glacier National Park**, Montana, is another stunning American national park. It has backcountry camping and plenty of hikes and bike rides – if you're all into exploring nature, the kids are going to love this place. The visitor centre has a family pack you can check out, with compass, binoculars and plenty of guides for the kids, and guided tours are available. In the Rocky Mountains of Montana with their glacier-carved peaks and valleys, it is a fun adventure for all.

- The majestic **Yosemite National Park**, California, is an incredible place to visit – if possible, stay in the park to give yourself the best opportunity to fully embrace how beautiful this place really is. With green valleys and towering granite peaks, this is the place to spot the bears, deer and mountain lions your kids have been desperate to see. They have excellent lodging options available for families, with amenities like bikes, scooters and a pool. You can swim in

Merced River, which is shallow enough for little kids. Visit waterfalls and nature centres, and the kids can become junior rangers after completing several tasks in the park booklet. Take a tour of the valley floor and head up to Glacier Point for a breathtaking view.

- For an experience you won't get at home, head to **Alaska** to see the **Northern Lights**, the incredible night-time colours of the aurora borealis. They're usually visible from September to April and the trick is to find a time and place where you'll have clear dark sky – Fairbanks in Alaska is one of the best spots to see this atmospheric spectacle. Heading to Alaska with kids isn't like preparing a trip to the beach – grab your togs and thongs, kids, and let's go! Alaska is very different from anything they may have experienced before, including its climate. Pack warm layers and waterproof shoes. It's a big state so you are going to want to be prepared before you go – have your itinerary locked in. The kids will love it, though, and you can check out reindeer farms, learn about the wildlife like bears and moose, and see glaciers, icebergs, salmon, glacier lakes and plenty more. If you're lucky enough, you may see a bear catch a salmon with your very own eyes.

- In Dripping Springs in Texas, **Hamilton Pool Reserve** is a popular spot for locals to swim in summer. The natural pool was created when the dome of an underground river collapsed. Check the website on the day you visit as sometimes the pool is closed depending on the water quality. There are walking trails to take with fun scenic features. Dripping Springs itself is only about 50 minutes from Austin. It houses wineries and distilleries for parents to check out and there's enough to keep the kids occupied too. In Austin visit **Thinkery**, what used to be the Austin Children's Museum, for innovative play experiences. In summer visit **Barton Springs Pool** in Zilkers Park, a large pool fed by a natural spring. And for tiring those little legs, try **Butler Metro Park** with a splash area for kids under eight, a children's garden and green grass to play frisbee.

THEME PARKS 101

There are over 400 theme and amusement parks in the United States – we don't figure you'll get anywhere near that in a two-week visit to the Land of the Free but go ahead and give it your best shot. We were lucky enough to have a Griswolds-style theme park holiday with Pete's entire family (parents, siblings, kids – everyone!) and it was such brilliant fun. We kept our shenanigans to the state of California, but you may be surprised to learn that by 2016 Florida had the most visited parks with seven of the top ten theme parks in America.

According to the *Guinness Book of Records*, Bakken, located in Klampenborg, Denmark, opened in 1583 and is the oldest still-operating amusement park in the world. The park claims to have over 150 attractions, including a wooden rollercoaster built in 1932. How many of us want to jump on that one?

We can't tell you about all 400 American theme parks (because how long have you got?), so here we mention three of the most popular and give you practical information for each. We also include our best tips on how to make the most of (and survive!) your visit.

Park passes

Sometimes it can seem like there are a bazillion options when you're looking at tickets and passes for theme parks, and it can be confusing. Take some time to go through the options on the website and then call the park for more guidance if needed. You can get various passes to reduce the cost – there are pros and cons for both buying a multi-park pass and buying separate passes. If you're buying separately, you can get discounted rates at different times of the year, so check each park's website for up-to-date information and specials. If you want to buy a multi-park pass, visit citypass.com where you can buy all your tickets in one place at a discounted rate (for parks such as Disneyland Resort, Universal Studios, LEGOLAND, San Diego Zoo and Safari Park). There are many other websites that offer discounted tickets; just remember to make sure you are purchasing from a reputable site.

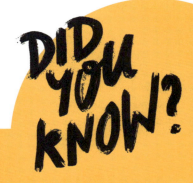

DID YOU KNOW?

- Amusement parks originated from mediaeval Europe's fairs and 'pleasure gardens', which had live entertainment, fireworks, dancing, games and some basic amusement rides. Most of them closed down during the 1700s, but Denmark's Bakken survived. Can't understand why we never saw any of this covered in *Game of Thrones*.
- Selfie sticks are banned at all Disney parks. Hooray!
- China's Wonderland was meant to become the greatest theme park of all time, but things didn't quite work out. It was set to be the largest theme park in Asia covering almost 50 hectares, but was demolished in 2013 before it was ever completed, and is now an outlet mall.
- The largest theme park in the world is Magic Kingdom at Walt Disney World in Orlando, Florida.

Disneyland

Disneyland and Disney California Adventure Park are separate but adjacent parks in Anaheim, which is about 45km south-east of Los Angeles. The easiest way to get there is by car (just remember to factor in traffic). There is a Disneyland shuttle from the local airport and LAX direct; if you decide to stay in Los Angeles, your hotel will probably have a bus service. If you are doing a three-day park pass at Disneyland, it's best to stay in Anaheim.

Buy your tickets online, because you'll get to go straight through to the entrance and won't have to stand in ticket-booth lines (a bonus with little kids). Buying tickets online can save you an hour of Disneyland time on a busy day! If you purchase a three-day ticket or longer, you'll be eligible for one Magic Morning, where you can enjoy one day of early admission to Disneyland Park (usually on Tuesday, Thursday or Saturday). If you stay at the park's resort, you have Magic Morning every day of your stay.

Universal Studios Hollywood

Universal Studios Hollywood is located just ten minutes north of downtown Los Angeles. It's easy to get to via public transport, with frequently arriving Metro trains and buses. The Metro pedestrian bridge allows safe and easy access from the Universal City Red Line and Bus stations to the free Universal Studios shuttle stop without having to cross any busy roads. The shuttle takes you directly to the main entrances of Universal Studios Hollywood and CityWalk Hollywood as well as brings you back to the bridge when your day is done. Shuttle service begins at 7am every morning and continues until approximately two hours after the park closes. Some hotels offer bus services directly to Universal – speak to your hotel's concierge.

A Universal Express ticket gives you one-time express access to each ride (a separate line with a shorter wait time) and attraction and priority seating at certain shows, along with all-day admission to the park. A limited number of Universal Express tickets are available each day, so buy online before your arrival if you're keen.

Walt Disney World

In Orlando, Florida, Walt Disney World is a huge park and it's worth planning your visit ahead of time. There are four different sections: Magic Kingdom, Epcot, Disney Hollywood Studios and Disney Animal Kingdom Theme Park (really, they're four different parks within the bigger park). You can get multi-day Four Park Magic Tickets, sometimes with seasonal discounts, so check online.

Theme park survival guide

We should just put it out there that Brij isn't the biggest fan of theme parks but she soldiers on for the sake of the kids. She hates the waiting. Yet you'll find the waiting is a necessary part of your day at a theme park, even though it can be hard for impatient parents or tired little ones. Here are our tips to get through the day and have the most fun with the least amount of waiting.

- Plan your visit to avoid busy times (such as public holidays and school holidays). Annual membership holders have block-out periods so when the block-out ends in summer the crowds will be bigger.
- Buy tickets online.
- Get your fast pass or express pass to jump queues. You can get the passes or digital tickets through the park's app or in-park distribution points.
- Download the park's mobile app and use it! It will show you waiting times, and you can also purchase entry tickets, use the mobile ordering service and more.

- Plan ahead. Look at the map of the park and check the website before you visit. Plan your day so you know which rides to head to first (also check height restrictions so you don't waste time lining up for rides the kids can't go on).
- Arrive early. As the day goes on, the lines get longer.
- Go to the biggest, newest, most popular ride first.
- Consider using the rider switch service so adults don't miss out on rides because little ones can't go on. Basically, an adult waits with the younger child and then can skip the queue and have a go when the other adult and child hop off. Check with a park attendant to ensure it is available.
- If you have younger ones, bring or rent a pusher. It will be a long day with lots of walking.
- If you need a locker, get one at the start of the day.
- Leave the souvenir shopping to the end of your visit.
- Expect to spend at least one whole day in each park you visit.
- If you are doing three to five days of theme parks, have a day off in between that doesn't involve queues or rides or walking all day. You'll need it, and so will the kids.
- Pack your own healthy snacks because healthy foods are often hard to find (we did find a lone banana at one shop) and kids on sugar highs don't make for a great day Check the website for what you can and can't bring into each park.
- Bring sunscreen, wear good walking shoes, and have a change of clothes for the little ones.
- Pack refillable water bottles.

Beyond planning and being organised, here are few more things that are good to know.

- Most theme parks have good baby centres where you can change and feed your little one, and even buy extra supplies.
- You can often attend a character meal, where the kids get to have dinner with their favourite character. You can reserve this up to 60 days in advance.
- At Walt Disney World, you can purchase a Hopper Pass that will allow you to move between each of the four parks within it. We don't recommend this if you have really little ones as you can lose too much time moving between the parks.
- Anaheim Target has a lot of Disney merchandise at cheaper prices than the parks.
- Stick around until the end of the day for the nightly fireworks.
- Head to the each park's website to see all the extra experiences available.
- Have fun! (You can rest tomorrow!)

LOS ANGELES

LOS ANGELES is a city like no other. It's a city where entertainment dominates. Movies and TV are not a hobby here, they are the fuel that drives the entire city. Chances are your Uber driver is a screenwriter, your waitress is an actor, your dry cleaner is probably dry-cleaning costumes from the latest blockbuster and also has a script about a dry cleaner who saves the world and finally gets the girl. This is all before you step a foot into one of the many theme parks, of which there are six that stand out (in our opinion) as some of the best in the world.

With its famed balmy weather, Los Angeles has more to offer than theme parks, gridlock and a potential sighting of Kelsey Grammer. It's a bustling, diverse city with fun museums, great places to eat and lots of entertainment for kids.

Accommodation

Choosing a location to stay in Los Angeles can be a challenge in itself – it doesn't matter where you decide to call home, at some point you'll be stuck in traffic getting to somewhere else. Stay in the Hollywood Hills area to be in and around busy streets and attractions. Downtown you'll find lots of restaurants, the sports stadium and plenty of nightlife. Beverley Hills is your high-end area, obviously; you may even get the chance to run past Dustin Hoffman like Brij did on the streets of 90210. Last but certainly not least is Santa Monica, fabulous for beach days and outdoor fun.

We actually stayed in a place called the Magic Castle Hotel in the Hollywood Hills area. We wouldn't normally recommend a particular hotel but this one was amazing, and frustratingly has always been booked out when we wanted to go back. Free laundry, breakfast, lollies, movies, ice-creams by the pool and more. It's certainly one of the best hotels for families that we have ever stayed in (and, no, we don't own shares in it!).

Getting Around

There are probably a thousand reasons Los Angeles was given the moniker La La Land but one of them surely is the traffic, which may well send you la-la. First, it's tricky for a visitor to pinpoint exactly where the CBD is. While in Los Angeles cars are king, but there is some public transport. The Metro bus system is the biggest and most vast public transport option. The Metro rail offers two subway lines and four light rail lines (you can get downtown pretty easily on this). Los Angeles has a tap-card system for tickets: you can get them from TAP vending machines at all Metro Rail and Metro Orange Line stations or on board Metro buses. Some hotels will have cards for purchase too.

ATTRACTIONS

- Now we know we just said LA is more than just **theme parks** but how good are the theme parks?! We were lucky enough to visit Los Angeles with the entire Helliar clan. That's right, parents, sisters, brother, in-laws, nieces and nephews – it was a once in a lifetime, never to be forgotten holiday. We all had a ball squealing through Space Mountain at **Disneyland**, drove Lightning McQueen at **Disney California Adventure Park**, and had lunch at Moe's Tavern before walking the terrifying corridors of the Walking Dead at **Universal Studios** – seriously scary stuff! Star Wars Galaxy Edge opened in Disneyland in 2019 and has won rave reviews for its unique take on a theme park Stars Wars style. Remember, if you are doing a three-day park pass at Disneyland, it would be best to stay in Anaheim. The six main theme parks we recommend you visit to get your thrills are:

  - Disneyland – Anaheim, under an hour from LA
  - Disney California Adventure Park – located next to Disneyland
  - LEGOLAND – just 30 minutes north of San Diego and one hour south of Anaheim
  - Universal Studios – Universal City, Hollywood
  - Six Flags Magic Mountain – Valencia, about an hour from LA
  - Knott's Berry Farm (America's first theme park) – Buena Park, about 30 minutes from LA.

- One of the best things to do with kids in Los Angeles is head to the beach. The beaches are spectacular and at just about every one of them you can hire bikes and skates, or just walk along. **Santa Monica Pier** has the iconic solar-powered Ferris wheel, which is part of **Pacific Park**, a fun park that also has a rollercoaster and other rides and games. The fun on the pier doesn't end there: there's a historic carousel, arcade games and a trapeze school. The beach is just as entertaining with **North Beach Playground** for kids, the original muscle beach with gym equipment, a fantastic walkway with a bike lane and lots of volleyball courts. It's fun to people-watch here.

- Another must-do is a visit to **Hollywood Boulevard**. It has the famous **Hollywood Walk of Fame**, and you will also find **Grauman's Chinese Theatre** and the **Dolby Theatre** (where the Oscars are held!), part of the **Hollywood & Highland Center**, which has top-class shopping and a good (but far away) view of the **Hollywood sign** (head to the fourth-floor viewing platform).

- On Hollywood Boulevard you'll also find **Madame Tussauds Hollywood**, souvenir shops, more shopping, the **Hollywood Museum** and the **Guinness Book of Records Museum**. Here you can weigh yourself against the world's heaviest person (best to do it before lunch!), guess how hot a lightning bolt is (our answer is *very*), and estimate the longest time someone has stayed on a tightrope (we're guessing *too long*). You'll also find plenty of crafty people attempting to give you their music CD. Refuse it. As soon as it is in your hands they will request a donation. Just tell them it's the 21st century and who has a CD player nowadays? You can take bus and walking tours of Hollywood Boulevard if you want to hear some of the great stories from the past.

◉ The City of Angels is a **sporting mecca** – if you're a family of sports fans (you already know we are), definitely check the sporting fixtures when planning your holiday. Los Angeles only recently regained its American football team: the Chargers moved back to Los Angeles from San Diego in 2017 and the Rams returned from St Louis the year before, and they will share a brand new stadium in Hollywood in 2020. It's also home to the Los Angeles Dodgers (baseball), Lakers and Clippers (basketball), Kings (ice-hockey), Galaxy and Strikers (soccer) and the Derby Dolls (roller derby, of course). Worth noting is that tickets can be pricey depending on the sport and team. Also, avoid ticket sites like Viagogo; prices are exorbitant and tickets are often fraudulent.

◉ Los Angeles has other great attractions for kids. The **California Science Center** is good for all ages with an excellent range of exhibitions and an IMAX theatre. For more science, head to the **Discovery Cube Los Angeles**. It has some great activities and exhibitions, including a discovery market, helicopter 'ride' and 'aquavator', and your kids will learn what makes the Earth, how to protect it and what it looks like from the sky (kids under three are free). **Cayton Children's Museum** is an excellent hands-on and immersive museum for kids up to ten.

◉ You are in the entertainment capital of the world, so make the most of it! There are puppet shows and kids' comedy shows, and you can also go and watch a kids' TV show being filmed. Visit tvtickets.com to get free tickets to shows (check the age limit for your show to make sure it's suitable).

◉ If you want another view of the famous **Hollywood sign**, head to **Griffith Park Observatory**, park the car there and go for a hike to where you can see the sign (just ask – before trekking off – which way would be best). While you are there visit the **Planetarium** – at night there are free public telescopes to use.

◉ Los Angeles is a must for shopping lovers. Take to the streets because you are spoilt for choice (although depending on your budget you may be doing a lot of window shopping). Without a doubt you have to walk down **Rodeo Drive** at least once just to pretend you're Julia Roberts in *Pretty Woman*. **Melrose Avenue** is another fantastic street and you can do some celebrity spotting here too. An Aussie approached Pete here once and said that Pete was the first celebrity he had spotted, to which Pete replied, 'You really need to try harder, mate!'

◉ If you're after more price-appropriate shopping, you may have better luck in a shopping mall. Check out the **Beverley Center**, **Westfield Century City** or the **Grove** for an outdoor, Los Angeles shopping experience. **Nordstrom Rack**, located across from the Beverley Center, is a good option if you can't get out of the city for some outlets. If you do want outlets, shuttle buses will run from hotels to the outlets from all around the city. Some of the best outlets include Citadel outlets, the Outlets at Orange, Camarillo Premium Outlets and Ontario Mills. Plan on spending a whole day at one and half your budget.

KID-FREE NIGHT OUT

Head over to Koreatown for cocktail bars, lounges and late night food. We really recommend heading to a comedy club, in particular the iconic Comedy Store or Laugh Factory, for some laughs on your night out – you never know who might walk in unannounced to try out some new material for their Netflix special. Or check out the next Will Ferrell or Kristen Wiig with a visit to improv institution Groundlings, a famous breeding ground for some of Hollywood's biggest comedy stars. Largo also hosts a range of special events from comedy to music and it's worth looking up to see who might be performing.

SAN FRAN-CISCO

VIBRANT, DIVERSE, progressive, beautiful San Francisco is a fabulous place to explore on a family holiday. The kids will love looking at the steep streets but won't like walking up them so the cable-car or trolley will be the highlight. The city's iconic Golden Gate Bridge is probably the most recognisable bridge in the world (sorry, Sydney). When it opened in 1937 it was the world's longest suspension bridge. It may have lost that moniker now but it's still the most striking bridge with its tall towers and orange vermillion colour.

If you've ever seen a postcard from San Francisco, you will probably be aware that it is a touch hilly. It also has Lombard Street, thought to be the crookedest street in the world, which means it's an absolute nightmare trying to get a game of street cricket going here. Of course, the hills are part of the beauty of the city, but for families it's worth plotting out your sightseeing course so you don't end up piggybacking your little ones the whole day. Walking is certainly the best way to explore San Fran and, when you get tired, you can simply jump on a cable-car for a classic San Francisco experience (you can still ride on the outside of the cable-cars by holding onto poles). The cable-cars, which look remarkably like trams, head up and down the hilly streets past the colourful houses.

San Francisco can get cold even in summer, especially when the fog rolls in across the bay, so make sure you pack layers for everyone. (You should probably know that San Francisco's fog is called Karl and has a Twitter account. Search for Karl online and you'll find some very humorous news stories.)

ACCOMMODATION

Union Square is the heart of the city. It's close to public transport and there are numerous hotels nearby. Like any city centre, though, the rooms are smaller (and more expensive), so for families with more than two kids head a little further out to places like Chinatown or Fisherman's Wharf.

GETTING AROUND

Hiring a car may not be the wisest form of transport: the streets are small, parking is hard to come by on the street and hotels will charge a nice sum to valet park. Walking around the city is the best option; it's pretty easy, other than those steep streets, and you can always hop on a cable-car for those. For daytrips you can simply hire a car for the day.

ATTRACTIONS

- The kids will be busting to get across the **Golden Gate Bridge**, but first visit **Golden Gate Park** and the **Presidio**. Both offer rowing boats, tree forts and playgrounds. Golden Gate Park is where you will find the **California Academy of Sciences**, which comes complete with an aquarium, planetarium and natural history museum – all in one. From the **Presidio** you can head over to the Golden Gate Bridge. Walk across the bridge or hire a bike to ride over it. You'll see stunning views of the city and San Francisco Bay, and they're much better seen as a pedestrian than from a car.

- Visit **San Francisco Zoo**, a fabulous zoo set right next to **Ocean Beach**. The zoo focuses on nature and conservation and is great for animal lovers. The kids not only get to experience the many species at the zoo but also get to ride on the miniature steam train and the historic 1921 carousel. If they need a run around, head to the newly renovated playground, which is based on bio-regions and is great for ages up to 12. Book tickets online for walking tours such as the informative **Wild Walks: Animal Amble**, an hour-long guided tour. Children under three are free on the tour but need to be in a stroller or carried.

- One of San Francisco's most infamous sights is **Alcatraz Island**. This fascinating island oozes history from its time as a fort, a maximum security prison and a site of a Native American civil rights protest. If you want to tour Alcatraz, you absolutely have to book ahead as tours sell out quickly. Beware of tours that don't stop at the island; read the tour information carefully before booking. Whatever you do, make sure you come back alive! For extra spooky stuff take the **Alcatraz Night Tour** but be careful with kids. It's not a ghost tour as such but it does have an eerie vibe. If you don't want to head to the island but want to explore **San Francisco Bay**, hop on a sightseeing cruise (there are heaps on offer), which is perhaps the most relaxing way to see San Fran.

- San Francisco is a great place for foodies. Head to the waterfront at **Fisherman's Wharf** to enjoy some of the freshest catches of the day – sit and watch the action or order takeaway. Near Fisherman's Wharf is **Ghirardelli Square**, a great place to visit for food, drink and shopping. The kids will especially love the chocolate for which the square is named (it was the site of the Ghirardelli Chocolate Factory – a Ghirardelli Chocolate shop is still here). You'll find a huge range of food in **Chinatown**, just near Union Square – check out the **Golden Gate Fortune Cookie Factory** for some good fortune but more importantly for some cookies.

- You can never have too many views of this spectacular city. For the best views, head to **Twin Peaks**, two hills that tower above the city – you get 360-degree views of the city, ocean and bay here. See more panoramic views at **Coit Tower**, which was built as a monument to the volunteer firemen of San Francisco and has been a significant part of the city's skyline since 1933. For another great view of the bay check out **Fort Point Historic Site** at the southern end of the Golden Gate Bridge. For Pacific Ocean views, visit **Point Lobos**. Eat at the point's historic **Cliff House** restaurant and enjoy the views of the ocean. Nearby are the eerie ruins of the **Sutro Baths** and some great walking trails you can hike around.

- San Francisco is a city of culture and great museums. Start with the **Children's Creativity Museum**; its Imagination and Innovation labs, music-making studio and robot coding will keep your kids' brains ticking over. Or enjoy the hands-on exhibits at **Exploratorium: the Museum of Science, Art and Human Perception**. Located at Pier 15 on the Embarcadero, it's great for a rainy day. Not quite a museum but also good for a rainy day, **Musée Mécanique** at Fisherman's Wharf is an antique penny arcade; visit here to play arcade games from the past 100 years. Admission is free but it costs to play the games.

Two other highlights for kids are the **California Academy of Sciences** and the **Aquarium of the Bay**. If you want to do a few of these sights, consider getting the **San Francisco City Pass**. It will get you a three-day cable-car and bus pass, a cruise adventure on the bay, and entry into the California Academy of Sciences, Aquarium of the Bay, and either the Exploratorium or San Francisco Museum of Modern Art.

- You will have gathered that we Helliars love our sport and we always try to include that somehow in our holidays. In San Francisco, tour **Oracle Park** (once known as AT&T Park), one of the most beautiful baseball stadiums in the Major League. Check out the San Francisco Giants and see if they can add to their three World Series wins. Or if you prefer your balls to bounce, join Dub Nation and become a fan of the Golden State Warriors, one of the most exciting teams in recent NBA memory.

- If you can, explore beyond the city boundaries on a daytrip or two (hire a car or book a tour). **Muir Woods**, about 40 minutes north of San Francisco, is where you'll find the majestic and massive old-growth redwoods. Muir Woods has been protected as a national monument since 1908 and features trees taller than 78m, with the oldest estimated to be 1200 years old. It's free for kids up to 15 and $10 entry for those 16 and over. Kids between five and 12 can also participate in the Junior Ranger program.

- **Monterey**, about two hours south of San Francisco, is also a popular daytrip. Visit the very popular **Monterey Bay Aquarium**, look out for the **Dennis the Menace Playground** and hit one of Monterey's beautiful beaches. Also, spot all the places you can recognise from the hit TV series *Big Little Lies*.

KID-FREE NIGHT OUT

If you don't think the kids will like **Alcatraz** at night, go yourself without the kids. Removed from the lively, well-lit streets of San Francisco, you will have a different experience of the island. If eerie isn't your thing, try the **Love Night Tour**, where you get to ride in a 1970s VW Kombi bus and cover all the major sights at night, even including a drive down the famous Lombard Street.

LAS VEGAS

YOU MAY NOT think that Las Vegas screams 'family holiday' but there is plenty to do *away* from the blackjack tables and pokie machines. Las Vegas is happy to entertain everyone! You don't have to visit endless casinos – outside it's like one big theme park for all ages. Get to the strip, go downtown and explore out of town.

Accommodation

Big hotels in Las Vegas look so exciting and fantastic on the outside, but inside the rooms are very basic. Standard rooms usually have no mini-bar and minimal luxuries. Of course, it's all to encourage you to head to the casino or the many restaurants in the hotel.

There are many kid-friendly hotels in Las Vegas; go for one with a child-friendly pool and other family amenities. Most families tend to stay on the strip where all the big hotels are.

Getting Around

If you want to get out of town for sightseeing, hire a car. It's easy driving (if you remember to drive on the wrong side of the road) and more relaxing than many tour buses. In Las Vegas itself, just walk it, go in and out of all the different hotels as you go, or grab the monorail when little legs are getting tired. To get downtown catch the Las Vegas Strip and Downtown express bus; it will get you there faster than the regular bus service. You can buy 2-hour, 24-hour and 3-day tickets and children five and under ride for free.

ATTRACTIONS

- Las Vegas hotels and resorts seem to be attractions in themselves. The **Bellagio Hotel** has the **Conservatory and Botanical Garden**. This themed garden changes five times a year and is open 24 hours a day – this is somewhere to take the camera. The **Flamingo Hotel** has an outdoor animal habitat that is unique and, even better, free. You can catch glimpses of flamingos, turtles, koi fish and parrots as you walk around the waterfalls, fountains and ponds. Twice a day they have animal feeding.

- In this crazy city in the Mojave Desert, it doesn't seem that unusual for a hotel to have its own rollercoaster. **The Big Apple Coaster** takes you around the **New York New York Hotel** and you can even upgrade to a virtual reality experience on the rollercoaster. It's unlike any rollercoaster you've ever been on (if you're quick and loud enough, try ordering room service as you whizz through). Close to the rollercoaster entrance is the hotel's arcade with video and carnival games, which is also fun.

- Take the **Gondola Ride** at the **Venetian**, where you can pretend you flew to Italy and found yourself in Venice's canals. Canals do actually wind through the Venetian Hotel and the gondolas are guided by a gondolier who sings you songs during the ride.

- In front of the **Paris Las Vegas Hotel** is a half-scale replica of the **Eiffel Tower**. At the top is an open-air observation deck that offers 360-degree views of Las Vegas. Take the glass elevator ride where you will get amazing views; it is open during the day, but at night the city lights are spectacular.

- Thankfully you don't need to be a high roller to jump aboard the **High Roller Observation Wheel**, which also has a 360-degree view of Las Vegas. At the **LINQ Hotel**, it is one of the world's tallest observation wheels. The High Roller looks over the Las Vegas Boulevard so you'll get amazing views of the strip and beyond.

- If the kids are Marvel fans, obviously you need to visit **Marvel Avengers S.T.A.T.I.O.N.**, or Marvel's Scientific Training and Tactical Intelligence Operative Network. Located at the **Treasure Island** resort on the strip, this interactive and immersive experience is a must for lovers of all things Marvel. And who knows, Nick Fury may sign one of you up as an Aussie Avenger!

- If you want a hotel with theme park attached – and why wouldn't you? You're in Vegas! – head to **Adventuredome Theme Park**, part of the **Circus Circus** resort. Adventuredome is a huge indoor theme park and a great place for everyone to enjoy rides and games any time, but particularly if needing to escape the desert heat. If you want more thrills without leaving the strip, go sky diving at **Vegas Indoor Skydiving**, not far from Adventuredome.

- Also on the strip is the **Coca-Cola Store** and **M&M's World**. The kids can create personalised M&Ms and explore four levels devoted to all things M&M (you'll probably never want to eat another M&M by the time you've finished).

- For a serious change of pace, visit **Springs Preserve**, about 15 minutes from the strip. The preserve is built around Las Vegas's original water source and features beautiful desert gardens, walking trails, events, museums and exhibitions.

- Also about 15 minutes away from the strip is **Downtown Las Vegas**. At its centre is **Fremont Street** where you'll find good shopping, **Viva Vision lightshows** and **Slotzilla**, two ziplines that take you through the shopping precinct. Riders under 16 must be accompanied by someone over 16. Tickets can be booked online. Also on Fremont Street is **Downtown Container Park**, an open-air shopping centre that is the place to get your shopping fix. It also has an interactive play area. In the nearby Symphony Park, **Discovery Children's Museum** is worth a visit for some great interactive exhibits and activities.

- You might be mesmerised by the shiny lights of the strip but aim to explore outside the city limits if you have the time. Visit **Boulder City** and **Bootleg Canyon**, just 30 minutes from the strip, for outdoor adventure, mountain-biking and thrilling ziplines over a desert canyon. Twenty minutes further on, stop at the engineering feat that is **Hoover Dam** – you can do a tour if you're keen to know more.

- About an hour's drive north-east from the strip, the slightly ominously named **Valley of Fire State Park** glows red thanks to its ancient red-sandstone formations. There are a few easy hikes to do for a half-day. Do the short **Atlatl Rock Trail** to see prehistoric petroglyphs. Check the weather before you go as it can get hot during the day and freezing at night. Take plenty of water and make sure someone knows where you're going.

- For an iconic American experience, take a daytrip to the **Grand Canyon**. There are many ways to get there from Las Vegas. You can take a helicopter, small plane, motorcycle or bus. Check the weather for when you are going, but even in winter the canyon will be beautiful. If you want to venture into the Grand Canyon itself, you can hike in, take a river cruise, ride a mule or do a ranger-led trip. It's a must-see. Can you imagine going to Alice Springs and *not* checking out Uluru?

KID-FREE NIGHT OUT

Even if you're not into nightclubs, you have to go to at least one in Vegas. Cover charges are high, and even higher if you try to bribe your way into a VIP lounge – but you just have to try. The **VIP lounges** are where it's all at: celebrities, social influencers and crazy Australians trying to act cool. Let's be honest, you most likely won't get into any VIP lounge, but the nightclubs are still good and, hey, it's your kid-free night out! Keep in mind that in America the legal drinking age is 21, so crowds in bars and nightclubs feel much older than in Australia. Ask around to find out which club is 'so hot right now' when you visit, as the Vegas scene changes all the time. Some hotels and resorts offer on-site childcare during the day (note that Nevada law has immunisation requirements for childcare); this is great for some day-time adult time. For night-time babysitters, there are reputable companies that offer in-room sitting. Do your research – usually companies recommended by hotels are the ones to pick.

NEW YORK CITY

YES, it is about time somebody finally wrote about New York! This insomniac city can be overwhelming, with skyscrapers resembling elevators to the clouds, endless horns honking, different smells around each corner – sometimes cuisine, sometimes dumpsters. It's a city that unreservedly attacks every one of your senses and it is so damn amazing it'll spin you round and flip you out. The kids were met with minus-eight-degree weather and snow on the sidewalks when they came up from the underground of Grand Central Terminal. Eyes wide and arms crossed to keep warm, they quickly found their way around New York and made getting a pizza pie their top priority (they had been talking about pie for months). This is a great time to explain what a pizza pie is: it's just what Americans call a whole pizza. Pete disappointed the kids by buying a pizza, coming out with one slice (for five people); he just thought the kids were joking about wanting pie. There is simply no city in the world like New York City. You will swear you are in the middle of the world and everyone and everything is simply orbiting around you.

The winter can get nose-bitingly cold and the summer can get nose-blisteringly hot. We arrived in January 2018 after a storm famously dubbed a 'bomb cyclone' had hit the East Coast; it was so cold that sharks were pulled out of the ocean completely frozen.

During peak times, New York can get a little squeezy, which means hotel prices get jacked up (like all cities really) and cafes and restaurants become crowded. You may want to consider travelling in the off-peak season so you'll be able to explore more freely – this can certainly make it easier sometimes when you have kids in tow.

ACCOMMODATION

Your choice of where to stay in New York will be based on budget and what you want to get out of your visit. We have found apartments are the best option for kids; hotel rooms are often too small, and having a kitchen is very helpful on long touring days.

GETTING AROUND

Getting around New York is easy: the subway is simple to navigate, and ride shares and taxis are easy to get. It is a big long city that has express trains, so double-check you're on a stop-all-stations train when you want to be.

ATTRACTIONS

- One only has to check out *Home Alone 2* to see that New York is great for kids, whether they're enjoying a family holiday or trying to outwit the recently released Wet Bandits so that every kid can enjoy Christmas. Perhaps more than any other city, New York offers so many options that kids and parents can both enjoy equally. Who doesn't want to look out from the top of the **Empire State Building**? Sure, your 16-year-old may be listening to Jay-Z with his AirBuds while Mum fantasises about meeting Tom Hanks on Valentine's Day, but still, the family's together, right? The Empire State Building actually has two observation decks, one on the 86th floor (the Main Deck) and one on the 102nd floor (the Top Deck), and there's also a gallery/museum with immersive exhibitions on the second floor. You can choose what you want to see when you buy your tickets.

- For more views over the Big Apple, head to **Top of the Rock Observation Deck** at the top of the iconic **Rockefeller Centre**.

- Of course there is Lady Liberty herself – the **Statue of Liberty**. You can either simply cruise around Lady Liberty, which is nice and easy, or you can actually get off the ferry at Liberty Island and explore her up close. The statue, which measures a towering 93m from the ground to the tip of the torch, was a gift to the American people from France. If you want to do more than just explore the grounds of the statue, note that it's a strenuous climb to visit the crown and kids have to be more than 120cm tall to do it. If this is something you want to do, book your ticket when you book your flights, as there is usually a long waiting list.

- No other city has this many definitely-*not*-boring-and-actually-*lots*-of-fun museums. Make sure the kids check out at least one of the *Night of the Museum* movies, which should be enough to entice them to the **American Museum of Natural History**. We spent most of a whole day here – it really is rather incredible. Note that it is huge, so if you can have a sense of what you all most want to see, this will help you plan your time here. You can buy your tickets online for general admission and extra exhibits to skip the queue. The kids loved exploring all the rooms. Liam loves most museums and his tip is to use the map and get to every room, and take the extra option to see one of the special exhibitions.

- Add to this the **Metropolitan Museum of Art** aka the Met and the **Museum of Modern Art** aka MoMA for art and culture; and the **Intrepid Sea, Air and Space Museum** for history, science, technology and an actual space shuttle. You can get a pass called the **New York Pass**, which provides discounted entry to over 85 city attractions including these museums and other tours, cruises and many more experiences.

- The **9/11 Memorial and Museum** is a beautifully touching and sobering reminder of one of humanity's very worst days. We took our children – our youngest, Oscar, was nine – but we encourage you to do a little research on the content of each component of the museum and decide whether your kids are going to be okay with it. The museum's website has information about how to speak to children about terrorism as well as an interactive tour of the museum.

- If you've had a gutful of school drama productions and student ballet recitals, you've earned yourselves some **Broadway** action. There are plenty of shows on offer that the kids will love – we were lucky enough to have *School of Rock* on when we were there. It was amazing, the actors were incredible and the kids loved it! On a date night, we organised a babysitter through a friend and snuck out to see *Hamilton* and, yes, it's every bit as good as they say – coming soon to Australia! If you want spur-of-the-moment budget tickets, you can queue at the Discount Booth in Times Square for last-minute same-day tickets, though sometimes it's hard to get a family-sized number of tickets together. We have taken the option to split the family sometimes, because two and three tickets together are usually easier to get than five.

- Another New York icon, **Central Park** is a place where, once you've been there, no park will ever compare. Ride the carousel, visit the Shakespeare garden and read the quotes on the plaques, go to the zoo ... the list goes on. You could spend days here and each day could have a different focus. Try downloading the map, or pick up a map at the visitor centre, and make a family Central Park visit plan. Because we have been in New York in winter it was a must to take the kids ice-skating in Central Park. It was questionable if they could actually do it, but they had a go. We saw Christopher McDonald walking through Central Park and embarrassed ourselves by screaming 'Shooter McGavin' and pointing our fingers like the character always did (Shooter is a character Chris played in the Adam Sandler film *Happy Gilmore*). We promise we will never call out to a big Hollywood star in public again.

- There is so much to do in New York City that you'll leave feeling like you haven't even begun! Here are a few more tidbits to consider doing ... if you have the time. Visit the **Brooklyn Navy Yard** after walking the **Brooklyn Bridge**, of course. Satisfy your sweet tooth by catching a cupcake tour or go freestyle on a hip-hop tour representing a prime opportunity for dads to embarrass their children. Feeling brave? Of course you are, you're in New York, so why not take a trapeze class? Feeling hungry? How does a pizza-eating tour sound, taking you to places for some of that famous New York pizza pie. You name it, you'll find it – that's New York for you.

BOSTON

IN THE AFTERMATH

of the Boston Marathon bombings in 2013, a hashtag began trending on Twitter: it was #BostonStrong. Most hashtags have the life expectancy of a cheeseball but this one stuck. Bostonians wear it with pride and as a badge of honour, and the meaning of it is well and truly felt in this amazing city. The people are delightful and helpful even if their New England accents can make them sound not so delightful and not so helpful. The Boston accent is one of the most parodied of all the American accents and mastering it can be 'wicked hahd'. Practise saying *Park your car in Harvard Yard*. But pronounce it more like *Paak the cah in Hahvahd Yahd*, and you may be a chance to master it.

Accommodation

You'll find plenty of family-friendly hotels with rooms that connect and a lounge to rest up in – having the extra space can be helpful for snowed-in days. Stay near Boston Common for shorter walks to key attractions. You can find plenty of apartments for short stays; just make sure the one you choose is local and close to transport.

Getting Around

If you are staying near the T, it's easy to get around. The T is Boston's Public Transport system. The Blue, Green, Orange and Red lines run beneath the city. Green, Orange and Red lines can be used to reach the Boston Common, which is the start of the Freedom Trail, in downtown Boston. Trains on the T aren't exactly state of the art bullet trains; rather, they are rickety old carriages full of character.

There are plenty of Amtrak trains heading from Boston to New York to Washington DC. You can get a few connecting trains and end up in Montreal, so if you have some time you could get to Canada. The trains aren't as well connected as Europe but still, a two-hour train trip from Boston to New York is much nicer than airport security and tiny seats.

ATTRACTIONS

📍 Bostonians care about their city and love welcoming locals. And we love it too. Adding to our love of this great city is the fact that it's the home of the greatest basketball team in the NBA, the Boston Celtics. We state this not just because we are a Boston Celtics household but because they have won the most NBA championship titles of any team – 17 in all, one more than arch-rival the LA Lakers. If you get a chance, go see the Celts play at **TD Garden**. It's a fun experience and a great glimpse of Boston pride. You may even be lucky enough to be there on a day where the Boston Bruins ice-hockey team have a home game too. The teams share TD Stadium and they simply up the famous parquet floor and put the ice down! We had tickets for the Bruins but the game was postponed due to a Snow Day – yep, that's how cold it was, the ice-hockey was put off because it was too cold.

Snow Days are declared when the snow is considered so bad it will affect public safety. Schools are closed and many workers work from home so the council can clear the snow off the streets and get life back to normal as early as possible.

Boston winters can get very cold, but the city is so pretty in the snow. If you are visiting in winter, make sure you have cold-weather gear, and get off the plane or train with your jackets and gloves at the ready. We are no stranger to thermals in Australia because Brij is always cold and has bought them for everyone in the family. It's great that she did that because thermals are a necessity in a Boston winter. If the cold isn't your thing, the summers can be lovely and in the summertime you can catch the train to Cape Cod or drive to Maine, about a four-hour trip. It's all beautiful countryside and worth a look, whatever the season.

📍 Boston has a lot to offer, but a great place to start is with the **Freedom Trail**. This 4km long trail passes 16 historically significant sites, including monuments, museums and parks, and is an excellent way to help the kids understand Boston's history. You can walk it yourself or join a free tour. Plan on taking all day so you can take your time at the various sites. You can walk back or catch the Charlestown water shuttle to downtown Boston. The Freedom Trail was originally suggested by a local journalist, William Schofield, as a way of connecting important local landmarks for visitors and became a reality in 1951. By 1953, 40,000 people were walking the trail every year and now it brings over four million people annually to the trail's sites.

📍 One of the most popular attractions in Boston, especially with kids, is the **Museum of Science**. With many fascinating exhibitions, a planetarium, a wind-turbine lab, a butterfly garden and an electricity centre, it will keep everyone enthralled for ages. It also has the Live Animal Care Center and a 4D film theatre. Another

On the famous parquet floor with Aussie great Aron Baynes – go Celtics!

top museum, the **Boston Children's Museum** is a perfect place to spend time if the weather isn't great. There are so many different hands-on and immersive exhibits, along with a play space for younger kids, that you'll find something to keep everyone happy.

- For another kid-friendly activity, hire bikes and ride along **Charles River Esplanade** and stop at the **Esplanade Playground**. You also get great views of the city along the river.

- Head to **Quincey Market** for a true Boston experience (and to hear more of that fabulous accent). The market first opened in 1826 and has hundreds of shops in its three market buildings. It's a colourful place to pick up some local produce, artisan crafts and locally made souvenirs, or to relax and people-watch at one of the many cafes in the market.

- Not to harp on too much about it but not only do Bostonians truly love their sport, the city also boasts some of the most successful franchises in American sport. Did we mention Boston has won 17 NBA championships? Outside our beloved Celtics and Bruins, the famed Boston Red Sox (baseball), winners of the 2018 World Series, play at **Fenway Park**. You can take a guided tour of Fenway Park year-round; the guides are great at telling the stories and history of this much-loved ballpark. Or check out the 2019 Super Bowl Champions, the Patriots (American football) at Gillette Stadium just south-west of Boston. You may even bump into Terrific Tom Brady and Giselle. You probably won't, but you might.

- For fans of classic TV sitcoms, check out the **Cheers bar** on Beacon Street. Sam, Woody and Carla sadly no longer work there but there are plenty of barflies imitating Norm and Cliff. There's been a bar here since 1969; it used to be called the Bull and Finch Pub until it was 'discovered' by producers looking for a location for *Cheers*. It's fun for a quick stop and photo op (probably more for the parents than the kids!).

CHICAGO

REALLY, we have to recommend you visit Chicago for **St Patrick's Day** to see the Chicago River turn green to mark the famed Irish Celebration (turning the river green is a tradition that started over 60 years ago). The process starts at 9am and the river keeps its colour for around five hours. But keep an eye on what date it will happen: while St Pat's Day is on 17 March, the fun usually happens on 16 March. Chicago has one of the largest Irish communities in America and the city is proud of its Irish heritage – it's actually home to the **Irish American Heritage Center**. There are also great beaches and lovely parks; there is beautiful architecture to admire; and the city is known for deep-dish pizza and hotdogs and jazz. The friendly locals love their sport and culture and apparently they have the best drinking water in the country. Let us know if you agree.

Accommodation

Staying around Lincoln Park is great for kids who want wide open spaces and lots of green – it's close to the zoo and an ideal neighbourhood for kids. The lively downtown area is where you stay if you want to be in the middle of all the action, and there are plenty of food and accommodation options for families. A hotel like the Four Seasons will have the kids excited – an ice-cream person visits the rooms with a trolley full of goodies, there are kids' clubs, manicures and pedicures for ages 12 to 18 and a games room.

Getting Around

If you are planning on spending a few days in Chicago, it's worth getting a Chicago Go Card or Explorer Pass, which gives you entry to numerous attractions at a discount. Trains and buses will get you around the city easily; download the downtown transit sightseeing guide to help you get to all the attractions and find information about tracking trains and buses (find it at transitchicago.com).

ATTRACTIONS

If St Pat's day isn't on your family's wishlist, Chicago is still worth visiting – it's a fun city for kids. The **Chicago Botanic Garden** has a nature-play garden and wonderful gardens to explore. The **Chicago Children's Museum** is heaps of fun – it has a dinosaur expedition space, an art studio, a tinkering hub and fascinating exhibitions. And the very good **Lincoln Park Zoo** is free for everyone year-round. The museum is in the **Navy Pier** precinct, which is also home to an IMAX theatre and **Pier Park** with the Centennial Wheel (a huge Ferris wheel) and other rides. For adults, the precinct has cafes, restaurants and a beer garden, as well as some interesting public art. It's on the edge of Lake Michigan and is the spot to hop on cruises of the lake and the Chicago River.

Lake Michigan means that Chicago has some lovely beaches (26 in all) – try **Oaks Street Beach**, which is near Navy Pier, **31st Street Beach** and **Loyola Beach**. Swimming is allowed when the lifesavers are on duty.

The **606 Trail**, a network of paths for pedestrians and bikes, is great to explore and an excellent example of urban regeneration. Part of it was the Bloomingdale Line, an elevated train line; rather than leave it abandoned when the trains stopped running, the city turned it into a wonderful green space and linear park for everyone. Another good way to explore the city is the **Chicago Riverwalk**; wander the riverside path, hire a kayak, stop at a cafe, admire the public art or let the kids loose on the pop-up play cubes that are sometimes installed.

Millennium Park, part of Chicago's Loop, is a cultural and community hub. Here you'll find **Cloud Gate**. Now, it would be weird if you didn't ask, what exactly is Cloud Gate? Well, it's the shiny bean-like sculpture that you see in all the photos of the city – in fact, the locals often simply call it the Bean. Created by British artist Anish Kapoor, the massive sculpture has a mirror-like surface, meant to look like liquid mercury, and is a very popular photo op. For more park action, try **Maggie Daley Park**, which is connected to Millennium Park by a pedestrian bridge. It's a great park any time of year and has fun areas for kids, an outdoor climbing park and gardens.

NEW ORLEANS

COMEDIAN Will Durst once called **Bourbon Street** in New Orleans 'Disneyland for drunks' and, yes, if that is what you're after then Bourbon Street will deliver – but there is plenty more on offer in New Orleans beyond its famed boozy street.

New Orleans is in the state of Louisiana and is loved for many reasons. The New Orleans tourism catch-cry has been 'Come to New Orleans and experience 300 years' worth of stories, celebrations and one-of-a-kind culture', and that's exactly what it felt like for us when we visited. There is an unmistakeable New Orleans attitude that floats through the streets like a light breeze. The music you hear on almost every corner is not being blasted from shopfront outdoor speakers; it's actually live music played by real musicians ranging from spectacular to still working on it. But the one thing they all have in common is they play with passion, an unbridled sense of fun and a bouncy energy that tells you this is a unique and special city.

Accommodation

You will find many accommodation options when staying in New Orleans. Stay in the French Quarter for old-world charm and character. If you have the budget, choose one of the district's dazzling hotels like the Bourbon New Orleans; you'll need two rooms or for a family of four get a double room, which has two double beds. The suburban hotels have great family options and easy parking and are close to malls. Some hotels have connecting rooms, otherwise look for apartment hotels because they usually offer a lounge with pull-out sofa beds. Apartment booking websites have plenty of places available too.

Getting Around

We pretty much walked everywhere, but you can get around easily on buses or the more romantic streetcar (pretend you are on your own streetcar named 'Desire'). Purchase a Jazzy Card if you plan on using a lot of public transport because it will allow access to many attractions as well. Children under three are free, and children between three and 12 can ride on a child ticket, all with unlimited bus and streetcar trips.

ATTRACTIONS

- The Big Easy, which is what New Orleans is often called, is a fun and easy place to explore with kids, and the food is outstanding – quality home-style comfort food that you can't pass up. The food is a reason to visit itself. You simply cannot leave New Orleans without first feeding your face with **gumbo**, a thickish stew-like soup, which is the official dish of Louisiana. It's warm, comforting and feels like your mother's hug on a cold day. If gumbo were to have a rival, it would be **jambalaya**, which is more like a paella and is the Katy Perry to gumbo's Taylor Swift.

- Like most of America, New Orleans loves to barbecue, particularly using Creole and Cajun spices. Try some smoked pork, chicken wings, pulled pork and, of course, ribs. They *love* their ribs. For breakfast, grab some coffee and some **beignets**, French-style doughnuts with no hole in the middle, which means MORE beignet! We loved them for breakfast – the kids couldn't believe they were getting doughnuts for breakfast! Beignets are easy to find so try a few different places – they are da bomb.

- To walk off those eight beignets you scoffed down like Tom Hanks in *Castaway*, why not walk down to the **National WWII Museum**, which captivatingly recounts the stories of World War II through immersive experiences and expansive exhibitions. A highlight is seeing the museum's 4D film *Beyond the Boundaries*, narrated by none other than *Saving Private Ryan*'s Tom Hanks. There is even a chair in the auditorium with a plaque that reads TOM HANKS to mark the seat the great man sat in at the film's opening night. Oscar found it and sat in it. He humble-bragged the whole rest of the day.

- Visit the **French Quarter**, the vibrant historic heart of the city and home of **Bourbon Street**. Explore **Jackson Square**, a favourite park and landmark in the French Quarter. You can actually do a kids' tour of the French Quarter – try **French Quartour Kids** for lots of themed and age-specific tours. Another great thing to do with kids in New Orleans is to visit **Storyland**, a fairytale-themed amusement park in **City Park**, which is a green oasis in the centre of New Orleans. It's easy to spend a day in City Park as it's also home to the **Louisiana Children's Museum**, which has both indoor and outdoor interactive activities for kids, and the **New Orleans Museum of Art**. If you're lucky enough to be in New Orleans for the **Mardi Gras** festival, grab some beads and masks and join in on the fun – it is a fabulous celebration and is family friendly, especially if you plan ahead and research the best spots to see the parade when you have kids. For more must-see classic New Orleans experiences, ride a streetcar, head to **Royal Street** for amazing food, book a swamp tour to see alligators in the wild, and cruise the famed Mississippi River.

HAWAII

THERE WOULDN'T be too many travel destinations in the Northern Hemisphere that are easier to visit than Hawaii. Brij has a not so secret dream of living in Hawaii – she loves the people, the weather, the beaches ... there is almost nothing she doesn't love. Except perhaps active volcanos. Because that's how Hawaii was created – its more than 100 islands were formed by volcanos in the Pacific Ocean, hence the dramatic scenery, lush vegetation and, um, at times flowing lava. Of those 100 islands, there are eight main ones, with seven of those inhabited by people. Here we tell you about five of our favourites.

ACCOMMODATION

When booking your resort, remember an 'ocean view' room doesn't always mean a view of the ocean. An 'ocean front' room will guarantee the view. Our ocean view was only available if we leaned dangerously out over the balcony. Just the tricks of the trade. Also, if you're travelling with teenagers ask for your room to be away from the toddlers' pool, as toddlers are up and about much earlier than a teenager.

If you want to avoid resorts, you can rent apartments and houses for short stays; however, before booking a property, confirm with the owner or manager that the property is operating in compliance with the short-stay laws.

GETTING AROUND

Getting to all the different islands is easier by plane; they are short flights that won't eat into your day on the next island. Boats are a fun way to do it but would probably only be a great option if you are cruising, as you are limiting your time on land by a fair bit.

ATTRACTIONS

📍 The island of **Hawaii**, or **Big Island** as it is usually called, is one of Brij's favourites and where she will grab real-estate vouchers 'just out of interest'. This island has so much to offer and, if the name doesn't give it away, it's the biggest of all the islands. You can fit two islands' worth of fun here – don't just stop at the beaches.

You must go to a black-sand beach such as **Punalu'u**, where you might also get to see turtles. The black sand is actually tiny fragments of lava (it can get really hot in the sun, so have beach shoes, especially for the kids). If you want the chance to see actual lava, go on a lava tour on Big Island, which is home to the active volcano **Kilauea** – you can do the tours by boat, helicopter or walking. The lava doesn't feel quite as threatening when it's crawling towards you at a snail's pace. **Hawai'i Volcanoes National Park** has the world's most active volcanos. We recommend doing a ranger-guided activity here as there is so much more to see than just bubbling lava and you will learn heaps about the amazing geology of the area. Remember to leave the national park as you found it, and don't remove any plants or rocks to take as souvenirs.

As you make your way around the island you will find good local shops and farmers' markets, waterfalls, black-sand beaches, lava trees, golf and taro farms. Keep in mind this is a big island, so staying in different towns (to make the travel time shorter) will be better with kids. Little kids will love the different scenery and all the things to do on this island, but it's also a fantastic island for teenagers, catering to many interests.

📍 **Oahu** is a favourite tourist spot and **Honolulu** on Oahu is the most frequented place to visit for Australians, with high-rises and luxury shops running alongside one of the most famous beaches in the world: **Waikiki**, where our kids learnt to surf for the first time on the famous Hawaiian longboards. You can head around the island of Oahu pretty easily. **North Shore** is a great place to visit, and in December and January check out the surfing competitions (remember, don't get in the way of the camera operators and photographers as they get a bit narky – at least the one we accidentally stood in front of did). **Kaneohe** is another popular place on Oahu, with a beautiful bay to snorkel in and great hiking. We also loved snorkelling in **Hanauma Bay** near Honolulu, which is easy to get to whether you catch a shuttle bus, taxi or drive there. It's a very popular beach. If driving, get there early as the carpark fills up quickly. You can hire gear there if you don't already have some. Hanauma Bay is part of a nature preserve and is closed on Tuesdays; you also have to pay a fee at the entry and watch a video on what you can and can't do. It's a beautiful spot and makes for a great day out. Check the website before you go to see what is and isn't allowed at the beach. For a bit of history, head to **Pearl Harbor**, site of the World War II bombing. You can tour a warship and see a moving memorial, but it gets busy so plan ahead and definitely pre-book tickets.

📍 If you want to chill a little more head to **Maui**, the second largest island in Hawaii. It's the in-between country and city of the islands and a wonderful place to go whale-watching. **Lahaina** has a lot of big resorts, plenty of shopping and nice places to eat too. **Wailea** is another part of Maui to check out. Both have options for tours and shopping. It's also home to **Haleakala**, the largest dormant volcano in the world, and a sacred site in traditional Hawaiian culture.

📍 **Kauai** is the Garden Isle. There are lots of rainforests, cliffs, canyons and walking tracks. Hiking is great here – definitely check out **Wailua Falls**. For a great beach, visit the popular **Poipu Beach**. Get in some snorkelling and body-boarding while you're here.

📍 Visit **Molokai** if you want a traditional Hawaiian experience. Half the population of Molokai has native Hawaiian ancestry and the place feels very authentic and less touristy than many of the other islands. It also has the highest sea cliffs in the world, which you can get up close to on a boat tour.

HAWAIIAN MISSILE CRISIS
(BY PETE)

New Year's Eve and Brij and I were on our back deck chatting about a subject that a lot of parents had been talking about in recent times: how to get our kids off their screens? We quickly realised that to do this we needed to get off our screens too. So, over white wine, seafood and cheese, our New Year's Resolution was hatched: Less Screen Time For Everybody.

The timing was perfect, because we were just two days away from heading to Boston, New York and Hawaii for a holiday (we just love to pack for two climates when we travel).

Fast forward to almost two weeks later. We arrive late to our resort accommodation in Maui. The kids sleep in but Brij and I rise early as the sun peeks through the closed curtains of our hotel room. After two weeks of experiencing one of the coldest winters ever on the American east coast, our bodies were crying out for some of that sweet vitamin D.

With the kids fast asleep, we decide to enjoy a romantic stroll along a Hawaiian beach. Instinctively, I move to grab my phone, charging on my bedside table.

No. Stop. You don't need it. Less Screen Time For Everybody.

This is the perfect opportunity to make good on our resolution. We leave a handwritten note on the kitchen bench informing our kids we will be back in 30 minutes.

We leave our phones behind. Well, Brij takes one that is purely for photos. It isn't connected. This is allowed.

What's the worst that could happen?

We stroll along the beach and it is heaven. Unusually quiet, which we take to be a win. Look at us getting up earlier than everyone else, sauntering hand-in-hand like newlyweds. We walk for about half an hour, take a selfie and head back to our room.

Little did we know ...

While we were strolling the sand talking about how great life is, the rest of Hawaii was going berserk. An official text message had been sent to all mobile phones. It read:

Emergency Alert

BALLISTIC MISSILE THREAT INBOUND TO HAWAII. SEEK IMMEDIATE SHELTER. THIS IS NOT A DRILL.

People were reportedly in stairwells sobbing and calling loved ones, parents were putting their children down manholes in the streets. The emptiness of the beach that morning now made perfect sense. Everybody but us and our slumbering children was preparing for the end of the world.

But the beach, the beach had been so peaceful. How blissful not to have this magical moment disrupted by text messages or notification pings.

Thirty-eight minutes after the alert, a second alert was sent out declaring it a false alarm. Apparently some dude had pressed the wrong button! (This is why you don't put the nuclear missile alert button on the Foxtel remote.)

Funny thing is, we still didn't know.

About 20 minutes after the second alert, Brij ducks back into the room to check on the kids and grab some sunscreen. That Hawaiian sun has some kick to it today, we had observed. She comes back and I notice she is laughing. She has a look on her face like she has just been told something amazing. She has a story to tell.

And now we all do.

When we look back at that selfie we took on the empty beach in Maui on 13 January 2018, life could have turned out very different. We could have been photobombed by an actual bomb.

So glad we didn't take our phones.

Bombs away! Well, thankfully not!

ABOUT THE AUTHORS

PETER HELLIAR is one of Australia's favourite comedians. Since first appearing on *Rove Live* in the late '90s, Pete's extraordinary entertainment and comedy career has spanned everything from radio to screenwriting, producing and co-starring in feature films (*I Love You Too*) and television series (*It's a Date, How To Stay Married*). Pete lives in Melbourne with his wife (and co-author) and three kids, and currently co-hosts the award-winning news and current affairs program *The Project* on Network Ten. He is also the best-selling author of the *Frankie Fish* series for children.

BRIDGET HELLIAR has spent much of her life planning trips, going on trips and then repeating those two steps again and again. Determined not to allow motherhood and marriage to stop her from travelling, Bridget first pitched the idea for this book during a family trip to France in 2010. As usual, it took her husband a long time to recognise what a brilliant idea it was. Bridget's favourite travel destinations include France, Japan and the Mornington Peninsula. She once lost her bikini top jumping off a yacht in the Greek Islands and is eternally grateful this occurred before the advent of the iPhone.

INDEX

9/11 Memorial and Museum, New York City, New York, USA 284
31st Beach Street, Chicago, Illinois, USA 289
606 Trail, Chicago, Illinois, USA 289

Abriachan Forest Trails, Inverness, Scotland 193
AC/DC Lane, Melbourne, Vic. 45
Acland Street, St Kilda, Vic. 46
Adelaide, SA 104–7
Adelaide Central Market, SA 105
Adelaide Oval, SA 106
Adelaide Oval Roof Climb, SA 105
Adelaide Park Lands, SA 105
Adelaide River, NT 96
Adventure Forest, Whangarei, New Zealand 126
Adventure World, Perth, WA 86
Adventuredome Theme Park, Circus Circus resort, Las Vegas, Nevada, USA 279
Aiguille du Midi, France 219
Airlie Beach, Qld 66
Alaska, USA 266
Alberobello, Italy 224
Alcatraz Island, San Francisco, California, USA 275
Alcatraz Night Tour, San Francisco, California, USA 275, 276
Alice Springs, NT 99
Alice Springs Desert Park, NT 99
Alice Springs School of the Air Visitor Centre, NT 99
Allansford, Vic. 40
Alps, Vic. 41
Amalfi, Italy 228
Amalfi Coast, Italy 228
Amaze'n Margaret River, WA 89
Amazonia, Singapore 146
American Mura, Osaka, Japan 179
American Museum of Natural History, New York City, New York, USA 283
An Bang Beach, Hoi An, Vietnam 160
Andy's Bar, Copenhagen, Denmark 247
Annecy, France 219
Antigua Boat Sheds, Christchurch, New Zealand 127
Anzac Hill, Alice Springs, NT 99
Aquapark, Chaweng, Koh Samui, Thailand 152

Aquarium of the Bay, San Francisco, California, USA 276
Araluen Arts Centre, Alice Springs, NT 99
Araluen Cultural Precinct, Alice Springs, NT 99
Arashiyama – The Bamboo Forest, Kyoto, Japan 176
Arc de Triomphe, Paris, France 211, 212
Armoury in Action experience, Tower of London, England 189
Army Museum of Western Australia, Fremantle, WA 88
Art Gallery of South Australia, Adelaide, SA 105
Arthur Waterhouse Lounge, Adelaide Hills, SA 107
Arthur's Seat, Edinburgh, Scotland 195
Arthurs Seat Eagle, Vic. 48
ArtVo, Docklands, Vic. 45
Asia Park Da Nang Amusement Park, Da Nang, Vietnam 160
Asobono, Tokyo, Japan 183
Astronomical Clock, Prague, Czech Republic 253
Atlatl Rock Trail, Valley of Fire State Park, Nevada, USA 280
Auckland, New Zealand 123–5
Auckland War Memorial Museum, New Zealand 124
Auckland waterfront, New Zealand 123
Augusta, WA 89
Australia 34–117
Australia Zoo, near Glass House Mountains National Park, Qld 77
Australian Age of Dinosaurs Museum, Winton, Qld 66
Australian Capital Territory 59–64
Australian Dinosaur Trail, Qld 66
Australian Institute of Sport, Canberra, ACT 63
Australian Maritime Museum, Sydney, NSW 54
Australian Museum, Sydney, NSW 54
Australian War Memorial, Canberra, ACT 62
Avalon, NSW 55
Aviation Heritage Museum, Fremantle, WA 88

Avon River, Christchurch, New Zealand 127
Avoriaz, France 220

Ba Vi National Park, Vietnam 159
Baan Teelanka Baan, Phuket, Thailand 152
Bakken Deer Park, Copenhagen, Denmark 245
Bali 132–7
Ballarat, Vic. 41
Bamboo Bar, Kuta, Bali 136
Bangalow Market, NSW 58
Bangkok, Thailand 153–5
Barchetta, Cottesloe, WA 86
Bargara, Qld 67
Barron Falls, Kuranda, Qld 80
Barron Gorge National Park, Qld 80
Bartolucci, Rome, Italy 227
Barton Springs Pool, Austin, Texas, USA 266
Basin rockpool, Bargara, Qld 67
Bath, England 185
Bathers Beach, Fremantle, WA 88
Bathers Beach House, Fremantle, WA 88
Battle of Bannockburn Visitor Centre, Stirling, Scotland 195
Bay of Islands, New Zealand 126
Beachhouse, Glenelg, SA 106
Bean, Brisbane, Qld 72
Beaune, France 218
Beerenberg Farm, Hahndorf, SA 106
beignets, New Orleans, Louisiana, USA 291
Belfast, Northern Ireland 196–7
Belfast Children's Festival, Northern Ireland 197
Belfast International Arts Festival, Northern Ireland 197
Belfast International Film Festival, Northern Ireland 197
Belgian Beer Cafe, Adelaide, SA 107
Bellagio Hotel, Las Vegas, Nevada, USA 279
Bellarine Peninsula, Vic. 48
Bells Beach, Vic. 40
Belongil Beach, NSW 58
Ben Tre, Vietnam 162
Bendigo, Vic. 41
Berghain, Berlin, Germany 237

Berlin, Germany 232, 235–8
Berlin Zoo, Germany 236
Berry Springs Nature Park, NT 96
Beverley Center, Los Angeles, California, USA 272
BeWILDerwood, Hoveton, Norfolk, England 185
Bia Hoi Junction, Hanoi, Vietnam 159
Big Apple Coaster, New York New York Hotel, Las Vegas, Nevada, USA 279
Big Banana, Coffs Harbour, NSW 50
Big Barra, Daintree, Qld 67
Big Barra, Normanton, Qld 67
Big Cane Toad, Sarina, Qld 67
Big Captain Cook, Cairns, Qld 67
Big Goose, Moorooduc, Vic. 48
Big Island, Hawaii, USA 293
Big Lobster, Kingston, SA 106
Big Mango, Bowen, Qld 67
Big Orange, Gayndah, Qld 67
Big Pineapple, Woombye, Qld 67
Big Rocking Horse, Gumeracha, SA 106
Big Scotsman, Medindie, SA 106
Big Tree, Mawbanna, Tas. 112
Big Wine Bottle, McLaren Vale, SA 106
Billund, Denmark 242
Bio Mio, Copenhagen, Denmark 244
Bios no Oka, Okinawa, Japan 168
Bitter Springs, Elsey National Park, NT 98
Black Light Theatre, Prague, Czech Republic 253
Blackbutt Nature Reserve, NSW 50
Blarney Castle and Gardens, Cork, Ireland 204
Blarney Stone, Blarney Castle and Gardens, Cork, Ireland 204
Blenheim, New Zealand 130
Blowhole, Eaglehawk Neck, Tas. 111
Blue Lagoon, Nusa Ceningan, Bali 135
Blue Lake, Mount Gambier, SA 109
Blue Mountains, NSW 56
Blue Mountains National Park, NSW 56
BMW Museum, Munich, Germany 239

BMW Welt, Munich, Germany 239
boat ride, Copenhagen, Denmark 245
Bob's Peak, Queenstown, New Zealand 128
Bombo Headland, Kiama, NSW 51
Bondi, NSW 55
Bo'ness and Kinneil Railway, Edinburgh, Scotland 195
Bootleg Canyon, Nevada, USA 280
Borough Market, London, England 189
Boston, Massachusetts, USA 285–7
Boston Celtics, Massachusetts, USA 265
Boston Children's Museum, Massachusetts, USA 287
Botanic Gardens, Bundaberg, Qld 67
Botanic Gardens, Wellington, New Zealand 122
Bottle Beach, Koh Phangan, Thailand 151
Boulder City, Nevada, USA 280
Bourbon Street, New Orleans, Louisiana, USA 290, 291
Bowali Visitor Centre, Jabiru, NT 97
Bowen, Qld 67
Brandenburg Gate, Berlin 236
Brazen Head, Dublin, Ireland 205
Bridge 277 (Bridge over River Kwai), Thailand 154
Bridgewater Bay, Vic. 48
Brighton, England 190
Brighton Beach, Dunedin, New Zealand 130
Brighton Beach, England 190
Brighton Palace Pier, Brighton, England 190
Brisbane, Qld 68–72
Brisbane Botanic Gardens Mount Coot-tha, Mount Coot-tha, Qld 70
British Airways i360, Brighton, England 190
British Museum, London, England 188
Broadbeach, Qld 74, 75
Broadway, New York City, New York, USA 284
Bronte, NSW 55
Brooklyn Bridge, New York City, New York, USA 284
Brooklyn Navy Yard, New York City, New York, USA 284
Broome, WA 90

Brunswick Fairy Trail, Brunswick Heads, NSW 58
Brunswick Heads, NSW 58
Buccaneer Archipelago, WA 91
Buckingham Palace, London, England 188
Buda Hill, Budapest, Hungary 261
Budapest, Hungary 259–61
Budapest Puppet Theatre, Hungary 261
Budapest walking tour, Hungary 261
Buddha Tooth Relic Temple, Singapore 148
Bundaberg, Qld 67
Bundy Barrel, Bundaberg, Qld 67
Bungle Bungles, Purnululu National Park, WA 91
Bunker Bay, Dunsborough, WA 89
Burgundy, France 218
Burma Railway, Thailand 154
Burnett Lane, Brisbane, Qld 72
Burnie, Tas. 112
Burrungkuy (Nourlangie Rock), Kakadu, NT 97
Bushrangers Bay, Vic. 48
Busselton Jetty, WA 89
Butler Metro Park, Austin, Texas, USA 266
Butterfly Creek, Auckland, New Zealand 124
Butterfly House, Tama Zoological Park, Tokyo, Japan 172
Byrdhouse Beach Club, Sanur, Bali 135
Byron Bay, NSW 57–8
Byron Bay Writers Festival, NSW 58

Cable Beach, Broome, WA 90
Cable Car Museum, Wellington, New Zealand 122
cafe culture, Melbourne, Vic. 45
Cafe St Honore, Edinburgh, Scotland 194
Cairns, Qld 67, 80
Cairns Aquarium, Qld 80
California Academy of Sciences, San Francisco, California, USA 275, 276
California Science Center, Los Angeles, California, USA 272
Caloundra, Qld 76
Cambridge, England 185
Camera Obscura and World of Illusions, Edinburgh, Scotland 195
Canberra, ACT 60–4

Canberra Reptile Zoo, ACT 63
Cania Gorge National Park, Qld 67
Canyon Flyer, Tamborine Mountain, Qld 74
Cape Byron Lighthouse, NSW 58
Cape Le Grand National Park, WA 84
Cape Leeuwin Lighthouse, WA 89
Cape Leveque, WA 91
Cape Range National Park, WA 83
Cape Reinga, New Zealand 126
Cape Schanck, Vic. 48
Cape Schanck Lighthouse, Vic. 48
Cape Schanck Lighthouse Reserve, Vic. 48
Cape Tribulation, Qld 81
Cape York Peninsula, Qld 66
Capitol Bar and Grill, Canberra, ACT 64
Carnarvon, WA 83
Carnarvon Blowholes, WA 83
Carnarvon National Park, Qld 67
Castle Road, Germany 233
Catacombs of Rome, Rome, Italy 227
Cataract Gorge, Tas. 112
Cathedral Quarter, Belfast, Northern Ireland 197
Cayton Children's Museum, Los Angeles, California, USA 272
Ceduna, SA 103
Centara Grand Beach resort, Phuket, Thailand 152
Central Australian Museum of Aviation, Alice Springs, NT 99
Central Coast, NSW 50
Central Deborah Gold Mine, Bendigo, Vic. 41
Central Park, New York City, New York, USA 284
Centre Place, Melbourne, Vic. 45
Cervantes, WA 83
Český Krumlov, Czech Republic 253
Chamonix, France 219
Champ de Mars, Paris, France 212
Champs-Élysées, Paris, France 211
Changing of the Guard Ceremony, Buckingham Palace, London, England 188
Charles Bridge, Prague, Czech Republic 253
Charles River Esplanade, Boston, Massachusetts, USA 287
Chatuchak Weekend Market, Bangkok, Thailand 154
Chaweng, Koh Samui, Thailand 152
Cheers bar, Boston, Massachusetts, USA 287

Chiang Mai, Thailand 152
Chiang Mai Night Safari, Thailand 152
Chicago, Illinois, USA 288–9
Chicago Botanic Garden, Illinois, USA 289
Chicago Children's Museum, Illinois, USA 289
Chicago Riverwalk, Illinois, USA 289
Childers, Qld 67
Childers Historical Complex, Qld 67
Children's Creativity Museum, San Francisco, California, USA 276
Children's Peace Monument, Hiroshima, Japan 181
Children's Railway, Budapest, Hungary 261
Chinatown, Broome, WA 90
Chinatown, Fortitude Valley, Qld 71
Chinatown, San Francisco, California, USA 275
Chinatown, Singapore 145, 146
Chinatown Heritage Centre, Singapore 146
Cholon (Binh Tay market), Ho Chi Minh City, Vietnam 162
Christchurch, New Zealand 127
Christchurch Botanic Gardens, New Zealand 127
Christchurch Gondola, New Zealand 127
Churchill War Rooms, London, England 188
Circular Quay, NSW 54
Circus Arts Byron Bay, NSW 58
Circus Circus resort, Las Vegas, Nevada, USA 279
Cittie of Yorke, London, England 191
City Botanic Gardens, Brisbane, Qld 70
City Park, New Orleans, Louisiana, USA 291
CityCat, Brisbane, Qld 79
Clare Valley, SA 103
Cliff House, Point Lobos, California, USA 276
Clifford's Honey Farm, Haines, SA 108
Cliffs of Moher, County Clare, Ireland 202
Cloth Hall, Krakow, Poland 257
Cloud 9, Fiji 141
Cloud Gate, Millennium Park, Chicago, Illinois, USA 289
Club Med Bali, Laguna, Bali 134

Coca-Cola Store, Las Vegas, Nevada, USA 279
Cockatoo Island, NSW 55
Cockington Green Gardens, Canberra, ACT 63
Coffin Bay, SA 103
Coffin Bay National Park, SA 103
Coffs Harbour, NSW 50
Coit Tower, San Francisco, California, USA 275
Coles Bay, Tas. 117
Collingwood Children's Farm, Vic. 45
Colosseum, Rome, Italy 227
Colossus of the Apennines, Pratolino, Italy 224
Comedy Store, Los Angeles, California, USA 273
Computer Spiele Museum, Berlin, Germany 236
concentration camps 234, 257
Conservatory and Botanical Gardens, Bellagio Hotel, Las Vegas, Nevada, USA 279
Coonabarabran, NSW 51
Copenhagen, Denmark 244-7
Coral Bay, WA 83
Coral Coast, WA 83
Cork, Ireland 204
Cornwall, England 185
Cornwall Park, Auckland, New Zealand 124
Côte d'Azur, France 217
Cottesloe Beach, WA 86
Cottesloe Beach Hotel, WA 86
County Clare, Ireland 202
County Galway, Ireland 202
County Kerry, Ireland 202
Cradle Mountain, Tas. 111
Cradle Mountain-Lake St Clair National Park, Tas. 111
Crocosaurus Cove, Darwin, NT 96
Crown Jewels, Tower of London, England 189
C.S. Lewis Square, Belfast, Northern Ireland 197
C.S. Lewis Trail, Belfast, Northern Ireland 197
Cu Chi Tunnels, Ho Chi Minh City, Vietnam 162
Cul De Sac, Rome, Italy 229
Cultural Centre, Uluru-Kata Tjuta National Park, NT 100
Curtis Falls, Tamborine National Park, Qld 74
Cutta Cutta Caves Nature Park, NT 98
cyclo tour, Ho Chi Minh City, Vietnam 162
Czech Republic 252-4

D-Day beaches, France 216
Da Nang, Vietnam 160
Daintree, Qld 79, 80
Daintree Discovery Centre, Qld 80
Dam Sen Water Park, Ho Chi Minh City, Vietnam 162
Dampier Peninsula, WA 91
Dance-O-Mat, Christchurch, New Zealand 127
Dandenong Ranges, Vic. 46
Dandenong Ranges Botanic Garden, Vic. 46
Danube River sightseeing cruise, Budapest, Hungary 261
Darling Harbour, NSW 54
Darwin, NT 94-6
Darwin Military Museum, East Point, NT 95
Darwin's Top End Tourism Visitor Centre, NT 95
Death and Taxes, Brisbane, Qld 72
Death Railway Museum, Thailand 154
Deckchair Cinema, Darwin, NT 96
Defence of Darwin Experience, East Point, NT 95
Denham, WA 83
Denmark 240-9
Dennis the Menace Playground, Monterey, California, USA 276
Derby, WA 91
Derrycunnihy Falls, Killarney, Ireland 202
Devil's Kitchen, Eaglehawk Neck, Tas. 111
Dijon, France 218
Dinosaur Park, Wanaka, New Zealand 129
Dip Falls, Mawbanna, Tas. 112
Discovery Children's Museum, Las Vegas, Nevada, USA 280
Discovery Cube Los Angeles, Los Angeles, California, USA 272
Discovery Parks Water Park, Byron Bay, NSW 58
Dismounting Ceremony, Buckingham Palace, London, England 188
Disney California Adventure Park, Anaheim, California, USA 268, 271
Disneyland, Anaheim, California, USA 268, 271

Disneyland Paris, Chessy, France 213
Dolby Theatre, Los Angeles, California, USA 271
Dong Ba Market, Hue, Vietnam 161
Donovans, St Kilda, Vic. 44
Dotonbori, Osaka, Japan 179
Downtown Container Park, Las Vegas, Nevada, USA 280
Downtown Las Vegas, Nevada, USA 280
Dr Rudi's Rooftop Brewing Co., Auckland, New Zealand 125
Dragon Bridge, Da Nang, Vietnam 160
Drayton Manor Theme Park, Tamworth, Staffordshire, England 186
Dream Beach, Bali 135
Dreamworld, Gold Coast, Qld 73
Dublin, Ireland 201, 203-5
Dublin Discovery Trails app, Ireland 204
Dublin Zoo, Ireland 204
Dublinia, Dublin, Ireland 204
Duck and Cover, Copenhagen, Denmark 247
Duke of Clarence, Sydney, NSW 53
Dunedin, New Zealand 130

Eagle Street Pier, Brisbane, Qld 72
Eaglehawk Neck, Tas. 111
Easey's, Collingwood, Melbourne 44
East End Cellars, Adelaide, SA 107
East Frame pump track, Christchurch, New Zealand 127
East Point Reserve, NT 95
Eastern Europe 250-61
EatStreet Northshore markets, Hamilton, Qld 71
Eatyard, Dublin, Ireland 205
Ebenezer Place, Adelaide, SA 107
Ebor Falls, NSW 50
Eden Project, Cornwall, England 185
Edinburgh, Scotland 194-5
Edinburgh Castle, Scotland 195
Eger, Hungary 261
Egsekov Castle, Kværndrup, Denmark 243
Egyptian Museum, Turin, Italy 224
Eiffel Tower, Paris, France 211
Eiffel Tower, Paris Las Vegas Hotel, Las Vegas, Nevada, USA 279
El Kabron, Bali 136
El Questro Station and Wilderness Park, WA 91

Elephant Jungle Sanctuary, Chiang Mai, Thailand 152
Ellenborough Falls, NSW 50
Ellery Creek Big Hole, Tjoritja-West MacDonnell Ranges National Park, NT 99
Elliston, SA 103
Elsey National Park, NT 98
Empire State Building, New York City, New York, USA 283
Employees Only, Singapore 149
Enchanted Adventure Garden, Arthurs Seat, Vic. 48
Engelbrecht Cave, Mount Gambier, SA 109
England 184-91
Enoteca Bulzoni, Rome, Italy 229
Enoteca Corsi, Rome, Italy 229
Entrecote, Berlin, Germany 232
EPIC: the Irish Emigration Museum, Dublin, Ireland 204
Espace Dali, Montmartre, France 213
Esperance, WA 84
Esperance Museum, WA 84
Esplanade, Cairns, Qld 80
Esplanade Playground, Boston, Massachusetts, USA 287
Étretat, France 216
Ettalong Beach, NSW 50
Eumundi Markets, Qld 76
Eureka Skydeck, Melbourne, Vic. 45
Europa-Park, Rust, Germany 233
EuroPark Milano, Milan, Italy 224
Evolve Spirits Bar, Hobart, Tas. 116
Exmouth, WA 83, 84
Experimentarium, Copenhagen, Denmark 246
Explora, Rome, Italy 228
Exploratorium: the Museum of Science, Art and Human Perception, San Francisco, California, USA 276
Eyre Peninsula, SA 103

Fairy Tale Road, Germany 233
Fairytale Garden, Odense, Denmark 243
Farm, the, Byron Bay, NSW 58
Fenway Park, Boston, Massachusetts, USA 287
Fern Glade Reserve, Burnie, Tas. 112
festivals, Vietnam 158

Field of Lights (art installation), Uluṟu, NT 100
Fiji 138–43
Fingal's Cave, Staffa, Scotland 193
fish pedicure, Tokyo, Japan 172
Fisherman's Wharf, San Francisco, California, USA 275, 276
Flamingo Hotel, Las Vegas, Nevada, USA 279
Flinders, Vic. 48
Flinders Blowhole, Vic. 48
Flinders Chase National Park, SA 108
Flinders Ranges, SA 103
Floating Market tour, Bangkok, Thailand 154
Florence Falls, Litchfield National Park, NT 96
Flying Fox Adventure, O'Reilly's Rainforest Retreat, Qld 74
Fort George, Inverness, Scotland 193
Fort Nepean, Vic. 48
Fort Point Historic Site, San Francisco, California, USA 276
Fortitude Valley, Qld 70
Fortune of War, Sydney, NSW 54
Four Mile Beach, Port Douglas, Qld 66, 80
Fowlers Bay, SA 103
France 206–21
Frank Kitts Park, Wellington, New Zealand 122
Fraser Island, Qld 78
Fratelli Belfast, Belfast, Northern Ireland 196
Frederiksborg Castle, Hillerød, Denmark 246
Freedom Beach, Phuket, Thailand 151
Freedom Trail, Boston, Massachusetts, USA 286
Fremantle, WA 88
Fremantle Prison, WA 88
Fremont Street, Las Vegas, Nevada, USA 280
French Alps, France 219
French Quarter, New Orleans, Louisiana, USA 291
French Quartour Kids, New Orleans, Louisiana, USA 291
French Riviera, Côte d'Azur, France 217
Freycinet Marine Farm, Coles Bay, Tas. 117
Freycinet National Park, Tas. 117

Friendly Beaches, Freycinet National Park, Tas. 117
Fullerton Bay Hotel, Singapore 148
Funfields Theme Park, Whittlesea, Vic. 46
Funky Dragon Dumplings, Hamilton, Qld 71
Funny Funny, Brisbane, Qld 72
Furano, Japan 169
Fushimi-Inari-Taisha Shrine, Kyoto, Japan 175

Galway, Ireland 202
Galway Farmers' Market, Galway, Ireland 202
Gap Filler, Christchurch, New Zealand 127
Gardeners Falls, Maleny, Qld 77
Gardens by the Bay, Singapore 146
GC Wake Park, Gold Coast, Qld 74
Gear Theatre, Kyoto, Japan 177
Geelong, Vic. 40
George Brown Darwin Botanic Gardens, Darwin, NT 95
Germany 230–9
Ghilbi Museum, Kichijoji, Japan 172
Ghirardelli Square, San Francisco, California, USA 275
Giant Prismatic Spring, Yellowstone National Park, USA 265
Giant's Causeway, Northern Ireland 197
Gibb River Road, WA 91
Gion, Kyoto, Japan 173, 177
Giverny, France 216
Givskud Zoo, Give, Denmark 242
Glacier National Park, Montana, USA 261
Glass House Mountains National Park, Qld 77
Gleisdreieck, Berlin, Germany 236
Glenelg Beach, SA 106
Glenfinnan Viaduct, Scotland 193
Glenrowan, Vic. 40
Globe Theatre Family Tour, London, England 189
Glow Worm Cave, Tamborine Mountain, Qld 74
Gold Bar, Hobart, Tas. 116
Gold Coast, Qld 73–5
Gold Coast hinterland, Qld 74
Gold Creek Village, ACT 63
Golden Beach, Qld 76
Golden Gate Bridge, San Francisco, California, USA 275
Golden Gate Fortune Cookie Factory, San Francisco, California, USA 275

Golden Gate Park, San Francisco, California, USA 275
gondola ride, Venice, Italy 224
Gondola Ride at the Venetian, Las Vegas, Nevada, USA 279
Gorge Scenic Chairlift, Launceston, Tas. 112
Grampians, Vic. 41
Grand Canyon, Arizona, USA 280
Grand Palace, Bangkok, Thailand 153
Grauman's Chinese Theatre, Los Angeles, California, USA 271
Gravity Discovery Centre, Yeal, WA 86
Great Barrier Reef, Qld 79, 81
Great Keppel Island, Qld 66
Great Ocean Road, Vic. 40
Great Orme Bronze Age Mines, Llandudno, North Wales 186
Great Orme Tramway, Llandudno, North Wales 186
Greenhouse, Dublin, Ireland 205
Greenly Beach, SA 103
Grenen, Denmark 243
Griffith Park Observatory, Los Angeles, California, USA 272
Groundlings, Los Angeles, California, USA 273
Grove, Los Angeles, California, USA 272
Guinness Book of Records Museum, Los Angeles, California, USA 271
Guinness Storehouse, Ireland 204
gumbo, New Orleans, Louisiana, USA 291
Gunlom Falls, Kakadu, NT 97
Gunlom Falls Plunge Pool, Kakadu, NT 97

Haad Yao, Koh Phangan, Thailand 151
Hahndorf, SA 106
Hahndorf Farm Barn, SA 106
Haigh's Chocolates, Adelaide, SA 105
Hakuba, Nagano, Japan 169
Haleakala, Maui, Hawaii, USA 294
Halong Bay, Vietnam 159
Hamelin Pool, WA 83
Hamilton Pool Reserve, Dripping Springs, Texas, USA 266
Hanauma Bay, Oahu, Hawaii, USA 293
Hanoi, Vietnam 159
Hanshin Koshien Stadium, Osaka, Japan 179

harbour cruise, Sydney, NSW 54
Hard Rock Hotel, Kuta, Bali 134
Hardy's Verandah Restaurant, Adelaide Hills, SA 107
Harry Potter Warner Bros Studio Tour, London, England 188
Haw Par Villa, Singapore 148
Hawaii, USA 292–6
Hawaii (Big Island), Hawaii, USA 293
Hawai'i Volcanoes National Park, Hawaii, USA 293
hawker centres, Chinatown, Singapore 145
Hazards, Freycinet National Park, Tas. 117
Hazards Beach, Freycinet National Park, Tas. 117
Healesville Sanctuary, Vic. 46
Heath Ledger Theatre, Perth, WA 86
Heide Park, Soltau, Germany 233
Hell's Gate, Rotorua, New Zealand 126
Henley Beach, SA 106
heritage tram, Christchurch, New Zealand 127
Hever Castle, Kent, England 189
High Roller Observation Wheel, LINQ Hotel, Las Vegas, Nevada, USA 279
Highball Express, Canberra, ACT 64
Highlanders Museum, Inverness, Scotland 193
Hiroshima, Japan 180–1
Hiroshima Castle, Japan 181
Hiroshima Children's Museum, Japan 181
Hiroshima Peace Memorial, Japan 180
Hiroshima Peace Memorial Museum, Japan 181
Hiroshima Peace Memorial Park, Japan 181
Ho Chi Minh City, Vietnam 162–3
Hobart, Tas. 113–15
Hobart's waterfront, Tas. 114
Hobbiton, New Zealand 124
Hofbräuhaus, Munich, Germany 239
Hoi An, Vietnam 160
Hoi An Lantern Festival, Vietnam 158
Hokianga Harbour, New Zealand 126
Hokkaido, Japan 169
'hole in the rock' formation, Motu Kōkako, New Zealand 126

Holey Moley Golf Club, Adelaide, SA 105
Hollybank Forest Reserve, Launceston, Tas. 112
Hollybank Wilderness Adventures, Launceston, Tas. 112
Hollywood & Highland Center, Los Angeles, California, USA 271
Hollywood Boulevard, Los Angeles, California, USA 271
Hollywood Museum, Los Angeles, California, USA 271
Hollywood sign, Los Angeles, California, USA 271, 272
Hollywood Walk of Fame, Los Angeles, California, USA 271
Holocaust museums 234
Holyrood Park, Edinburgh, Scotland 195
homestay, Vietnam 158, 162
Hon Chong Beach, Nha Trang, Vietnam 161
Honfleur, France 216
Honolulu, Oahu, Hawaii, USA 293
Hoover Dam, Nevada, USA 280
hop-on hop-off bus tour, Rome, Italy 227
Horizontal Falls, WA 91
Hosier Lane, Melbourne, Vic. 45
Hospoda 99, Český Krumlov, Czech Republic 253
Hot Water Beach, New Zealand 124
House of Terror museum, Budapest, Hungary 261
Howard Springs Nature Park, NT 96
Hozugawa River Cruise, Kyoto, Japan 176
Hue, Vietnam 161
Hughenden, Qld 66
Hugo's, Berlin, Germany 238
Hungarian Parliament Building, Budapest, Hungary 261
Hungary 259–61
Hyde Park, Sydney, NSW 54
Hyden, WA 84

Ichiran Hiroshima Hondori Ekimae, Hiroshima, Japan 166
Idroscalo Park, Milan, Italy 224
iFLY Indoor Skydiving, Surfers Paradise, Qld 74
iFLY Perth, WA 86
Ikara–Flinders Ranges National Park, SA 103
Il Goccetto, Rome, Italy 229
Illawarra Fly Treetop Adventures, Knights Hill, NSW 51

Imagination Station, Christchurch, New Zealand 127
Imperial City, Hue, Vietnam 161
In the Moon, Gion, Kyoto, Japan 177
Ingham, Qld 80
Injidup Beach, WA 89
Inokashira Park, Kichijoji, Japan 172
Insectarium, Tama Zoological Park, Tokyo, Japan 172
Intercontinental Koh Samui resort, Koh Samui, Thailand 152
International Antarctic Centre, Christchurch, New Zealand 127
Intrepid Sea Air and Space Museum, New York City, New York, USA 284
Inverness, Scotland 193
Ireland 198–205
Irish American Heritage Center, Chicago, Illinois, USA 288
Irish Fairy Trails, Killarney, Ireland 202
Irish Village market, Dublin, Ireland 201
Isle of Skye, Scotland 193
Italy 222–9
Itsukushima, Hiroshima, Japan 181

Jabiru, NT 97
Jackson Square, New Orleans, Louisiana, USA 291
Jacobite Steam Train, Scotland 193
Jakub, Český Krumlov, Czech Republic 253
jambalaya, New Orleans, Louisiana, USA 291
Jamberoo Action Park, NSW 51
Japan 164–81
Japanese Alps, Nagano, Japan 169
Japanese Pizza, Hamilton, Qld 71
Jardin des Plantes, Toulouse, France 216
Jardin du Luxembourg, Paris, France 212
J.C. Slaughter Falls, Mount Coot-tha, Qld 70
Jean-Michel Cousteau resort, Savusavu, Fiji 140
Jenolan Caves, NSW 56
Jervis Bay, NSW 51
Jetty Road, Glenelg, SA 106
Jewel Cave, Augusta, WA 89
Jewish Museum Berlin, Germany 236
Jim Jim Falls, Kakadu, NT 97
John Forrest National Park, WA 87

Jorvik Viking Centre, York, England 186
Jurien Bay, WA 83

Kaipupu Wildlife Sanctuary, Picton, New Zealand 130
Kaiser Wilhelm Memorial Church, Berlin, Germany 235
Kaiyukan Aquarium, Osaka, Japan 178
Kakadu, NT 97
Kakadu National Park, NT 97
Kakahi Falls, Rotorua, New Zealand 126
Kamo River, Kyoto, Japan 175
Kanchanaburi, Thailand 154
Kanchanaburi War Cemetery, Thailand 154
Kaneohe, Oahu, Hawaii, USA 293
Kangaroo Island, SA 108
Karensminde Agricultural Museum, Grinsted, Denmark 242
Karijini National Park, WA 84
Kata Tjuta, NT 100
Katathani Phuket Beach resort, Phuket, Thailand 152
Katherine, NT 98
Katherine Hot Springs Reserve, NT 98
Katherine Visitor Centre, NT 98
Katoomba, NSW 56
Kauai, Hawaii, USA 294
Kecskemét, Hungary 261
Kelburn Lookout, Wellington, New Zealand 122
Kerosene Creek, Rotorua, New Zealand 126
Kiama, NSW 51
kids' cooking classes, Paris, France 213
Kids Plaza Osaka, Osaka, Japan 179
KidZania, Bangkok, Thailand 154
KidZania, Tokyo, Japan 171
Kila Eco Adventure Park, Fiji 140
Kilauea, Hawaii, USA 293
Killarney, Ireland 202
Killarney National Park, Ireland 202
King George Falls, WA 91
Kings Beach, Qld 77
Kings Park, Perth, WA 86
Kingscote, SA 108
Kiyomizu-dera Temple, Kyoto, Japan 175
Koala Hospital, Port Macquarie, NSW 50
Kobe, Japan 176

Koh Phangan, Thailand 151
Koh Phi Phi, Thailand 151
Koh Samui, Thailand 151, 152
Kokomo Private Island, Fiji 140
Kondalilla National Park, Qld 77
Kooljaman, Cape Leveque, WA 91
Korakuen Garden, Okayama, Japan 176
Koreatown, Los Angeles, California, USA 273
Krakow, Poland 254–8
Kryal Castle, Ballarat 41
Kuchu Teien, Umeda Sky Building, Osaka, Japan 179
Kula WILD Adventure Park, Fiji 140
kunanji/Mount Wellington, Tas. 114
Kununurra, WA 91
Kuranda, Qld 80
Kuranda Scenic Railway, Qld 80
Kurrawa Park, Broadbeach, Qld 74
Kuta, Bali 134
Kyoto, Japan 174–7
Kyoto Rail Museum, Kyoto, Japan 175

Labyrinth Kinder Museum, Berlin, Germany 236
Laguna Resort and Spa, Bali 134
Lahaina, Maui, Hawaii, USA 294
Laibon, Český Krumlov, Czech Republic 253
Lake Alexander, East Point Reserve, NT 95
Lake Annecy, France 219
Lake Argyle, WA 91
Lake Burley Griffin, ACT 62
Lake Hillier, Middle Island, WA 84
Lake MacDonnell, SA 103
Lake Wakatipu, New Zealand 128
Lake Wanaka, New Zealand 129
Lalandia Aquadome, Billund, Denmark 242
Lamb and Flag, London, England 191
Lamington National Park, Qld 74
Lancelin, WA 86
Lanes district, Brighton, England 190
Largo, Los Angeles, California, USA 273
Lark Quarry Dinosaur Trackways, Qld 66
Larnach Castle, Dunedin, New Zealand 130
Las Vegas, Nevada, USA 278–80
Lau Pa Sat satay street, Singapore 145

Laugh Factory, Los Angeles, California, USA 273
Launceston, Tas. 112
Le Bois des Lutins, Villeneuve-Loubet, France 217
Le Havre, France 216
Leaning Tower of Pisa, Italy 224
Leanyer Recreation Park, NT 95
learn to surf, Byron Bay, NSW 58
Leeman, WA 83
Leglan, Bali 134
LEGO Factory, Billund, Denmark 242
LEGO House, Billund, Denmark 242
LEGOLAND, Billund, Denmark 242, 248-9
LEGOLAND Germany, Günzburg, Germany 233
LEGOLAND Japan, Nagoya, Japan 173
Leolandia, Milan, Italy 224
Leura, NSW 56
Liakoeb, Copenhagen, Denmark 247
Lincoln National Park, SA 103
Lincoln Park Zoo, Chicago, Illinois, USA 289
LINQ Hotel, Las Vegas, Nevada, USA 279
Litchfield National Park, NT 96
Little Gravelly Beach, Freycinet National Park, Tas. 117
Little Hay Street, Sydney, NSW 53
Little India, Singapore 146
Little Sahara, Seal Bay, SA 108
Lizard Island, Qld 81
Llandudno, North Wales 187
Loch Ness, Scotland 193
Loch Ness Monster, Scotland 193
London, England 187-91
London Bridge, Portsea, Vic. 48
London Dungeon, England 189
London Eye, England 188
Long Beach, Phu Quoc island, Vietnam 158
Lord Howe Island, NSW 51
Lord Nelson Brewery Hotel, Sydney, NSW 54
Los Angeles, California, USA 270-3
Lost City, Litchfield National Park, NT 96
Louisiana Children's Museum, New Orleans, Louisiana, USA 291
Louvre Museum, Paris, France 211, 212
Love Land, Dublin, Ireland 205
Love Night Tour, San Francisco, California, USA 276

Loyola Beach, Chicago, Illinois, USA 289
Lucca, Italy 224
Lucky Bay, WA 84
Lucky's Speakeasy, Canberra, ACT 64
Luna Park, St Kilda, Vic. 46
Luna Park, Sydney, NSW 54
Lunar New Year, Vietnam 158

M&M's World, Las Vegas, Nevada, USA 279
Macaco Tour, Venice, Italy 224
Madame Tussauds Hollywood, Los Angeles, California, USA 271
Mae Nam Beach, Koh Samui, Thailand 152
Maggie Daley Park, Chicago, Illinois, USA 289
Magic Mountain, Merimbula, NSW 51
Magna Carta, Salisbury Cathedral, England 185
Maguk (falls), Kakadu, NT 97
Main Beach, Byron Bay, NSW 58
Main Beach, Noosa, Qld 66
Main Market Square, Krakow, Poland 256, 257
Maleny, Qld 77
Malolo Island resort, Fiji 141
Mammino Gourmet Ice Cream, Childers, Qld 67
Manly, NSW 55
Marble Mountains, Da Nang, Vietnam 160
Mardi Gras, New Orleans, Louisiana, USA 291
Margaret Mahy Family Playground, Christchurch, New Zealand 127
Margaret River, WA 89
Margaret River Farmers' Markets, WA 89
Margaret River Fudge Factory, WA 89
Margaret River Skate Park, WA 89
Marina Barrage, Singapore 147
Marina Bay Sands, Singapore 147
Marina Pier, Glenelg, SA 106
Mark's Square, Venice, Italy 224
Marksie's Stockman's Camp Tucker Night, Katherine, NT 98
Marlborough region, New Zealand 130
Marlborough Sounds, New Zealand 130
Marshmallow Park, Adelaide, SA 105

Maruyama-koen Park, Kyoto, Japan 175
Marvel Avengers S.T.A.T.I.O.N., Treasure Island resort, Las Vegas, Nevada, USA 279
Mary Cairncross Scenic Reserve, Maleny, Qld 77
Marzipan Museum, Szentendre, Hungary 261
Mataranka, NT 98
Mataranka Thermal Pool, Elsey National Park, NT 98
Maui, Hawaii, USA 294
Mauku Waterfall, Auckland, New Zealand 124
Maya Bay, Phi Phi, Thailand 151
Mayfair, England 191
Mazda Museum, Hiroshima, Japan 181
Meiji Jingu, Tokyo, Japan 173
Mekong Delta river cruise, Ho Chi Minh City, Vietnam 162
Melbourne, Vic. 43-6
Melbourne Cricket Ground, Vic. 45
Melbourne Museum, Vic. 46
Melbourne Star Observation Wheel, Vic. 45
Melbourne Zoo, Vic. 45
Melrose Avenue, Los Angeles, California, USA 272
Merimbula, NSW 51
Metropolitan Museum of Art (Met), New York City, New York, USA 284
Mettams Pool, WA 86
Mid Autumn Festival, Vietnam 158
Middle Island, WA 84
Mike's Bike Tours, Munich, Germany 239
Milan, Italy 224
Milan Cathedral, Italy 224
Milford Sound, New Zealand 128
Millennium Park, Chicago, Illinois, USA 289
Mimi Aboriginal Art and Craft, Katherine, NT 98
Mindil Beach, NT 95
Mindil Beach Sunset Market, NT 95
Mintaro Maze, SA 103
Mitchell Falls, WA 91
Miyajima, Hiroshima, Japan 181
MOD, Adelaide, SA 105
Model Engineers miniature railway, Clare, SA 103
Molokai, Hawaii, USA 294
Mon Repos Conservation Park, Qld 67

MONA (Museum of Old and New Art), Hobart, Tas. 114
Monkey Mia, WA 83
Monster Kitchen and Bar, Canberra, ACT 64
Mont Blanc, France 219
Mont-Saint-Michel, Normandy, France 216
Monterey, California, USA 276
Monterey Bay Aquarium, California, USA 276
Montmartre, France 213
Montville, Qld 77
Mooloolaba, Qld 76
Moonta Bay, SA 103
Mornington Peninsula, Vic. 47-8
Mossman Gorge, Qld 80
MOTAT (Museum of Transport and Technology), Auckland, New Zealand 124
Mother Vine, Adelaide, SA 107
Motu Kōkako, New Zealand 126
Motuara Island, New Zealand 130
Mount Aspiring National Park, New Zealand 129
Mount Buller, Vic. 41
Mount Coot-tha, Qld 70
Mount Fuji, Japan 173
Mount Gambier, SA 109
Mount Kosciuszko, NSW 51
Mount Lofty House, Adelaide Hills, SA 107
Mount Misen, Hiroshima, Japan 181
Mount Tomanivi, Viti Levu, Fiji 140
Mount Walsh National Park, Qld 67
Mouth of Truth, Santa Maria in Cosmedin church, Rome, Italy 227
Movenpick Resort Phuket, Phuket, Thailand 152
Movie World, Gold Coast, Qld 73
Muckross Traditional Farms, Killarney, Ireland 202
Mui Ne Beach, Vietnam 158
Muir Woods, California, USA 276
Mungalla Aboriginal Tours, Ingham, Qld 80
Munich, Germany 239
Murray River, Vic./NSW 41
Musée de la Magie, Paris, France 212
Musée d'Orsay, Paris, France 212
Musée Mécanique, San Francisco, California, USA 275
Museum and Art Gallery Northern Territory, Darwin, NT 96
Muséum de Toulouse, Toulouse, France 216

Museum of Australian Democracy, Canberra, ACT 62
Museum of the Brothers Grimm, Steinau, Germany 233
Museum of Central Australia, Alice Springs, NT 99
Museum of Modern Art (MoMA), New York City, New York, USA 284
Museum of Old and New Art (MONA), Hobart, Tas. 114
Museum of Science, Boston, Massachusetts, USA 286
Museum of Transport and Technology (MOTAT), Auckland, New Zealand 124
Museum of Waitangi, New Zealand 126
Mustafa Centre, Little India, Singapore 146
My Khe Beach, Da Nang, Vietnam 160

Nagano, Japan 168
Naha, Okinawa, Japan 168
Nairn Beach, Nairn, Scotland 193
Nambung National Park, WA 83
Nara, Japan 176
Nara Park, Japan 176
Naracoorte Caves National Park, SA 109
National Arboretum, Canberra, ACT 63
National Capital Exhibition, Canberra, ACT 62
National Dinosaur Museum, Canberra, ACT 63
National Gallery of Australia, Canberra, ACT 63
National History Museum, Berlin, Germany 236
National Leprechaun Museum of Ireland, Dublin, Ireland 203
National Museum of Australia, Canberra, ACT 62
National Museum of Denmark, Copenhagen, Denmark 245
National Museum of Scotland, Edinburgh, Scotland 195
National Road Transport Hall of Fame, Alice Springs, NT 99
National Sporting Museum, Melbourne, Vic. 45
National Transport and Toy Museum, Wanaka, New Zealand 129

National War Museum, Edinburgh Castle, Edinburgh, Scotland 195
National Wine Museum, Szentendre, Hungary 261
National WWII Museum, New Orleans, Louisiana, USA 291
National Zoo and Aquarium, Canberra, ACT 63
Nature Playground, Copenhagen, Denmark 244
Navy Pier, Chicago, Illinois, USA 289
Neuschwanstein Castle, Schwangau, Germany 239
New Farm Park, Fortitude Valley, Qld 71
New Orleans, Louisiana, USA 290–1
New Orleans Museum of Art, Louisiana, USA 291
New South Wales 49–58
New York City, New York, USA 282–4
New York New York Hotel, Las Vegas, Nevada, USA 279
New York Pass 284
New Zealand 118–31
Newcastle, NSW 50
Ngadiku Dreamtime Walk, Mossman Gorge, Qld 80
Nha Trang, Vietnam 161
Nha Trang Beach, Vietnam 161
Nice, France 217
night markets, Vietnam 158
9/11 Memorial and Museum, New York City, New York, USA 284
Ninety Mile Beach, New Zealand 126
Ningaloo Marine Park, WA 83
Ningaloo Reef, WA 83
Ninh Binh, Vietnam 159
Ninja House, Nagano, Japan 168
Ninja Village, Nagano, Japan 168
Niseko, Japan 169
Nishiki Market, Kyoto, Japan 175
Nitmiluk Centre, NT 98
Nitmiluk National Park, NT 98
NOLA, Adelaide, SA 107
Non Nuoc Beach, Da Nang, Vietnam 160
Nonna Gina, Český Krumlov, Czech Republic 253
Noosa, Qld 66, 76
Noosa Chocolate Factory, Qld 76
Nordstrom Rack, Los Angeles, California, USA 272
Normandy, France 216

North Beach Playground, Los Angeles, California, USA 271
North Island, New Zealand 121–6
North Jutland, Denmark 243
North Shore, Hawaii, USA 293
Northern Ireland 196–7, 201
Northern Lights, Alaska, USA 266
Northern Territory 93–101
Northland, New Zealand 126
Notre-Dame Cathedral, Paris, France 211, 213
Nourlangie Rock Walk, Kakadu, NT 97
Nozawa Onsen, Nagano, Japan 169
Nusa Ceningan, Bali 135
Nusa Dua, Kuta, Bali 134
Nusa Lembongan, Bali 135
Nyhaven Harbour, Copenhagen, Denmark 245
Nymphenburg Palace, Munich, Germany 239

Oahu, Hawaii, USA 293
Oaks Street Beach, Chicago, Illinois, USA 289
Ocean Beach, San Francisco, California, USA 275
Odense, Denmark 243
Oedo-onsen-Monogatari, Tokyo, Japan 173
Okayama, Japan 176
Okinawa, Japan 168
Okinawa Island, Japan 168
Okonomi-mura, Hiroshima, Japan 166
Oktoberfest, Munich, Germany 239
Old Ghan Heritage Railway and Museum, Alice Springs, NT 99
Old Hobart Town, Richmond, Tas. 115
Old Parliament House, Canberra, ACT 62
Old Town Hall, Prague, Czech Republic 253
Old Town Square, Prague, Czech Republic 253
Omaka Aviation Heritage Centre, Blenheim, New Zealand 130
One Tree Hill, Auckland, New Zealand 124
Operation Dagger, Singapore 149
Oracle Park, San Francisco, California, USA 276
Orchard Road, Singapore 146, 149
O'Reilly's Rainforest Retreat, Lamington National Park, Qld 74

O'Reilly's Treetop Walk, Lamington National Park, Qld 74
Ormiston Gorge, Tjoritja–West MacDonnell Ranges National Park, NT 99
Orokonui Ecosanctuary, Dunedin, New Zealand 130
Ørstted Ølbar, Copenhagen, Denmark 247
Osaka, Japan 178–9
Osaka Castle, Osaka, Japan 179
Oskar Schindler Factory, Krakow, Poland 257
Ostia Lido, Italy 228
Otowa Waterfall, Kiyomizu-dera Temple, Kyoto, Japan 175
Outback Spectacular, Gold Coast, Qld 73
Outrigger Fiji Beach resort, Viti Levu, Fiji 141
Outrigger Laguna Phuket Beach, Phuket, Thailand 152
Ovolo Nishi, Canberra, ACT 64
Owl of Notre Dame de Dijon, Dijon, France 218
Owl's Trail, Dijon, France 218
Oxbow Playspace, Adelaide, SA 105

Pablo, Dotonbori, Osaka, Japan 179
Pacific Park, Los Angeles, California, USA 271
Palace of Holyroodhouse, Edinburgh, Scotland 195
Palmerston Water Park, NT 95
Panoramic Mont Blanc cable-car, France 219
Pantheon, Paris, France 212
Pantheon, Rome, Italy 227
Paradise Cave, Phong Nha-ke Bang National Park, Vietnam 161
Paradise Country, Gold Coast, Qld 73
Parc des Buttes-Chaumont, Paris, France 212
Paris, France 209–15
Paris Las Vegas Hotel, Las Vegas, Nevada, USA 279
Parkavonear Castle, Killarney, Ireland 202
Pass, the, Byron Bay, NSW 58
Pavilion Gardens Cafe, Brighton, England 190
Pearl Harbour, Oahu, Hawaii, USA 293
Penneshaw, SA 108
Penong, SA 103
Penong Windmill Museum, SA 103

Perfume Festival, Vietnam 158
Perth, WA 85–8
Perth Zoo, South Perth, WA 87
pet cafes, Tokyo, Japan 173
Peter Rabbit Garden, Richmond, Tas. 115
Pham Ngu Lao Street, Ho Chi Minh City, Vietnam 163
Phantasialand, Brühl, Germany 233
Phap Lam Pagoda, Da Nang, Vietnam 160
Phillip Island, Vic. 40
Pho City, Brisbane, Qld 72
Phong Nha-ke Bang National Park, Vietnam 161
Phu Quoc island, Vietnam 158
Phuket, Thailand 151, 152
Piazza della Rotunda, Rome, Italy 227
Picton, New Zealand 130
Picton Foreshore, New Zealand 130
Pier Park, Chicago, Illinois, USA 289
Pillaga National Park, NSW 51
Pink Elephant Samui, Koh Samui, Thailand 152
Pinnacles Desert, Nambung National Park, WA 83
Pirate Bay Lookout, Eaglehawk Neck, Tas. 111
Pisa, Italy 224
Piss Alley, Tokyo, Japan 172
Pizzarium La Gatta Mangiona, Rome, Italy 229
Plac Nowy, Krakow, Poland 256
Planetarium, Los Angeles, California, USA 272
Planetarium, Melbourne, Vic. 46
Plantation Island resort, Malolo LaiLai Island, Fiji 141
Play Forest, Egsekov Castle, Kværndrup, Denmark 243
Pod Playground, Canberra, ACT 63
Pōhutu Geyser, Rotorua, New Zealand 126
Point Lobos, California, USA 276
Poipu Beach, Hawaii, USA 294
Polish art and craft stalls, Krakow, Poland 257
Pont des Arts, Paris, France 211
Pontocho, Kyoto, Japan 177
Pooseum, Richmond, Tas. 115
Popper Pete's Popcorn, Hamilton, Qld 71
Poppy Kettle Playground, Geelong, Vic. 40
Port Arthur, Tas. 111
Port Arthur Ghost Tour, Tas. 111

Port Campbell, Vic. 40
Port Douglas, Qld 66, 80
Port Lincoln, SA 103
Port Macquarie, NSW 50
Port Noarlunga, SA 106
Port Noarlunga Reef, SA 106
Port Road Playground, Killarney National Park, Ireland 202
Port Stephens, NSW 50
Port Vincent, SA 103
Portsea, Vic. 48
Positano, Italy 228
Prague, Czech Republic 252–4
Pratolino, Italy 224
Preacher Bar, Battery Point, Tas. 116
Presidio, San Francisco, California, USA 275
Promenade des Anglais, Nice, France 217
Puffing Billy, Dandenong Ranges, Vic. 46
Puglia, Italy 224
Pulau Ubin, Singapore 148
Punalu'u, Hawaii, USA 293
Purnululu National Park, WA 91
Puzzling World, Wanaka, New Zealand 129

QT, Canberra, ACT 64
Quake City, Christchurch, New Zealand 127
Queen Anne Garden, Stirling Castle, Scotland 195
Queen Charlotte View Lookout, Picton, New Zealand 130
Queen Sirikit Botanical Garden, Chiang Mai, Thailand 152
Queen Vic Market, Melbourne, Vic. 46
Queenscliff, Vic. 48
Queensland 65–81
Queenstown, New Zealand 128
Questacon: the National Science and Technology Centre, Canberra, ACT 63
Quincey Market, Boston, Massachusetts, USA 287

Raffles Long Bar, Singapore 147
Raging Waters Sydney, NSW 54
Rainbows End, Auckland, New Zealand 123
Rainforest Canopy Walkway, Eden Project, Cornwall, England 185
Rallye Mômes, Dijon, France 218
Ramen Museum, Tokyo, Japan 172
Rangitoto Island, New Zealand 124

Rauora Park, Christchurch, New Zealand 127
Realm VR, Wanaka, New Zealand 129
Recreation Lagoon, Darwin, NT 95
Red Hill Market, Vic. 48
Red Peak Station, Barron Gorge, Qld 80
Reffen, Copenhagen, Denmark 244
Remarkable Rocks, Flinders Chase National Park, SA 108
Remarkables, New Zealand 128
Richmond, Qld 66
Richmond, Tas. 114
Richmond Gaol, Tas. 115
Richmond Park, Wimbledon, England 188
Ring of Kerry, Ireland 202
Ripley's Believe It or Not, Surfers Paradise, Qld 74
river-drift snorkelling, Port Douglas, Qld 81
Riversdale Estate, Richmond, Tas. 115
Robot Restaurant, Tokyo, Japan 171
Rockefeller Building, New York City, New York, USA 283
Rodeo Drive, Los Angeles, California, USA 272
Rollerball, Phuket, Thailand 152
Roman Baths, Bath, England 185
Roman Forum, Rome, Italy 227
Rome, Italy 225–9
Roosevelt Lounge, Broadbeach, Qld 75
Rosenborg Castle, Copenhagen, Denmark 246
Ross Castle, Killarney National Park, Ireland 202
Rotorua, New Zealand 126
Rottnest Island, WA 88
Rouen, France 216
Royal Australian Mint, Canberra, ACT 62
Royal Botanic Gardens, Melbourne, Vic. 46
Royal Flying Doctor Service Museum's Bombing of Darwin exhibit, Darwin, NT 95
Royal Pavilion, Brighton, England 190
Royal Street, New Orleans, Louisiana, USA 291
Royal Tasmanian Botanic Gardens, Hobart, Tas. 114
Rubjerg Knude lighthouse, Lokken, Denmark 243
Ruby, Copenhagen, Denmark 247

Rundle Mall, Adelaide, SA 105
Rusutsu, Japan 169
Rye, England 190
Rye Castle Museum, England 190

Sacré-Coeur, Montmartre, France 213
Sagano Scenic Railway, Kyoto, Japan 176
Sai Yok National Park, Thailand 154
Saigon Saigon, Ho Chi Minh City, Vietnam 163
St Clair Beach, Dunedin, New Zealand 130
St George's Market, Belfast, Northern Ireland 196
St Louis House of Fine Ice-cream and Dessert, Adelaide, SA 104
St Margaret's Chapel, Edinburgh Castle, Edinburgh, Scotland 195
St Mary's Basilica, Krakow, Poland 257
St Patrick's Cathedral, Melbourne, Vic. 45
St Patrick's Day, Chicago, Illinois, USA 288
St Vitus Cathedral, Prague, Czech Republic 253
Salamanca Market, Hobart, Tas. 114
Salamanca Place, Hobart, Tas. 116
Salisbury, England 185
Salisbury Cathedral, England 185
Salthill Promenade, Salthill, Ireland 202
Samurai and Ninja Museum, Kyoto, Japan 175
San Francisco, California, USA 274–7
San Francisco Bay, California, USA 275
San Francisco City Pass 276
San Francisco Zoo, California, USA 275
sand dunes of Mui Ne, Vietnam 158
Santa Maria in Cosmedin church, Rome, Italy 227
Santa Marinella, Italy 228
Santa Monica Pier, Los Angeles, California, USA 271
Sanur, Bali 134
Sarina, Qld 67
scavenger hunts, Venice, Italy 224
Scenic Cableway, Katoomba, NSW 56
scenic flight, Kakadu, NT 97

Scenic Railway, Katoomba, NSW 56
Scenic Skyway, Katoomba, NSW 56
Scenic Walkway, Katoomba, NSW 56
Scenic World, Katoomba, NSW 56
ScienceWorks, Melbourne, Vic. 46
Scitech, West Perth, WA 86
Scotland 192–5
Sculpture Garden, Canberra, ACT 63
Sea World, Gold Coast, Qld 73, 74
Seal Bay Conservation Park, SA 107
Seminyak, Bali 134
Sentosa Island, Singapore 148
Serpentine National Park, WA 87
Seven Mile Beach, Tas. 114
Shakespeare's Globe, London, England 189
Shangri-La Fijian resort, Yanuca Island, Fiji 141
Shark Bay, WA 83
Shell Beach, WA 83
shell middens, Freycinet National Park, Tas. 117
Shitennoji Temple flea market, Osaka, Japan 179
Shoes on the Danube exhibit, Budapest, Hungary 261
Shukkeien Garden, Hiroshima, Japan 181
Shuri Castle, Okinawa, Japan 168
Siam Paragon, Bangkok, Thailand 154
Simon-Dach-Straße, Berlin, Germany 237
Simpsons Falls, Mount Coot-tha, Qld 70
Simpsons Gap, Tjoritja–West MacDonnell Ranges National Park, NT 99
Singapore 144–9
Singapore Botanic Gardens, Singapore 146
Singapore Wake Park, Singapore 147
Singapore Zoo, Singapore 147
Six Forgotten Giants, Copenhagen, Denmark 245
Six Senses Fiji, Malolo Island, Fiji 141
606 Trail, Chicago, Illinois, USA 289
Skagen, Denmark 243
skiing
 in France 220
 in Japan 169

Sky Circus, Tokyo, Japan 171
Sky Tower, Auckland, New Zealand 123
Sky Wire, Eden Project, Cornwall, England 185
Skybar, Lebua State Tower, Bangkok, Thailand 155
SkyJump, Auckland, New Zealand 123
Skyline Gondola, Queenstown, New Zealand 128
Skyrail Rainforest Cableway, Wet Tropics, Qld 80
Skytree, Tokyo, Japan 171
SkyWalk, Auckland, New Zealand 123
Sleepy Bay, Freycinet National Park, Tas. 117
Slideways, Eagle Farm, Qld 71
Slotzilla, Las Vegas, Nevada, USA 280
Smeaton, Vic. 41
Snout Track, Picton, New Zealand 130
Snowplanet, Auckland, New Zealand 123
Snowtown, Bangkok, Thailand 154
Soho, England 191
Son Doong Cave, Phong Nha-ke Bang National Park, Vietnam 161
Sora Margherita, Rome, Italy 229
Sorrento, Italy 228
Sorrento, Vic. 48
South Australia 102–9
South Australian Museum, Adelaide, SA 105
South Bank, Brisbane, Qld 70
South Bank Arbour, Brisbane, Qld 70
South Coast, NSW 51
South Island, New Zealand 127–30
South Kensington, England 191
Southern Ridges, Singapore 148
Sovereign Hill, Ballarat, Vic. 41
Space Kitchen, Woden, ACT 61
Space Place at Carter Observatory, Wellington, New Zealand 122
Spaniards Inn, London, England 191
Spanish Arch, Galway, Ireland 202
Spanish Steps, Rome, Italy 227
Sperlonga, Italy 228
Spice Alley, Sydney, NSW 53
Splash Jungle Water Park, Phuket, Thailand 152
Sporting Globe, Richmond, Vic. 44
sporting mecca, Los Angeles,
 California, USA 272
Springs Preserve, Las Vegas, Nevada, USA 280
Sri Mariamman Temple, Chinatown, Singapore 148
Staffin Dinosaur Museum, Isle of Skye, Scotland 193
State Cinema, Hobart, Tas. 116
Statue of Liberty, Liberty Island, New York City, New York, USA 283
Steam Mill Lane, Sydney, NSW 53
Steamranger Heritage Railway, Mount Barker, SA 106
Stirling Castle, Stirling, Scotland 195
Stockton Bight Sand Dunes, Anna Bay, NSW 50
Stonehenge, England 185
Storyland, New Orleans, Louisiana, USA 291
Street Art Trail, Dunedin, New Zealand 130
stromatolites, Hamelin Pool, WA 83
Stromovka Park, Prague, Czech Republic 253
Summit Restaurant and Bar, Mount Coot-tha, Qld 70
sumo wrestlers, Tokyo, Japan 173
Sunrise Beach, Phuket, Thailand 151
Sunshine Coast, Qld 76–7
Suoi Tien Cultural Theme Park, Ho Chi Minh City, Vietnam 162
Super Street Arcade, Christchurch, New Zealand 127
Super Whatnot, Brisbane, Qld 72
Surf House Flow Rider, Kata Beach, Phuket, Thailand 152
Surfers Paradise Beach, Qld 74
Surfers Point, Prevelly, WA 89
SurfWorld, Torquay, Vic. 40
Sutro Baths, San Francisco, California, USA 276
Suva, Fiji 140
Suva Markets, Fiji 140
Swan River, WA 86
Swedish Candy Bar, Hamilton, Qld 71
Sydney, NSW 54–5
Sydney Harbour Bridge, NSW 54
Sydney Observatory, NSW 54
Sydney Opera House, NSW 54
Sydney Tower Eye, NSW 54
Szentendre, Hungary 261

tagliatelle al ragu, Italy 224
Takeshita Street, Tokyo, Japan 173
Talia Caves, Elliston, SA 103
Tama Zoological Park, Tokyo, Japan 172
Tamaki Drive Promenade, Auckland, New Zealand 123
Tamborine Mountain, Qld 74
Tamborine National Park, Qld 74
Tan, Melbourne, Vic. 46
Taronga Zoo, Sydney, NSW 54
Tasmania 110–17
Tasmanian Devil Unzoo, Taranna, Tas. 111
Tasmanian Museum and Art Gallery, Hobart, Tas. 114
Tasmazia, Promised Land, Tas. 112
Tasting Room, East End Cellars, Adelaide, SA 107
TD Garden, Boston, Massachusetts, USA 286
Te Papa Tongarewa, Wellington, New Zealand 121
Te Puia, Rotorua, New Zealand 126
Tegenungan Waterfall, Bali 134
Temple Bar food market, Dublin, Ireland 201, 205
Temple de la Sibylle, Paris, France 212
Tessellated Pavement, Eaglehawk Neck, Tas. 111
Thac Bac Waterfalls, Hanoi, Vietnam 159
Thailand 150–5
Thang Long Water Puppets Theatre, Hanoi, Vietnam 159
Thap Ba Spa, Nha Trang, Vietnam 161
the Farm, Byron Bay, NSW 58
The Kimberley, WA 90–1
the Pass, Byron Bay, NSW 58
The Rocks, NSW 54
theme parks, USA 267–8, 271
Thian Hock Keng Temple, Singapore 148
Thinkery, Austin, Texas, USA 266
31st Beach Street, Chicago, Illinois, USA 289
Thomas Brisbane Planetarium, Brisbane, Qld 70
Thomas Land, Drayton Manor Theme Park, Tansworth, England 186
Thredbo, NSW 51
Three Blue Ducks, Byron Bay, NSW 58
Three Sisters, NSW 56
Tiergarten Park, Berlin, Germany 236

Tili Wiru Tjuta Nyakutjaku (art installation), Uluru, NT 100
Titania's Palace, Egeskov Castle, Kværndrup, Denmark 243
Titanic Belfast, Belfast, Northern Ireland 197
Tivoli Gardens, Copenhagen, Denmark 245
Tjaynera Falls, Litchfield National Park, NT 96
Tjoritja–West MacDonnell Ranges National Park, NT 99
Togakure Ninja Museum, Nagano, Japan 168
Tokyo, Japan 170–3
Tokyo Disneyland, Japan 171
Tokyo Dome, Japan 171
Tonbori River cruise, Dotonbori, Osaka, Japan 179
Top Didj Cultural Experience, Katherine, NT 98
Top of the Rock Observation Deck, Rockefeller Building, New York City, New York, USA 283
Torquay, Vic. 40
Torvehallerne Food Hall, Copenhagen, Denmark 244
Toulouse, France 216
Toulouse Cite de l'espace, France 216
Tower of London, London, England 189
Toy Factory, Gumeracha, SA 106
Traitors' Gate, Tower of London, England 189
Treasure Island resort, Las Vegas, Nevada, USA 279
TreeClimb Adelaide, SA 105
TreeTop Challenge, Tamborine Mountain, Qld 74
Trevi Fountain, Rome, Italy 227
Trinity College, Ireland 204
Tropical Islands, Krausnick, Germany 236
Tropical North, Qld 79–81
truffle hunting, Piedmont, Italy 224
trulli, Alberobello, Italy 224
Tuki Trout Farm, Smeaton, Vic. 41
turtle stepping stones, Kamo River, Kyoto, Japan 175
Twelve Apostles, Port Campbell, Vic. 40
Twilight Beach, Esperance, WA 84
Twin Falls Gorge, Kakadu, NT 97
Twin Peaks, San Francisco, California, USA 275
U Dwau Maryi, Český Krumlov, Czech Republic 253

Ubirr, Kakadu, NT 97
Ubud, Bali 134
Ueno Zoological Gardens, Tokyo, Japan 172
Uluru, NT 100
Uluru Base Walk, NT 100
Uluru–Kata Tjuta National Park, NT 100
Uluwatu Temple, Bali 135
Umeda Sky Building, Osaka, Japan 179
Umpherston Sinkhole, Mount Gambier, SA 109
Underwater Observatory, Busselton, WA 89
United Kingdom 182–97, 201
Universal Studios, Osaka, Japan 178
Universal Studios Hollywood, Los Angeles, California, USA 268, 271
Urquhart Castle, Loch Ness, Scotland 193
USA 262–96
Utopia rockpools, Waterfall Creek, Qld 67

Val Thorens, France 220
Valley of Fire State Park, Nevada, USA 280
Vatican City, Italy 228
Vegas Indoor Skydiving, Las Vegas, Nevada, USA 279
Velence Lake, Hungary 261
Venetian, Las Vegas, Nevada, USA 279
Venice, Italy 224
Victoria, Australia 39–48
Vietnam 156–63
Vietnam Museum of Ethnology, Hanoi, Vietnam 159
Viking Museum, Roskilde, Denmark 246
Village of Lower Crackpot, Tasmazia, Promised Land, Tas. 112
Villages des Fouls, Villeneuve-Loubet, France 217
Villefranche-sur-Mer, France 217
Vinpearl Amusement Park, Nha Trang, Vietnam 161
Vinpearl Cable Car, Nha Trang, Vietnam 161
Viti Levu, Fiji 140
Viva Vision lightshows, Las Vegas, Nevada, USA 280
Vivonne Bay, SA 108

VizioVirtù Cioccolateria, Venice, Italy 224
Vltava River, Prague, Czech Republic 253
Volks Electric Railway, Brighton, England 190
Vomo resort, Vomo Island, Fiji 141

W5 Discovery and Science Centre, Belfast, Northern Ireland 197
Wadandi Track, WA 89
Waikiki, Oahu, Hawaii, USA 293
Wailea, Maui, Hawaii, USA 294
Wailua Falls, Kauai, Hawaii, USA 294
Waitakere Ranges Regional Park, Auckland, New Zealand 124
Waitangi, New Zealand 126
Waitangi Treaty Grounds, New Zealand 126
Walkabout Cultural Adventures, Daintree region, Qld 80
Walpa Gorge Walk, Kata Tjuta, NT 100
Walt Disney Studios Park, Chessy, France 213
Walt Disney World, Orlando, Florida, USA 268
Waltzing Matilda Centre, Winton, Qld 66
Walunga National Park, WA 87
Wanaka, New Zealand 129
Wanaka Lavender Farm, New Zealand 129
Wanaka Station Park, New Zealand 129
Wanaka Wastebusters, New Zealand 129
Warrumbungle Observatory, NSW 51
Wat Pho, Bangkok, Thailand 153
Waterbom Bali, Kuta, Bali 134
Watergate, Berlin, Germany 237
watersports, Bali 135
Wave Lagoon, Darwin, NT 95
Wave Rock, Hyden, WA 84
Wellington, New Zealand 121–2
Wellington Cable Car, New Zealand 121
Wellington Park, Tas. 114
Wellington Underground Market, New Zealand 122
Wellington Zoo, New Zealand 122
Werribee Open Range Zoo, Vic. 45
Weserstraße, Berlin, Germany 237
West End, London, England 188
Western Australia 82–92

Western Australian Maritime Museum, Fremantle, WA 88
Western Australian Shipwreck Museum, Fremantle, WA 88
Westfield Century City, Los Angeles, California, USA 272
Westminster Abbey, London, England 188
Wet 'n' Wild, Gold Coast, Qld 73
Wet Tropics, Qld 79, 80
Whakarewarewa Forest, Rotorua, New Zealand 126
Wheel of Brisbane, Qld 70
Whitehaven Beach, Qld 66
WhiteWater World, Gold Coast, Qld 73
Wieliczka Salt Mine, Poland 258
Wild Walks: Animal Amble, San Francisco Zoo, California, USA 275
Wilpena, SA 103
Wilpena Pound, Ikara–Flinders Ranges National Park, SA 103
Wilsons Promontory National Park, Vic. 40
Windjana Gorge, WA 91
Wineglass Bay, Coles Bay, Tas. 117
Wineglass Bay Lookout, Tas. 117
Winter Village, Melbourne, Vic. 44
Winton, Qld 66
Wolfe Creek Crater, WA 84
Wolfe Creek Crater National Park, WA 84
Woodgate Beach, Qld 67
Workshops Rail Museum, Ipswich Qld 71

Yallingup, WA 89
Yanbaru, Okinawa, Japan 168
Yanchep National Park, WA 87
Ye Olde Cheshire Cheese, London, England 191
Yellow Water Cruises, Kakadu, NT 97
Yellow Water (Ngurrungurrudjba) Billabong, Kakadu, NT 97
Yellowstone National Park, Wyoming, USA 265
Yeoman Warder tour, Tower of London, England 189
York, England 186
Yorke Peninsula, SA 103
Yosemite National Park, California, USA 265
Yulara, NT 100

Zealandia, Wellington, New Zealand 122

Published in 2020 by Hardie Grant Travel, a division of Hardie Grant Publishing

Hardie Grant Travel (Melbourne)
Wurundjeri Country
Building 1, 658 Church Street
Richmond, Victoria 3121

Hardie Grant Travel (Sydney)
Gadigal Country
Level 7, 45 Jones Street
Ultimo, NSW 2007

www.hardiegrant.com/au/travel

All rights reserved. No part of this publication may be reproduced, stored in a retrieval system or transmitted in any form by any means, electronic, mechanical, photocopying, recording or otherwise, without the prior written permission of the publishers and copyright holders.

The moral rights of the author have been asserted.

Copyright text © Peter and Bridget Helliar 2020
Copyright concept and design © Hardie Grant Publishing 2020

A catalogue record for this book is available from the National Library of Australia

Trippin' with Kids
ISBN 9781741176858

10 9 8 7 6 5 4 3 2

The paper this book is printed on is certified against the Forest Stewardship Council® Standards and other sources. FSC® promotes environmentally responsible, socially beneficial and economically viable management of the world's forests.

Publisher
Melissa Kayser
Project editor
Megan Cuthbert
Editor
Alexandra Payne
Proofreader
Susan Keogh
Trainee book editor
Jessica Smith
Research assistance
Hayley Rochford
Design
Astred Hicks, Design Cherry
Typesetting
Kerry Cooke
Index
Max McMaster
Prepress
Kerry Cooke and Splitting Image Colour Studio

Printed and bound in China by LEO Paper Products LTD.

Photo credits:
All images © Peter and Bridget Helliar, except the following:

Front cover (left), 52 Adrian Rem/Unsplash; front cover (right) Anton Karatkevich/Unsplash; iii (bottom) Ashim D Silva/Unsplash; 41 Cindy C/Unsplash; 49 April Pethybridge/Unsplash; 57, 77 Jade Stephens/Unsplash; 61 Kylie de Guia/Unsplash; 69 Weiqi Xiong/Unsplash; 71 Alice Duffield/Unsplash; 87 Dylan Alcock/Unsplash; 88 Christine Mendoza/Unsplash; 92 Tourism Australia; 94, 112, 131, 134, 186, 246 iStock Images; 101 Simon Watkinson/Unsplash; 115 Unsplash; 122 Jil Beckham/Unsplash; 134 Sebastian Pena/Unsplash; 137 Jarrad Horne/Unsplash; 143 Timothy Ah Koy/Unsplash; 147 Yeo Khee/Unsplash; 154 Evan Krause/Unsplash; 160 Rene Deanda/Unsplash; 168 Julie Fader/Unsplash; 173 Masaaki Komori/Unsplash; 174 Svetlana Gumerova/Unsplash; 178 Han Min/Unsplash; 181 Fezbot2000/Unsplash; 190 Alex Block/Unsplash; 193 Bjorn Snelders/Unsplash; 200 Saad Chaudhry/Unsplash; 201 Gabriel Ramos/Unsplash; 203 Diogo Palhais/Unsplash; 209 Sebastien Gabriel/Unsplash; 225 Meejin Choi/Unsplash; 228 Christopher Czermak/Unsplash; 232 Marius Serban/Unsplash; 234 Shutterstock; 243 Max Adultanukosol/Unsplash; 254 Alamy; 265 Yannick Menard/Unsplash; 266 Unsplash; 269 Aaron Burden/Unsplash; 278 James Walsh/Unsplash; 280 Mike Boening/Unsplash; 289 Unsplash; 292 Marcus Lenk/Unsplash; 294 Luke McKeown/Unsplash.